Culture

A Critical Review of Concepts and Definitions – The History of Human Culture, its Role in Social Sciences

By A. L. Kroeber and Clyde Kluckhohn

Published by Pantianos Classics

ISBN-13: 978-1-78987-276-7

First published in 1952

Contents

Acknowledgments

WE ARE indebted to Professor Robert Bierstedt for access to his master's thesis, only a small portion of which has been published. His extensive bibliography through 1935 greatly lightened our task, and his text was also suggestive to us at many points. We have also benefited from the memoranda and records, largely unpublished, of the Committee on Conceptual Integration of the American Sociological Society (Albert Blumenthal, Chairman) of which one of us (C. K.) was a member in its later stage. Dr. Alfred Meyer was very helpful, especially with the Germ.an materials. To Professor Leslie White we owe several references that we probably would not have discovered ourselves. Professor Jerome Bruner has made clarifying suggestions. Dr. Walter Taylor and Paul Friedrich kindly read the manuscript and made suggestions.

Wayne Untereiner, Richard Hobson, Clifford Geertz, Jr., Charles Griffith, and Ralph Patrick (all graduate students in anthropology at Harvard University) have not only done unusually competent work as research assistants; each has made significant criticisms of content and style. We have placed the name of Mr. Untereiner on the title-page because he made major contributions to our theoretical formulations. We are also grateful for the scrupulously careful work of Hermia Kaplan, Mildred Geiger, Lois Walk, Muriel Levin, Kathryn Gore, and Carol Trosch in typing various versions of the manuscript, and to the four first-named in collating bibliographical references and editorial checking and to Cordelia Gait and Natalie Stoddard who edited the monograph.

We thank the following publishers for permission to quote from copyrighted materials:

Addison-Wesley Press, Inc.: G. K. Zipfs *Human Behavior and the Principle of Least Effort* (1949),
Appleton-Century-Crofts, Inc.: A. A. Goldenweiser's *Anthropology* (1937).
The Century Co.: C. A. Ellwood's *Cultural Evolution* (1927),
Cohen & West, Ltd. (British Edition) and The Free Press (American Edition): E. E. Evans-Pritchard's *Social Anthropology* (1951).
Columbia University Press: Abram Kardiner's *The Individual and His Society* (1959) and Ralph Linton's *The Science of Man in the World Crisis* (1945).
E. P. Dufton & Co., Inc.: Alexander Leighton's *Human Relations in a Changing World* (1949).
Farrar, Straus, and Young, Inc.: Leslie White's *The Science of Culture* (1949).
The Free Press: S. F. Nadel's *The Foundations of Social Anthropology* (1950).
Harcourt, Brace and Company, Inc.: A. L. Kroeber's and T. T. Waterman's *Source Book in Anthropology* (1931), Kroeber's *Anthropology* (1948), and Lewis Mumford's *The Culture of Cities* (1938).
D. C. Heath and Company: Franz Boas and others' *General Anthropology* (1938).
The Hogarth Press: Geza Roheim's *The Riddle of the Sphinx* (1934).
A. A. Knopf, Inc.: .M. J. Herskovits' *Man and His Works* (1948), and A. A. Goldenweiser's *History, Psychology and Culture* (1933).
The Macmillan Company: G. P. Murdock's *Social Structure* (1949).
McGraw-Hill Book Company, Inc.: Ellsworth Faris's *The Nature of Human Nature* (1937), Talcott Parsons' *The Structure of Social Action* (1937), and W. D. Wallis's *Culture and Progress* (1930).
Methuen & Company: R. R. Marett's *Psychology and Folklore* (1920).
Oxford University Press: Meyer Fortes' *The Web of Kinship Among the Tallensi* (1949).
Routledge and Kegan Paul, Ltd.: Raymond Firth's *Primitive Polynesian Economy* (1939).
University of California Press: Edward Sapir's *Selected Writings of Edward Sapir in Language, Culture, and Personality* (edited by D. G. Mandelbaum) (1949).
The Viking Press, Inc.: W. F. Ogburn's *Social Change* (1950)
Watts & Company: Raymond Firth's *Elements of Social Organization* (1951).
Yale University Press: C. S. Ford's "A Simple (Comparative Analysis of Material Culture," and G. P. Murdock's Editorial Preface, both of which appear in *Studies in the Science of Society Presented to Albert Galloway Keller* (1937).

Introduction

THE "culture concept of the anthropologists and sociologists is coming to be regarded as the foundation stone of the social sciences." This recent statement by Stuart Chase [1] will not be agreed to, at least not without reservation, by all social scientists, [2] but few intellectuals will challenge the statement that the idea of culture, in the technical anthropological sense, is one of the key notions of contemporary American thought. In explanatory importance and in generality of application it is comparable to such categories as gravity in physics, disease in medicine, evolution in biology. Psychiatrists and psychologists, and, more recently, even some economists and lawyers, have come to tack on the qualifying phrase "in our culture" to their generalizations, even though one suspects it is often done mechanically in the same way that mediaeval men added a precautionary "God Willing" to their utterances. Philosophers are increasingly concerned with the cultural dimension to their studies of logic, values, and aesthetics, and indeed with the ontology and epistemology of the concept itself. The notion has become part of the stock in trade of social workers and of all those occupied with the practical problems of minority groups and dependent peoples. Important research in medicine and in nutrition is oriented in cultural terms. Literary men are writing essays and little books about culture.

The broad underlying idea is not new, of course. The Bible, Homer, Hippocrates, Herodotus, Chinese scholars of the Han dynasty — to take only some of the more obvious examples — showed an interest in the distinctive fife-ways of different peoples. Boethius' Consolations of Philosophy contains a crude statement of the principle of cultural relativity: "The customs and laws of diverse nations do so much differ that the same thing which some commend as laudable, others condemn as deserving punishment." We find the notion in more refined form in Descartes' *Discourse on Method:*

...While traveling, having realized that all those who have attitudes very different from our own are not for that reason barbarians or savages but are as rational or more so than ourselves, and having considered how greatly the self-same person with the self -same mind who had grown up from infancy among the French or Germans would become different from what he would have been if he had always lived among the Chinese or the cannibals...I found myself forced to try myself to sec things from their point of view.

In Pico della Mirandola, Pascal, and Montesquieu one can point to some nice approximations of modern anthropological thinking. Pascal, for example, wrote:

I am very much afraid that this so-called nature may itself be no more than an early custom, just as custom is second nature...Undoubtedly nature is not altogether uniform. It is custom that produces this, for it constrains nature. But sometimes nature overcomes it, and confines man to his instinct, despite every custom, good or bad.

Voltaire's [3] "Essai sur les moeurs et l'esprit des nations" is also to the point. To press these adumbrations too far, however, is like insisting that Plato anticipated Freud's crucial concept of the unconscious because he made an insightful remark about the relation between dreams and suppressed desire.

By the nineteenth century the basic notion was ready to crystallize in an explicit, generalized form. The emergence or the Gentian word, Kultur, is reviewed in the next section. Part I. In developing the notion of the "superorganic," Spencer presaged one of the primary anthropological conceptions of culture, although he himself used the word "culture" only occasionally and casually. [4] The publication dates of E. B, Tylor's *Primitive Culture* and of Walter Bagehot's *Physics and Politics* are 1871 and 1872. Bagehot's "cake of custom" is, in essence, very similar to Tylor's "culture." The latter slowly became established as the technical term because of the historical associations of the word and because Tylor defined its generic implications both more sharply and more abstractly.

Even in this century after "culture" was fairly well established in intellectual circles as a technical term, certain well-known thinkers have not used the word though employing highly similar concepts. Graham Wallas, while familiar with anthropological literature, avoids the term "culture" (he occasionally uses "civilization" — without definition) in his books, *The Great Society* (1914) and *Our Social Heritage* (1921). However, his concept of "social heritage" is equivalent to certain definitions of culture:

Our social heritage consists of that part of our "nurture" which we acquire by the social process of teaching and learning. (1921, 7)

The anthropologist, M. F. Ashley-Montagu, has recently asserted that Alfred Korzybski's concept of time-binding (in *Manhood of Humanity,* 1921) "is virtually identical with the anthropologist's concept of culture." (1951, 251)

The editorial staff of the Encyclopedia of the Social Sciences (vol. I, p. 202) in their article on "War and Reorientation" correctly describes the position reached by the anthropological profession at about 1930:

The principal positive theoretical position of the early decades of the 20th century was the glorification of culture. The word loomed more important than any other in the literature and in the consciousness of anthropologists. Culture traits, culture complexes, culture types, culture centers, culture areas, culture circles, culture patterns, culture migrations, cultural convergences, cultural diffusion — these segments and variants point to an attempt to grapple rigorously with an elusive and fluid concept and suggest incidentally the richness of such a concept. Concern was rife over the birth of culture, its growth and wanderings and contacts, its matings and fertilizations, its maturity and decay. In direct proportion to their impatience with the classical tradition anthropologists became the anatomists and biographers of culture.

To follow the history of a concept, its diffusion between countries and academic disciplines, its modifications under the impact of broader intellectual movements, is a characteristically anthropological undertaking. Our purpose is several-fold. First, we wish to make available in one place for purposes of reference a collection of definitions by anthropologists, sociologists, psychologists, philosophers, and others. The collection is not exhaustive, but it perhaps approaches exhaustiveness for English and American social scientists of the past generation. We present, thus, some sources for a case study in one aspect of recent intellectual history. Second, we are documenting the gradual emergence and refinement of a concept we believe to be of great actual and still greater potential significance. Third, we hope to assist other investigators in reaching agreement and greater precision in definition by pointing out and commenting upon agreements and disagreements in the definitions thus far propounded. Considering that the concept has had a name for less than eighty years and that until very recently only a handful of scholars were interested in the idea, it is not surprising that full agreement and precision has not yet been attained. Possibly it is inevitable and even desirable that representatives of different disciplines should emphasize different criteria and utilize varying shades of meaning. But one thing is clear to us from our survey: it is time for a stock-taking, for a comparing of notes, for conscious awareness of the range of variation. Otherwise the notion that is conveyed to the wider company of educated men will be so loose, so diffuse as to promote confusion rather than clarity." [5] Moreover, as Opler has pointed out, the sense given the concept is a matter of considerable practical importance now that culture theory underlies much psychiatric therapy as well as the handling of minority problems, dependent peoples, and even some approaches in the field of international relations:

The discovery and popularization of the concept of culture has led to a many-sided analysis of it and to the elaboration of a number of diverse theories. Since aberrants and the psychologically disturbed are often at loggerheads with their cultures, the attitude toward them and toward their treatment is bound to be influenced by the view of culture which is accepted...it is obvious that the reactions which stem from different conceptions of culture may range all the way from condemnation of the unhappy individual and confidence in the righteousness of the cultural dictate, to sharp criticism of the demanding society and great compassion for the person who has not been able to come to terms with it. (1947, 14)

Indeed a few sociologists and even anthropologists have already, either implicitly or explicitly, rejected the concept of culture as so broad as to be useless in scientific discourse or too tinged with valuations. The German sociologist, Leopold von Wiese, says "...the word should be avoided entirely in descriptive sociology..." (1939, pp. 593-94). Lundberg characterizes the concept as "vague" (1939, p. 179). In the glossary of technical terms in Chapple and Coon's *Principles of Anthropology* the word "culture" is conspicuous by its deliberate absence. [6] Radcliffe-Brown and certain British social anthropologists influenced by him tend to avoid the word.

We begin in Part One with a semantic history of the word "culture" and some remarks on the related concept "civilization." In Part Two we then list definitions, grouped according to principal conceptual emphasis, though this arrangement tends to have a rough chronological order as well. Comments follow each category of definitions, and Part Two concludes with various analytical indices. Part Three contains statements about culture longer or more discursive than definitions. These are classified, and each class is followed by comment by ourselves. Part Four consists of our general conclusions.

[1] Chase, 1948, 59.

[2] Malinowski has referred to culture as "the most central problem of all social science" (1939, 588). Curiously enough, this claim has also been made by a number of sociologists — in fact, by more sociologists than anthropologists, so far as our evidence goes.

[3] Cf. Honigsheim, 1945.

[4] In a secondary source we have seen the following definition of culture attributed to Spencer: "Culture is the sum total of human achievement." No citation of book or page is made, and we have been unable to locate this definition in Spencer's writings. Usually, certainly, he treats culture in roughly the sense employed by Matthew Arnold and other English humanists. For example, "taken in its widest sense culture means preparation for complete living" (1895, 514). Cf. George Eliot's *Silas Marner,* Chapter I: "...Silas was both sane and honest, though, as with many honest fervent men, culture had not defined any channels for his sense of mystery, and it [*sic*] spread itself over the proper pathway of inquiry and knowledge."

[5] One sometimes feels that A. Lawrence Lowell's remarks about the humanistic concept of culture is almost equally applicable to the anthropological: '...I have been entrusted with the difficult task of speaking about culture. But there is nothing in the world more elusive. One cannot analyze it, for its components are infinite. One cannot describe it, for it is a Protean in shape. An attempt to encompass its meaning in words is like trying to seize the air in the hand, when one finds that it is everywhere except within one's grasp." (1934, 115)

[6] Except that on p. 695 two possible deletions were overlooked, and on p. 580 the adjective cultural survived editing.

Part One - General History of the Word Culture

1. Brief Survey

As a preliminary to our review of the various definitions which have been given of culture as a basic concept in modern anthropology, sociology, and psychology, we submit some facts on the general semantic history of the word culture — and its near-synonym civilization — in the period when they were gradually acquiring their present-day, technical social-science meaning.

Briefly, the word culture with its modern technical or anthropological meaning was established in English by Tylor in 1871, though it seems not to have penetrated to any general or "complete" British or American dictionary until more than fifty years later — a piece of cultural lag that may help to keep anthropologists humble in estimating the tempo of their influence on even the avowedly literate segment of their society. Tylor, after some hesitation as against "civilization," borrowed the word culture from German, where by his time it had become well recognized with the meaning here under discussion, by a growth out of the older meaning of cultivation. In French the modern anthropological meaning of culture [1] has not yet been generally accepted as standard, or is admitted only with reluctance, in scientific and scholarly circles, though the adjective cultural is sometimes so used. [2] Most other Western languages, including Spanish, as well as Russian, follow the usage of German and of American English in employing culture. [3]

Jan Huizinga says: [4]

"What do we mean by Culture? The word has emanated from Germany. It has long since been accepted by the Dutch, the Scandinavian and the Slavonic languages, while in Spain, Italy, and America it has also achieved full standing. Only in French and English does it still meet with a certain resistance in spite of its currency in some well-defined and traditional meanings. At least it is not unconditionally interchangeable with civilization in these two languages. This is no accident. Because of the old and abundant development of their scientific vocabulary, French and English had far less need to rely on the German example for their modern scientific nomenclature than most other European languages, which throughout the nineteenth century fed in increasing degree on the rich table of German phraseology.

According to Germán Arciniegas, Paul Hazard observes that the German word Kultur does not occur in 1774 in the first edition of the German dictionary, but appears only in the 1793 one. [5] For some reason, Grimm's Deutsches Wörterbuch [6] does not give the word either under "C" or "K" in the volumes that appeared respectively in 1860 and 1873, although such obvious loan words as Creatur and cujoniren are included, and although the word had been in wide use by classic German authors for nearly a century before, Kant, for instance, like most of his contemporaries, still spells the word *Cultur,* but uses it repeatedly, always with the meaning of cultivating or becoming cultured — which, as we shall see, was also the older meaning of civilization.

The earlier usages of the word culture in German are examined in detail below.

The ethnographic and modern scientific sense of the word culture, which no longer refers primarily to the process of cultivation or the degree to which it has been carried, but to a state or condition, sometimes described as extraorganic or superorganic, in which all human societies share even though their particular cultures may show very great qualitative differences — this modern sense we have been able to trace back to Klemm in 1843, from whom Tylor appears to have introduced the meaning into English.

Gustav E, Klemm, 1802-67, published in 1843 the first volume of his *Allgemeine Culturgeschichte der Menschheit,* which was completed in ten volumes in 1852. In 1854 and 1855 he published *Allgemeine Culturwissenschaft in* two volumes. The first of these works is a history of Culture, the latter a science of it. The first sentence of the 1843 work says that his purpose is to represent the gradual development of mankind as an entity — "die allmähliche Entwickelung der Menschheit als eines Individuums." On page 18 of the same volume Klemm says that "it was Voltaire who first put aside dynasties, king lists, and battles, and sought what is essential in history, namely culture, as it is manifest in customs, in beliefs, and in forms of government." Klemm's understanding and use of the word "culture" are examined in detail in § 9 of Part One.

That Klemm [7] influenced Tylor is unquestionable. In his *Researches,* 1865, at the end of Chapter I on page 13, Tylor's references include "the invaluable collection of facts bearing on the history of civilization in the

'Allgemeine Cultur-geschichte der Menschheit,' and 'Allgemeine Culrurwissenschaft,' of the late Dr. Gustav Klemm, of Dresden." In his *Researches* Tylor uses the word culture at least twice (on pages 4 and 369) as if trying it out, or feeling his way, though his usual term still is civilization (pp. 1, 2, 3, 4, etc...361).

The tenth volume (1920) of Wundt's *Völkerpsychologie* [8] is entitled "Kultur und Geschichte," and pages 3-36 are devoted to The Concept of Culture. Wundt gives no formal definition, but discusses the origin of the term and the development of the concept. The word is from colere, whence cultas, as in cultus deorum and cultus agri, which latter became also cultura agri. From this there developed the mediaeval cultura mentis; [9] from which grew the dual concepts of geistige and materielle Kultur. Wundt also discusses the eighteenth-century nature-culture polarity (l'homme naturel, Naturmensch); and he finds that the historian and the culture historian differ in evaluating men's deeds respectively according to their power or might and according to their intellectual performance — which last seems a bit crudely stated for 1920; however, it is clear that in actually dealing with cultural phenomena in his ten volumes, Wundt conceived of culture in the modern way. [10]

[1] Tonnelat (*Civilisation: Le Mot et l'Idée,* p. 61. See Addendum of this monograph) says of the development of the more general sense of culture in French: "...il faudrait distinguer entre l'emploi du xviie siècle et cclui du xviiie: au xviie siècle, le mot 'culture' — pris dans son sense abstrait — aurait toujours été accompagne d'un complément grammatical désignant la matière cultivée: de même que l'on disait 'la culture du blé,' on disait 'la culture es lettres, la culture des sciences.' Au contraire, des écrivains du xviiie siècle, comme Vauvenargues et Voltaire, auraient été les premiers à employer le mot d'une façon en quelque sorte absolue, en lui donnant le sense de 'formation de l'esprit.' Voltaire, par exemple, écrit dans la *Henriade,* en parlant de Charles IX:
> Des premiers ans du roi la funeste culture
> N'avait que trop en lui combattu la nature."

Febvre (1930, discussion on Tonnelat, p. 74) remarks: "La notion allemande de *Kultur* enrichit et complete la notion française de *civilisation*." In the same discussion Saen adds: "Le mot *culture,* dans l'acception de Herder, a passé en France par l'intermédiaire d'Edgar Quinet. Cependant Condorcet a déjà propagé en France des idées analogues à celles de Herder."

[2] The French Academy's Eighth or 1932 edition of its Dictionary gives "l'application qu'on met à perfectionner..."; then: "*culture genérale, ensemble de connaissances....*"; and finally: "par extension de ces deux dernier sens, *Culture* est quelquefois maintenant synonyme de Civilisation. *Culture* gréco-latine...." Today many of the younger French anthropologists use the word as freely as do English and American.

[3] Tonnelat (*Civilisation: Le Mot et l'Idée,* p. 61. See Addendum to our Part One) says that Kultur is "certainement un caique direct du français *culture*." Febvre (1930, pp. 38-39) takes a similar view, citing especially the parallels between the 1762 definition of the Academy's dictionary and that in Adelung's (1793 edition). The present authors agree that both civilization and culture were probably used in French before they were used in either English or German. Our main point here is that for the generalized concept — sometimes called the ethnographic or anthropological sense, which did not emerge until the nineteenth century — the French came to use the word Civilization, the Germans Cultur and later Kultur, and that English usage divided, the British unanimously employing Civilization until Tylor, and in part thereafter to Toynbee, but Americans accepting Culture without reluctance.

[4] Huizinga, 1936, pp. 39-40. Huizinga does not proceed to a systematic definition of his own.

[5] Arciniegas, 1947, p. 146. "Le mot 'Kultur' — qui, en allemand, correspond en principe a 'civilisation'..." The 1774 and 1793 dictionaries are presumably Adclung's. He spells Cultur, not Kultur. His definition is given below.

[6] Grimm, 1860, contains *curios* as well as *Creatur.* In the lengthy introduction by J. Grimm there is nothing said about deliberate omission of words of foreign origin (as indeed all with initial "C" are foreign). There is some condemnation of former unnecessary borrowings, but equal condemnation of attempts at indiscriminate throwing out of the language of well-established and useful words of foreign origin.

[7] An evaluation of Klemm's work is given by R. H. Lowie, 1937, pp. 11-16.

[8] Not to be confused, of course, with his one-volume *Elemente der Völkerpsychologie,* 1912, which on account of its briefer compass and translation into English is often mis-cited for the larger work. This latter is described in its subtitle as: An Inquiry into Laws of Development; the shorter work as: Outline of a Psychological History of the Development of Mankind. The one-volume work is actually an evolutionistic quasi-history in the frame of four stages — the ages of primitiveness, totemism, heroes and gods, and development to humanity.

[9] Actually, Cicero (Tusculan Disputations, 2, 5, 13) wrote "cultura animi philosophia est." Cultus meant "care directed to the refinement of life" and was also used for "style of dress," "external appearance and the like."

[10] In the remainder of the section on The Concept of Culture, Wundt discusses nationality, humanity, and civilization. Here he makes one distinction which is sometimes implicit as a nuance in the English as well as the German usage of the words. Culture, Wundt says, tends to isolate or segregate itself on national lines, civilization to spread its

content to other nations; hence cultures which have developed out of civilizations, which derive from them, remain dependent on other cultures. Wundt means that, for instance, Polish culture which in the main is derivative from European civilization, thereby is also more specifically derivative from ("dependent on") the French, Italian, and German cultures.

2. Civilization

Civilization is an older word than culture in both French and English, and for that matter in German. Thus, Wundt [1] has Latin civis, citizen, giving rise to *civitas,* city-state, and *civilitas,* citizenship; whence Medieval *civitabilis* (in the sense of entitled to citizenship, urbanizable), and Romance language words based on *civilisatio.* [2] According to Wundt, Jean Bodin, 1530-96, first used civilization in its modern sense. In English, civilization was associated with the notion of the task of civilizing others. In eighteenth-century German, [3] the word civilization still emphasized relation to the state, somewhat as in the English verb to civilize, viz., to spread political [sic] [4] development to other peoples. So far Wundt.

Grimm's *Wörterbuch* gives: civilisieren: erudire, ad humanitatem informare, and cites Kant (4:304): "Wir sind...durch Kunst und Wissenschaft cultiviert, wir sind civilisiert...zu allerlei gesellschaftlicher Artigkeit und Anständigkeit..." (We become cultivated through art and science, we become civilized [by attaining] to a variety of social graces and refinements [or decencies]).

If Kant stuck by this distinction, his *cultivated* refers to intrinsic improvement of the person, his *civilized* to improvements of social interrelations (interpersonal relations). He is perhaps here remaining close to the original sense of French *civiliser* with its emphasis on pleasant manners (cf. poli, politesse) and the English core of meaning which made Samuel Johnson prefer "civility" to civilization.

The French verb *civiliser* was in use by 1694, according to Havelock Ellis, [5] with the sense of polishing manners, rendering sociable, or becoming urbane as a result of city life.

According to Arciniegas, the Encyclopédie Française says: "Civiliser une nation, c'est la faire passer de l'état primitif, naturel, à un état plus évolué de culture [6] morale, intellectuelle, sociale... [car] le mot civiliser s'oppose à barbarie." [7] As to the noun *civilisation,* Arciniegas says that the dictionary of the French Academy first admitted it in the 1835 edition. C. Funck-Brentano makes the date 1838 for French "dictionaries," but adds that there is one pre-nineteenth-century use known, Turgot's: "Au commencement de la civilisation." [8]

We find in the Encyclopédie [9] only a juristic meaning for *Civiliser,* namely co change a criminal legal action into a civil one. The following article is on civilité, politesse, affabilité. Incidentally, culture appears as a heading only in culture des terres, 20 pages long. In the French of the nineteenth century, *civilisation* is ordinarily used where German would use *Kultur.* One can point to a few examples of the use of *culture* like Lavisse's: "leur culture était toute livresaue et scolaire;" [10] but it is evident that the meaning here is education, German Bildung, not culture in the anthropological sense.

The English language lagged a bit behind French. In 1773, Samuel Johnson still excluded *civilization* from his dictionary Boswell had urged its inclusion, but Johnson preferred *civility.* Boswell [11] notes for Monday, March 23, 1772:

I found him busy, preparing a fourth edition of his folio Dictionary. He would not admit "civilization," but only "civility." With great deference to him, I thought "civilization" from "to civilize," better in the sense opposed to "barbarity," than "civility."

This seems indicative of where the center of gravity of meaning of the word then lay. John Ash, in his 1775 dictionary defines civilization as "the state of being civilized, the act of civilizing." Buckle's use of the noun in the title of his *History of Civilization* in England, 1857, might still be somewhat ambiguous in implication, but Lubbock's (Avebury's) *The Origin of Civilization,* 1870, which dealt with savages and not with refinement, means approximately what a modern anthropologist would mean by the phrase. [12] Neither of these titles is referred to by the Oxford Dictionary, though phrases from both Buckle and Lubbock are cited — with context of Egypt and ants! It must be remembered that Tylor's *Researches into the Early History and Development of Mankind* was five years old when Lubbock published. The Oxford Dictionary's own effort — in 1933! — comes to no more than this: "A developed or advanced state of human society; a particular stage or type of this."

Huizinga [13] gives a learned and illuminating discussion of the Dutch term, *beschaving,* literally *shaving* or *polishing,* and of its relations to *civilization* and *culture. Beschaving* came up in the late eighteenth century with the sense of *cultivation,* came to denote also the condition of being cultivated, blocked the spread of *civilisatie* by acquiring the sense of culture, but in the twentieth century was increasingly displaced by *cultuur.*

Huizinga also points out that Dante, in an early work, "Il Convivio," introduced into Italian *civiltà* from the Latin *civilitas,* adding a new connotation to the Latin original which made it, in Huizinga's opinion, a "specific and clear" term for the concept of culture.

[1] Wundt, 1910-20, vol. 10, ch. I, § I.

[2] To which Huizinga, 1945, p. 20, adds that the French verb civiliser preceded the noun civilisation — that is, a word for the act of *becoming* civilized preceded one for the condition of *being* civilized.

[3] However, we find that the 1733 *Universal-Lexicon aller Wissenschaften und Künste,* Halle und Leipzig, has no articles on either civilization or culture.

[4] Governmental control as a means to Christianity, morality, trade?

[5] Ellis, 1923, p. 288.

[6] In the sense of cultivation, cultivating.

[7] Arciniegas, 1947, pp. 145-46. He does not state under what head this quotation is to be found, and we have not found it — see next paragraph.

[8] Funck-Brentano, 1947, p. 64. Both Arciniegas and Funck-Brentano are in error as to the date — it was the 1798 edition; Turgot did not use the word; and there was not only one instance but many of pre-nineteenth century French usage of *civilisation.* The history of the French word has been most exhaustively reviewed by Lucien Febvre in his essay "Civilisation: Evolution d'un Mot et d'un Groupe d'Idées," forming pages 1-55 of the volume *Civilisation: Le Mot et l'Idée,* 1930, which constitutes the Deuxième Fascicule of the Première Semaine of Centre International de Synthèse, and which presents the best-documented discussion we have seen. We summarize this in an Addendum to the present Part One. On pages 3-7 Febvre concludes that Turgot himself did not use the word, that it was introduced into the published text by Turgot's pupil, Dupont de Nemours. The first publication of the word *civilisation* in French, according to Febvre, was in Amsterdam in 1766 in a volume entitled *L'Antiquite Devoilée par ses Usages.* Febvre also establishes by a number of citations that by 1798 the word was fairly well established in French scholarly literature. Finally (pp. 8-9), he makes a case for the view that the English word was borrowed from the French.

[9] We had available the 1780-82 edition published in Lausanne and Berne. *Civiliser* is in vol. 8. According to Berr's discussion on Febvre, 1930 (as just cited in full), p. 59, the participle from this verb is used already by Descartes (Discourse on Method, Part II).

[10] Lavisse, 1900-11, vol. VII, I, p. 30, cited by Huizinga, 1945, p. 24. The reference is to the seventeenth-century "noblesse de robe."

[11] Quoted in Huizinga, 1945, p. 21; also in New English (Oxford) Dictionary, vol. 2, 1893, "Civilization," under "1772 — Boswell, Johnson, XXV."

[12] For instance, Goldenweiser, *Early Civilization,* 1922.

[13] Huizinga, 1945, pp. 18-33. Dante's *Civiltà,* p. 22.

3. Relation of Civilization and Culture

The usage of "culture" and "civilization" in various languages has been confusing. [1] Webster's Unabridged Dictionary defines both "culture" and "civilization" in terms of the other. "Culture" is said to be a particular state or stage of advancement in civilization. "Civilization" is called an advancement or a state of social culture. In both popular and literary English the tendency has been to treat them as near synonyms, [2] though "civilization" has sometimes been restricted to "advanced" or "high" cultures. On the whole, this tendency is also reflected in the literature of social science. Goldenweiser's 1922 introduction to anthropology is called *Early Civilization* and all index references to "culture" are subsumed under "civilization." Some writers repeatedly use the locutions "culture, or civilization," "civilization, or culture." Sumner and Keller follow this practice, but in at least one place make it plain that there is still a shade of difference in their conception:

The adjustments of society which we call civilization form a much more complex aggregation than does the culture that went before... (1917, 2189)

Occasional writers incline to regard civilization as the culture of societies characterized by cities — that is, they attempt or imply an operational definition based upon etymology. Sometimes there is a tendency to use the term civilization chiefly for literate cultures: Chinese civilization but Eskimo culture — yet without rigor or insistence of demarcation.

[1] For a thoughtful discussion, see Dennes, 1942.

[2] This statement, of course, does not apply to one popular usage, namely that which identifies "culture" with "refinement," "sophistication," "learning" in some individuals as opposed to others.

4. The Distinction of Civilization from Culture in American Sociology

Certain sociologists have attempted a sharp opposition between the two terms. These seem to have derived from German thought. Lester Ward writes:

We have not in the English language the same distinction between civilization and culture that exists in the German language. Certain ethnologists affect to make this distinction, but they are not understood by the public. The German expression *Kulturgeschichte* is nearly equivalent to the English expression history of civilization. Yet they are not synonymous, since the German term is confined to the material conditions [*sic!*], while the English expression may and usually does include psychic, moral, and spiritual phenomena. To translate the German *Kultur* we are obliged to say material civilization [*sic!*]. Culture in English has come to mean something en" rely different, corresponding to the humanities [*sic*]. But *Kultur* also relates to the arts of savages and barbaric peoples, which are not included in any use of civilization since that term in itself denotes a stage of advancement higher than savagery or barbarism. These stages are even popularly known as stages of culture, where the word culture becomes clearly synonymous with the German *Kultur.*

To repeat again the definition that I formulated twenty years ago: *material civilization consists in the utilization of the materials and forces of nature.* (1903. 18)

In a book published two years later, Albion Small expresses himself along not dissimilar lines:

What, then, is "culture" (Kultur) in the German sense? To be sure, the Germans themselves are not wholly consistent in their use of the term, but it has a technical sense which it is necessary to define. In the first place, "culture" is a condition or achievement possessed by *society.* It is not individual. Our phrase "a cultured person" does not employ the term in the German sense. For that, German usage has another word, *gebildet,* and the peculiar possession of the *gebildeter Mann* is not "culture," but *Bildung.* If we should accept the German term "culture" in its technical sense, we should have no better equivalent for *Bildung,* etc., than "education" and "educated," which convey too much of the association of school discipline to render the German conception in its entire scope. At all events, whatever names we adopt, there is such social possession, different from the individual state, which consists of adaptation in thought and action to the conditions of life.

Again, the Germans distinguish between "culture" and "civilization." Thus "civilization is the ennobling, the increased control of the elementary *human* impulses by society. Culture, on the other hand, is the control of *nature* by science and art." That is, civilization is one side of what we call politics; culture is our whole body of technical equipment, in the way of knowledge, process, and skill for subduing and employing natural resources, and it does not necessarily imply a high degree of socialization. (1905, 59-60)

Another American sociologist, writing some twenty-five years later, seizes upon an almost opposite German conception, that developed primarily by Alfred Weber in his *Prinzipielles zur Kultursoziologie.* MacIver thus equates "civilization" with means, and "culture" with ends:

...The contrast between means and ends, between the apparatus of living and the expressions of our life. The former we call civilization, the latter culture. By civilization, then, we mean the whole mechanism and organization which man has devised in his endeavor to control the conditions of life...Culture on the other hand is the expression of our nature in our modes of living and thinking, in our everyday intercourse, in art, in literature, in religion, in recreation and enjoyment...The realm of culture...is the realm of values, of styles, of emotional attachments, of intellectual adventures. Culture then is the antithesis of civilization. (1931, 126) [1]

Merton has criticized MacIver's position, provided a restatement of Weber, and supplied some refinements of his own:

...The essential difficulty with such a distinction [as MacIver's] is that it is ultimately based upon differences in motivation. But different motives may be basic to the same social activity or cultural activity...Obviously, a set of categories as flexible as this is inadequate, for social products tend to have the same social significance whatever the motivation of those responsible for them.

Weber avoids this difficulty. Civilization is simply a body of practical and intellectual knowledge and a collection of technical means for controlling nature. Culture comprises configurations of values, of normative principles and ideals, which are historically unique...

Both these authors [MacIver and A. Weber] agree in ascribing a series of sociologically relevant attributes to civilization and culture. The civilizational aspects tend to be more accumulative, more readily diffused, more susceptible of agreement in evaluation and more continuous in development than the cultural aspect...Again, both avoid a narrow determinism and indicate that substantial interaction occurs between the two realms.

This last point is especially significant. For insofar as he ignores the full significance of the *concrete* effects of such interdependence, Weber virtually reverts to a theory of progress. The fact which must be borne in mind is that accumulation is but an *abstractly* immanent characteristic of civilization. Hence, concrete movements which always involve the interaction with other spheres need not embody such a development. The *rate* of accumulation is influenced by social and cultural elements so that in societies where cultural values are inimical to the cultivation of civilization, the rate of development may be negligible...

The basis for the accumulative nature of civilization is readily apparent. Once given a cultural animus which positively evaluates civilizational activity, accumulation is inevitable. This tendency is rooted deep in the very nature of civilization as contrasted with culture. It is a peculiarity of civilizational activities that a set of operations can be so specifically defined that the criteria of the attainment of the various ends are clearly evident. Moreover, and this is a further consideration which Weber overlooks entirely, the "ends" which civilization serves are empirically attainable [2]...

Thus civilization is "impersonal" and "objective." A scientific law can be verified by determining whether the specified relations uniformly exist. The same operations will occasion the same results, no matter who performs them...

Culture, on the other hand, is thoroughly personal and subjective, simply because no fixed and clearly defined set of operations is available for determining the desired result...It is this basic difference between the two fields which accounts for the cumulative nature of civilization and the unique (noncumulative) character of culture. (1936, 109-12)

Among others, Howard Odum, the well-known regional sociologist, makes much the same distinction as Merton (cf. e.g., Odum, 1947, esp. pp. 123, 281, 285). To him also civilization is impersonal, artificial, often destructive of the values of the folk. Odum was heavily influenced by Toennies.

However, the anthropological conception, stemming back to Tylor, has prevailed with the vast majority of American sociologists as opposed to such special contrasts between "culture" and "civilization." Talcott Parsons — also under the influence of Alfred and Max Weber — still employs the concept of "culture" is a sense far more restricted than the anthropological usage, bur, as will be seen in Part II, almost all of the numerous definitions in recent writings by sociologists clearly revolve about the anthropological concept of culture. This trend dates only to the nineteen-twenties. Previously, culture was little used as a systematic concept by American sociologists. [3] If it appeared in their books at all, it was as a casual synonym for "civilization" or in contradistinction to this term.

Ogburn's *Social Change: With Respect to Culture and Original Nature* (1922) seems to have been the first major work by an American sociologist in which the anthropological concept of culture was prominently employed. Ogburn studied with Boas and was influenced by him. He appears also to have been cognizant of Kroeber's *The Superorganic,* 1917. He cites Kroeber's *The Possibility of a Social Psychology* (1918). The appearance of Lowie's little book. *Culture and Ethnology* (1917), and Wissler's *Man and Culture* (1923), seems to have made a good deal of difference. At any rate, the numerous articles [4] on culture and "cultural sociology" which make their appearance in sociological journals in the next ten years cite these books more frequently than other anthropological sources, although there is also evidence of interest in Boas and in Wissler's culture area concept.

To summarize the history of the relations of the concepts of culture and civilization in American sociology, there was first a phase in which the two were contrasted, with culture referring to material products and technology; then a phase in which the contrast was maintained but the meanings reversed, technology and science being now called civilization; and, beginning more or less concurrently with this second phase, there was also a swing to the now prevalent non-differentiation of the two terms, as in most anthropological writing, culture being the more usual term, and civilization a synonym or near-synonym of it. In anthropology, whether in the United States or in Europe, there has apparently never existed any serious impulse to use culture and civilization as contrastive terms.

[1] This conception is followed also in *The Modern State* and in articles by MacIver, and is modified and developed in his *Social Causation* 1942, which we have discussed in Part Three, Group *b.*

[2] [Merton's footnote] This fundamental point is implied by MacIver but is not discussed by him within the same context.

[3] Chugerman (1939) in his biography of Lester Ward states that *Pure Sociology* (1903) marks Ward's transition from a naturalistic to a cultural approach. C. A. Ellwood and H. E. Jensen in their introduction to this volume also comment "In effect. Ward holds in *Pure Sociology* that sociology is a science of civilization or 'culture' which is built up at first accidentally and unconsciously by the desires and purposes of men, but is capable of being transformed by intelligent social purposes" (p. 4). But the anthropologist who reads *Pure Sociology* will hardly recognize the concept of culture as he knows it.

[4] See Bernard (1926, 1930, 1931); Case (19Z4b, 1917); Chapin (1925); Ellwood (1927a, 1917b); Frank (1931); Krout (1932); Price (1930); Smith (1929); Stem (1929); Wallis (1929); Willcy (1927a, 1927b, 1931). Abel (1930) views this trend with alarm as does Gary in her chapter in the 1929 volume *Trends in American Sociology*. Gary cites Tylor's definition and one of Wissler's.

5. The Attempted Distinction in Germany

This American sociological history is a reflection of what went on in Germany, with the difference that there the equation of culture and civilization had been made before their distinction was attempted, and that the equating usage went on as a separate current even while the distinction was being fought over. The evidence for this history will now be presented. We shall begin with the contrast of the two concepts, as being a relatively minor incident which it will be expedient to dispose of before we examine the main theme and development of usage in Germany.

The last significant representative known to us of the usage of the noun culture to denote the material or technological component is Barth. [1] He credits Wilhelm von Humboldt, in his *Kawisprache,* 1836, [2] with being the first to delimit the "excessive breadth" which the concept of culture had assumed. Humboldt, he says, construed culture as the control of nature by science and by "Kunst" (evidently in the sense of useful arts, viz., technology); whereas civilization is a qualitative improvement, a "Veredelung," the increased control of elementary human impulses (Triebe) by society. As a distinction, this is not too sharp; and Humboldt's own words obscure it further. He speaks of civilization as "die Vermenschlichung der Völker in ihren äusseren Einrichtungen und Gebräuchen und der darauf Bezug nabenden Gesinnung." This might be Englished as "the humanization of peoples in their outer [manifest, visible, tangible, overt?] arrangements [institutions] and customs and in their [*sc.* inner, spiritual] disposition relating to these [institutions]."

Next, Barth cites A. Schaeffle, 1875-78, [3] who gives the name of "Gesittung" to what eventuates from human social development. There is more connotation than denotation in this German word, so that we find it impossible to translate it exactly. However, a "gesitteter" man is one who conducts himself according to Sitte, custom (or mores), and is therefore thoroughly human, non-brutish. The word Gesittung thus seems essentially an endeavored substitution for the older one of culture. Schaeffle then divides Gesittung into culture and civilization, culture being, in his own words, the "sachliche Gchalt aller Gesittung." "Sachlich" varies in English sense from material to factual to relevant; "sachliche Gehalt" probably means something close to the "concrete content" of "Gesittung." Schaeffle's "civilization," according to Barth, refers to the interior of man, "das Innere des Menschen"; it is the "attainment and preservation of the [cultural] sachliche Gehalt in the nobler forms of the struggle for existence." This is as nebulous as Humboldt; and if we cite passages of such indefiniteness from forgotten German authors, it is because it seems worthwhile to show that the culture-civilization distinction is essentially a hang-over, on both sides of the argument, of the spirit-nature dichotomy — Geist und Natur — which so deeply penetrated German thought from the eighteenth to the twentieth century. Hence the ennoblements, the inwardnesses, the humanizations as opposed to the factual, the concrete, and the mechanical arts.

Barth also reckons on the same side Lippert — whose *Kulturgeschichte der Menschheit,* 1886, influenced Sumner and Keller — on the ground that he postulates "Lebensfürsorge" as "Grundantrieb" (subsistence provision constituting the basal drive), and then derives from this primary impulse tools, skills, ideas [*sic*], and social institutions. [4]

Barth's own resumé of the situation is that "most often" culture refers to the sway of man over nature, civilization to his sway over himself; though he admits that there is contrary usage as well as the non-differentiating, inclusive meaning given to culture. It is clear that in the sway-over-nature antithesis with sway-over-himself, the spirit of man is still being preserved as something intact and independent of nature.

15

It was into this current of nomenclature that Ward and Small dipped.

Now for the contrary stream, which, although overlapping in time, began and perhaps continued somewhat later, and to which MacIver and Merton are related. Here it is civilization that is technological, culture that contains the spiritualities like religion and art.

Toennies, in his *Gemeinschaft und Gesellschaft,* first published in 1887, [5] makes his primary dichotomy between community' and society, to which there corresponds a progress from what is socially "organic" to what is "mechanical," a transition from the culture of folk society (Volkstum) to the civilization of state organization (Staatstum). Culture comprises custom (Sitte), religion, and art: civilization comprises law and science. Just as psychological development is seen as the step from Gemüt to Verstand and political development that from Gemeinschaft to Gesellschaft, so Kultur is what precedes and begets Zivilisation. There is some similarity to Irwing's distinction between Kultur des Willens and Kultur des Verstandes. While Toennies' culture-civilization contrast is formally secondary to the Gemeinschaft-Gesellschaft polarity in Toennies' thought, it is implicit in this from the beginning. His frame of distinction is social in terms, but the loading of the frame is largely cultural (in the anthropological sense of the word).

Alfred Weber's address "Der Soziologische Kulturbegriff," first read at the second German "Soziologentag" in 1912, [6] views the process of civilization as a developmental continuation of biological processes in that it meets necessities and serves the utilitarian objective of man's control over nature. It is intellectual and rational; it can be delayed, but not permanently prevented from unfolding. By contrast, culture is superstructural, produced from feeling; it works toward no immanent end; its products are unique, plural, non-additive.

Eight years later Weber reworked this thesis in *Prinzipielles zur Kultursoziologie* [7] in language that is equally difficult, but in a form that is clearer than his first attempt, perhaps both because of more thorough thinking through and because of a less cramping limitation of space. In this philosophical essay Weber distinguishes three components: social process, civilizational process, and cultural movement (or flow: Bewegung). It is this work to which MacIver and Merton refer in the passages already cited. [8] It should be added that Weber's 1920 essay contains evident reactions — generally negative — to Spengler's *Untergang* that had appeared two years before.

Spengler in 1918 [9] made civilization merely a stage of culture — the final phase of sterile crystallization and repetition of what earlier was creative. Spengler's basic view of culture is discussed below (in § 10).

Oppenheimer in 1922, [10] reverting to Schaeffle's "Gesittung," makes civilization to be the material, culture the spiritual content (geistige Gehalt) of "Gesittung." To art and religion, as expressions of culture, Oppenheimer adds science. [11]

Meanwhile, the Alfred Weber distinction, with civilization viewed as the technological, subsistential, and material facies, and culture as the spiritual, emotional, and idealistic one, maintained itself in Germany. See Menghin, 1931, and Tessmann in 1930, as cited and discussed in Part Three, *b.* Thurnwald, who always believed in progress in the sense of accumulation on physically predetermined stages, determined the locus or this as being situate in technology and allied activities, and set this off as civilization. In his most recent work (1950) the contrast between this sphere of "civilization" and the contrasting one of residual "culture" is the main theme, as the subtitle of the booklet shows: man's "ascent between reason and illusion." See especially our tabulation at the end of Part Three, *b.* [12]

Nevertheless, it is evident that the contrasting of culture and civilization, within the scope of a larger entity, was mainly an episode in German thought. Basically it reflects, as we have said, the old spirit-nature or spirit matter dualism carried over into the field of the growing recognition of culture. That it was essentially an incident is shown by the fact that the number of writers who made culture the material or technological aspect is about as great as the number or those who called that same aspect civilization. More significant yet is the fact that probably a still greater number of Germans than both the foregoing together used culture in the inclusive sense in which we are using it in this book. We therefore return to consideration of this major current, especially as this is the one that ultimately prevailed in North America and Latin America, in Russia and Italy, in Scandinavia and the Netherlands, partially so in England, and is beginning to be felt in long-resistive France.

[1] Barth, 1922.
[2] Barth, 1922, vol. I, p. xxxvii.
[3] *Bau und Leben des sozialen Körpers.*
[4] Bernheim's *Lehrbuch* (6th edition, 1914, p. 60) also has culture and civilization refer to man's mastery respectively over nature and over himself.

[5] Later editions in 1912, 1920 — Barth's summary in 1922, pp. 441-44.

[6] Published, he says in "Verhandlungen I Serie II." It is reprinted in his *Ideen zur Staats- und Kultursoziologie,* 1927, pp. 31-47.

[7] Weber, 1920, vol. 47, pp. 1-49. Primarily historical in treatment is Weber's book *Kulturgeschichte als Kultursoziologie,* 1935.

[8] A comment by Kroeber is being published under the title *Reality Culture and Value Culture,* No. 18 of *The Nature of Culture,* University of Chicago Press, 1952.

[9] Untergang des Abendlandes. The standard translation by C. F. Atkinson as *The Decline of the West* was published in 1926 (vol. 1), 1928 (vol. 2), 1939 (2 vols, in 1).

[10] Oppenheimer, 1922, vol. 1.

[11] For Wundt's distinction, see § 1, especially its footnote 8.

[12] Thurnwald, 1950, p. 38: "The sequence of civilizational horizons represents progress." Page 107: "Civilization is to be construed as the equipment of dexterities and skills through which the accumulation of technology and knowledge takes place. Culture operates with civilization as a means." Legend facing plate 11: "Civilization is to be understood as the variation, elaboration, and perfection of devices, tools, utensils, skills, knowledge, and information. Civilization thus refers to an essentially temporal chain of variable but accumulative progress — an irreversible process...The same [civilizational] object, when viewed as component of an associational unity at a given time, that is, in synchronic section of a consociation of particular human beings, appears as a component in a culture."

6. Phases in the History of the Concept of Culture in Germany

At least three stages may be recognized in the main stream of use of the term culture in Germany.

First, it appears toward the end of the eighteenth century in a group of universal histories of which Herder's is most famous. In these, the idea of progress is well tempered by an intrinsic interest in the variety of forms that culture has assumed. The slant is therefore comparative, sometimes even ethnographic, and inclined toward relativism. Culture still means progress in cultivation, toward enlightenment; but the context is one from which it was only a step to the climate of opinion in which Klemm wrote and the word culture began to take on its modern meaning.

Second, beginning contemporaneously with the first stage but persisting somewhat longer, is a formal philosophic current, from Kant to Hegel, in which culture was of *decreasing* interest. This was part of the last florescence of the concept of spirit.

The third phase, since about 1850, is that in which culture came increasingly to have its modern meaning, in general intellectual as well as technical circles. "Among its initiators were Klemm the ethnographer and Burckhardt the culture historian; and in its development there participated figures as distinct as the neo-Kantian Rickert and Spengler.

M. Heyne's *Deutsches Wörterbuch,* 189095, illustrates the lag of dictionary makers in all languages in seizing the modern broad meaning of culture as compared with its specific technical senses. After mentioning "pure cultures of bacilli," the Dictionary says that the original meaning was easily transferred to the evocation or finishing (Ausbildung) and the refining of the capabilities (Kräfte) of man's spirit and body — in other words, the sense attained by the word by 1780. No later meaning is mentioned, although the compound "culture history" is mentioned.

H. Schulz, *Deutsches Fremdwörterbuch,* 191 3, says that the word Kultur was taken into German toward the end of the seventeenth century to denote spiritual culture, on the model of Cicero's cultura animi, or the development or evocation (Ausbildung) of man's intellectual and moral capacities. In the eighteenth century, he says, this concept was broadened by transfer from individuals to peoples or mankind. Thus it attained its modern sense of the totality (as E. Bernheim, 1889, *Lehrbuch,* p. 47, puts it) "of the forms and processes of social life, of the means and results of work, spiritual as well as material."

This seems a fair summary of the history of the meanings of the word in German; as Bernheim's definition k the fair equivalent, for a German and a historian, of Tylor's of eighteen years earlier.

The earliest appearance of the term "culture history," according to Sehultz, is in Adelung's *Geschichte der Cultur,* 1782 and, (discussed in §7 and note 49), in the reversed order of words, in D. H. Hegewisch, *Allgemeine Uebersicht der teutschen Culturgeschichte,* 1788.

7. Culture as a Concept of Eighteenth-Century General History

In its later course, the activity of eighteenth-century enlightenment found expression in attempts at universal histories of the development of mankind of which Herder's is the best-known. This movement was particularly strong in Germany and tended to make considerable use of the term culture. It was allied to thinking about the "philosophy of history," but not quite the same. The latter term was established in 1765 by Voltaire when he used it as the title of on essay that in 1769 became the introduction of the definitive edition of his *Essai sur les Moems et FEsprit des Nations.''* [1] Voltaire and the Encyclopedists were incisive, reflective, inclined to comment philosophically. Their German counterparts or successors tended rather to write systematic and sometimes lengthy histories detailing how man developed through time in all the continents, and generally with more emphasis on his stages of development than on particular or personal events. Such stages of development would be traceable through subsistence, arts, beliefs, religion of various successive peoples: in short, through their customs, what we today would call their culture. The word culture was in fact used by most of this group of writers of universal history'. To be sure, a close reading reveals that its precise meaning was that of "degree to which cultivation has progressed." But that meaning in turn grades very easily and almost imperceptibly into the modern sense of culture. In any event, these histories undoubtedly helped establish the word in wide German usage; the shift in meaning then followed, until by the time of Klemm, in 1843, the present-day sense had been mainly attained and was ready-made for Tylor, for the Russians, and others.

In the present connection, the significant feature of these histories of. mankind is that they were actual histories. They were permeated by, or aimed at, large ideas; but they also contained masses of concrete fact, presented in historical organization. It was a different stream of thought from that which resulted in true "philosophies of history," that is, philosophizings about history, of which Hegel became the most eminent representative. By comparison, this latter was a deductive, transcendental movement; and it is significant that Hegel seems never to have used the word culture in his *Philosophy of History*, and civilization only once and incidentally. [2] This fact is the more remarkable in that Hegel died only twelve years [3] before Klemm began to publish. He could not have been ignorant of the word culture, after Herder and Kant had used it: it was his thinking and interests that were oriented away from it.

It must accordingly be concluded that the course of "philosophy of history" forked in Germany. One branch, the earlier, was interested in the actual story of what appeared to have happened to mankind. It therefore bore heavily on customs and institutions, became what we today should call culture-conscious, and finally resulted in a somewhat diffuse ethnographic interest. From the very beginning, however, mankind was viewed as an array or series of particular peoples. The other branch of philosophy of history became less interested in history and more in its supreme principle. It dealt increasingly with mankind instead of peoples, it aimed at clarifying basic schemes, and it operated with the concept of "spirit" instead or that of culture. This second movement is of little further concern to us here. But it will be profitable to examine the first current, in which comparative, cultural, and ethnographic slants are visible from the beginning.

The principal figures to be reviewed are Irwing, Adelung, Herder, Meiners, and Jenisch; their work falls into the period from 1779 to 1801. First, however, let us note briefly a somewhat earlier figure.

Isaac Iselin, a Swiss, published in Zurich in 1768 a *History of Mankind,* [4] which seems not to contain the words culture or civilization. The first of eight "books" is given over to a Psychological ("psychologische") Consideration of Man, the second to the Condition (Stand) of Nature (of Man — in Rousseau's sense, but not in agreement with him), the third to the Condition of Savagery, the fourth to the Beginnings of Good Breeding (Gesittung, i.e., civilization). Books five to eight deal with the Progress of Society (Geselligkeit — sociability, association?) toward Civil (bürgerlich, civilized?) Condition, the Oriental peoples, the Greeks and Romans, the Nations of Europe. The implicit idea of progress is evident. The polar catchwords are Wildheit and Barbarey (Savagery and Barbarism), on the one hand; on the other, Milderung der Sitten, Policirung, Erleuchtung, Verbesserung, that is, Amelioration of Manners, Polishing (rather than Policing), Illumination (i.e.. Enlightenment), Improvement. The vocabulary is typical mid-eighteenth century French or English Enlightenment language put into German — quite different from the vocabulary of Adelung and Herder only twenty-five to thirty years later: Cultur, Humanität, Tradition are all lacking. While Europe was everywhere groping toward concepts like those of progress and culture, these efforts were already segregating into fairly diverse streams, largely along national speech lines.

K. F. von Irwing, 1725-1801, an Oberconsistorialrat in Berlin, who introduces the main Gentian series, attempted, strictly speaking, not so much a history of mankind as an inquiry into man, [5] especially his individual and social springs or impulses ("Triebfedern" or "Triebwerke"). He is of interest in the present connection on account of a long section, his fourteenth, devoted to an essay on the culture of mankind. [6] Culture is cultivation, improvement, to Irwing. Thus: The improvements and increases of human capacities and energies, or the sum of the perfectings (Volkkommenheiten) to which man can be raised from his original rudest condition — these constitute "den allgemeinen Begriff der ganzen Kultur ueberhaupt" — a very Kantian-sounding phrase. Again: The more the capacities of man are worked upon ("bearbeitet werden") by culture ("dutch die Kultur") the more does man depart from the neutral condition ("Sinnesart") of animals. Here the near-reification of culture into a seemingly autonomous instrument is of interest. Culture is a matter and degree of human perfection (Vollkommenheit) that is properly attributable only to the human race or entire peoples: individuals are given only an education (Erziehung), and it is through this that they are brought to the degree (Grade) of culture of their nation. [7]

Johann Christoph Adelung, 1732-1806, already mentioned as the author of the dictionaries of 1774 and 1793, published anonymously in 1782 an *Essay on the History of Culture of the Human Species.* [8] This is genuine if highly summarized history, and it is concerned primarily with culture, though political events are not wholly disregarded. The presentation is in eight periods, each of which is designated by a stage of individual human age, so that the idea of growth progress is not only fundamental but explicit. The comparison of stages of culture with stages of individual development was of course revived by Spengler, though Spengler also used the metaphor of the seasons. [9] Adelung's periods with their metaphorical designations are the following:

1. From origins to the flood. Mankind an embryo.
2. From the flood to Moses. The human race a child in its culture.
3. From Moses to 683 B.C. The human race a boy.
4. 683 B.C. to A.D. 1. Rapid blooming of youth of the human race.
5. A.D. 1 to 400 (Migrations). Mankind an enlightened man (aufgeklaerter Mann).
6. 400-1096 (Crusades). A man's heavy bodily labors.
7. 1096-1520 (1520, full enlightenment reached). A man occupied in installation and improvement of his economy (Hauswesen).
8. 1510 (1782). A man in enlightened enjoyment (im aufgeklaerten Genusse). [10]

Adelung is completely enlightened religiously. In § 1 he does not treat of the creation of man but of the origins of the human race ("Ursprung seines Geschlechts"). Moses assures us, he says, that all humanity' is descended from a single pair, which is reasonable; but the question of how this pair originated cannot be answered satisfactorily, unless one accepts, along with Moses, their immediate creation by God. But man was created merely with the disposition and capacity ("Anlage") of what he was to become (§ 3). Language was invented by man; it is the first step toward culture (§5 foll.). The fall of man is evaded (§ 13); but as early as Cain a simultaneous refinement and corruption of customs ("Verderben der Sitten") began (§ 24). The Flood and the Tower of Babel are minimized (Ch. 2, § 1-4), not because the author is anticlerical but because he is seeking a natural explanation for the growth of culture. Throughout, he sees population increase as a primary cause of cultural progress. [11]

While there are innumerable passages in Adelung in which his "Cultur" could be read with its modern meaning, it is evident that he did not intend this meaning — though he was unconsciously on the wav to it. This is clear from his formal definitions in his Preface. These are worth quoting.

Cultur ist mir der Uebergang aus dem mehr sinnlichen und thierischen Zustande in enger verschlungene Verbindungen des gesellschaftlichen Lebens. (Culture is the transition from a more sensual and animal condition to the more closely knit interrelations of social life.)

Die Cultur bestehet...in der Summe deutlicher Begriffe, und...in der...Milderung und Verfeinerung des Koerpers und der Sitten. (Culture consists of the sum of defined concepts and of the amelioration and refinement of the body and of manners.)

The word "sum" here brings this definition close to modern ones as discussed in our Part II; it suggests that Adelung now and then was slipping into the way of thinking of culture as the *product* of cultivation as well as the *act* of cultivating.

Die Cultur des Geistes bestehet in einer immer zunehmenden Summe von Erkenntnissen, welche nothwendig wachsen muss...(Spiritual culture consists in an ever increasing and necessarily growing sum of understandings.)

And finally:

Gerne hactte ich für das Wort *Cultur* einen deutschen Ausdruck gewähiet; allein ich wciss keinen, der dessen Begriff erschocpfte. *Verfeinerung, Aufklaerung, Entwinckelung der Faehigkeiten,* sagen alle erwas, aber nicht alles. (I should have liked to choose a German expression instead of the word culture; but I know none that exhausts its meaning. *Refinement, enlightenment, development of capacities* all convey something, but not the whole sense.)

Again we seem on the verge of the present-day meaning of culture.

Adelung's definition of Cultur in his 1793 German dictionary confirms that to him and his contemporaries the word meant improvement, rather than a state or condition of human social behavior, as it does now. It reads:

Cultur — die Veredlung oder Verfeinerung der gesammten Geistes- and LeibesKraeftec eines Menschen oder eines Volkes, so dass dieses Wort so wohl die Aufklaerung, die Veredlung des Verstandes durch Befreyung von Vorurtheilen, aber auch die *Politur,* die Veredlung und Verfeinerung der Sitten unter sich begreift. (Culture: the improvement [ennoblement] or refining of the total mental and bodily forces of a person or a people; so that the word includes not only the enlightening or improving of understanding through liberation from prejudices, but also polishing, namely [increased] improvement and refinement, of customs and manners.)

Veredlung, literally ennoblement, seems to be a metaphor taken from the improvement of breeds of domesticated plants and animals.

It is significant that the application of the term culture still is individual as well as social.

Adelung's definition is of interest as being perhaps the first formal one made that includes, however dimly, the modern scientific concept of culture. However, basically it is still late eighteenth century, revolving around polish, refining, enlightenment, individual improvement, and social progress.

Johann Gottfried Herder's (1744-1803) *Ideas on the Philosophy of History of Mankind* [12] is the best-known and most influential of these early histories of culture. The title reverts to the "Philosophy of History" which Voltaire had introduced twenty years before; but the work itself deals as consistently as Adelung's with the development of culture. The setting, to be sure, is broader. The first section of Book I has the heading: "Our Earth is a Star Among Stars." Books II and III deal with plants and animals; and when man is reached in Book IV', it is to describe his structure, what functions he is organized and shaped to exercise. Book V deals with energies, organs, progress, and prospects. In Books VI and VII racial physiques and geographical influences are discussed. A sort of theory of culture, variously called Cultur, Humanitat, Tradition, is developed in VIII and IX; X is devoted to the historic origin of man in Asia, as evidenced by "the course of culture and history" in its § 3. Books XI to XX then settle down to an actual universal history of peoples — of their cultures, as we would say, rather than of their politics or events. These final ten books deal successively [13] with East Asia, West Asia, the Greeks, Rome, humanization as the purpose of human nature, marginal peoples of Europe, origin and early development of Christianity, Germanic peoples, Catholicism and Islam, modern Europe since Amalfi and the Crusades.

Herder's scope, his curiosity and knowledge, his sympathy, imagination, and verve, his enthusiasm for the most foreign and remote of human achievements, his extraordinary freedom from bias and ethnocentricity, endow his work with an indubitable quality of greatness. He sought to discover the peculiar values of all peoples and cultures, where his great contemporary Gibbon amused himself by castigating with mordant polish the moral defects of the personages and the corruption and superstition of the ages which he portrayed.

Basically, Herder construes Cultur as a progressive cultivation or development of faculties. Not infrequently he uses Humanitat in about the same sense. Enlightenment, Aufklärung, he employs less often; but Tradition frequently, both in its strict sense and coupled with Cultur. This approach to the concepts of culture and tradition has a modern ring: compare our Part Two.

Wollen wir diese zweite Genesis des Menschen die sein ganzes Leben durchgeht, von der Bearbeitung des Ackers *Cultur,* oder vom Bilde des Lichtes Aufklärung nennen: so stehet uns der Name frei; die Kette der Culrur und Aufklärung reicht aber sodann ans Ende der Erde. (13: 348; IX, 1)

Setzen wir gar noch willkührliche Unterschiede zwischen Cultur und Aufklärung fest, deren keine doch, wenn sie rechter Art ist, ohne die andere sein kann... (13: 348; IX, 1)

Die Philosophie der Geschichte also, die Kette der Tradition verfolgt, ist eigentlich die wahre Menschengeschichte. (13: 352; IX, 1)

Die ganze Geschichte der Menschheit...mit alien Schätzen ihrer Tradition und Cultur... (13: 355; IX, 2)

Zum gesunden Gebrauch unsres Lebens, kurz zur Bildung der Humanität in uns... (13: 361; IX, 2)

Die Tradition der Traditionen, die Schrift. (13: 366; IX. 2)

Tradition ist [also auch hier] die fortplanzende Mutter, wie ihrer Sprache und wenigen Cultur, so auch ihrer Religion und heiligen Gebräuche (13: 388; IX 3)

Der religiösen Tradition in Schrift und Sprache ist die Erde ihre Samenkörner aller höheren Cultur schuldig. (13: 391; IX, 5)

Das gewisseste Zeichen der Cultur einer Sprache ist ihre Schrift. (13: 408; X, 3)

Wenn...die Regierungsformen die schwerste Kunst der Cultur sind... (13: 411; X, 3)

Auch hüte man sich, allen diesen Völkern gleiche Sitten oder gleiche Cultur zuzueignen. (14: 175; XVI, 3)

Von selbst hat rich kein Volk in Europa zur Cultur erhoben. (14: 289; XVI, 6)

Die Städte sind in Europe gleichsam stehende Heerlager der Cultur. (14: 486; XX, 5)

Kein Thier hat Sprache, wie der Mensch sie hat, noch weniger Schrift, Tradition, Religion, willkührliche Gesetze und Rechte. Kein Tier endlich hat auch nur die Bildung, die Kleidung, die Wohnung, die Künste, die unbestimmte Lebensart, die ungebundenen Triebe, die flatterhaften Meinungen, womit sich beinahe jedes Individuum der Menschheit auszeichnet. (13: 109; III, 6)

The enumeration in this last citation is a good enough description of culture as we use the word. If it had the modern meaning in his day. Herder would probably have clinched his point by adding "culture" to sum up the passage.

C. Meiners, 1747-1810, published in 1785 a *Grundriss der Geschichte der Menschheit.* We have not seen this work and know of it through Stoltenberg, [14] Muehlmann, and Lowie. [15] It aims to present the bodily formation, the "Anlagen" of the "spirit and heart," the various grades of culture of all peoples, especially of the unenlightened and half-cultivated ones. This comes, as Meiners himself admits, close to being a "Völkerkunde" [16] or ethnography. [17] Like most of his contemporaries, Meiners saw culture as graded in completeness, but since he rejected the prevalent three-stage theory (hunting, herding, farming) he was at least not a unilinear devclopmentalist.

D. Jenisch, 1762-1804, published in 1801 a work called *Universal-historical Review of the Development of Mankind viewed as a Progressing Whole.* [18] This book also we have not seen, and know of it through Stoltenberg's summary. [19] It appears to bear a subtitle "Philosophie der Kulturgeschichte." [20] Stoltenberg quotes Jenisch's recognition of the immeasurable gap between the actual history of culture and a rationally ideal history of human culture marked by progressive perfection. He also cites Jenisch's discussion of the "developmental history of political and civilizing culture." It would seem that Jenisch, like his German contemporaries, was concerned with culture as a development which could be traced historically, but still weighted on the side of the act of rational refining or cultivation rather than being viewed as a product or condition which itself serves as a basic influence on men.

[1] As usually stated; e.g., in E. Bernheim, *Lehrbuch,* 6th edition, 1914. But dates and titles are given variously, due no doubt in part to alterations, inclusions, and reissues by Voltaire himself. Febvre, 1930, summarized in Addendum to our Part I, credits the *Philosophie de l'Histoire* to 1736.

[2] "Es ist femer cin Faktum, dass mit fortschreitender Zivilisation der Gesellschaft und des Staats diese systemadsche Ausführung des Verstandes [in gebildeter Sprache] sich abschleift und die Sprache hieran ärmer und ungebildeter wird." (1920, 147; Allgem. Einleitung, III, 2.)

[3] His Philosophy of History is a posthumous work, based on his lecture notes and those of his students It was first published in 1837.

[4] Iselin, 1768 (Preface dated 1764, in Basel).

[5] Irwing, 1777-85.

[6] Vol. 3, § 184-207, pp. 88-372 (1779). This Abtheilung is entitled: "Von der allgemeinen Veranlassung zu Begriffen, oder von den Triebwerken, wodurch die Mcnschen zum richdgen Gebrauch ihrer Geisteskraefte gebracht werden. Ein Versuch ueber die Kulmr der Menschheit ueberhaupt." The word is spelt with K — Kultur.

[7] The three passages rendered are from pp. 122-23, 127 of § 188, "Von der Kultur ueberhaupt."

[8] Adelung, 1782. Sickel, 1933, contains on pp. 145209 a well-considered analysis of "Adelungs Kulturtheorie." Sickel credits Adelung with being the first inquirer to attribute cultural advance to increased population density (pp. 151-55).

[9] A fundamental difference is that Spengler applies the metaphor only to stages within particular cultures, never to human culture as a whole; but Adelung applies it to the totality seen as one grand unit.

[10] The metaphorical subtitles appear in the Table of Contents, but not in the chapter headings. For the first five periods, reference is to "mankind" (der Mensch) or to "the human race" (das menschliche Geschlecht); for the last three, directly to "a man" (der Mann), which is awkward in English where "man" denotes both "Mensch" and "Mann."

[11] Preface: "Die Cultur wird durch Volksmenge...bewirkt"; "Volksmenge im eingeshraenkten Raume erzeuget Cultur"; and *passim* to Chapter 8, § 2, p. 413.

[12] Herder, 1744-1803, 4 vols., 1784, 1785, 1787, 1791. These constitute vols. 13 and 14 of Herder's *Sämmtliche Werke* edited by Bernhard Suphan, 1887, reprinted 1909, pagination double to preserve that of the original work. We cite the Suphan paging.

[13] The books are without titles as such; we are roughly summarizing their contents.

[14] As cited, 1937, vol, I, 199-201.

[15] Mühlmann, 1948, pp. 63-66; Lowie, 1937, pp. 5, 10-11.

[16] The word Völkerkunde had been previously used by J. R. Forster, *Beiträge zür Volker- und Länderkunde,* 1781 (according to Stoltenberg, vol. I, 200).

[17] According to Muehlmann, just cited, p. 46, the word ethnography was first used in Latin by Johann Olorinus in his "Ethnographia Mundi," Magdeburg, 1608.

[18] *Universalhirtorischer Ueberlick der Envwicklung des Menschengeschlechts, als eines sich fortbildenden Ganzen,* 2 vols., 1801.

[19] Stoltenberg, 1937, vol. i, pp. 289-92.

[20] The original may have been "Cultur," Stoltenberg modernizes spellings except in titles of works.

8. Kant to Hegel

[1]

The great German philosophy of the decades before and after 1800 began with some recognition of enlightenment culture and improvement culture, as part of its rooting in the eighteenth century; but its general course was away from Cultur to Geist. This is evident in the passage from Kant to Hegel.

Kant says in his *Anthropologie:* [2]

Alle Fortschritte in der Cultur...haben das Ziel diese erworbenen Kentnisse und Geschicklichkeiten zum Gebrauch für die Welt anzuwenden.

Die pragmatische Anlage der Civilisirung durch Cultur. (p. 323)

"Künste der Cultur" are contrasted with the "Rohigkeit" of man's "Natur." (p. 324)

With reference to Rousseau, Kant mentions the "Ausgang aus der Natur in die Culrur," "die Civilisirung," "die vermeinte Moralisirung." (p. 326)

The national peculiarities of the French and English are derivable largely "aus der Art ihrer verschiedenen Cultur," those of other nations "vielmehr aus der Anlage ihrer Natur dutch Vermischung ihrer urspriinglich verschiedenen Stamme." (p. 315)

In this last passage Cultur might possibly seem to have been used in its modern sense, except that on page 311 Kant calls the French and English "die zwei civilisirtestcn Völker auf Erden," which brings the word back to the sense of cultivation.

In *Critique of Pure Reason,* 1781, Kant says, "metaphysics is the completion of the whole culture of reason." [3] Here again, culture must mean simply cultivation.

Fichte deals with Cultur and "Vernunftcultur" largely from the angle of its purpose: freedom. Cultur is "die Uebung aller Kraefte auf den Zweck der voelligen Freiheit, der voelligen Unabhaengigkeit von allem, was nicht wir selbst, unset reines Selbst ist." [4]

Hegel's transcendental philosophy of history, viewed with reference only to "spirit," a generation after a group of his fellow countrymen had written general histories which were de facto histories of culture, [5] has already been mentioned.

Schiller also saw culture unhistorically, added to a certain disappointment in the enlightenment of reason. [6] "Culture, far from freeing us, only develops a new need with every power it develops in us...It was culture itself which inflicted on modern humanity the wound [of lessened individual perfection, compared with ancient times]" (1883, 4: 566, 568). He takes refuge in "the culture of beauty," or "fine [schoene] culture," evidently on the analogy of fine arts or belles lettres. Lessing does not appear to use the word. Goethe uses it loosely in opposition to "Barbarei."

[1] Kant's position as an "anthropologist" is relevant to consideration of his treatment of "Cultur." Bidney (1949, pp. 484, 485, 486) remarks: "It is most significant, as Cassirer observes, that Kant was 'the man who introduced anthropology as a branch of study in German universities and who lectured on it regularly for decades.'...It should be noted, however, that by anthropology Kant meant something different from the study of human culture or comparative anatomy of peoples. For him the term comprised empirical ethics (folkways), introspective psychology, and 'physiology.' Empirical ethics, as distinct from rational ethics, was called 'practical anthropology.' ...Kant reduced natural philosophy or theoretical science to anthropology. Just as Kant began his critique of scientific knowledge by accepting the fact of mathematical science, so he began his ethics and his *Anthropologie* by accepting the fact of civilization." Kant's view, as defined by Bidney, seems very similar to the contemporary "philosophical anthropology" of Wein (1948) and the "phenomenological anthropology" of Binswanger (1947).

[2] References are to Kant's *Werke,* Reimer 1907 edition: the Anthropologie of 1798 is in vol. 7.

[3] Muller's translation. New York, 1896, p. 730. The original (Kritik, 2nd ed., Riga, 1787, p. 879) reads: "Eben deswegen ist Metaphysik auch die Vollendung aller Cultur der Menschlichen Vernunft."

[4] Cited from Eucken, 1878, p. 186.

[5] We have found one use of Zivilisation in Hegel as cited in footnote 43 above.

[6] *Briefe ueber die aesthetische Erziehung des Menschen,* 1795. Citations are from *Saemmtliche Werke,* vol. 4.

9. Analysis of Klemm's Use of the Word "Cultur"

It seems worth citing examples of Klemm's use of the word Cultur, because of his period being intermediate betvveen the late eighteenth-century usage by Herder, Adelung, etc., in the sense of "cultivation," and the modern or post-Tylorian usage. We have therefore gone over the first volume, 1843, of his *Cultur-geschichte,* and selected from the hundreds of occurrences of the word some that seem fairly to represent its range of meaning.

Very common are references to stages (Stufen) of culture. These can generally be read as referring to conditions of culture, as we still speak of stages; but they may refer only to steps in the act of becoming cultivated. We have: very low stage of culture, up to the stage of European culture, middle stages, higher stages, an early stage, our stage, a certain degree of culture (1: 2, 184, 185, 186, 199, 207, 209, 211, 220, 227, etc.).

Similar are combinations which include step or progress of culture: erste Schritt, fortschreitende, zuschreitet, Fortschritt zur Cultur (1: 185, 206, 209, 210). These are also ambiguous.

Also not certain are true culture (1: 204), purpose of culture (1: 205), yardstick of culture (1: 214), spiritual culture (1: 221), sittliche Cultur (1: 221), resting places (Anhaltepuncte) of culture (1: 224).

The following are typical passages in which culture is used as if in the modern sense:

My effort is to investigate and determine the gradual development of mankind from its rudest...first beginnings to their organization into organic nationalities (Volkskörper) m all respects, that is to say with reference to customs, arts (Kentnisse) and skills (Fertigkeiten), domestic and public life in peace or war, religion, science (Wissen) and art... (1: 21) [While the passage begins with mention of development, the list of activities with which it concludes is very similar to that in which Tylor's famous definition ends.]

We regard chronology as part of culture itself. (1: 25)

The means (or mechanisms, Mittel) of culture rooted first in private life and originally in the family, (1: 205)

We shall show...that possessions are the beginning of all human culture, (1: 206)

[With reference to colonies and spread of the "active race,"] the emigrants brought with them to their new homes the sum (Summe) of the culture which they had hitherto achieved (erstrebt) and used it as foundation of their newly florescent life, (1: 210)

Among nations of the "passive race," custom (Sitte) is the tyrant of culture, (1: 220)

South American Indians...readily assume a varnish (Firniss) of culture...But nations of the active race grow (bilden sich) from inside outward...Their culture consequently takes a slower course but is surer and more effective, (1: 288)

A blueprint (Fantasie) of a Museum of the culture history of mankind, (1: 352)

The last section of the natural history collection [of the Museum] would be constituted by [physical] anthropology...[and]...[materials illustrating] the rudest cultural beginnings of the passive race, (1: 356-57)

The next section comprises the savage hunting and fishing tribes of South and North America.... A system could now be put into effect which would be retained in all the following sections...about as follows: 1) Bodily constitution...2) Dress...3) Ornament...4) Hunting gear...5) Vehicles on land and water...6) Dwellings...7) Household utensils...8) Receptacles...9) Tools...10) Objects relating to disposal of the dead...11) Insignia of public life...batons of command, crowns, wampum, peace pipes, models of assemblies...12) War...13) Religious objects...14) Culture [*sic*]. Musical instruments, decorative ornament, petroglyphs, maps, drawings; illustrations (Sammlungen) of speech, poetical and oratorical products of the various nations, (1: 357-58)

Most of these ten cited passages read as if culture were being used in its modern anthropological sense — as indeed Klemm is de facto doing an ethnography, even though with reminiscences of Herder and Adelung as regards general plan. Whenever he adds or lists or summates, as in the first, fifth, and last of these citations, the ring is quite contemporary. Moreover, the "enlightenment," "tradition," "humanity" of Herder and his contemporaries have pretty well dropped out. [1] It is difficult to be sure that Klemm's concept of culture was ever fully the same as that of modern anthropologists. On the other hand, it would be hard to believe that he is never to be so construed. Most likely he was in an in-between stage, sometimes using the term with its connotations of 1780, sometimes with those of 1920 — and perhaps never fully conscious of its range, and, so far as we know, never formally defining it. [2]

In that case, the more credit goes to Tylor for his sharp and successful conceptualization of culture, and for beginning his greatest book with a definition of culture. He found Klemm doing ethnography much as it is being presented today, and using for his data a general term that was free of the implication of advancement that clung to English civilization. So Tylor substituted Klemm's "cultur" for the "civilization" he had himself used before, gave it formal definition, and nailed the idea to his masthead by putting the word into the title of his book. By his conscious explicitness, Tylor set a landmark, which Klemm with all his ten volumes had not done.

[1] We do not find civilization, and only one passing use of "civilisirt": "in the rest of civilized Europe" (1: 221)
[2] What Klemm does make clear is that he proposes to treat of the "gradual development of mankind as an individual" (1: 1): "I consider mankind as an individual...which...has its childhood, youth, maturity." (1: 21) But he does very little to follow out this Adelung idea.

10. The Concept of Culture in Germany Since 1850

By mid-nineteenth century, the Hegelian active preference for dealing with Geist in preference to Cultur was essentially over, and the latter concept became increasingly, almost universally, dominant in its own field. The term Zivilisation languished in Germany, much as Culture did in England, as denotation of the inclusive concept. It had some vogue, as we have seen, in two attempts — diametrically opposite ones, characteristically — to set it up as a rival to Culture by splitting off one or the other part of this as contrastive. But the prevailing trend was toward an inclusive term; and this became Cultur, later generally written Kultur. In this movement, philosophers, [1] historians, and literary men were more active and influential than anthropologists.

The following list of book titles suggests the course of the trend.

1843, Klemm, *Allgemeine Cultur-geschichte*
1854, Klemm, *Allgemeine Culturwissenschaft*
1860, Burckhardt, *Die Cultur der Renaissance in Italien*
1875, Hellwald, *Kultur in ihrer Natürlichen Entwickelung bis zur Gegenwart*
1878, Jodl, *Die Kulturgeschichtschreibung*
1886, Lippert, *Kultur der Menschheit*
1898, Rickert, *Kulturwissenschaft und Naturwissenschaft*
1899, Frobenius, *Probleme der Kultur*
1900, Lamprecht, *Die Kulturhistorische Methode*
1908, Vierkandt, *Stetigkeit im Kultunvandel*
1908, Mueller-Lyer, *Phasen der Kultur*
1910, Frobenius, *Kulturtypen aus dem Westsudan*
1914, Prcuss, *Die Geistige Kultur der Naturvölker*
1923, Lederer, *Aufgaben einer Kultursoziologie*
1923, *Die Kultur der Gegenwart:* Part III, Section 5, "Anthropologie," Eds., Schwalbe and Fischer
1923, Simmel, *Zur Philosophie der Kultur*
1924, Schmidt and Koppers, *Völker und Kulturen,* vol. I
1930, Bonn, *Die Kultur der Vereinigten Staaten*
1931, Buehler, *Die Kultur des Mittelalters*
1933, Frobenius, *Kulturgeschichte Afrikas*

Rickert's basic thesis, to the effect that what has been called Geisteswissenschaft really is Kulturwissenschaft and that it is the latter and not Geisteswissenschaft that should be contrasted with Naturwssenschaft — this thesis proves that Rickert's concept of kultur is as broad as the most inclusive anthropologist or "culturologist" might make claim for. Rickert's Wissenschaft of culture takes in the whole of the social sciences plus the humanities, in contemporary American educational parlance.

Spengler's somewhat special position in the culture-civilization dichotomy has already been touched on. For Spengler, civilization is the stage to which culture attains when it has become unproductive, torpid, frozen, crystallized. A culture as such is organismic and creative; it becomes. Civilization merely is; it is finished. Spengler's distinction won wide though not universal acceptance in Germany at least for a time, and is included in the 1931 edition of Brockhaus' *Konversationlexicon.* [2] In spite of the formal dichotomy of the words, Spengler's basic concept, the one with which his philosophy consistently operates, is that of culture. The monadal entities which he is forever trying to characterize and compare are the Chinese, Indian, Egyptian, Arabic-Magian, Classic, and Occidental cultures, as an anthropologist would conceive and call them. Civilization is to him merely a stage which every culture reaches: its final phase of spent creativity and wintry senescence, with fellaheen-type population. Cultures are deeply different, all civilization is fundamentally alike: it is the death of the culture on which it settles. Spengler's theory concerns culture, culture in at once the most inclusive and exclusive sense, and nothing else. He sees culture manifesting itself in a series almost of theophanies, of wholly distinct, uncaused, unexplainable realizations, each with an immanent quality and predestined career and destiny (Schicksal). Spengler's view is certainly mystic, but it is so because in trying to seize the peculiar nature of culture he helps his sharpness of grasp by not only differentiating but insulating culture from the remainder of the cosmos: in each of its occasional realizations, it is self-sufficient, self-determining and uncaused, hardly even perceivable. In fact, no culture really is wholly intelligible to members of other cultures. Culture in short is something wholly irreducible and unrelatable, for Spengler. This is an extreme view, unquestionably. But it can also be construed as an exaggeration of the view of some modern anthropologists that culture constitutes a distinctive aspect, dimension, or level with which for certain purposes it is most profitable to operate in terms of inter-cultural relations, even though ultimately the relations of cultural to non-cultural phenomena can never be disregarded. Pushed to the limit, this concept of the operational distinctiveness of culture, which is still relative, becomes the concept of its absolute distinctness and complete self-sufficiency. Spengler does not feel this distinctness and self-sufficiency as merely marking the limit of the concept of culture but as constituting the ultimate essence of its quality.

Spengler acknowledges his indebtedness to Nietzsche who wrote, "Kultur ist Einheit des künstlerischen Stils in allen Lebensäusserungen eines Volkes." [3] This accent on style recurs in Spengler.

We have already dealt (§4) with Alfred Weber's attempted distinction between "culture" and "civilization." A few words must be said here of Weber's "cultural sociology," particularly as set forth in his article in the 193 1 "Sociological Dictionary."'[4] Sociology, Weber writes, can be the science of social structures. But, he continues, as soon as you try to write sociology of religion, art, or knowledge, structural sociology must be transcended. And the Wesengehalt (reality' content), of which social structure is only one Ausdrucksform (expression), is Kultur. In its intent, therefore, Kultursoziologie is much the same as cultural anthropology. The irrationalist trend inherent in German Kultur ideas is perhaps perpetuated in the sharp stand Weber takes against all materialist conceptions of history which make cultural phenomena into mere superstructure. [5]

We close this section by commenting on the core of a definition by a philosopher in a German philosophical dictionary: [6]

Kultur ist die Daseinsweise der Menschheit (wie Leben die Daseinsweise des Protoplasmas und Kraft die Dasceinsweise der Materie) sowie das Resultat dieser Daseinsweise, der Kulturbesitz odor die Kulturerrungenschaften. (Culture is the mode of being of mankind — as life is the mode of being of protoplasm and energy the mode of being of matter — as well as the result of this mode of being, namely, the stock of culture possessed or cultural attainments.)

With culture construed as the characteristic mode of human existence or manifestation, as life is of organisms and energy of matter, we are close to the recent theory of integrative levels of organization, each level, in the words of Novikoff, [7] "possessing unique properties of structure and behavior, which, though dependent on the properties of the constituent elements, appear only when these elements are combined in the new system...The laws describing the unique properties of each level are qualitatively distinct, and their discovery requires methods of research and analysis appropriate to the particular level," This view, sometimes spoken of as a theory of emergent levels, seems to have been developed largely by biologists, first Lloyd Morgan, then Needham, Emerson, Novikoff, Herrick, etc., for the phenomena of life; though it was explicitly extended to the phenomena of society by W. M. Wheeler, also a biologist, but specially interested in social insects. For culture as a distinct level of organization, the most avowed proponents in American anthropology have probably been Kroeber and White. In Germany, culture as a level has been explicitly recognized chiefly by non-anthropologists such as Rickert and Spengler — by the latter with the unnecessary exaggerations mentioned.

Just when, by what German, and in what context Cultur was first unequivocally used in this fundamental and inclusive sense, as distinct from the previous meanings in which nurture or cultivation or progressive enlightenment are dominant, is interesting, but can be most securely worked out by a German well read in the generic intellectual literature of his people. [8]

Why it was the Germans who first attained, however implicitly, to this fundamental and inclusive concept and attached it to the vocable Cultur, is equally interesting and perhaps even more important. Almost certainly their priority is connected with the fact that in the decades following 1770 Germans for the first time began to contribute creatively to general European civilization abreast of France and England, and in certain fields even more productively; but at the same time they remained a nationality instead of an organized or unified nation. Being politically in arrears, their nationalism not only took solace in German cultural achievement, but was led to appraise culture as a whole above politics as a portion thereof; whence there would derive an interest in what constituted culture.

Some further suggestions are made by us below (§ 11, and by Dr. Meyer in Appendix A). But to follow out our hints fully, or try to discover other possible factors, would require a more intimate and pervasive acquaintance with the whole of German thought between about 1770 and 1870 than we possess. We therefore relinquish the problem at this point.

[1] There is an extensive literature in this century on Kulturphilosophie. See, for example, Kroner (1918) and the critique of Kroner's system by Marck (1929).

[2] Huizinga, 1945, p. 28.

[3] Geburt der Tragödie (Band I, Gesammelte Werke, Grossoktav-Ausgabe: Leipzig, 1924, p. 183. The identical sentence is repeated on p. 314 of the same work. Nietzsche (1844-1900) falls in the period when culture had acquired its modern meaning. At any rate, it is clear that Nietzsche is wholly out of the Kant-to-Hegel su'ing away from cognizance of culture. The *Nietzsche-Register* by Richard Oehler (Leipzig: Alfred Kroner V'erlag, 1926) lists hundreds of references to Kultur (pp. 182-87). Cf. also N. von BubnofT, Friedrich Nietzsches Kulturphilosophie und Unrwertungslehre, 1924, pp. 38-82.

[4] Handworterbuch der Soziologie, Stuttgart, 1931, pp. 284-94. Article "Kultursoziologie."

[5] Hans Freyer in his article (pp. 294-308) of the same *Handwörterbuch* offers a sociological concept of culture as opposed to Alfred Weber's cultural concept of sociology. He says, for example, "Das Problem Typen und Stufen der Kultur verwandelt sich...in die Frage nach den Struktur- und Entwicklungsgesetzen des gesellschaftlichen Lebens." (p. 307)

[6] Schmidt, 1922, p. 170.

[7] Novikoff, 1945, pp. 209-15. Compare also, Herrick, 1949, pp. 222-42.

[8] Barth, after discussing cultura animi in Cicero, Thomas More, Bacon, gives it up too: "Aber wo Cultura absolut, ohne Genitiv, zuerst gebraucht wird, nicht als Ackerbau wie bei den Alten, sondern im heutigen Sinne. habe ich nicht finden konnen." (1922, 1, 599, fn. 1)

11. "Kultur" and ""Schrecklichkeit"

Just before, during, and after World War I, the Germans became notorious among the Allied nations for alleged insistence on their having discovered something superior and uniquely original which they called Kultur. Thirty years later it is clear what underlay this passionate and propagandist quarrel. The Germans, having come to their modern civilization belatedly and self-consciously, believed that this civilization was more "advanced," of greater value, than that of other Western nations. French, British, and Americans believed the same for their national versions of the common Western civilization; but the French and British having had an integrated, standardized, and effective civilization longer than the Germans, took their position more for granted, were more secure in it, had spread much more of their civilization to other societies, and on the whole were enough in a status of superiority' to have to do no ill-mannered boasting about it. The other difference was that in both the French and English languages the ordinary word referring to the totality of social attainments, achievements, and values was civilization, whereas in German it had come to be Kultur. Here accordingly was a fine chance, in war time, to believe that the enemy claimed to have invented something wholly new and original which however was only a crude barbarism. Had the customary German word been civilization, we Allies would no doubt have argued back that our brand of it was superior, but we could hardly have got as indignant as we did become over the bogey meanings which seemed to us to crystallize around the wholly strange term Kultur.

This episode is touched on here because it confirms that in the Germany of 1914 the word culture had a popular meaning essentially identical to that with which anthropologists use it, whereas in spite of Tylor, the British, American, and French people, including even most of their upper educated level, were ignorant of this sense of the word, for which they then generally used civilization instead. [1]

[1] That this was the situation is shown also by the fact that the 1917 paper of Kroeber, *The Superorganic,* uses this term, superorganic, synonymously with "the social," when it is obvious that it is essentially culture that is being referred to throughout. h is not that Kroeber was ignorant of culture in 1917 but that he feared to be misunderstood outside of anthropology if he used the word.

12. Danilevsky

The Russians apparently took over the word and the concept of culture from the Germans (see Appendix A). This was pre-.Marxian, about mid-nineteenth century. In the late eighteen-sixties N. I. Danilevsky published first a series of anicles and then a book, *Russia and Europe,* [1] which was frankly Slavophile but has also attracted attention as a forerunner of Spengler. [2] He deals with the greater civilizations much in the manner of Spengler or Toynbee, but calls them culture-historical types [3] instead of cultures or civilizations. They are supernational, and while ethnically limited, they differ culturally in their quality.

We are not certain whether Danilevsky was the first Russian to employ culture in the sense which it had acquired in German, but it has come into general usage since his day. The noun is kul'tura; [4] the adjective kul'turnyi seems to mean cultural as well as cultured or cultivated. Kul'turnost' is used for level or stage of culture as well as for high level.

[1] Rossiia i Evropa, 1869 in the journal Zaria; 1871 in book form. Sorokin, 1950, pp. 49-71, summarizes Danilevsky's work, and on pp. 205-43 he critically examines the theory along with those of Spengler and Toynbee.
[2] Danilevsky acknowledges a debt to Heinrich Rückert's *Lehrbuch der Weltgeschichte in organischer Darstellung* (Leipzig, 1857). Ruckert defines Cultur as "die Totalität der Erscheinungen...in welcher sich die Selbständigkeit und Eligenthümlichkeit der höheren menschlichen Anlage ausspricht...." p. iii. Rueckert also uses the terms "Culturkreis," "Culturreihe," "Culturindividuum" (a particular culture), and "Culturtypus," pp. 92-97 and elsewhere. The last appears to be the origin of Danilevsky's "cultur-historical types."
[3] Kul'tumo-istoricheskie tipy.
[4] This is the standard method of transcription adopted by the Library of Congress. In it, the apostrophe following a consonant indicates the palatalization of that consonant. It is hence a direct transcription of the *miagkii znak* (soft sign) in the Russian alphabet.

13. "Culture" In the Humanities in England and Elsewhere

Curiously enough, "culture" became popularized as a literary word in England [1] in a book which appeared just two years before Tylor's. Matthew Arnold's familiar remarks in Culture and Anarchy (1869) were an answer to John Bright who had said in one of his speeches, "People who talk about culture...by which they mean a smattering of the two dead languages of Greek and Latin..." Arnold's own definition is primarily in terms of an activity on the part of an individual:
...a pursuit of total perfection by means of getting to know, on all the matters which most concern us, the best which has been thought and said in the world...I have been trying to show that culture is, or ought to be, the study and pursuit of perfection; and that of perfection as pursued by culture, beauty and intelligence, or, in other words, sweetness

and light, are the main characters... [culture consists in]...an inward condition of mind and spirit, not in an outward set of circumstances...

Arnold's words were not unknown to social scientists. Sumner, in an essay probably written in the eighties, makes these acid comments:

Culture is a word which offers us an illustration of the degeneracy of language. If I may define culture, I have no objection to produce it; but since the word came into fashion, it has been stolen by the dilettanti and made to stand for their own favorite forms and amounts of attainments. Mr. Arnold, the great apostle, if not the discoverer, of culture, tried to analyze it and he found it to consist of sweetness and light. To my mind, that is like saying that coffee is milk and sugar. The stuff of culture is all left out of it. So, in the practice of those who accept this notion, culture comes to represent only an external smoothness and roundness of outline without regard to intrinsic qualities. (Sumner, 1934, 12-23.)

Since Arnold's day a considerable literature on culture as humanistically conceived has accumulated. John Cowper Powys [2] in The Meaning of Culture lays less stress on formal education and more on spontaneity, play — in brief, on the expression of individual personality rather than the supine following of custom:

Culture and self-control are synonymous terms...What culture ought to do for us is to enable us to find somehow or other a mental substitute for the traditional restraints of morality and religion.... It is the application of intelligence to the difficult imbroglio of not being able to live alone upon the earth. (1929, 235)
What has been suggested in this book is a view of culture, by no means the only possible one, wherein education plays a much smaller part than does a certain secret, mental and imaginative effort of one's own, continued...until it becomes a permanent habit belonging to that psyche of inner nucleus of personality which used to be called the soul. (1929, 275)

Robert Bierstedt sums up as follows:

John Cowper Powys understands by culture that ineffable quality which makes a man at case with his environment, that which is left over after he has forgotten everything he deliberately set out to learn, and by a cultured person one with a sort of intellectual finesse, who has the aesthete's deep feeling for beauty, who can find quiet joy in a rock-banked stream, a peewee's call, a tenuous wisp of smoke, the warmth of a book format, or the serene felicity of friendship. (Bierstedt, 1936, 93)

The humanistic or philosophical meanings of culture tended to be the only ones treated in standard reference works for a long period. For example, John Dewey's article, "Culture," in the Cyclopaedia of Education (1911) does not cite Tylor or any other anthropologist, though he had been in contact with Boas at Columbia and later evidenced considerable familiarity with anthropological literature. Here Dewey says (239): "From the broader point of view culture may be defined as the habit of mind which perceives and estimates all matters with reference to their bearing on social values and aims." The Hastings Encyclopaedia of Religion and Ethics (1912) contains articles by anthropologists and a good deal of material on primitive religion, but C. G. Shaw, a philosopher who wrote the article, "Culture," makes no reference to the anthropological concept and comes only as close as Wundt to citing an anthropologist. Shaw, incidentally, attributes the introduction of the term "culture" into England to Bacon, citing his *Advancement of Learning*, 1605, II, xix 2F. [3]
The Spanish philosopher, Ortega y Gasset, operates within the humanistic tradition (in its German form) but gives a vitalistic twist:

We can now give the word, culture, its exact significance. There are vital functions which obey objective laws, though they are, inasmuch as they are vital, subjective facts, within the organism; they exist, too, on condition of complying with the dictates of a *régime* independent of life itself. These are culture. The term should not, therefore, bo allowed to retain any vagueness of content. Culture consists of certain biological activities, neither more nor less biological than digestion or locomotion.... Culture is merely a special direction which we give to the cultivation of our animal potencies. (1933, 41, 76)

He tends to oppose culture to spontaneity:
...culture cannot be exclusively directed by its objective laws, or laws independent of life, but is at the same time subject to the laws of life. We are governed by two contrasted imperatives. Man as a living being must be good, orders the one, the cultural imperative: what is good must be human, must be lived and so compatible with and necessary to

life, says the other imperative, the vital one. Giving a more generic expression to both, we shall reach the conception of the double mandate, life must be cultured, but culture is bound to be vital.... Uncultured life is barbarism, devitalized culture is byzantinism. (1933, 45-46)

To oppose life to culture and demand for the former the full exercise of its rights in the face of the latter is not to make a profession of anti-cultural faith...The values of culture remain intact; all that is denied is their exclusive character. For centuries we have gone on talking exclusively of the need that life has of culture. Without in the slightest degree depriving this need of any of its cogency, I wish to maintain here and now that culture has no less need of life...Modern tradition presents us with a choice between two opposed methods of dealing with the antinomy between life and culture. One of them — rationalism — in its design to preserve culture denies all significance to life. The other — relativism — attempts the inverse operation: it gets rid of the objective value of culture altogether in order to leave room for life. (1933, 86)

In other passages he makes points which are essential aspects of the anthropological conception of culture:

...the generations are born one of another in such a way that the new generation is immediately faced with the forms which the previous generation gave to existence. Life, then, for each generation is a task in two dimensions, one of which consists in the reception, through the agency of the previous generation, of what has had life already, e.g., ideas, values, institutions, and so on...(1933, 16)

The selection of a point of view is the initial action of culture. (1933, 60)

...Culture is the system of vital ideas which each age possesses; better yet, it is the system of ideas by which each age lives. (1944, 81)

F. Znaniecki's *Cultural Reality* (1919), though written in English by a Polish sociologist, is essentially a philosophical treatise. The basic point of view and argument can be indicated by brief quotations:

For a general view of the world the fundamental points are that the concrete empirical world is a world in evolution in which nothing absolutely permanent can be found, and that as a world in evolution it is first of all a world of culture, not of nature, a historical, not a physical reality. Idealism and naturalism both deal, not with the concrete empirical world, but with abstractly isolated aspects of it. (1919, 21)

We shall use the term "culturalism" for the view of the world which should be constructed on the ground of the implicit or explicit presuppositions involved in reflection about cultural phenomena...

The progress of knowledge about culture demonstrates more and more concretely the *historical relativity* of all human values, including science itself. The image of the world which we construct is a historical value, relative like all others, and a different one will take its place in the future, even as it has itself taken the place of another image.... The theories of the old type of idealism are in disaccordance with experience, for they conceive mind, individual consciousness or super-individual reason, as absolute and changeless, whereas history shows it relative and changing. (1919, 15-16)

The German philosopher, Ernst Cassirer, states (p. 52) that the objective of his *Essay on Man* is a *"phenomenology of human culture."* But, though he was familiar with modern anthropology, particularly the writings of Malinowski, his conception remains more philosophical than anthropological:

Human culture taken as a whole may be described as the process of man's progressive self-liberation. Language, art, religion, science are various phases in this process. In all of them man discovers and proves a new power — the power to build up a world of his own, an "ideal" world. (1944, 228)

At the moment many of the younger American philosophers are accepting one of the various anthropological definitions of culture. For example, the anthropologist finds himself completely at home reading Richard McKcon's treatment of culture in two recent articles in the "Journal of Philosophy" and "Ethics." One may instance a passage from *Philosophy and the Diversity of Cultures:*

If political problems have cultural and ideological dimensions, philosophies must treat not only ethical and esthetic judgments but must also examine the form which those judgments must take in terms of the operation of political power and relevant to actions accessible to the rule of law and their possible influence on the social expectations which make conventional morality. The study of cultures must present not merely the historically derived systems of designs for living in their dynamic interactions and interrelations in which political and ideological characteristics are given their place, but must also provide a translation of those designs of living into the conditions and conventional understandings which are the necessities and material bases of political action relative to common ends and an abstraction from them of the values of art, science, religion and philosophy which are the ends of human life and the explanations of cultures. (1950b, 239-40)

Werner Jaeger, the classicist, reflects both the dissatisfaction of most Western humanists with the anthropological habit of extending "culture" to encompass the material, humble, and even trivial, and also the tendency of one strain of German scholarship to restrict culture to the realm of ideals and values. He equates culture with the classical Greek concept of *paideia* and is quick to contrast the anthropological notion unfavorably:

We are accustomed to use the word culture not to describe the ideal which only the Hellenocentric world possesses, but in a much more trivial and general sense, to denote something inherent in every nation of the world, even the most primitive. We use it for the entire complex of all the ways and expressions of life which characterize any one nation. Thus the word has sunk to mean a simple anthropological concept, not a concept of value, a consciously pursued ideal. (1945, xviii)
...the distinction...between culture in the sense of a merely anthropological concept, which means the way of life or character of a particular nation, and culture as the conscious ideal of human perfection. It is in this latter, humanistic sense that the word is used in the following passage. The "ideal of culture" (in Greek areté and paideia) is a specific creation of the Greek mind. The anthropological concept of culture is a modern extension of this original concept; but it has made out of a concept of value a mere descriptive category which can be applied to any nation, even to "the culture of the primitive" because it has entirely lost its true obligatory sense. Even in Matthew Arnold's definition of culture...the original paideutic sense of the word (as the ideal of man's perfection) is obscured. It tends to make culture a kind of museum, i.e., paideia in the sense of the Alexandrian period when it came to designate *learning* (1945, 416)

The Arnold-Powys-Jaeger concept of culture is not only ethnocentric, often avowedly Hellenocentric; it is absolutistic. It knows perfection, or at least what is most perfect in human achievement, and resolutely directs its "obligatory" gaze thereto, disdainful of what is "lower." The anthropological attitude is relativistic, in that in place of beginning with an inherited hierarchy of values, it assumes that every society through its culture seeks and in some measure finds values, and that the business of anthropology includes the determination of the range, variety, constancy, and interrelations of these innumerable values.

Incidentally, we believe that when the ultramontane among the humanists renounce the claim that their subject matter is superior or privileged, and adopt the more catholic and humble human attitude — that from that day the humanities will cease being on the defensive in the modern world.

The most recent humanistic statement on culture is that of T. S. Eliot [4] who attempts to bridge the gap between the conception of the social sciences and that of literary men and philosophers. He quotes Tylor on the one hand and Matthew Arnold on the other. In rather a schoolmasterish way he reviews the meanings of "culture": (1) the conscious self-cultivation of the individual, his attempt to raise himself out of the average mass to the level of the elite; (2) the ways of believing, thinking, and feeling [5] of the particular group within society to which an individual belongs; and (3) the still less conscious ways of life of a total society. At times Eliot speaks of culture in the quite concrete denotation of certain anthropologists:

It includes all the characteristic activities and interests of a people: Derby Day, Henley Regatta, Cowes, the twelfth of August, a cup final, the dog races, the pin table, the dart board, Wensleydale cheese, boiled cabbage cut into sections, beetroot in vinegar, nineteenth-century Gothic churches and the music of Elgar. (1948, 31)

He also accepts the contemporary anthropological notion that culture has organization as well as content: "...culture is not merely the sum of several activities, but a way of life." (p. 40) On the other hand, he says "Culture may even be described as that which makes life worth living." (p. 26) Finally, he seems to be saying that, viewed concretely, religion is the way of life of a people and in this sense is identical with the people's culture. Anthropologists are not likely to be very happy with Eliot's emphasis on an elite and his reconciliation of the humanistic and social science views, and the literary reviews [6] have tended to criticize the looseness and lack of rigor of his argument.

[1] So deeply entrenched is this usage that as late as 1946 a distinguished anthropologist. Sir Arthur Keith, used "culture" in this humanistic sense (1946, 117-18).
[2] For other representative recent treatments from the point of view of the humanities, see Bums (1929), Patten (1916), Lowell (1934).
[3] Siebert (1905, p. 579) cites Bacon "cultura sive georgica animi" and gives the reference as De Augm. Scient., VII, 1. Neither citation conforms to the editions available to us.

[4] Eliot, 1948. Vogt (1951) has linked both the personal and "societal" conceptions of culture to the cult or cultus idea.
[5] Cf. "...culture — a peculiar way of thinking, feeling, and behaving." (p. 56) "Now it is obvious that one unity of culture is that of the people who live together and speak the same language: because speaking the same language means thinking, and feeling, and having emotions rather differently from people who use a different language." (pp. 120-21)
[6] Irwin Edman in *New York Times Book Review,* March 6, 1949; W. H. Auden in *The New Yorker,* April 23, 1949; John L. Myers in *Man,* July, 1949; William Barrett in *Kenyon Review,* summer, 1949.

14. Dictionary Definitions

The anthropological meaning of "culture" had more difficulty breaking through into wider public consciousness than did the word "civilization." This is attested by the history of "culture" in standard dictionaries of English. We summarize here what the Oxford dictionary has to say about the history of the word. [1]

Culture is derived from Latin cultura, from the verb colere, with the meaning of tending or cultivation. [It may also mean an honoring or flattering; husbandry — Short's Latin dictionary.] In Christian authors, ciiltiira has the meaning of worship. The Old French form was coumre, later replaced by culture. In English, the following uses are established: 1420, husbandry, tilling; 1483, worship; [2] 1510, training of the mind, faculties, manners. More (also, 165 1, Hobbs; 1752, Johnson; 1848, Macaulay); 1628 training of the humr-n body, Hobbes. Meaning 5 is: "The training, development, and refinement of mind, tastes, and manners; the condition of being thus trained and refined; the intellectual side of civilization." This is illustrated by citations from Wordswoith, 1805, and Matthew Arnold. [3] "A particular form of intellectual development," evidently referring to a pairing of language and culture, is illustrated from Freeman, 1867. Then there are the applications to special industries or technologies, with culture meaning simply "the growing of." Such are silk culture, 1796; oyster culture, 1862; bee culture, 1886; bacterial cultures, 1884.

There is no reference in the original Oxford Dictionary of 1893 to the meaning of culture which Tylor had deliberately established in 1871 with the title of his most famous book, *Primitive Culture,* and had defined in the first paragraph thereof. This meaning finally was accorded recognition sixty-two years after the fact, in the supplement [4] of 1933. The entry reads:

5b. *spec.* The civilization of a people (especially at a certain stage of its development in history).
1871, E. B. Tylor (title), *Primitive Culture.*
[1903, C. Lumholtz, *Unknown Mexico* is also cited.]

Webster's New International Dictionary in 1929 seems the first to recognize the anthropological and scientific meaning which the word had acquired:

7. A particular state or stage of advancement in civilization; the characteristic attainments of a people or social order: as, Greek culture; primitive culture [Examples from Tylor and Ripley follow; but that from Tylor is not his famous fundamental definition.] [5]

In the 1936 Webster, there appear three separate attempts to give the scientific meaning of the word culture, numbered 5a, 5b, 6. Of these, 5a is the 7 of 1929, with minor revisions of phrasing. The two others follow:

5b. The complex of distinctive attainments, beliefs, traditions, etc., constituting the background of a racial, religious, or social group; as, a nation with many *cultures.* Phrases in this sense are culture area, culture center, culture complex, culture mixing, culture pattern, culture phenomenon, culture sequence, culture stage, culture trait.
6. *Anthropol.* The trait complex manifested by a tribe or a separate unit of mankind.

These statements certainly at last recognize the fact that the word culture long since acquired a meaning which is of fundamental import in the more generalizing segments of the social sciences. Yet as definitions they are surely fumbling. "Particular state or *stage* of advancement"; "characteristic *attainments* of a...*social order*"; "distinctive attainments...*constituting the background* of a...group"; "the *trait complex manifested* by a tribe" — what have these to do with one another? What do they really mean or refer to — especially the vague terms here italicized? And what do they all build up to that a groping reader could carry away? — compared for instance with Tylor's old dictum that culture is civilization, especially if supplemented by a statement of the implications or nuances by which the two differ m import in some of their usages. It is true that anthropologists and sociologists also have differed widely in their definitions: if they had not, our Part Two would have been much briefer than it is. But these professionals were generally trying to find definitions that would be both full and exclusive, not merely adumbrative; and they often differ deliberately in their distribution of emphasis of meaning, where the dictionary makers seem to be trying to avoid distinctive commitment. [6]

Yet the main moral is the half-century of lag between the common-language meanings of words and the meanings which the same words acquire when they begin to be used in specific senses in professional disciplines like the social sciences. Dictionary makers of course are acute, and when it is a matter of something technical or technological, like a culture in a test tube or an oyster culture, or probably ergs or mesons, they are both prompt and accurate in recognizing the term or meaning. When it comes to broader concepts, especially of "intangibles," they appear to become disconcerted by the seeming differences in professional opinion, and hence either leave out altogether, as long as they can, the professional meaning which a word has acquired, or they hedge between its differences in meaning even at the risk of conveying very little that makes useful sense. Yet, primarily, the lag is perhaps due to students in social fields, who have gradually pumped new wine into skins still not empty of the old, in their habit of trying to operate without jargon in common-language terminology even while their concepts become increasingly refined. However, each side could undoubtedly profit from the other by more cooperation.

It will be of comparative interest to cite a definition of culture in a work which is both a dictionary and yet professionally oriented. This is the Dictionary of Sociology edited by H. P. Fairchild, 1944. The definition of culture was written by Charles A. Ellwood.

Culture: a collective name for all behavior patterns socially acquired and socially transmitted by means of symbols; hence a name for all the distinctive achievements of human groups, including not only such items as language, tool making, industry, art, science, law, government, morals, and religion, but also the material instruments or artifacts in which cultural achievements are embodied and by which intellectual cultural features are given practical effect, such as buildings, tools, machines, communication devices, art objects, etc.

...The essential part of culture is to be found in the patterns embodied in the social traditions of the group, that is, in knowledge, ideas, beliefs, values, standards, and sentiments prevalent in the group. The overt part of culture is to be found in the actual behavior of the group, usually in its usages, customs, and institutions...The essential part of culture seems to be an appreciation of values with reference to life conditions. The purely behavioristic definition of culture is therefore inadequate. Complete definition must include the subjective and objective aspects of culture. Practically, the culture of the human group is summed up in its traditions and customs; but tradition, as the subjective side of culture, is the essential core.

While this is somewhat prolix, it is enumeratively specific. In condensation, it might distill to something like this:

Culture consists of patterns of and for behavior acquired and transmitted by symbols, constituting the distinctive achievements of human groups, including their embodiments in artifacts; the essential core of culture consists of traditional [=historically derived and selected] ideas and especially their attached values.

It will be shown that this is close to the approximate consensus with which we emerge from our review that follows in Part II.

[1] *A New English Dictionary on Historical Principles,* ed. by J. A. H. Murray, vol. II, 1893.
[2] Elliot (1948) cites from the Oxford Dictionary another (rare) meaning of 1483: "The setting of bounds; limitation."
[3] Culture is "the study and pursuit of perfection;" and, of perfection, "sweetness and light" are the main characters.
[4] "Introduction,. Supplement, and Bibliography."
[5] Which we cite as A1 in Part Two.
[6] For instance. Funk and Wagnall's New Standard Dictionary, 1947, under Culture: "3. The training, development, or strengthening of the powers, mental or physical or the condition thus produced; improvement or refinement of mind, morals, or taste; enlightenment or civilization." By contrast, the Random House American College Dictionary of the same year does give a specific and modern definition: "7. *Sociol.,* the sum total of ways of living built up by a group of human beings, which is transmitted from one generation to another..." There are also definitions of culture area, change, complex, diffusion, factor, lag, pattern, trait.

15. General Discussion

The most generic sense of the word "culture" — in Latin and in all the languages which have borrowed the Latin root — retains the primary notion of cultivation [1] or becoming cultured. This was also the older meaning of "civilization." The basic idea was first applied to individuals, and this usage still strongly persists in popular and literary English to the present time. [2] A. second concept to emerge was that of German *Kultur,* roughly the distinctive "higher" values or enlightenment of a society. [3]

The specifically anthropological concept crystallized first around the idea of "custom." Then — to anticipate a little — custom was given a time backbone in the form of "tradition" or "social heritage." However, the English anthropologists were very slow to substitute the word "culture" for "custom." On March 10th, 1885, Sir James G. Frnzcr presented his first anthropological research to a meeting of the Royal Anthropological Society. In the discussion following the paper, he stated that he owed his interest in anthropology to Tylor and had been much influenced by Tylor's ideas. Nevertheless, he [4] speaks only of "custom" and "customs" and indeed to the end of his professional life avoided the concept of culture in his writings. R. R. Marett's Home University Library *Anthropology* also uses only the word custom. Radcliffe-Brown writing in 19:3 does not use "custom" but is careful to say rather consistently "culture or civilization." In 1940 he no longer bothers to add "or civilization." The implication is that by roughly 1940 "culture" in its anthropological sense had become fairly familiar to educated Englishmen.

The contemporary influence of learning theory and personality psychology has perhaps brought the anthropological idea back closer to the Kantian usage of the individual's becoming cultured, with expressions like "enculturation" and "the culturalization of the person." Perhaps instead of "brought back" we should say that psychological interest, in trying better to fund the idea of culture, and to understand and explain its basic process, has reintroduced the individual into culture.

The history of the word "culture" presents many interesting problems in the application of culture theory' itself. Why did the concept "Kultur" evolve and play such an important part in the German intellectual setting? Why has the concept of "culture" had such difficulty in breaking through into public consciousness in France and England? Why has it rather suddenly become popular in the United States, to the point that such phrases as "Eskimo culture" appear even in the comic strips?

We venture some tentative hypotheses, in addition to the suggestion already made as to the imbalance in Germany of 1800 of cultural advancement and political retardation. In the German case, there was first — for whatever reasons — a penchant for large abstractions in eighteenth- and nineteenth-century thought. Second, German culture was less internally homogeneous — at least less centralized in a dominant capital city — than the French and English cultures during the comparable period. France and England, as colonial powers, were aware, of course, of other ways of life, but — perhaps precisely because of imperialism — the English and French were characteristically indifferent to the intellectual significance of cultural differences — perhaps resistant to them. Similarly, the heterogeneous cultural backgrounds of Americans — plus the fact that the new speed of communication and political events forced a recognition of the variety of social traditions in the world generally — quite possibly have helped create a climate of opinion in the United States unusually congenial to the cultural idea.

Not that a precise anthropological concept of culture is now a firm part of the thinking of educated citizens. [5] If it were, there would be no need for this monograph. No, even in intellectual and semi-intellectual circles the distinction between the general idea of culture and a specific culture is seldom made. "Culture" is loosely used as a synonym for "society." In social science literature itself the penetration of the concept is far from complete, though rapidly increasing. Mr. Untcreiner surveyed the tables of contents and indices in about six hundred volumes in the libraries of the Department of Social Relations and the Peabody Museum of Harvard University. Anthropology, sociology, social psychology, and clinical psychology were represented in about that order, and dates of publication ranged back as far as 1900 but with heavy concentration on the past two decades. In more than half of these books "culture" was not even mentioned. In the remainder surprisingly few explicit definitions were given. Usage was rather consistently vague, and denotation varied from very narrow to very broad. Mr. Untereiner's impression (and ours) is that the neighboring social science disciplines have assimilated, on the whole, little more than the notion of variation of customs. There are important individual exceptions, of course, and there does seem to be a much greater effort at explicitness and rigor in some recent sociological and psychological works.

The lack of clarity and precision is largely the responsibility of anthropology. Anthropologists have been pre-occupied with gathering, ordering, and classifying data. Apart from some nineteenth- and early twentieth-century "armchair" speculations which were largely of the order of pseudo-historical reconstructions, anthropology has only very' recently become conscious of problems of theory and of the logic of science. A fully systematic scientific theory' of man, society, and culture has yet to be created. While there has been greater readiness to theorize in psychology and sociology than in anthropology, the results as yet show neither any marked agreement nor outstanding applicability to the solution of problems. The lack of mooring of the concept of culture in a body of systematic theory is doubtless one of the reasons for the shyness of the dictionary' makers. They have not only been puzzled by the factoring out of various sub-notions and exclusive emphasis upon one of these, but they have probably sensed that the concept has been approached from different methodological assumptions — which were seldom made explicit.

We have made our taxonomy of definitions in the next section as lengthy as it is because culture is the central concept of anthropology' and inevitably a major concept in a possible eventual unified science of human behavior. We think it is important to discuss the past, the present, and the prospects of this crucial concept. Its status in terms of refinements of the basic idea, and the organization of such refinements into a corpus or theory, may serve as a gauge of the development of explicit conceptual instruments in cultural anthropology. Definitions of culture can be conceived as a "telescoping" or "focussing" upon these conceptual instruments.

[1] A philosophy of history published in 1949 by an agriculturalist (H. B. Stevens) bears the title *The Recovery of Culture.*
[2] One may instance the little book by Herbert Read (1941) *To Hell with Culture: Democratic Values are New Values.*
[3] This is reflected even in anthropological literature of the first quarter of this century in the distinction (e.g., by Vierkandt and by Schmidt and Koppers) between "Naturvölker" and "Kulturvölker."
[4] Frazer, 1885.
[5] An example of confusion is the interpretation of "Ethical Culture" as stemming from anthropology. The Ethical Culture movement has nothing to do with culture in the anthropological sense. It refers to cultivation of ethics: the meaning being the older one that gave rise to terms like horticulture, pearl culture, bee culture, test-tube culture. The movement was founded and long led by Felix Adler as a sort of deistic or agnostic religion, with emphasis on ethics in place of the deity. The parent society was, and is still, flourishing in New York. Other societies were established in several American cities, and in Germany; until Hitler abolished them there. The term "Ethische Kultur" was so out of step with the by then general use of Kultur in Germany that the movement was sometimes misunderstood there as having reference to a special kind of proposed civilization-culture, instead of the mere fostering of ethical behavior.

Addendum: Febvre on Civilisation

A work published as far back as 1930 which attempts for civilization much the sort of inquiry, though somewhat more briefly, which we are instituting as regards culture, eluded us (as it did certain writers in French — see § 2, notes 15, 16, 17) until after our text was in press — partly because few copies of the work seem to have reached American libraries and partly because of certain bibliographical ambiguities of its title. It has a pretitle: *Civilisation: le Mot et l'Idée,* without mention of author or editor; and then a long full title: "Fondation Pour la Science: Centre International de Synthèse. Première Semaine International de Synthèse. Deuxième Fascicule. Civilisation: Le Mot et l'Idée. Exposés par Lucien Febvre, Émile Tonnelat, Marcel Mauss, Alfredo Niceforo, Louis Weber. Discussions. [Publ. by] La Renaissance du Livre. Paris. 1930." The Director of the Centre, active participant in the discussions, and editor of the volume of 144 pages was Henri Berr. The contained article of special relevance to our inquiry is the first one by Lucien Febvre, entitled ""Civilisation: Évolution d'un Mot et d'un groupe d'Idées," covering pages 1-55, including full documentation in 124 notes. In the following paragraphs we summarize this important and definitive study, which has already been referred to several times. [1]

Febvre, after distinguishing the "ethnographic" concept of civilization from the idea of higher civilization loaded with values of prestige and eminence, searches for historic evidences of first use of the word as a noun — to civilize and civilized are earlier in both French and English. A 1752 occurrence attributed to Turgot is spurious, being due to the insertion by an editor, probably Dupont de Nemours (Ed. 1884, II, p. 674). The earliest printed occurrence discovered by Febvre is by Boulanger, who died in 1759, in his *L'Antiquite Devoilée par ses Usages,* printed in Amsterdam in 1766 (vol. III, pp. 404-05), in a sentence which contains the phrases "mettre fin à l'acte de civilisation" and "une civilisation continuée." In both cases the reference is to a becoming, not to a state of being civilized. The second recorded usage is by Baudeau, 1767, *Ephémérides du Citoyen*, p. 82. After that, occurrences are, 1770, Raynal, *L'Histoire Philosophique...dans les deux Indes*; 1773, d'Holbach, *Système Social*; 1773-74, Diderot, *Réfutation*; 1793, Billaud-Varennes; June 30, 1798, Bonaparte ("une conquête dont les effets sur la civilisation et les commerces du monde sont incalculable," where the meaning seems to have passed from that of "becoming" to "a condition of activity' in," as in the coupled "commerces"). Finally, in 1798, the work also "forces the gates" of the Academy's Dictionary, Littre being in error when he says that this was not until 1835.

Voltaire, Rousseau, Turgot, Helvetius, de Chastellux in 1772, Buffon in *Epoques de la Nature* in 1774-79 do not use the noun, although the verb or participle occurs in Voltaire in 1740 and Rousseau in 1762 — in fact long before them in Montaigne and Descartes. A near-synonym in the mid-eighteenth century was police, policed, favored by Rousseau, and used by Voltaire in 1736 in his *Philosophie de l'Histoire*, [2] though in his Chapters 9 and 19 "civilisé" occasionally replaces it. Allied qualities, since at least the seventeenth century, were expressed by "civilité" — sometimes as being arbitrary or a mere varnish, while Montesquieu rates it above "politesse." All three words, however, were ultimately displaced by "civilisation" as regards the broadest meaning.

The first use of the plural "civilisations" — a significant step — which Febvre has been able to find is in 1819, by Ballanche in *Le Veillard et le Jeune Homme* (p. 102 of 1868 edition). The idea of a plurality of civilizations is already implicit when Volney in his *Eclaircissements sur les États-Unis* (before 1814, p. 718 of the 1868 edition) speaks almost ethnographically of "la civilisation des sauvages."

While Febvre leaves the question open, British use seems to follow on French, Murray traces the English verb and participle back only to 1631-41, as against sixteenth-century use by Montaigne. The Boswell reference of 1772 about Johnson excluding civilization in favor of civility (our §2) is cited. Two apparent occurrences in the 1771 French translation of Robertson's *History of Charles V* have "refinement" in the English original of 1769. The first use of the noun, in English as in French, is in its legal procedural sense of turning a criminal into a civil suit, as we too have noted in §2.

So far, Febvre's precise and illuminating account of the word civilization. This extends our comments in §2, which were incidental to the history of the word culture and its meanings.

The second essay in the volume, by E. Tonnelat, on *Kultur: Histoire du Mot, Évolution du Sens,* is much briefer (pp. 61-73) and somewhat sketchy. He regards the German usage as a direct *calque* or copy of the French. In the seventeenth century, in French, the noun "culture" is always accomplished by the object of action — culture of wheat or letters or what not. In the eighteenth, it is used by itself, to denote "formation de l'esprit." In German, Tonnelat cites the 1793 dictionary definition by Adelung which we have discussed, and the 1807-13 one by Campe, who equates Cultur with Bildung, geistige Entwickelung, and proposes Anbau, Geistesanbau as a German equivalent. Tonnelat then briefly discusses usage in Herder, Kant, Schiller, Goethe, and the growing emphasis on relation of Cultur to Staat in the romantics Novalis, Fichte, and Schlegel.

The remaining essays in the volume, by Mauss on elements and forms of civilization, by Niceforo on cultural values and the possibility of an objective scale for measuring these, by Weber on technology, discuss aspects of civilization itself rather than the history of the concept and word as such.

[1] In notes of §1, above.
[2] As to the date see footnote §7, above.

Part Two - Definitions

Groups of Social Science [1] Definitions in English [2]

Group A. Enumeratively descriptive
Group B. Historical
Group C Normative
   C-I. Emphasis on Rule or Way
   C-II. Emphasis on Ideals or Values plus Behavior
Group D. Psychological
   D-I. Emphasis on Adjustment, on Culture as a Problem-Solving Device
   D-II. Emphasis on Learning
   D-III. Emphasis on Habit
   D-IV. Purely Psychological Definitions
Group E. Structural
Group F. Genetic
   F-I. Emphasis on Culture as a Product or Artifact
   F-II. Emphasis on Ideas
   F-III. Emphasis on Symbols
   F-IV. Residual Category Definitions
Group G. Incomplete Definitions

[1] The definers (in addition to anthropologists, sociologists, psychologists, psychiatrists, one chemist, one biologist, one economist, one geographer, and one political scientist) include several philosophers. The latter, however, are operating within the social-science area of the concept.
[2] Only four definitions not in the English language are included.

Introduction

IT IS impossible, without an enormous number of categories and great artificiality, to group definitions of culture with complete consistency. We think, however, that some ordering both reflects meaningful historical fact and makes for a measure of conceptual enlightenment. As the physiologist, L. J. Henderson, used to say to his students, "In science any classification is better than no classification — provided you don't take it too seriously." We recognize that an clement of arbitrariness has entered into many of our assignments, and we are quite aware that an excellent case could be made for a radical shifting of some mixed or borderline definitions. In certain (but not all) cases we have indicated possible alternative assignments.

We have tried to categorize on the basis of principal emphasis rather than by, as it were, averaging the total content of the definition. This emphasis, in some instances, we have judged in a broader context than that supplied by the quotation given. Yet this does not mean that a given emphasis is constant for a particular author throughout his professional life. Indeed we present examples of definitions from the same publication which differ importantly in emphasis. The fact of the matter is that many of the definitions we cite are only very crudely comparable. Some were constructed for the purpose of making one kind of legitimate point or for dealing with highly specialized materials; others for very different points and materials. Some definitions are from books, some from articles in professional journals, a few from monographs or popular essays or literary pieces. Some were hardly intended as formal definitions at all but rather as convenient encapsulations of what was taken as generally agreed upon. Nevertheless, it seemed important to us to document fully the range and variety of nuclear ideas and their possible combinations. We hope the reader will remember that we do not take our classification at all insistently in its details, and that we consider it useful for heuristic purposes only.

The objective of our taxonomy is to illustrate developments of the concept and to bring out the convergences and divergences in various definitions. In our classification and our critical comments we realize that we are taking brief statements out of the larger context of the authors' thinking. But our purpose is not to make an over-all critique of certain writers. It is rather to point up the important and useful angles from which the central idea has been approached. This can, in part, be achieved by grouping together those statements which seem to stress one or more of the same fundamental criteria.

In the operation of definition one may see in microcosm the essence of the cultural process: the imposition of a conventional form upon the flux of experience. And, as I. A. Richards has remarked, some words must bear a much heavier weight of meaning than others. It is the basic concepts like "value," "idea," and "culture" that are the hardest to circumscribe. There is a scattering of denotations and connotations that might be compared to the clustering of steel filings around a magnet. This analogy might be pursued further: as a magnet is a point of reference, so are the key concepts centers of symbolic crystallization in each culture. Charged with affect, almost impossible to delimit and hence susceptible to considerable projection, these fundamental concepts are the ultimate conscious and unconscious references in a culture. Accepted as a currency for explanation, they may be viewed as the boundary lines of symbolic development in a culture. Scientific definition represents a sharpening of the same process that occurs more slowly and less rationally in culture generally.

We do not think it profitable in this study to haggle over the logical and metaphysical aspects of a "definition of definition." The (1941) statement of the Committee on Conceptual Integration does not seem very helpful for our purposes:

A definition is a statement of a definiendum (the thing defined) which indicates its genus (next most inclusive class), indicates its species (the class in which the definiendum lies), differentiates it (the definiendum) from all other phenomena in the same species and which indicates no more than these things about the definiendum — the choice of genus, species, and intra-species differentiae being determined by and adequate to fulfill the purposes for which the statement was devised.

We prefer the view expressed by Freud:

The fundamental concepts or most general ideas in any of the disciplines of science are always left indeterminate at first and are only explained to begin with by reference to the realm of phenomena from which they were derived; it is only by means of a progressive analysis of the material of observation that they can be made clear and can find a significant and consistent meaning. It is plain that a science based upon observation has no alternative but to work out its findings piecemeal and to solve its problems step by step..." (1946, 106-07)

Indeed scientists reject more and more the old recipe "define your terms" in favor of the prescription "state explicitly and clearly your undefined terms." For, as Woodger has remarked:

It is clear that we cannot define all our terms. If we start to define all our terms, we must by necessity soon come to a set of terms which we cannot define any more because we will have no terms with which to define them. (1937, 159)

Moreover, all "definitions" are constructed from a point of view — which is all too often left unstated. Not all definitions are substantive or descriptive. Nor is explanatory the only other alternative. Some of the definitions of culture which we shall present have been "functional" in intent. Others may be characterized as epistemological — that is, they have been intended to point to the phenomena and process by which we gain our knowledge of culture. Some definitions look towards the actions of the individual as the starting point of all generalizations, whereas others, while perhaps admitting individual acts as ultimate referents, depart from abstractions posited for groups.

Our own procedure may be stated simply: One of the reasons "culture" has been so hard to delimit is that its abstractness makes any single concrete referent out of the question, and, up to this time, the notions that have accreted around the concept have not been well enough organized to cross-relate them. Our hope is that by grouping and dissecting the varying notions that have been subsumed under this label we can show the interconnections of the related abstractions. As L. L. Bernard (1941a, p. 501, *Definition of Definition*) has remarked: "Definition becomes...at one and the same time a process of condensation and simplification on the one hand and of precision and formulation on the other hand."

Group A: Descriptive - Broad Definitions with Emphasis on Enumeration of Content: Usually Influenced By Tylor

1. *Tylor, 1871: 1.*

Culture, or civilization,...is that complex whole which includes knowledge, belief, art, law, morals, custom, and any other capabilities and habits acquired by man as a member of society.

2. *Wissler, 1920: 5.*

...all social activities in the broadest sense, such as language, marriage, property system, etiquette, industries, art, etc....

3. *Dixon, 1928: 5.*

(a) The sum of all [a people's] activities, customs, and beliefs.

(b) That totality of a people's products and activities, social and religious order, customs and beliefs which...we have been accustomed to call their civilization.

4. *Benedict, (1929)* [1] *1931: 806.*

...that complex whole which includes all the habits acquired by man as a member of society.

5. *Burkitt, 1929: 231.*

...the sum of the activities of a people as shown by their industries and other discoverable characteristics.

6. *Bose, 1929: 23.*

We can now define Culture as the crystallized phase of man's life activities. It includes certain forms of action closely associated with particular objects and institutions; habitual attitudes of mind transferable from one person to another with the aid of mental images conveyed by speech-symbols. Culture also includes certain material objects and techniques...

7. *Boas, 1930: 79.*

Culture embraces all the manifestations of social habits of a community, the reactions of the individual as affected by the habits of the group in which he lives, and the products of human activities as determined by these habits. [2]

8. *Hiller, 1933: 5.*

The beliefs, systems of thought, practical arts, manner of living, customs, traditions, and all socially regularized ways of acting are also called culture. So defined, culture includes all the activities which develop in the association between persons or which are learned from a social group, but excludes those specific forms of behavior which are predetermined by inherited nature.

9. *Winston, 1933: 25.*

Culture may be considered as the totality of material and non-material traits, together with their associated behavior patterns, plus the language uses which a society possesses.

10. *Linton, 1936: 288.*

...the sum total of ideas, conditioned emotional responses, and patterns of habitual behavior which the members of that society have acquired through instruction or imitation and which they share to a greater or less degree.

10a. *Lowie, 1937: 3.*

By culture we understand the sum total of what an individual acquires from his society — those beliefs, customs, artistic norms, food habits, and crafts which come to him not by his own creative activity but as a legacy from the past, conveyed by formal or informal education.

11. *Panunzio, 1939: 106.* (could also justifiably be assigned to D-I)

It [culture] is the complex whole of the system of concepts and usages, organizations, skills, and instruments by means of which mankind deals with physical, biological, and human nature in satisfaction of its needs.

12. *Murray, 1943: 346.*

The various industries of a people, as well as art, burial customs, etc., which throw light upon their life and thought.

13. *Malinowski. 1944: 36.*

It [culture] obviously is the integral whole consisting of implements and consumers' goods, of constitutional charters for the various social groupings, of human ideas and crafts, beliefs and customs.

14. *Kluckhohn and Kelly, 1945a: 82.*

Culture is that complex whole which includes artifacts, beliefs, art, all the other habits acquired by man as a member of society and all products of human activity as determined by these habits.

15. *Kluckhohn and Kelly, 1945a: 96.*

...culture in general as a descriptive concept means the accumulated treasury of human creation: books, paintings, buildings, and the like; the knowledge of ways of adjusting to our surroundings, both human and physical; language, customs, and systems of etiquette, ethics, religion, and morals that have been built up through the ages.

16. *Bidney, 1947: 376.*

...functionally and secondarily, culture refers to the acquired forms of technique, behavior, feeling and thoaght of individuals within society and to the social institutions in which they cooperate for the attainment of common ends.

17 *Kroeber, 1948a: 8-9.*

...the mass of learned and transmitted motor reactions, habits, techniques, ideas, and values — and the behavior they induce — is what constitutes *culture.* Culture is the special and exclusive product of men, and is their distinctive quality in the cosmos.... Culture...is at one and the same time the totality of products of social men, and a tremendous force affecting all human beings, socially and individually.

18. *Herskovits, 1948: 154.*

Culture [3] ...refers to that part of the total setting [of human existence] which includes the material objects of human manufacture, techniques, social orientations, points of view, and sanctioned ends that are the immediate conditioning factors underlying behavior.

19. *Herskovits, 1948: 625.*

...culture is essentially a construct that describes the total body of belief, behavior, knowledge, sanctions, values, and goals that mark the way of life of any people. That is, though a culture may be treated by the student as capable of objective description, in the final analysis it comprises the things that people have, the things they do, and what they think.

20. *Thurnwald, 1950: 104.*

[Culture:] The totality of usages and adjustments which relate to family, political formation, economy, labor, morality, custom, law, and ways of thought. These are bound to the life of the social entities in which they are practiced and perish with these; whereas civilizational horizons are not lost.

Comment

The distinctive criteria of this group are (a) culture as a comprehensive totality, [4] (b) enumeration of aspects of culture content. All of these definitions, save two, use one or more of the following words explicitly: complex whole, totality, sum, sum total, all. A12 speaks merely of "various." The phrase "accumulated treasury" in A15 clearly implies "totality." Every definition except A-4 is enumerative.

Tylor's definition appears at the very beginning of his *Primitive Culture.* It has been, and continues to be, quoted numberless times — and not only by anthropologists and sociologists. Klineberg uses it in his *Social Psychology* (1940, p. 62). Another important recent textbook in psychology (Gardner Murphy's *Personality,* 1948) gives Tylor's as the sole definition in the glossary under "culture" (p. 983).

Boas expanded and refined Tylor's definition, but without breaking away from it. He had met Tylor and was evidently impressed by him; and if direct influencing is not traceable, that tends to be true of Boas generally. Wissler, Benedict, Dixon, Linton, and Kroeber were all students of Boas. The influence of Tylor — often through Boas — appears also in the phrasing of definitions not included in this group (cf. B-1, B-7, B-8, B-10, B-11, C-I-1, C-I-4, C-I-5, C-II-2, C-II-4, D-II-8, etc.).

Customs (group referent), habits (individual referent), customs and habits, or habitual behavior enter into the majority of the definitions in this group. This was probably inevitable for a conception emanating from ethnologists, for customs are the obvious phenomena presented by history-less and non-literate peoples. Learning and tradition were no doubt implicit in the idea of custom, but learning is made explicit in only one definition by an anthropologist prior to 1930 (Wissler, 1916; D-II-i). Linton (1936, A-10) says "acquired through instruction or imitation." After the formal "learning theory" of psychologists began to reach anthropologists, "learning" as consciously distinct from "tradition" besrins to enter into an increasing number of definitions (Mead, 1937, B-10; Miller and Dollard, 1941, D-II-3; Linton, 1945a, C-I-8; Opler, 1947, D-II-8; Ford, 1942, D-I10; Benedict, 1947, D-II-6; Davis, 1948, D-II-9; etc. Symbolism was formally injected by sociologists, though one anthropologist, Leslie White, has emphasized it in his definitions. Behavior as such enters the scene long after behaviorism was launched in psychology: with the sociologists Hiller and Winston (both 1933), with Linton (1936), Mead (1937,

B-10), and Thomas (1937, C-II-2). Activity is mentioned by Wissler (1920) and Dixon (1928). It is certainly contained in Boas' "reactions of the individual" and implied in Benedict's (and of course Tylor's) "habits acquired by man." Tylor's term "capabilities" is perhaps to be construed in the sense of "capabilities *as realized* in achievements." But the enumeration — "knowledge, belief, art, morals, customs" — seems today curiously ambiguous as between products of activity and activities as such. It is probable that Tylor would have said that the products implied activities, and the activities resulted in products. This is the position implicit in the two definitions in this group by archeologists (A-5, A-12).

Boas' definition, which is careful, is also unusually comprehensive and explicit. He takes in, separately: (1) customs and their manifestations; (2) individual behavior ("reactions") as determined by customs; (3) the products of activity as so determined. We have not been able to find an earlier explicit definition by Boas, nor in his long teaching at Columbia does he seem to have entered into a systematic discussion of the concept. In the first edition of The Mind of Primitive Man (1911) he uses the word frequently, sometimes as interchangeable with "civilizacion." Occasionally he slips into popular terminology as in "highly cultured families," "most cultured class." On the whole, his usage reveals a conception substantially identical with the formal definition quoted above, though his quasi-definition on page 139 is archaic or at least incomplete.

Linton's definition, which is only one of several by him, does not use "customs;" "habits" have become "habitual behavior;" and "conditioned responses" enter as further indication of influencing by social psychology. There may be a remnant of Tylor-Boas type of definition, but the orientation is away from it.

Malinowski (A13) takes Tylor's notions of comprehensive totality and enumeration of content and adds a dash of economic jargon and his own favorite locution "constitutional charters" which implies "rule or way" (see C-I). Kluckhohn and Kelly (A-15) link enumeration with social heritage (B) and adjustment (D-I). Kroeber (A-17) is enumerative but theoretically his is one of the more inclusive of the statements in this group, for learning, transmission, behavior, and the significance for human life are all included.

Thurnwald's recent definition (20) is still enumerative. It differs from the others in this group in that Thurnwald restricts culture by *excluding* civilization, which he sees as an irreversible, human-wide accumulation of technology and knowledge which proceeds (in the Alfred Weberian not the Spenglerian sense of civilization — Part I, § 5, Part III, *b*), independently of the more transient and perishable cultures and their societies.

The principal logical objection to the definitions in this group is that definitions by enumeration can never be exhaustive and what is not explicitly mentioned tends to get left out of consideration. Culture is an abstraction and the listing of any relatively concrete phenomena confuses this issue. As Bernard (1941a, *Definition of Definition,* p. 501) says:

The precision of a definition does not usually consist in the accuracy of a detailed description, but rather in that of a representative conceptualized inclusive formula which serves as a base for control operations. That is, the precision resides in a synthetic conceptualized norm which is always in some degree artificial and projective and may be and frequently is in large measure hypothetical and ideal formation.

Certain abstract and (today) generally agreed upon properties of culture — e.g., the fact that it has organization as well as content — do not enter into any of the definitions in this group.

[1] The year in parentheses represents date of first publication, the second year the date of source cited.
[2] An expansion of this definition by Boas in 1938 is cited by us in a footnote to his quoted statement on culture in Part III, *b*-4.
[3] When a single word or words in a definition are italicized by the author, this is reproduced, but where the whole definition is italicized we present it in ordinary type.
[4] This is now almost universal. Odum (1947), though distinguishing culture from civilization somewhat as Merton does, nevertheless says "...culture is the sum total of the characteristics of a society..." (p. 13)

Group B: Historical - Emphasis on Social Heritage or Tradition

1. *Park and Burgess, 1921: 72.*
    The culture of a group is the sum total and organization of the social heritages which have acquired a social meaning because of racial temperament and of the historical life of the group.
2. *Sapir, 1921: 221.*

...culture, that is,...the socially inherited assemblage of practices and beliefs that determines the texture of our lives....

3. *Sapir, 1924a: 402. (1949: 308-09.)*

[Culture is technically used by the ethnologist and culture historian to embody] any socially inherited element in the life of man. material and spiritual.

4. *Tozzer, 1925: 6.*

...the cultural, that which we inherit by social contact. . , .

4a. *Myres, 1927: 16.*

..."culture" is not a state or condition only, but a process; as in *agriculture* or *horticulture* we mean not the condition of the l.md but the whole round of the farmer's year, and all that he does in it; "culture," then, is what remains of men's past, working on their present, to shape their future.

5. *Bose, 1929: 14.*

...we may describe culture as including such behaviour as Is common among a group of men and which is capable of transmission from generation to generation or from one country to another.

6. *Malinowski, 1931: 621.*

This social heritage is the key concept of cultural anthropology. It is usually called culture...Culture comprises inherited artifacts, goods, technical processes, ideas, habits, and values.

7. *Winston, 1933: 4.*

...we may regard culture as the sum total of the possessions and the patterned ways of behavior which have become part of the heritage of a group.

8. *Lowie, 1934: 3.*

The whole of social tradition. It includes, as...Tylor put it, "capabilities and habits acquired by man as a member of society'"...

9. *Linton, 1936: 78.*

...the social heredity is called *culture.* As a general term, *culture* means the total social heredity of mankind, while as a specific term *a culture* means a particular strain of social heredity.

10. *Mead, 1931: 17.*

Culture means the whole complex of traditional behavior which has been developed by the human race and is successively learned by each generation. *A culture* is less precise. It can mean the forms of traditional behavior which are characteristic of a given society, or of a group of societies, or of a certain race, or of a certain area, or of a certain period of time.

11. *Sutherland and Woodward, 1940: 19.*

Culture includes everything that can be *communicated* from one generation to another. The culture of a people is their *social heritage,* a "complex whole' which includes knowledge, belief, art, morals, law, techniques of tool fabrication and use, and method of communication.

12. *Davis and Dollard, 1940: 4.*

...the difference between groups is in their cultures, their social heritage. Men behave differently as adults because their cultures are different; they are born into different habitual ways of life, and these they must follow because they have no choice.

13. *Groves and Moore, 1940: 14.*

Culture is thus the *social heritage,* the fund of accumulated knowledge and customs through which the person "inherits" most of his behavior and ideas.

14. *Angyal, 1941: 187.*

Culture can be defined as an organized body of behavior patterns which is transmitted by social inheritance, that is, by tradition, and which is characteristic of a given area or group of people.

15. *Kluckhohn, 1942: 2.*

Culture consists in those abstracted elements of action and reaction which may be traced to the influence of one or more strains of social heredity.

16. *Jacobs and Stern, 1947: 2.*

Humans, as distinct from other animals have a culture — that is, a social heritage — transmitted not biologically through the germ cells but independently of genetic inheritance.

17. *Dietschy, 1947: 121.*

C'est cette perpétuation des données de l'histoire qui nous sont transmises d'abord par la génération qui nous précède que nous nommons civilisation.

18. *Kroeber, 1948a: 253.*

...culture might be defined as all the activities and non-physiological products of human personalities that are not automatically reflex or instinctive. That in turn means, in biological and physiological parlance, that culture consists of conditioned or learned activities (plus the manufactured results of these); and the idea of learning brings us back again to what is socially transmitted, what is received from tradition, what "is acquired by man as a member of societies." So perhaps *how it comes to be* is really more distinctive of culture than what it is.

19. *Parsons, 1949: 8.*

Culture...consists in those patterns relative to behavior and the products of human action which may be inherited, that is, passed on from generation to generation independently of the biological genes.

20. *Kluckhohn, 1949a: 17.*

By "culture" anthropology means the total life way of a people, the social legacy the individual acquires from his group.

21. *Henry, 1949: 218.*

I would define culture as *the individuals or group's acquired response systems*...the conception of culture as *response systems acquired through the process of domestication...*

22. *Radcliffe-Brown, 1949: 510-11.*

As a sociologist the reality to which I regard the word "culture" as applying is the process of cultural tradition, the process by which in a given social group or social class language, beliefs, ideas, aesthetic tastes, knowledge, skills and usages of many kinds are handed on ("tradition" means "handing on") from person to person and from one generation to another.

Comment

These definitions select one feature of culture, social heritage or social tradition, rather than trying to define culture substantively. Linton's "social heredity" obviously means the same and is etymologically equally valid, but is open to the tactical objection that "heredity" has acquired in biology the technical denotation of an organic process which is distinctly *not* involved in culture transmission. "Heritage" connotes rather what is received, the product; "tradition" refers primarily to the process by which receipt takes place, but also to what is given and accepted. Both terms view culture statically, or at least as more or less fixed, though the word "tradition" denotes dynamic activity as well as end product.

Several of the statements deviate somewhat. Sapir speaks of culture *embodying elements* that are socially inherited: elements "in the life of man, material and spiritual" — phrases that have a curiously old-fashioned or Germanic ring uncharacteristic of the later Sapir. .Margaret .Mead's statement looks both forward and back. Its "complex whole" is a reminiscence from Tylor, perhaps via Benedict. "Traditional" is what connects the definition with the others in the group; "behavior" and "learned," which differentiate it from the others, represent formal or conscious psychological influencing.

There are six definitions from sociologists in this group (1, 7, 11, 12, 13, 19). The first is perhaps the neatest and most interesting. "Historical life of the group" is a component which anthropologists long implied rather than formulated. "Racial temperament" is a factor that anthropologists have tended to shy away from since they became conscious of culture. "*Social* meaning" and "*social* heritage" are understandable emphases. This definition by Park and Burgess is one of the first to state that culture has organization as well as content. This note is also struck by Winston's "*patterned* ways of behavior" (7), Parsons' "patterns" (19), and by the psychiatrist Angyal's "*organized* body" (14).

Linton's and Mead's definitions (9 and 10) appear to be the first to make an explicit distinction between "culture" and "a culture." This point is simple but of great theoretical importance.

The definitions in this group have been of utility in drawing attention to the fact that human beings have a social as well as a biological heritage, an increment or inheritance that springs from membership in a group with a history of its own. The principal drawbacks to this conception of culture are that it implies too great stability and too passive a role on the part of man. It tends to make us think of the human being as what Dollard (1939) has called "the passive porter of a cultural tradition." Men are, as Simmons (1942) has reminded us, not only the carriers and creatures of culture — they are also creators and manipulators of culture. "Social heredity" suggests too much of the dead weight of tradition.

Group C: Normative - C-I. Emphasis on Rule or Way

1. *Wissler, 1929: 15, 341.*

The mode of life followed by the community or the tribe is regarded as a culture...[It] includes all standardized social procedures...a tribal culture is...the aggregate of standardized beliefs and procedures followed by the tribe.

2. *Bogardus, 1930: 336 (second sentence would justify assignment to B).*

Culture is the sum total of the ways of doing and thinking, past and present, of a social group. It is the sum of the traditions, or handed-down beliefs, and of customs, or handed-down procedures.

3. *Young, 1934: xiii (or F-1, second sentence; B, third sentence).*

The general term for these common and accepted ways of thinking and acting is culture. This term covers all the folkways which men have developed from living together in groups. Furthermore, culture comes down to us from the past.

4. *Klineberg, 1935: 255 (or A, second sentence).*

[culture] applies to that whole "way of life" which is determined by the social environment. To paraphrase Tylor it includes all the capabilities and habits acquired by an individual as a member of a particular society.

5. *Firth, 1939: 18.*

They [anthropologists] consider the acts of individuals not in isolation but as member^ of society and call the sum total of these modes of behavior "culture."

5a. *Lynd, 1940: 19.*

...all the things that a group of people inhabiting a common geographical area do, the ways they do things and the ways they think and feel about things, their material tools and their values and symbols.

6. *Gillin and Gillin, 1942: 20.*

The customs, traditions, attitudes, ideas, and symbols which govern social behavior show a wide variety. Each group, each society has a set of behavior patterns (overt and covert) which are more or less common to the members, which are passed down from generation to generation, and taught to the children, and which are constantly liable to change. These common patterns we call the *culture*...

7. *Simmons, 1942: 387.*

...the culture or the commonly recognized mores...

8. *Linton, 1945b: 203.*

The culture of a society is the way of life of its members; the collection of ideas and habits which they learn, share, and transmit from generation to generation.

9. *Linton, 1945a: 30.*

[Culture] refers to the total way of life of any society...

10. *Kluckhohn and Kelly, [1] 1945a: 84.*

...those historically created selective processes which channel men's reactions both to internal and to external stimuli.

11. *Kluckhohn and Kelly, 1945a: 97.*

By culture we mean all those historically created designs for living, explicit and implicit, rational, irrational, and non-rational, which exist at any given time as potential guides for the behavior of men.

12. *Kluckhohn and Kelly, 1945a: 91.*

Culture is...a set of ready-made definitions of the situation which each participant only slightly retailors in his own idiomatic way.

13. *Kluckhohn and Leighton, 1946: xviii.*

A culture is any given people's way of life, as distinct from the life-ways of other peoples.

14. *Herskovits, 1948: 29.*

A culture is the way of life of a people; while a society' is the organized aggregate of individuals who follow a given way of life. In still simpler terms a society' is composed of people; the way they behave is their culture.

15. *Lasswell, 1948: 203.*

"Culture" is the term used to refer to the way that the members of a group act in relation to one another and to other groups.

16. *Bennett and Tumin, 1949: 209.*

Culture: the behavior patterns of all groups, called the "way of life": an observable feature of all human groups; the fact of "culture" is common to all; the *particular pattern* of culture differs among all. "A culture": the specific pattern of behavior which distinguishes any society from all others.

17. *Frank, 1948: 171.*

...a term or concept for the totality' of these patterned ways or thinking and acting which are specific modes and acts of conduct of discrete individuals who, under the guidance of parents and teachers and the associations of their fellows, have developed a way of life expressing those beliefs and those actions.

18. *Titiev, 1949: 45.*

...the term includes those objects or tools, attitudes, and forms of behavior whose use is sanctioned under given conditions by the members of a particular society.

18a. *Maquet, 1949: 324.*

La culture, c'est la manière de vivre du groupe.

19. *Kluckhohn, 1951a: 86.*

"A culture" refers to the distinctive way of life of a group of people, their complete "design for living."

Addendum: When this monograph was already in press — and hence too late for inclusion in tabulations — we encountered the following definition belonging to this group, by the biologist, Paul Sears:

The way in which the people in any group do things, make and use tools, get along with one another and with other groups, the words they use and the way they use them to express thoughts, and the thoughts they think — all of these we call the group's culture. ('939. 78-79)

Comment

Wissler's 1929 statement, "the mode of life followed by the community," sets the pattern. It is the old "customs" concept (cf. Group A), raised from its pluralistic connotations into a totalizing generalization. The word "mode" or "way" can imply (a) common or shared patterns; (b) sanctions for failure to follow the rules; (c) a manner, a "how" of behaving; (d) social "blueprints" for action. One or more of these implications is made perfectly explicit in many of these definitions.

There are probably few contemporary anthropologists who would reject completely the proposition "A culture is the distinctive way of life of a people," though many would regard it as incomplete. Radcliffe-Brown has only recently committed himself to a definition of culture (B-22). Earlier in his professional career he appeared to accept the Tylorian conception but increasingly he has belittled "culture" as opposed to "social structure" (see p. 132). Even Radcliffe-Brown, however, in conversation and in his final seminar at Chicago in 1937 spoke of culture as a set of rules for behavior. If there is a difference with Wissler's position it is in Radcliffe-Brown's implication that there is something artificial in rules. This is an understandable enough attitude for an anti-culturalist of his day and generation. Wissler's "mode of life followed" is more neutral; or if it has a connotation, it is rather that of a natural phenomenon.

The idea of artificiality or arbitrariness becomes explicit in Redfield's "conventional understandings manifest in act and artifact" (E-4). This emphasis seems to pull the definition well off to one side — almost as if it were an echo of the *Contrat Social.* The "arbitrariness" of a cultural phenomenon is a function of its particular historical determination. "Artificiality" is related to a different set of problems hinging on the role of culture in human life. Is it a thwarting or fulfilling or both? Is man's "culturalness" just a thin film, an epiphenomenon, capping his naturalness? Or are cultural features in man's life so important that culture becomes the capstone to human personality'? Perhaps, however, there is no influence of either Rousseau or Radcliffe-Brown involved in Redfield's definition; it may be only a degree of stylization of phrase.

In any case there tends to be a close relationship between the definitions in this group and the group (E) to which Redfield's definition is assigned — those which emphasize the organization of culture. From Tylor's "complex whole" to Wissler's "mode of life" is one step. It is a next natural step to a "system" or "organization" (Redfield's word) of the common patterns, for the notion of stylization suggested by "mode" or "way" is easily extended to the totality of a culture.

There is also some linkage to the definitions in the D groups, particularly D-I, "Emphasis Upon Culture as a Problem-Solving Device." Ford (D-I-8) speaks of "regulations governing human behavior" (the "blueprints" idea) but emphasizes the fact that these rules constitute a set of solutions for perennial human problems. Morris (D-I-14) starts from "a scheme for living" but stresses the role of this in the adjustment process. Miller and Dollard (D-II-3) use the phrase "design of the human maze" but emphasize primarily the learning theory angle and secondarily the conception of adjustment. It is clear, however, that the "design for living" theme is, to greater or lesser extent, a feature common to Groups C-I, D-I, D-II, and E.

A few more specific comments are now in order.

Bogardus' definition (2) combines an echo of Tylor with the social heritage notion but stresses "the ways." Young (3) likewise includes the theme of tradition with a stress upon "ways" but combines these with Sumner's term "folkways." The Gillin and Gillin definition (6) seems to be the first to speak of the overt and covert aspects of culture, though it is probable that the younger Gillin drew this distinction from the lectures of his teacher, Linton.

Linton, in two books in 1945, drifts into three or four definitions or sub-definitions of culture. Most in accord with Wissler is "the total way of life of any society," though he says only that this is what culture "refers to." An amplified version (8) adds the "ideas and habits" which the members of the society "learn, share, and transmit." Two other statements in 1945 (E-5) completely leave out the way of living, and emphasize the psychological factors or organized repetitive responses and configurations of learned behavior — as is natural enough in a book professedly dealing with personality'.

Herskovits (A-19) includes the phrase "way of life" In his definition, but we have placed this in the Tylor group rather than here because it is specifically enumerative. An alternative definition from the same book of Herskovits belongs in F-I.

In general, the definitions in this group imply an "organicism" which becomes explicit in the "structural" definitions of Group E. Here is foreshadowed the notion of a network of rules, the totality rather than the parts (the discrete rules) being stressed.

[1] The multiplicity of definitions from the Kluckhohn and Kelly article is due to the fact that this was also, in part, a survey of current thinking about the concept of culture. In addition to the explanatory (10) and descriptive (11) definitions proposed by the authors, there is an attempt to state various positions reflecting different types of anthropological emphasis. Of these (12) is an example, and others will follow in later sections.

C-II. Emphasis on Ideals or Values plus Behavior

1. *Carver, 1935. 283.*
Culture is the dissipation of surplus human energy in the exuberant exercise or the higher human faculties.
2. *Thomas, 1937: 8.*
[Culture is] the material and social values of any group of people, whether savage or civilized (their institutions, customs, attitudes, behavior reactions)...
3. *Bidney, 1942: 452.*
A culture consists of the acquired or cultivated behavior and thought of individuals within a society, as well as of the intellectual, artistic, and social ideals which the members of the society profess and to which they strive to conform.
4. *Bidney, 1946: 535.*
An integral or holistic concept of culture comprises the acquired or cultivated behavior, feeling, and thought of individuals within a society as well as the patterns or forms of intellectual, social, and artistic ideals which human societies have professed historically.
5. *Bidney, 1947: 376.*
...genetically, integral culture refers to the education or cultivation of the whole man considered as an organism and not merely to the mental aspect of his nature or behavior.
6. *Sorokin, 1947: 313.*
[The social aspect of the superorganic universe is made up of the interacting individuals, of the forms of interaction, of unorganized and organized groups, and of the interindividual and intergroup relationships...] The cultural aspect of the superorganic universe consists of meanings, values, norms, their interaction and relationships, their integrated and unintegrated groups (systems and congeries) as they are objectified through overt actions and other vehicles in the empirical sociocultural universe.

Comment

These definitions come from an economist, two sociologists, and a philosopher concerned with the concept of culture. The definition by the economist (Carver) is probably of the "Geist" or "Kultur" type ("higher faculties");

we have included it only because of some slight historical interest. It may also be argued that Sidney's 1947 definition (5) has no genuine place in this group.

The remaining four definitions all name "behavior" or "overt actions" together with "ideals" or "values." However, the relation of behavior to ideals or values in these definitions appears to be not conceptually intrinsic, but to be historical — a function of the period when the definitions were framed (1937-1947).

Thomas is notable among sociologists perhaps most of all for his contribution of the "definition of the situation;" but this does not enter into his definition of culture. Basically this is: "material and social values" of a group; further elaborated by specification of "institutions, customs, attitudes, behavior reactions." As artifacts are not mentioned in the enumeration, the word "material" in the core of the definition perhaps refers to expression in physical form, whether in terms of tangible objects or of bodily actions. This core of the definition, as usual with Thomas, is trenchant: the essence of culture is values.

Sorokin's 1947 statement is elaborate because it is really part of a philosophical system. Thus he begins by separating the social aspect from the cultural aspect of the superorganic or sociocultural empirical universe. Within this universe, culture, or "the cultural aspect," consists first of all of "meanings, values, norms." The three together obviously equate more or less with Thomas's "values." However, that is only the beginning. With the meanings, values, and norms there are also included by Sorokin: (1) their interactions and relationships; (2) their respectively more or less integrated grouping into systems versus congeries; and (3) these systems and congeries "as they are objectified through overt actions and other vehicles." This lands us in the midst of a systematic terminology that Sorokin has coined but which it would be beyond the scope of this comparative review to examine or appraise in detail. It is however clear that "overt actions" means behavior; that "other vehicles" are or include artifacts or objects of material culture; and that "objectified through" means that both behavior and artifacts are expressions of the primary meanings, values, and norms in their variably integrated groupings. Values, in short, are primary. Sorokin's thought system is therefore idealistic. Nevertheless, both behavior and artifacts have room made for them as "objectifications" — that is, expressions or derivations — just as it is recognized that values may occur either integrated into systems or merely collocated in congeries. That is, the world of phenomena is fully recognized, though the thinking is idealistic. This is how we construe Sorokin's definition. It aims at being broader than most, and is more avowedly idealistic, but otherwise is less off-center in meaning than in the terminology chosen.

Of Sidney's three definitions, the 1946 one is an expansion of that of 1942 by the addition of "feelings" to "behavior and thought"; of "patterns or forms of to the "ideals" of various kinds; of "historically" to "profess": and by the omission of "to which they strive to conform," which presumably is already implied in the profession of ideals. We need therefore consider only the later definition. Sidney avows himself as in the humanist tradition. This fact no doubt accounts for his "acquired or cultivated" where most other definitions stress only acquisition itself, or its empirical method by social inheritance, learning, symbolism. To Bidney culture retains an element of its older sense of "cultivation" [1] — especially self-cultivation; culture is something sought. [2] It is no doubt this inclination that makes him specify "individuals within a society," where most other writers merely refer to the society or group. Seemingly also it is this same orientation that allows Bidney to couple behavior and values. The behavior, feelings, and thought being acquired or cultivated, in other words, being purposive or sought, relate to the patterns or forms of the social and other ideals — presumably partly shaping the ideals, partly being again influenced by them. Sorokin connects the same two elements by having behavior "objectify" ideals — express it or derive from it. Perhaps one may compare the expression of the "themes" of a personality in TAT stories. Thomas apparently was not conscious of a problem of relation: he simply redefines his values as *being* customs, attitudes, and behavior.

Such unity as exists in this group consists in the premise of the dynamic force of certain normative ideas on behavior in the cultural process. This conception is one to which anthropologists have openly given their allegiance only quite recently. In definitions of culture by anthropologists one must wait until Kroeber's 1948 definition (A-17) before the word "values" appears. On the other hand, the treatment given to religious and other ideas constitutes an implicit admission of the significance of such norms. And anthropologists have long recognized such concepts as Sumner's "mores" which clearly contain value implications.

[1] This is clear from his 1947 definition of "integral culture."
[2] Ortega y Gasset has somewhere said, "culture is that which is sought" (quoted by Frank, 1948).

Group D: Psychological - D-I. Emphasis on Adjustment, On Culture as a Problem-Solving Device

1. *Small, 1905: 344-45.*

"Culture"...is the total equipment of technique, mechanical, mental, and moral, by use of which the people of a given period try to attain their ends..."culture" consists of the means by which men promote their individual or social ends.

2. *Summer [10] and Keller, 1927: 46-41.*

The sum of men's adjustments to their life-conditions is their culture, or civilization. These adjustments...are attained only through the combined action of variation, selection, and transmission.

3. *Dawson, 1928: xiii-xiv (could also be assigned to C-I).*

A culture is a common way of life — a particular adjustment of man to his natural surroundings and his economic needs.

4. *Keller, 1931: 26.*

No civilization (sum or synthesis of mental adjustments) of any importance can be developed by the individual or by the limited group in isolation.... Culture [1] is developed when the pressure of numbers on land reaches a degree at which life exerts stress on man.

5. *Young, 1934: 18-19.*

These folkways, these continuous methods of handling problems and social situations, we call *culture.* Culture consists of the whole mass of learned behavior or patterns of any group as they are received from a previous group or generation and as they are added to by this group, and then passed on to other groups or to the next generation.

6. *Lundberg, 1939: 179.*

Through this process of inventing and transmitting symbols and symbolic systems and technologies as well as their non-symbolic counterparts in concrete tools and instruments, man's experience and his adjustment technique become cumulative. This societal behavior, together with its man-made products, in their interaction with other aspects of human environment, creates a constantly changing series of phenomena and situations to which man must continually adjust through the development of further habits achieved by the same process. The concrete manifestations of these processes are usually described by the vague word culture.

7. *Panunzio, 1939: 106.*

...culture is a man-made or superorganic order, self-generating and dynamic in its operation, a pattern-creating order, objective, humanly useful, cumulative, and self-perpetuating. It is the complex whole of the systems of concepts and usages, organizations, skills, and instruments by means of which mankind deals with physical, biological, and human nature in the satisfaction of its needs.

8. *Ford, 1939: 137 (could justifiably be assigned to C-I).*

Culture, in the form of regulations governing human behavior, provides solutions to societal problems.

9. *Blumenthal, 1941: 9.*

Culture consists of all results (products) of human learned effort at adjustment.

10. *Ford, 1942: 555, 557.*

Culture consists of traditional ways of solving problems...Culture...is composed of responses which have been accepted because they have met with success; in brief, culture consists of learned problem-solutions.

11. *Young, 1942: 35.*

Culture consists of common and more or less standardized ideas, attitudes, and habits which have developed with respect to man's recurrent and continuous needs.

12. *Kluckhohn and Leighton, 1946: xviii-xix.*

There are certain recurrent and inevitable human problems, and the ways in which man can meet them are limited by his biological equipment and by certain facts of the external world. But to most problems there are a variety of possible solutions. Any culture consists of the set of habitual and traditional ways of thinking, feeling, and reacting that are characteristic of the ways a particular society' meets its problems at a particular point in time.

13. *Morris, 1946: 205.*

The culture of a society may be said to consist of the characteristic ways in which basic needs of individuals are satisfied in that society (that is, to consist of the particular response sequences of various behavior-families which occur in the society)...

14. *Morris, 1948: 43.*

A culture is a scheme for living by which a number of interacting persons favor certain motivations more than others and favor certain ways rather than others for satisfying these motivations. The word to be underlined is "favor." For preference is an essential of living things.... To live at all is to act preferentially — to prefer some goals rather than others and some ways of reaching preferred goals rather than other ways. A culture is such a pattern of preferences held by a group of persons and Transmitted in time.

15. *Turney-High, 1949: 5.*

In its broadest sense, culture is coterminous with everything that is artificial, useful, and social employed by man to maintain his equilibrium as a biopsychological organism.

16. *Gorer, 1949: 2.*

...a culture, in the anthropological sense of the word: that is to say, shared patterns of learned behaviour by means of which their fundamental biological drives are transformed into social needs and gratified through the appropriate institutions, which also define the permitted and the forbidden.

17. *Piddington, 1950: 3-4.*

The culture of a people may be defined as the sum total of the material and intellectual equipment whereby they satisfy their biological and social needs and adapt themselves to their environment.

Comment

Although only four of the definitions in this group (2, 4, 8, 10) are directly traceable to William Graham Sumner, it seems likely that most of them show at least an indirect influence from him. Young (5), for example, uses Sumner's favorite word "folkways." It is notable that of the seventeen definitions ten come from sociologists, [3] two from a philosopher (13, 14), two from English general scholars who are hard to classify in academic terms (3, 16), one from an anthropologist [4] and psychiatrist (12), and but two from conventional anthropologists (15, 17).

At any rate, it is a fact that Sumner, once a dominating figure in American sociology, consistently stressed the point of adjustment. In defining his major concept — which is very close to anthropological "culture" but narrower, for "culture" embraces both "folkways" and "mores" — he says:

...folkways are habits of the individual and customs of the society which arise from efforts to satisfy needs; they are intertwined with goblinism and demonism and primitive notions of luck...and so they win traditional authority. Then they become a social force. They arise no one knows whence or how. They grow only to a limited extent by the purposeful efforts of men. In time they lose power, decline, and die, or are transformed. While they are in vigor they very largely control individual and social undertakings, and they produce and nourish ideas of world philosophy and life policy. Yet they are not organic or material. They belong to a superorganic system of relations, conventions, and institutional arrangements. The study of them is called for by their *social* character, by virtue of which they are leading factors in the science of society. (1906, iv)

The number of elements found in earlier, contemporary, and later definitions of culture present also in the above statement is remarkable. We have: customs, habits, tradition, values ("ideas of world philosophy and life policy"), the superorganic, the social, the cyclical nature or culture.

This group has an evident conceptual relationship to the "rule or way" group (C-I) on the one hand, and to the succeeding "learning" group (D-II), on the other. The Yale atmosphere was peculiarly congenial to the attempted synthesis of anthropology, sociology, and learning theory because of the Sumner tradition, as Dollard, Neal .Miller. Murdock, Ford, Whiting, and others have testified. This position is also close to Malinowski's [5] assumption that culture is solely the result of response to physiological drives and needs as modified by acquired drives. Indeed Malinowski apparently found himself intellectually at home in Yale during the last years of his life. Gorer was also at Yale for some time.

Clellan Ford's definitions express the modern central tendency of this group without deviation or qualification. His "traditional ways of solving problems" and "learned problem solutions" stem from Sumner, from Dollard, and from a specific psychological orientation. "Problem solutions" are the explicit way in which one strain of contemporary academic psychology (and some theoretical sociology) would approach the field of design, aim, or business of living. The "learned" also comes from a branch of psychology, learning theory. In fact ever\'thing characteristically cultural has been dissolved out of Ford's definitions, except for the hangover of alternative "traditional." The drift is to resolve or reduce culture into psychology. This is a principal distinction between a number of definitions in this group and some definitions (e.g., Opler, D-II-8; Kluckhohn and Kelly, E-6) which have certain points of similarity.

It is true that any culture is, among other things, a set of techniques for adjusting both to the external environment and to other men. Insofar as these definitions point to this fact, they are helpful; however, they are both incomplete and inaccurate as synoptic definitions. For cultures create problems as well as solving them. If the lore of a people states that frogs are dangerous creatures, or that it is not safe to go about at night because of were-animals or ghosts, threats are posed which do not arise out of the inexorable facts of the external world. This is why all "functional" definitions of culture tend to be unsatisfactory': they disregard the fact that cultures create needs as well as provide means of fulfilling them.

Moreover, we must not continue so glibly to posit "needs" on the basis of observed habits. We must, with Durkheim, take account of the possibility that even some "functional" necessities of societies are referable primarily to the collectivity rather than to the biologically derived needs of the component individuals. We require a way of thinking which takes account of the pull of expectancies as well as the push of tensions, which emphasizes perjuring values as well as immediate situation. As Dorothy Lee (1948, *Are Basic Needs Ultimate*) has noted: "Culture is not...'a response to the total needs of a society' but rather a system which stems from and expresses something had, the basic values of the society." Only in part is culture an adaptive and adjustive instrument.

Another weakness of most of this cluster of propositions is that in concern at why culture exists, and how it is achieved, they forget to tell what culture is. In short, they aim to find an explanatory definition without even troubling to find a descriptive one.

Finally, though these definitions attempt to relate the scientific idea of culture to the individual, culture often tends to disappear in the work of the proponents of this "school": culture is "reduced" to psychology. What is actually stressed is the acquisition of habits by individuals and why they retain or change habits. Then this analysis is projected into culture.

[1] Sumner's *Folkways* (1906) uses the term "civilization" but not "culture."
[2] The 1915 edition of this same book defines culture as "the sum or synthesis of mental adaptations." (11)
[3] Although C. S. Ford is considered an anthropologist degree was in "The Science of Society" at Yale.
[4] Kluckhohn has been deeply influenced by his contacts with the Yale Institute of Human Relations group in anthropology and psychology, and their thinking stems, in part, from Sumner.
[5] Piddington's definition would seem to stem directly from Malinowski, though cast more in the "Yale" framework than any actual definition by Malinowski.

D-II. Emphasis on Learning

1. *Wissler, 1916: 195.*
Cultural phenomena are conceived of as including all the activities of man acquired by learning.... Cultural phenomena may, therefore, be defined as the acquired activity complexes of human groups.
2. *Hart and Pantzer, 1925: 703, 705.*
Culture consists in behavior patterns transmitted by imitation or tuition.... Culture includes ail behavior patterns socially acquired and socially transmitted.
3. *Miller and Dollard, 1941: 5* (could justifiably be assigned to C-I).
Culture, as conceived by social scientists, is a statement of the design of the human maze, of the type of reward involved, and of what responses are to be rewarded.
4. *Kluckhohn, 1942: 2.*
Culture consists in all transmitted social learning.
5. *LaPiere, 1946: 68.*
A culture is the embodiment in customs, traditions, institutions, etc., of the learning of a social group over the generations. It is the sum of what the group has learned about living together under the particular circumstances, physical and biological, in which it has found itself.
6. *Benedict, 1947: 13.*
...culture is the sociological term for learned behavior, behavior which in man is not given at birth, which is not determined by his germ cells as is the behavior of wasps or the social ants, but must be learned anew from grown people by each new generation.

7. *Young, 1947: 7.*

The term refers to the more or less organized and persistent patterns of habits, ideas, attitudes, and values which are passed on to the newborn child from his elders or by others as he grow s up.

8. *Opler, 1947: 8* (could justifiably be assigned to D-I).

A culture can be thought of as the sum total of learned techniques, ideas, and activities which a group uses in the business of living.

9. *A. Davis, 1948: 59.*

...culture...may be defined as all behavior learned by the individual in conformity imth a group....

10. *Hoebel, 1949: 5, 4.*

Culture is the sum total of learned behavior patterns which are characteristic of the members of a society' and which are, therefore, not the result of biological inheritance.

11. *Haring, 1949: 29.*

Cultural behavior denotes all human functioning that conforms to patterns learned from other persons.

12. *Wilson and Kolb, 1949: 57.*

Culture consists of the patterns and products of learned behavior — etiquette, language, food habits, religious beliefs, the use of artifacts, systems of knowledge, and so on.

13. *Hockett, 1950: 113.*

Culture is those habits which humans have because they have been learned (not necessarily without modification) from other humans.

14. *Steward, 1950: 98.*

Culture is generally understood to mean learned modes of behavior which are socially transmitted from one generation to another within particular societies and which may be diffused from one society to another.

15. *Slotkin, 1950: 76.*

By definition, customs are categories of actions learned from others....A *culture* is the body of customs found in a society and anyone who acts according to these customs is a participant in the culture. From a biological viewpoint, its culture is the means by which a society' adjusts to its environment.... Artifacts are not included in culture.

16. *Aberle, et al,* 1950: 102.

Culture is socially transmitted behavior conceived as an abstraction from concrete social groups.

Comment

It is interesting that Wissier appears to have pioneered both the "rule or way" and the "learning" definitions, though it was many years before the latter caught on among his anthropological colleagues. Wissier was trained as a psychologist. The recent fashion of emphasizing learning in definitions of culture demonstrably comes from psychology, more especially from "learning theory," most especially from the Institute of Human Relations brand of learning theory.

LaPiere is of interest because he represents an attempt to combine the content of the old Tylor-type group A definitions with the recent psychological emphasis on learning. Culture becomes the sum or embodiment in customs of what a society has learned in its history about how to live. Not everything that might be mentioned is here; but what there is seems unexceptionable, provided one is ready to put its acquisition by learning into the forefront of consideration over what culture may be.

Opler's definition seems perhaps influenced by the substantive one of Kluckhohn and Kelly. "Uses in the business of living" is at least equally telic or functional in its emphasis. However, this is a less selective or purified definition. The "group" is in, "learning" is in, so are "ideas," "activities" include behavior. There is even a new element "techniques," which may have been meant to refer specifically to technologies, but also slants ahead to "use in the business of living."

Slotkin mentions action, learning, and adjustment, and his psychological accent is thus clear. His basic definition of a culture reduces to the body of actions learned from others in a society. Culture is also the means by which a society "adjusts" (see our preceding subgroup D-I) to its environment; but this is "from the biological viewpoint," that is, in non-sociocultural aspect. While artifacts are specifically excluded from culture by Slotkin, he does not state whether he includes in culture or excludes from it other "products" of human behavior such as ideas and values (our groups F-I and C-II).

Most of these definitions stress the element of inter-human learning, of non-genetic transmission, at the expense of other features of culture. That the learning element is important would not be questioned by contemporary anthropologists; it is mentioned in many other definitions without such preponderant emphasis. In the broad sense, of course, this was realized as long ago as 1871, for Tylor says, "acquired by man as a member of society." All human beings of whatever "races" seem to have about the same nervous systems and biological equipment generally; hence the basic processes of learning are very similar if not identical among all groups. Anthropologists look to the psychologists to discover these general laws of learning. On the other hand, anthropologists can show that that which is learned, from whom learning takes place, and when the learning of certain skills usually occurs, varies according to culture. However, while cultural behavior is always learned behavior, not all learned behavior is cultural; conversely, learning is only one of a number of differentia of culture.

A number of the definitions in the group, while emphasizing learning, do combine this with other features, LaPiere (5), Young (7), and Wilson and Kolb (12) are enumerative in Tylorian fashion. Others (1, 2, 3, 5, 9, 11) echo the "rule or way" theme by the use of words like "groups," "social," "conformity," and the like. Opler (8) combines "learning" with a suggestion of adjustment. Slotkin (15) has learning, customs, and adjustment — with an implication of rule or way. Steward (14) joins learning to social transmission with a characteristically anthropological emphasis on diffusion which he mentions explicitly.

D-III. Emphasis on Habit

1. *Tozzer, n.d. (but pre-1930).* Culture is the rationalization of habit.
2. *Young, 1934: 592 (Glossary)*
   Culture: Forms of habitual behavior common to a group, community, or society. It is made up of material and non-material traits.
3. *Murdoch, 1941: 141.*
   ...culture, the traditional patterns of action which constitute a major portion of the established habits with which an individual enters any social situation.

Comment

These three definitions belong with the other psychological groups because, whereas "custom" refers to a group, "habit" puts the locus in the individual. Perhaps the definition of Murdock [1] will serve at least as a conscious reminder that, in the last analysis, the social scientist's description of a culture must rest upon observation of the behavior of individuals and study of the products of individual behavior. The word "habits," however, is too neutral; a group is never affectively indifferent to its culture. "Socially valued habits" would seem minimal and again, like "learning," this is only part of the picture. Anthropologists would agree, though, that social habits and the alterations brought about in the non-human environment through social habits constitute the raw data of the student of culture.

It may legitimately be questioned whether Young's definition (2) belongs here or in C-I ("rule or way"). The second sentence is also the beginning of an enumerative definition.

[1] Roberts, a pupil of Murdock, says (1951, pp. 3, 6): "It [the study] is based on the major hypothesis that every small group, like groups of other sizes, defines an independent and unique culture...the description of any culture is a statement of ordered habit relationships.... "The data in the field were collected on the theory that the culture of a group could be defined in terms of its shared habits. On analysis, it was found that, although important because it implies common learning, understanding, and action, the shared habit relationship was not the only one which was significant." Roberts also (p. 3) speaks of a habit as "a way of behaving." There is thus a link to the C-I group.

D-IV. Purely Psychological Definitions

1. *Roheim, 1934: 216.*
   By culture we shall understand the sum of all sublimations, all substitutes, or reaction formations, in short, everything in society' that inhibits impulses or permits their distorted satisfaction.
2. *Katz and Schanck, 1938: 551.*

Society refers to the common objective relationships (non-attitudinal) between man and man and between men and their material world. It is often confused with culture, the attitudinal relationship between men...Culture is to society what personality is to the organism. Culture sums up the particular institutional content of a society. Culture is what happens to individuals within the context of a particular society, and...these happenings are personal changes.

Comment

These two definitions not only stress the psychological angle; they are couched in terms entirely outside the main stream of anthropological and sociological thought. The first is psychoanalytic; the second is from social psychology, as evidenced by the key word "attitudinal."

Roheim appears to be the only psychoanalyst who has attempted a formal definition in psychoanalytic terms. Freud occasionally used the word "Kultur" in its non-anthropological sense. In general, he seems to have had little sense of the significance of cultural diversity. His eye was upon the universal. The "Neo-Freudians" (Horney, Kardiner, Alexander, and Fromm) use the term "culture" freely enough but with little precision. Homey at least uses "cultural" as synonymous with "social."

Group E: Structural - Emphasis on the Patterning or Organization of Culture

1. *Willey, 1929: 207.*
   A culture is a system of interrelated and interdependent habit patterns of response.
2. *Dollard, 1939: 50.*
   Culture is the name given to [the] abstracted [from men] inter-correlated customs of a social group.
3. *Ogburn and Nimkoff, 1940: 63.*
   A culture consists of inventions, or culture traits, integrated into a system, with varying degrees of correlation between the parts.... Both material and non-material traits, organized around the satisfaction of the basic human needs, give us our social institutions, which are the heart of culture. The institutions of a culture are interlinked to form a pattern which is unique for each society,
4. *Redfield, 1940: quoted in Ogburn and Nimkoff, 1940: 25.*
   An organization of conventional understandings manifest in act and artifact, which, persisting through tradition, characterizes a human group. [1]
5. *Linton, 1945a: 5, 32.*
   a)...and cultures are, in the last analysis, nothing more than the organized repetitive responses of a society's members.
   b) A culture is the configuration of learned behavior and results of behavior whose component elements are shared and transmitted by the members of a particular society.
6. *Kluckhohn and Kelly, 1945a: 98.*
   A culture is a historically derived system of explicit and implicit designs for living, which tends to be shared by all or specially designated members of a group.
7. *Gillin, 1948: 191.*
   Culture consists of patterned and functionally interrelated customs common to specifiable human beings composing specifiable social groups or categories.
8. *Coutu, 1949: 358.*
   Culture is one of the most inclusive of all the configurations we call interactional fields — the way of life of a whole people like that of China, western Europe, and the United States. Culture is to a population aggregate what personality is to the individual; and the ethos is to the culture what self is to a personality, the core of most probable behaviors.
9. *Turney-High, 1949: 5.*
   Culture is the working and integrated summation of the non-instinctive activities of human beings. It is the functioning, patterned totality of group-accepted and -transmitted inventions, material and non-material.

Comment

Five of these nine definitions have been published within the past six years; only one antedates 1939. This may reflect only an intellectual fashion of the past decade or may indicate a deeper level of sophistication. The essential points are two. First, there is the distinction between the enumerative "sum" or "total" of Group A and the organized interrelation of the isolable aspects of culture. Second, most of the definitions in this group make it clear that a culture is inevitably an abstraction. Dollard (2) first explicitly separates "customs" from their concrete carriers or agents. Culture becomes a conceptual model that must be based on and interpret behavior but which is not behavior itself. The definitions in this group tend to be remote from the overt, observable uniformities of behavior. Culture is a design or system of designs for living; it is a plan, not the living itself; it is that which selectively channels men's reactions, it is not the reactions themselves. The importance of this is that it extricates culture as such from behavior, abstracts it from human activity; the concept is itself selective.

These concepts may be considered "advanced" also in the sense of inclusiveness and absence of one-sided weighting. While there is always a key word ("system," "organization," "configuration") justifying inclusion in this group, the concept never rests on this sole feature to the extent that some definitions rest on "tradition," "learning." "adjustment," and the like. Each of these definitions includes at least two of the emphases noted for previous groups.

The definition of Ogburn and Nimkoff (3) is tent-like and loose. Redfield (4) is tight and unusually thoughtful. He gets in: (1) the systematic property ("organization"); (2) the selective or arbitrary aspect of culture ("conventional understandings"); (3) the empirical basis ("manifest in act and artifact"); (4) social heritage ("tradition"); (5) distinctive way of life; and (6) hnrrnan group reference ("characterizes a human group"). The whole is tightly bound together. Linton (5) cements organization, habit, group, learning, heritage. But the content or kind of behavior, its idea or way, are not gone into as in Linton's earlier definitions.

Gillin (7) is reminiscent, perhaps accidentally, of Willey (1) 1929, and also suggests influence of Kluckhohn and Kelly (6). Gillin uses "customs" as the noun in the predicate of his definition. The customs are qualified as "patterned" and as "functionally interrelated"; and the larger half of the definition refers to the specifiable individuals and specifiable groups or social categories to whom the customs are common. This quantitative weighting reflects Gillin's psychological and sociological interests. The "specifiable" carriers suggest emphasis on cultural variability due to a viewing of it from the angle of personality rather than collectively. "Customs," though formally the key word, seems residual rather than pivotal in the definition.

The definition by Coutu (8), a social psychologist, is interesting and original. He links organization to "way of life" and to the concepts of the culture and personality field.

Kluckhohn and Kelly (6) mention historical creation or derivation — as a more conscious variant of the older tradition or heritage factor. This new variant is less explicit as to process, but is more inclusive in range of connotation and perhaps more specific as to effect. A new element is "system of...designs for living." This expresses purpose or end. So far as we know, this is the first injection of consideration of aim or end into formal definitions of culture, though of course the concept was not new in considerations of culture. The "explicit or implicit" is a modification of Linton's "overt and covert culture."

The analysis of a culture must encompass both the explicit and the implicit. The explicit culture consists in those regularities in word and deed which may be generalized straight from the evidence of the ear or eye. The implicit culture, however, is an abstraction of the second order. Here the anthropologist infers least common denominators which seem, as it were, to underlie a multiplicity of cultural contents. Only in the most sophisticated and self-conscious of cultures will his attention be called directly to these by carriers of the culture, and then only in part, probably. One may instance Radcliffe-Brown's well-known paper "The Position of the Mother's Brother in South Africa."

As Ernst Cassirer and Kurt Lewin, among others, have pointed out, scientific progress frequently depends upon changes in what is regarded as real and amenable to objective study. The development of the social sciences has been impeded by a confusion between the "real" and the concrete. Psychologists, typically, are reluctant to concede reality in the social world to anything but individuals. The greatest advance in contemporary anthropological theory is probably the increasing recognition that there is something more to culture than artifacts, linguistic texts, and lists of atomized traits.

Structural relations are characterized by relatively fixed relations between parts rather than by the parts or elements themselves. That relations are as "real" as things is conceded by most philosophers. It is also clear from ordinary experience that an exhaustive analysis of reality cannot be made within the limitations of an atomistic or narrowly positivistic scheme. Take a brick wall. Its "reality" would be granted by all save those who follow an idealism of Berkeley's sort — they would deny it even to the bricks. Then let us take each brick out of the wall. A radical, analytic empiricist would be in all consistency obliged to say that we have destroyed nothing. Vet it is clear that while nothing concrete has been annihilated, a form has been eliminated. Similarly, the student of culture change is forced to admit that forms may persist while content changes or that content remains relatively unaltered but is organized into new structures.

An analogy used by Freud for personality is equally applicable to cultural disintegration. If we throw a crystal to the ground, it breaks; however, its dissolution is not haphazard. The fragmentation accords with lines of cleavage predetermined by the particular structure of the crystal, invisible though it was to the naked eye. So, in culture, the mode in which the parts stand to each other cannot be indifferent from the standpoint of understanding and prediction. If a form ceases to exist, the resultant change is different from that of a purely subtractive operation. Each culture is, among other things, a complex of relations, a multiverse of ordered and interrelated parts. Parts do not cause a whole but they comprise a whole, not necessarily in the sense of being perfectly integrated but in the sense of being separable only by abstraction.

All nature consists of materials. But the manner in which matter is organized into entities is as significant as the substance or the function serviced within a given system. Recent organic chemistry has documented this fact. The self-same atoms present in exactly the same number may constitute either a medicine or a poison, depending solely upon the fashion in which they are arranged. Contemporary genetics and biology have come to the same conclusion. A famous geneticist has written, "All that matters in heredity is its pattern." Positivistic biologists have observed: "These results appear to demonstrate that statistical features or *organization* can be heritable...." [2] The behavioristic psychologist, Clark Hull, finds that behavior sequences are "strictly patterned" and that it is the pattern which is often determinative of adaptive or non-adaptive behavior.

That organization and equilibrium seem to prevail in nature generally is doubtless a matter of balance, economy, or least action of energy. Assuming that those aspects of behavior which we call cultural are part of a natural and not of a supernatural order, it is to be expected that exactness of relationship, irrespective of dimensions, must be discovered and described in the cultural realm. One of the most original of anthropological linguists, B. L. Whorf, [3] has put well the approach most suited to cultural studies:

...In place of apparatus, linguistics uses and develops *techniques.* Experimental does not mean quantitative. Measuring, weighing, and pointer-reading devices are seldom needed in linguistics, for quantity and number play little part in the realm of pattern, where there are no variables but, instead, abrupt alternations from one configuration to another. The mathematical sciences require exact measurement, but what linguistics requires is, rather, exact "patternment" — an exactness of relation irrespective of dimensions. Quantity, dimension, magnitude are metaphors since they do not properly belong in this spaceless, relational world. I might use this simile: Exact measurement of lines and angles will be needed to draw exact squares or other regular polygons, but measurement, however precise, will not help us to draw an exact circle. Yet it is necessary only to discover the principle of the compass to reach by a leap the ability to draw perfect circles. Similarly, linguistics has developed techniques which, like compasses, enable it without any true measurement at all to specify *exactly* the patterns with which it is concerned. Or I might perhaps liken the case to the state of affairs within the atom, where also entities appear to alternate from configuration to configuration rather than to move in terms of measurable positions. As alternants, quantum phenomena must be treated by a method of analysis that substitutes a point in a pattern under a set of conditions for a point in a pattern under another set of conditions — a method similar to that used in analysis of linguistic phenomena.

[1] Almost the same definition, but less complete and, in our opinion, a little less precise, is given in Redfield, 1941, p. 133. This work also amplifies as follows: "The 'understandings' are the meanings attached to acts and objects. The meanings are conventional, and therefore cultural, in so far as they have become typical for the members of that society by reason of intercommunication among the members. A culture is then an abstraction.... We may as well identify 'culture' with the extent to which the conventionalized behavior of members of the society is for all the same. Still more concretely we speak of culture, as did Tylor, as knowledge, belief, art, law, custom ,....The quality of organization...is probably a universal feature of culture and may be added to the definition."
[2] Crozier and Wolf, 1939, p. 178.
[3] Whorf, 1949, p. 11.

Group F: Genetic - F-I. Emphasis on Culture as a Product or Artifact

1. *Groves, 1928: 23.*
   A produce of human association.
1a. *Willey, 1927b: 500.*
   ...that part of the environment which man has himself created and to which he must adjust himself.
2. *Folsom, 1928: 15.*

Culture is the sum total of all that is artificial. It is the complete outfit of tools, and habits of living, which are invented by man and then passed on from one generation to another.

3. *Folsom, 1931: 476-77.*

Culture is not any part of man or his inborn equipment. It is the sum total of all that man has produced: tools, symbols, most organizations, common activities, attitudes, and beliefs. It includes both physical products and immaterial products. It is everything of a relatively permanent character [1] that we call artificial, everything which is passed down from one generation to the next rather than acquired by each generation for itself: it is, in short, civilization.

4. *Winston, 1933: 209.*

Culture in a vital sense is the product of social interaction.... Human behavior is cultural behavior to the degree that individual habit patterns are built up in adjustment to patterns already existing as an integral part of the culture into which the individual is born.

5. *Menghin, 1934: 68.*

Kultur ist das Ergebnis der geistigen Betätigung des Menschen, objectivierter, stoffgebundener Geist. [2]

6. *Warden, 1936: 22-23.*

Those patterns of group life which exist only by virtue of the operation of the threefold mechanism — invention, communication, and social habituation — belong to the cultural order...The cultural order is superorganic and possesses its own modes of operation and its own types of patterning. It cannot be reduced to bodily mechanisms or to the biosocial complex upon which it rests. The conception of culture as a unique type of social organization seems to be most readily explicable in terms of the current doctrine of emergent evolution.

7. *Sorokin, 1937: I: 3.*

In the broadest sense [culture] may mean the sum total of everything which is created or modified by the conscious or unconscious activity of two or more individuals interacting with one another or conditioning; one another's behavior.

8. *Reuter, 1939: 191.*

The term *culture* is used to signify the sum-total of human creations, the organized result of human experience up to the present time. Culture includes all that man has made in the form of tools, weapons, shelter, and other material goods and processes, all that he has elaborated in the way of attitudes and beliefs, ideas and judgments, codes, and institutions, arts and sciences, philosophy and social organization. Culture also includes the interrelations among these and other aspects of human as distinct from animal life. Everything, material and immaterial, created by man, in the process of living, comes within the concept of culture.

9. *Bernard, 1941: 8.*

Culture consists of all products (results) of organismic non-genetic efforts at adjustment.

10. *Dodd, 1941: 8 (could be assigned to D-II).*

Culture consists of all products (results) of interhuman learning.

11. *Hart, 1941: 6.*

Culture consists of all phenomena that have been directly or indirectly caused (produced) by both non-genetic and non-mechanical communication of phenomena from one individual to other.

12. *Bernard, 1942: 699.*

The term *culture* is employed in this book in the sociological sense, signifying anything that is man-made, whether a material object, overt behavior, symbolic behavior, or social organization.

13. *Young, 1942: 36.*

A precipitate of man's social life.

14. *Huntington, 1945: 7-8.*

By culture we mean every object, habit, idea, institution, and mode of thought or action which man produces or creates and then passes on to others, especially to the next generation.

15. *Carr, 1945: 137.*

The accumulated transmissible results of past behavior in association.

16. *Bidney, 1947: 387.*

...human culture in general may be understood as the dynamic process and product of the self-cultivation of human nature as well as of the natural environment, and involves the development of selected potentialities of nature for the attainment of individual and social ends of living.

17. *Herskovits, 1948: 17.*

A short and useful definition is: "Culture is the man-made part of the environment."

18. *Kluckhohn, 1949a: 17.*

...culture may be regarded as that part of the environment that is the creation of man.

19. *Murdoch, 1949a: 378.*

The interaction of learning and society thus produces in every human group a body of socially transmitted adaptive behavior which appears super-individual because it is shared, because it is perpetuated beyond the individual life span, and because its quantity and quality so vastly exceeds the capacity of any single person to achieve by his own unaided effort. The term "culture" is applied to such systems of acquired and transmitted behavior.

20. *Kluckhohn, 1951a: 86.*

Culture designates those aspects of the total human environment, tangible and intangible, that have been created by men.

Comment

F-I, F-II, and F-III are lumped together as "genetic" because all focus upon the question: how has culture come to be? what are the factors that have made culture possible or caused it to come into existence? Other properties of culture are often mentioned, but the stress is upon the genetic side.

This group of definitions (F-I) is Ln effect close to the B group that centers on tradition or heritage, but it emphasizes the result or product instead of the transmitting process. Groves says in 1928, "a product of human association"; Kimball Young fourteen years later: "a precipitate of man's social life." Sorokin — in a definition which he says is the broadest possible — also regards culture as the product of human interaction. This is a distinctively sociological emphasis, and twelve of the twenty definitions in this group come from sociologists, [3] Carr packs a tremendous lot into his nine words. The basing in society is there; the history and the accumulation; the products and their transmissibility.

The single definition by a psychologist. Warden (6), is perhaps more concerned to make the point of culture as an emergent than of culture as a product, but both notions are there. The geographer, Huntington (14), has enumerative and heritage aspects to his definition. The philosopher, Bidney (16), recurs to his favorite theme of "self-cultivation," mentions "process" as well as "product," and includes the properties of selection and "ends of living."

The four anthropological definitions in this group all date from the last four years. While agreeing upon culture as "product," the twist they give is quite different from that of the sociologists: while the environment influences the "way of life" which is culture, the most humanly relevant part of this environment is itself the product of cultural groups.

Some of these definitions, while quite vague, point up an important problem: the locus of abstraction. Certain definitions emphasize the effect aspect of culture; others localize the effects in the human mind; still others suggest the possibility of putting the effects out in the environment. This is a recurrent problem in the thinking of our culture; the Ogden and Richards' distinction between reference and referent hinges on it. Another example is the shifting of value from "inside" ("attitude") to outside the person.

[1] Cf. Folsom, 1931, p. 474: "...those relatively constant features of social life are called *culture*." P. 475: *"Culture as the more constant features of social life."*

[2] This definition by the archaeologist, Oswald Menghin, has a doubtful place in this group. Anything in terms of "Geist" really belongs at another level and does not fit properly within our scheme. We have put the definition here only because Ergebnis means product, result, outcome.

[3] Another sociologist, Leopold von Wiese (1932), while not defining culture, formally associates himself with the "product" criterion: "De la relation interhumaine resulte tout ce que nous appellons culture au sens le plus large possible." (24)

"Dans la structure des cultures, nous reconnaissons une accumulation et une continuité ininterrompus de séries de processus sociaux." (28)

F-II. Emphasis on Ideas

1. *Ward, 1903: 235.*

A culture is a social structure, a social organism, if any one prefers, and ideas are its germs.

2. *Wissler, 1916: 197.*

...a culture is a definite association complex of ideas.

3. *Schmidt, 1937: 131.*

Die Kultur besteht ihrem tiefsten Wesen nach in der inneren Formung des menschlichen Geistes; in der äussern Formung des Körpers and der Narur insofern, als diese durch den Geist gelenkt ist. Somit ist Kultur, wie alles Geistige, etwas Immanentes, etwas durchaus Innerliches und als soches der äussern Beobachtung direkt nicht zugänglich.

4. *Blumenthal, 1937: 3, 12.*

a) Culture is the world sum-total of past and present cultural ideas. [*Note:* As cultural ideas are said to be "those whose possessors are able to communicate them by means of symbols," symbolically-communicable should be substituted for cultural above.]

b) Culture consists of the entire stream of inactive and active cultural ideas from the first in the cosmos to the last. [*Note:* This includes ideas *once resident in human minds,* but now no longer held by living minds, though their former existence is ascertainable from surviving material symbols.] [1]

5. *Osgood, 1940: 25.*

Culture consists of all ideas concerning human beings which have been communicated to one's mind and of which one is conscious.

6. *Kluckhohn and Kelly, 1945a: 97.*

...a summation of all the ideas for standardized types of behavior.

7. *Feibleman, 1946: 73, 76.*

(a. Tentative definition.) Culture may be said to be the common use and application of complex objective ideas by the members of a social group.

(b. Final definition.) A culture is the actual selection of some part of the whole of human behavior considered in its effect upon materials, made according to the demands of an implicit dominant ontology and modified by the total environment. [Implicit dominant ontology is elsewhere said to be the common sense of a cultural group, or the eidos of a culture.]

8. *Taylor, 1948: 109-10.*

By [holistic] culture as a descriptive concept, I mean all those mental constructs or ideas which have been learned or created after birth by an individual...The term *idea* includes such categories as attitudes, meanings, sentiments, feelings, values, goals, purposes, interests, knowledge, beliefs, relationships, associations, [but] not...Kluckhohn's and Kelly's factor of "designs."

By [holistic] culture as an explanatory concept,. I mean all those mental constructs which are used to understand, and to react to, the experiential world of internal and external stimuli...Culture itself consists of ideas, not processes.

By *a* culture, i.e., by culture as a partitive concept, I mean a historically derived system of culture traits which is a more or less separable and cohesive segment of the whole-that-is-culture and whose separate traits tend to be shared by all or by specially designated individuals of a group or "society."

9. *Ford, 1949: 38.*

...culture may be briefly defined as a stream of ideas, [2] that passes from individual to individual by means of symbolic action, verbal instruction, or imitation.

10. *Becker, 1950: 251.*

A culture is the relatively constant nonmaterial content transmitted in a society by means of processes of sociation.

Comment

While this concept seems unnecessarily restricted, it does aim at what certain authors have thought cardinal. The underlying point is often expressed in conversation somewhat as follows: "Strictly speaking, there is no such thing as 'material culture.' A pot is not culture — what is culture is the idea behind the artifact. A prayer or a ceremony is merely the outward and visible manifestation of a cultural idea."

In this emphasis, as in two others, Wissler was first — or first among anthropologists. However, this appears to be another trial balloon — derived again from his psychological training — which he threw out in passing but did not develop systematically in his later writings.

Schmidt's somewhat cryptic definition has an echo of nineteenth-century German *Geist*. It does tie in with a consistent strain in his writing emphasizing internality and the dependence of culture upon the individual psyche. The note of "immanence" links with Sorokin's thinking.

Blumenthal, in a special and condensed paper on the subject in 1937, gives alternative definitions. Combined into one, these would read: "The entire stream (*or:* world sum-total) of past and present (*or:* inactive and active) symbolically-communicable ideas." The historic weighting is obvious. Ideas alone, in the strict sense, seem a narrow concept for embracing the whole of culture. Yet, if there is to be limitation to a single clement or term, ideas is perhaps as good as could be found. Blumenthal's definition further includes the feature of the method of communication or transmission ("symbolically communicable) which so characteristically sets off culture from other organically based aspects. What is lacking from the Blumenthal definition is, first, consideration of behavior, activity, or practice; second, that of design or mode or way, whether teleological-functional or empirically descriptive; and third, the element of ideal, norm, or value — unless this was intended to be comprised in "ideas." While the present definition by Blumenthal is perhaps anthropological in its slant, and certainly is historically oriented, his redefinition of four years later (D-I-9) is psycho-sociological (learned efforts at adjustment).

Osgood's statement — "all ideas...which have been communicated... [or are] conscious" — seems to belong here. But it contains features whose relevance is not evident ("ideas *concerning human beings*"!) or which are unclear (do "one," "one's mind" refer to members of the society having the culture or to the student of culture?). There appear to be elements belonging in the definition which have not been stated.

Feibleinan is a philosopher. Neither his tentative nor his final definition fits well into the classification we have made of the opinions of sociologists and anthropologists. We have put them here because the first one stresses ideas and the second one ontology. How these elements integrate with other elements in the same definitions is not wholly clear. Does "common use and application" refer to behavior? What are "complex objective" ideas? As to "the actual selection of some part of the whole of human behavior" — does this mean that a particular culture is a selection out of the total of possible human culture viewed as behavior, or is it intended merely to exclude non-cultural physiology like scratching an itch or digesting? "Behavior considered in its effects upon materials" would seem to be oriented away from ideas, but is obscure, unless the reference is to artifacts. However, an "implicit dominant ontology" is an integrating ideology, and the "selection," being "made according to [its] demands," would render this ontology formative.

We welcome the participation of philosophers in the problem of what culture is. Better trained in abstract terminology, they will not however be of much help to working social scientists until they either conform to the established terminology of these or reform it by explicit revision or substitution.

By contrast, Taylor comes from archeology, that branch of social studies most directly concerned with tangibles, and presents a set of definitions which are both clear and readily applicable to specific situations. His definitions number three because he makes a point of distinguishing between holistic culture and particular cultures, and then defines the first Doth descriptively and explanatorily, following Kluckhohn and Kelly. He also states that he essentially follows them in his definition of particular cultures. Nevertheless, Taylor differs from Kluckhohn and Kelly on the fundamental point that to him culture consists of ideas or mental constructs; to them, of designs or selective channeling processes. It would appear to us that while Taylor has been influenced by Kluckhohn and Kelly, he has emerged with something different, and that his definitions clearly belong in the present class where we have put them. This is primarily because Taylor restricts himself to cognitive or conscious processes ("mental constructs"), whereas "design" allows for feelings, unconscious processes, "implicit culture."

The distinction between culture holistically conceived and partitively conceived is of course not new. Linton explicitly makes the distinction (in our B-9) in the same book (1936: 78) in which Taylor sees him shifting from one level to another (1936: 274) on this point. There is probably little danger of confusion between the two aspects, the holistic and the partitive, becoming consequential in concrete situations; but theoretically, failure to observe the distinction might be serious. Taylor revolves the distinction largely around individual peculiarities, emergent or surviving. These he argues are cultural when culture is conceived holistically, but not cultural when it is conceived partitively — in that event only shared traits are cultural.

Taylor gives to the holistic concept of culture an emergent quality and says that it "hinges...against concepts of the same [*sic*] level such as the organic" and inorganic. By "same level" he does not of course mean that the cultural, the organic, and the inorganic represent phenomena of the same order, but that they are on the same "first level of abstraction" resulting from "the primary breakdown of data" (p. 99). The other or partitive concept of "*a*" culture he credits to "a secondary' level of abstraction." This distinction by Taylor of course holds true only on deductive procedure, from universals to particulars. Historically it is obvious that the procedure has been the reverse. Even savages know particular customs and culture traits, whereas culture as a defined holistic concept arose in the nineteenth century and is still being resisted in spots within the social sciences and ignored in considerable areas without. We would rather say that the first "level" or step in abstraction was represented by the mild common-sense generalization of customs from sensorily observed instances of behavior; that then the customs of particular societies were generalized into the cultures of those societies; and that culture conceived holistically, as an order of phenomena and an emergent in evolution, represented the to-date final "level" or step of abstraction, the one farthest removed from the raw data of experience.

In short, Taylor seems to us to have blurred two different meanings of the term "level" as currently used. One meaning is levels of abstraction, which are really *steps* in the process of abstracting. The other meaning refers to a hierarchy of *orders* of organization of the phenomenal world (like inorganic, organic, superorganic or sociocultural). These orders are often spoken of as levels, but do *not* differ one from the other in their degree of abstractness. And in any empirical context they obviously all represent the *last* and highest level of abstraction, as compared with more restricted concepts or categories such as particular cultures, behaviors, organisms, species.

Taylor's summary (p. 110) seems worth resummarizing, in supplement of his definition. Culture consists of the increments [of mental constructs] which have accrued to individual minds after birth. When the increments of enough minds are sufficiently alike, we speak of a culture. Culture traits are manifested by cultural agents through the medium of vehicles, as in Sorokin's terms. These agents are human beings; the vehicles are "objectifications of culture" — observable behavior and its results. Culture processes are the dynamic factors involving culture traits. They do not constitute culture but comprise the relationship between culture traits. (This would exclude formal and structural relationships and recognize only dynamic relationship.] Culture, consisting of mental constructs, is not directly observable; it can be studied solely through the objectifications in behavior and results of behavior. Culture traits are ascertainable only by inference and only as approximations (p. 111). It is for this reason that context is of such tremendous importance in all culture studies. — Thus Taylor.

Ford's definition (9) suggests influence from both Blumenthal and Taylor, but is original and carefully thought through. Ford, it is worth remarking, is also an archeologist.

These definitions emphasizing ideas form an interesting group, whatever specific defects may be felt to attach to any given definition. Perhaps this group and Group E are farthest out on the frontier of culture theory. Certain issues are raised (for instance Osgood's suggestion that culture must be restricted to phenomena above the level of consciousness) which anthropology must face up to. Many of these definitions deal explicitly with the problem of weighting. An attempt is made to extract what is central from looser conceptions of "custom," "form," "plan," and the like. The important distinction between participant and scientific observer is introduced. There are points of linkage with the analyses of the "premises" and "logics" of cultures recently developed by Dorothy Lee, B. L. Whorf, Laura Thompson, and others. In short, at least some of these definitions make genuine progress toward refinement of some hitherto crude notions.

[1] These two definitions are somewhat modified and commented upon in Blumenthal, 1938a and 1938b. Also, contrast his two definitions of 1941 which we cite as D-I-9 and F-IV-3.
[2] [Ford's footnote.] Webster's definition of "idea" does not quite serve here, yet the writer does not wish to use an obscure word or coin a new one. For the purposes of this paper, it is understood that individuals do not "create" ideas. The concept of "free will" seems to have no place in science. Individuals receive ideas from other humans, sometimes combine them, less frequently discover them in the natural world about them, and almost always pass them along to others.

F-III. Emphasis on Symbols

1. *Bain, 1942: 87.*
   Culture is all behavior mediated by symbols.
2. *White, 1943: 335.*
   Culture is an organization of phenomena — material objects, bodily acts, ideas, and sentiments — which consists of or is dependent upon the use of symbols.
3. *White, 1949b: 15.*
   The cultural category, or order, of phenomena is made up of events that are dependent upon a faculty peculiar to the human species, namely, the ability to use symbols. These events are the ideas, beliefs, languages, tools,

utensils, customs, sentiments, and institutions that make up the civilization — or culture, to use the anthropological term — of any people regardless of time, place, or degree of development.

4. *White, 1949a: 363.*

..."culture" is the name of a distinct order, or class, of phenomena, namely, those things and events that are dependent upon the exercise of a mental ability, peculiar to the human species, that we have termed "symbolling." To be more specific, culture consists of material objects — tools, utensils, ornaments, amulets, etc. — acts, beliefs, and attitudes that function in contexts characterized by symbolling. It is an elaborate mechanism, an organization of exosomatic ways and means employed by a particular animal species, man, in the struggle for existence or survival.

5. *K. Davis, 1949: 3-4 (could be assigned to D-II).*

...it [culture] embraces all modes of thought and behavior that are handed down by communicative interaction — i.e., by symbolic transmission — rather than by generic inheritance.

Comment

It has been held by some, including Leslie White, that the true differentium of man is neither that he is a rational animal nor a culture-building animal, but rather that he is a symbol-using animal. If this position be correct, there is much to he said for making reference to symbols in a definition of culture. However, we have found only two sociologists (Bain and Davis) and one anthropologist (White) [1] who have built their definitions around this idea.

Bain's definition is admirably compact. Its "behavior" suggests the adjustment efforts of the definitions in D-I. Its "mediation by symbols" implies inter-human learning and non-genetic communication. But the reader must project even these meanings into the definition. That which is characteristic of culture and is specific to it is not gone into by Bain. The larger class to which culture belongs is said to be behavior, and within this it consists of that part which is "mediated" by symbols — that is, is acquired through them or dependent on them for its existence; but w hat this part is like is not told.

White's statements all include enumerations. One (4) includes the words "organization" and "function," but the emphasis remains upon symbols.

A good case could be made for assigning Davis' definition to D-II ("learning"), but the explicit use of "symbol" or "symbolic" is so rare that we put it in this group. Ford (F-II-p) does include the word "symbolic" — but very casually.

This group has some affiliation with C-II ("values") because "symbol" implies the attachment of meaning or value to the externally given. There is also a connection with the group F-II ("ideas"), though "symbol" like "design" has connotations of the affective and the unconscious — in contradistinction to "idea."

[1] Three years earlier than his first formal definition we find that White wrote "A culture, or civilization, is but a particular kind of form (symbolic) which the biologic, life-perpetuating activities of a particular animal, man, assume." (1940: 463)

F-IV. Residual Category Definitions

1. *Ostwald, 1907: 510.*

That which distinguishes men from animals we call culture.

2. *Ostwald, 1915: 192.*

These specifically human peculiarities which differentiate the race of the Homo sapiens from all other species of animals is comprehended in the name culture...

3. *Blumenthal, 1941: 9.*

Culture consists of all non-genetically produced means of adjustment.

4. *Roheim, 1943: v.*

Civilization or culture should be understood here in the sense of a possible minimum definition, that is, it includes whatever is above the animal level in mankind.

5. *Kluckhohn and Kelly, 1945a: 87.*

...culture includes all those ways of feeling, thinking, and acting which are not inevitable as a result of human biological equipment and process and (or) objective external situations.

Comment

This group is "genetic" in the sense that it explains the origin of culture by stating what culture is not. Most logicians agree that residual category definitions are unsatisfactory for the purposes of formal definition, though they may be useful as additional expository statements.

Ostwald, the chemist, whose contributions to culture theory have been recently re-discovered by Leslie White, is an odd and interesting figure in the intellectual history of this century.

Roheim's phrase "minimum definition" maybe a conscious echo of Tylor's famous minimum definition of religion.

Group G: Incomplete Definitions

1. *Sapir, 1921: 233.*
   Culture may be defined as what a society does and thinks.
2. *Marett, 1928: 54.*
   Culture...is communicable intelligence.... In its material no less than in its oral form culture is, thca, as it were, the language of social life, the sole medium for expressing the consciousness of our common humanity.
3. *Benedict, 1934: 16.*
   What really binds men together is their culture — the ideas and the standards they have in common.
4. *Rouse, 1939: 17 (chart).*
   Elements of culture or standards of behavior.
5. *Osgood, 1942: 22.*
   Culture will be conceived of as comprising the actual artifacts, plus any ideas or behavior of the people who made them which can be inferred from these specimens.
6. *Morris, 1946: 207.*
   Culture is largely a sign configuration...
7. *Bryson, 1947: 74.*
   ...culture is human energy organized in patterns of repetitive behavior.

Comment

These are on-the-side stabs in passing or metaphors. They should not be judged in comparison with more systematic definitions. Sapir's phrase, for instance, is most felicitious in an untechnical way, but never comes to particulars and hence not to involvements. These statements are included precisely because of some striking phrase or possible germinal idea.

Osgood's sentence which on its face has shifted from ideas (cf. F-II-5) to artifacts as central core (in an archaeological monograph) seems to be incomplete. Perhaps it was not intended as a general definition but as a picture of the culture remnant available to the archaeologist. The definition of culture obviously presents a problem to the archaeologist. We have listed six definitions propounded by men who were — or are — primarily archaeologists (or concerned with "material culture"). Two (A-5, A-12) fall in the Tylorian group. Two (F-II-8, F-II-9) into the "ideas" bracket; for this Taylor has made a good case. Two (4, 5) fall in this incomplete group and were probably not intended as formal definitions.

The intent of Morris' remark (6) clearly places it within E, "structural."

Indexes to Definitions

A: Authors

Sapir, B-2 (1921). B-3 (1924a), G-1 (1921).
Schanck, D-IV-2; (with Katz, 1938).
Schmidt, F-II-3 (1937).
Sears, C-I-Addendum (1939).
Simmons, C-I-7 (1942).
Slotkin, D-II-15 (1950).
Small, D-I-1 (1905).
Sorokin, C-II-6 (1947), F-I-7 (1937).
Stem, B-16 (with Jacobs, 1947).
Steward, D-II-14 (1950).
Sumner, D-I-2 (with Keller, 1927).
Sutherland, B-11 (with Woodward, 1940).

Taylor, F-II-8 (1948). Thomas, C-II-1 (1937).
Thurnwald, A-20 (1950).
Titiev, C-I-18 (1949).

Tozzer. B-4 (1925), D-III-1 (n.d.).
Tumin, C-I-16 (with Bennett, 1949).
Turney-High, D-I-15 (1949), E-9 (1949).
Tylor, A-1 (1871).

Ward, F-II-1 (1903).
Warden, F-1-6 (1936).
White, F-III-2 (1943), F-III-3 (1949b), F-III-4 (1949a).
Willey, E-1 (1929), F-I-12 (1927b).
Wilson, D-II-12 (with Kolb, 1949).
Winston, A-9 (1933), B-7 (1933), F-I-4 (1933). Wissler A-2 (1920), C-I-1 (1929), D-II-1 (1916), F-II-2 (1916).
Woodward, B-11 (with Sutherland, 1940).

Young, C-I-3 (1934), D-I-5 (1934), D-I-11 (1942), D-lI-7 (1947), D-III-2 (1934), F-I-13 (1942).

B: Conceptual Elements in Definitions

acquisition (see *learning*)

acts, actions, and activities — act, C-I-15, C-I-17; act, C-I-5, F-III-4, bodily acts, F-III-2; acting, A-8, C-I-3, C-I-17, F-IV-5; actions, A-6, B-15, B-19, C-I-17, D-III-3. F-I-14; categories of actions, D-II-14; symbolic action, F-II-9; activities, A-3, A-5, A-8, B-18, D-II-1, D-II-8, F-I-5; human activity, A-7; activity complex, D-II-1; life activities, A-6; conscious and unconscious activities, F-I-7; non-instinctive activities, E-9; social activities, A-2; doing, C-I-2, C-I-5a.

adjustive-adaptive function of culture — societal problems, D-I-8, D-I-10, D-I-11; problem-solutions, D-I-10; solutions, D-I-8, D-I-I2; solving, D-I-10; adjustments, D-I-2, D-I-3, D-I-9, F-I-4, F-I-9, F-IV-3; adjusting, A-15; adjust, A-20, D-I-6, D-II-14; adjustment techniques, D-I-6; adaptation to environment, D-I-17, F-I-1a; adaptive behavior, F-I-19; culture is that which is useful, D-I-15; humanly useful, D-7; struggle for survival and existence, F-III-4; maintenance of equilibrium, D-I-15; attainment of ends, F-I-16; satisfaction, A-11, D-I-7, E-3; satisfying motivations, D-I-14; satisfied needs of individuals, D-I-13, D-I-16, D-I-17, D-IV-1; success of responses, D-I-10.

association between persons (see *common or shared patterns*)

attitudes and feelings - attitudes, A-6, C-I-6, C-I-18, C-II-2, D-I-11, D-II-7, F-I-3, F-I-8, F-II-8, F-III-4; attitudinal relationship, D-IV-2; feeling, A-16, C-I-5a, C-II-4, D-I-12, F-IV-5; non-rational, C-I-11; emotional responses, A-10; irrational, C-I-11; unconscious activity, F-I-7; sentiments, F-III-2, F-III-3.

behavior — behavior, A-16, A-17, A-18, B-7, B-10, C-I-5. C-I-6, C-I-11, C-I-18, C-II-2, C-II-3, C-II-4, D-I-8, D-II-9, D-III-2, F-I-7, F-I-19, F-II-6, F-II-7, F-III-1, F-III-5, G-4, G-5, G-7; overt behavior, F-I-12; societal behavior, D-I-6; learned behavior, D_I_5, D-I-16, D-II-6, D-II-10, D-II-12, E-5; learned modes of behavior, D-II-14; symbolic behavior, F-I-12; probable behavior, E-8; adaptive behavior, F-19; behavior patterns, A-9, A-10, A19, B-5, B-13. B-14, B-19, C-I-6, C-I-16, D-II-2, F-I-4; behavior families, D-I-13; behave, B-12, C-I-14; responses, D-I-10, D-II-3, E-1; emotional responses, A-10; response system, B-21; response sequences, D-I-14; repetitive responses, E-5; repetitive behavior, G-7; overt actions (behavior), C-II-6; reactions, A-7, B-15, C-II-2; reacting, D-I-12; motor reactions, A-17; expressing, C-I-17, G-2; conduct, C-I-17, socially transmitted behavior, D-II-16.

beliefs — beliefs, A-1, A-3, A-8, A-10a, A-13, A-14, A-19, B-2, B-11, B-22, C-I-1, C-I-2, C-I-17, F-I-3, F-I-8, F-II-8, F-III-3, F-III-4; religious beliefs, D-11-12; implicit dominant ontology, F-II-7.

biological heritage — biological nature, A-11; biological equipment, D-I-12; biological circumstances, D-II-5; human biological equipment and process, F-IV-5; biopsychological organism, D-I-15; biological drives (transformation of), D-I-16; biological needs, D-I-17.

capabilities (see *techniques, skills, and abilities*)

carriers of culture — individuals, A-7, A-16, B-20, B-21, C-I-4, C-I-5, C-I-17, C-II-3, C-II-4, D-I-13, D-II-9, D-III-3. D-IV-2, F-1-4, F-1-7, F-1-11, F-1-16, F-I-19, F-II-8; individually, A-17; persons, A-6, A-8, B-13, B-22, D-I-.4, D-II-11, D-III-4, F-I-19; personalities, B-18; participant, C-I-12, D-II-15; population aggregate, D-8; a people, A-3, A-5. A-12, A-19, B-14, B-20, C-I-13, C-I-14, C-I-19, C-II-2, D-I-1, E-8, F-III-3, G-5; members of a group, C-I-15, E-6; members of a society, A-1, A-4, A-10, A-14, B-8, B-18, C-I-4, C-I-5, C-I-6, C-I-8, C-II-3, D-II-10, E-17, F-II-7; social entities, A-20; possessors of ideas, F-II-4; generations, B-22, C-I-6, C-I-8, D-I-5, D-II-5, D-II-6, F-I-2, F-I-3, F-I-14.

63

civilization — civilization, A-1, A-3, B-17, D-I-2, F-I-3.

common or shared patterns — common, A-16, B-5, C-I-3, C-I-6, D-I-3, D-I-11, D-III-2, E-7, F-I-3, F-II-7, G-3; commonly recognized, C-7; shared, A-10, C-I-8, D-I-16, E-5, E-6, F-I-19, F-II-8; association between persons, A-8, C-I-17, F-I-1, F-I-15, F-II-8; social contact, B-4; social interaction, F-4; interaction of individuals, F-I-7; living together, D-II-5; attitudinal relationship, D-IV-2; accepted, C-I-3, D-I-10; group-accepted, E-9; cooperate, A-16; conventional understandings, E-4; conformity, D-II-9; conforms, D-II-ii; conform to ideals, C-II-3.

community (see *group reference*)

complex whole (see *totality, culture as comprehensive*)

configuration — E-5, E-8, G-6. (see also *patterns, systems, and organization*)

constancy — relatively constant, F-I-4 (note), F-II-10; relatively permanent, F-I-3; self -generating, D-I-7; self-perpetuating, D-I-7; persistent patterns, D-II-7; persisting, E-4; perpetuated, F-I-19.

creation and modification — human creation, A-15, F-I-8, F-I-18; created, F-I-7, F-I-8, F-II-8; creates, F-I-14; inventing, D-I-6; invented, F-I-2; invention, F-I-6; man-made, D-I-7, F-I-12, F-I-17; superorganic order, D-I-7, F-I-6; modification of learned habits, D-II-13; modified, F-I-7; modified by environment, F-II-7; retailored by individual participant, C-I-12; personal changes due to culture, D-IV-2; change, C-I-6; changing, D-I-6; added to (changed), D-I-5; transformation of biological drives, D-I-16; not created, A-10a.

cultivation, culture of self — cultivated, C-II-3, C-II-4; cultivation of the whole man, C-II-5, self-cultivation, F-I-16.

customs — customs, A-1, A-3, A-8, A-10a, A-12, A-13, A-15, A-20, B-13, C-I-2, C-I-6, C-II-2, D-II-5, E-2, E-7, F-III-3; practices, B-2; burial customs, A-12.

diffusion — D-II-14.

dynamic structural religions — social structure, F-II-1; relationships, C-II-6, F-II-8, interrelated patterns, E-1, E-7; interrelations, F-I-8; interdependent patterns, E-i; interaction, C-11-6, D-I-6, F-I-19; interacting, D-I-14; communicative interaction, F-III-5; interactional fields, F-8; interlinked institutions, E-3; correlation, E-3; intercorrelated customs, E-2; functioning, E-9; functionally interrelated, E-7.

elements and their enumeration — elements, B-3, B-15, E-5, G-4; knowledge, A-1, A-15, A-19, B-11, B-13, B-22, D-II-12, F-II-8; art, A-1, A-12, A-14, B-11, E-4; language, A-2, A-15, B-22, D-II-12, F-III-3; language uses, A-9; sciences, F-I-8; communicable intelligence, G-2; philosophy, F-I-8.

environmental conditions and situations — environment, D-I-17, D-II-15, F-I-17, F-I-18; area, B-10, B-14; natural surroundings, D-I-3; physical circumstances, D-II-5; life-conditions, D-I-2; biological circumstances, D-II-5; external world, D-I-12; manmade environment, F-I-1a; natural environment, F-I-16; social environment, C-1-4; human environment, D-I-6, F-I-20; physical nature, A-11; objective external situations, F-IV-5; social situation, D-III-3; events, F-III-5; internal and external stimuli, F-II-8; physical, biological, and human nature, A-11, D-I-7.

feelings (see *attitudes and feelings*)

forbidden, the — (definition by culture) D-I-16.

generations (see *carriers of culture*)

goals, ends, and orientations — goals, A-19, D-I-12; common ends, A-16, D-I-1; social ends, D-I-1; individual ends, D-I-1; individual and social ends, F-I-16; sanctioned ends, A-18; definitions of the situation, C-I-12; designs for living, C-I-10, C-I-19, E-6; design of the human maze, D-II-3; social orientations, A-18; points of view, A-18; eidos, common sense, implicit dominant ontology, F-II-7; ethos, E-8.

group reference — group, A-7, B-1, B-5, B-7, B-11, B-14, B-20, B-21, C-I-3, C-I-6, C-I-16, G-I-19, C-II-2, D-I-5, D-I-14; D-II-1, D-II-8, D-ll-9, D-III-2, E-2. E-4, E-6, E-9, F-I-6, F-I-19, F-II-7, F-II-8; social group, A-8, B-22, C-I-2, D-11-5, E-7; social groupings, A-13; integrated and unintegrated groups, C-I-5a, C-II-6; social, A-3, A-8, A-13, A-16, A-18, B-1, B-4, B-6, B-7, B-9, B-11, B-12, B-13, B-14, B-15, C-I-1, C-I-4, C-I-6, D-I-15, D-II-4, D-II-5, D-III-3, E-2, E-3, E-7, F-I-4, F-I-6, F-I-8, F-I-12, F-I-13, F-I-16, F-II-1, F-II-7, G-2; socially, A-8, A-17, B-2, B-3, D-II-2, F-I-19; society, A-1, A-4, A-9, A-10, A-10a, A-14, A-16, B-8, B-10, B-18, C-I-4, C-I-5, C-I-6, C-I-9, C-I-16, C-I-18, C-II-3, C-II-4, D-I-12, D-I-13, D-II-14, D-II-15, D-III-2, D-IV-1, D-IV-2, E-3, E-5, F-I-19, F-II-8, F-II-10; community. A-7, C-I-1, D-III-2; tribe, C-I-1; group of people inhabiting a common geographic area, C-I-5a; social categories, E-7; social class, B-22; societal problems, D-I-8, D-I-10, D-I-12; societal behavior, D-I-6.

habits — habits, A-1, A-4, A-7, A-14, A-17, B-6, B-8, C-I-4, C-I-8, D-I-6, D-I-11, D-II-7, D-II-13, D-III-1, F-I-2, F-I-14; habit patterns, E-1, F-I-4; social habits, A-7; food habits, D-II-12; established habits, D-III-3; habitual, A-6. A10, B-12, D-I-12, D-III-2; habituation. F-I-6.

holistic vs. partitive culture — culture common to all groups, C-I-16; holistic culture, F-II-8; segment ("a" culture), F-II-8; (a particular) strain (of social heredity), B-9, B-15.

history (see *time and historical derivation*)

ideas and cognitive processes — ideas, A-10. A-13, A-17, B-6, B-13, B-22, C-I-6, C-1-8, D-I-11, D-II-7, D-II-8, F-I-14, F-

II-1, F-II-2, F-II-3, F-II-5, F-II-6, F-II-8, F-II-9, F-III-2, F-III-3, G-3, G-5; complex objective ideas, F-II-7; symbolically-communicated ideas, F-II-4; inactive and active ideas, intellectual equipment, D-I-17; concepts. A-11, D-I-7; mental images, A-6; mental constructs, F-II-8; mental technique, D-I-1; consciously held ideas, F-II-5; thinking, C-I-2, C-I-3, C-I-5a, C-I-17, D-I-12, F_IV-5; thought, A-8, A-16, C-II-3, C-II-4, F-I-14, F-III-5; thought (of a people), A-12; mind, A-6, F-II-5; rational, C-I-11; rationalization, D-III-1; nonmaterial content, F-II-10.

ideals (see *values, ideals, tastes, and preferences*)

implicit culture — non-material traits, A-9, D-III 2, E-3; inventions, E-9; non-physiological products, B-18; intangible aspects of human environment, F-I-10; immaterial products, F-I-3; implicit, C-I-11; implicit dominant ontology, F-II-7; implicit design for living. D-7; covert behavior patterns, C-I-6.

individuals (see *carriers of culture*)

language — language, A-2, A-15, B-22, D-II-12, F-III-3; language uses, A-9.

learning — acquired, A-1, A-4, A-10, A-14, A-16, B-8. B-18, B-21, C-I-4, C-II-3, C-II-4, D-II-1, D-II-2, F-I-19; learning, A-8, A-17, B-10, B-18, C-1-8, D-I-9, D-I-10, D-II-1, D-II-4, D-II-5, D-II-8, D-II-11, D-II-13, F-I-10, F-I-19, F-II-8; learned behavior, D-I-5, D-I-16, D-II-6, D-II-9, D-II-10, D-II-12, D-II-14, D-II-15, E-5; learned patterns, D-I-5; conditioned, A-10, B-18; conditioning, A-18, F-I-7; tuition, D-II-2; taught, C-I-6; guidance, C-I-17; guides for behavior, C-I-11; education, C-II-5; domestication, B-21; use in the business of living, D-II-8; instruction, A-10; verbal instruction, F-II-9; imitation, A-10, D-II-2, F-II-9; reward, D-II-3; sanctions, A-19; sanctioned ends, A-18.

manners and morals — morals, A-1, A-15, B-11; etiquette, A-2, A-15, D-II-12; ethics, A-15; codes, F-I-8; standards, G-3, G-4; standardized, C-I-1, D-I-11, F-II-6; usages, A-11, B-22, D-I-7; regulations, D-I-8; socially regularized, A-8; morality, A-20; mores, C-I-7; manner of living, A-8; law, B-11; conventional understandings, E-4.

material culture — material objects, A-6, A-18, F-I-12, F-III-2, F-III-4; inventions, E-9; material traits, A-9, D-III-2, E-3; material goods, F-I-8; material processes, F-I-8; material element, B-3; material equipment, D-I-17; material tools, C-I-5a; artificial, D'-15, F-I-2, F-I-3; tangible aspects of human environment, F-I-20; physical products, F-I-3; manufactured results of learned activities, B-18; human manufacture, A-18.

means (see *processes and means*)

members of a group, a society (see *carriers of culture*)

modes — mode of life, C-I-1; modes of behavior, C-I-5, D-II-14; modes of conduct, C-I-17; modes of operation, F-I-6; modes of thought, F-I-14, F-III-5; modes of action, F-I-14 (see also *ways and life-ways*).

modification (see *creation and modification*)

needs — needs, A-11, D-I-7, D-I-11; basic needs, D-I-13, E-3; economic needs, D-I-3; recurrent and continuous needs, D-I-11; social needs, D-I-16, D-I-17; motivations, D-I-14; favor (motivations), D-I-14.

organization (see *patterns, systems, and organization*)

participants in learning process — children, C-I-6; child, D-II-7; parents, C-I-17; teachers, C-I-17, elders, D-II-7; grown people, D-II 6.

patterns, systems, and organization — patterns, C-I-16. C-II-4, D-I-14, D-I-16, D-II-7, D-II-11, D-II-11, D-III-3, E-3, F-i-6, G-7; patterning, F-I-6; learned patterns, D-I-5, D-II-10; habit patterns, E-i, F-I-4; behavior patterns, A-9, A10, B-14, B-19, C-I-^, C-I-16, D-II-10; patterned ways of behavior, B-7, C-I-4 7, E-7. E-9; pattern-creating, D-I-7; systems, A-11, A-15, B-21, C-II-6, D-I-7, E-1, E-3, E-6, F-I-19, F-II-8; systems of thought, A-8; systems of knowledge, D-II-11; organization, A-11, B-1, D-I-7, E-4, F-I-6, F-III-2, F-III-4; social organization, F-I-8,. F-I-12; organized, B-14, D-II-7, E-3, E-5. F-I-8, G-7; forms, A-6, B-10, C-II-4, D-III-2; configuration, E-5, E-8, G-6, channel, C-I-10; integrated, E-3, E-9.

people, a (see *carriers of culture*)

permitted, the — (definition of by culture) D-I-16.

persons (see *carriers of culture*)

press of culture on its agents — permits, D-IV-1; inhibits, D-IV-1; influence, B-15; force, A-17, govern, C-I-6.

processes and means — process, B-11, B-22, D-I-6, F-I-16; technical processes, B-6, F-I-8; selective processes, C-I-10; social procedures, C-I-1, C-I-2; means, D-I-1, D-I-7; means of adjustment, D-I-17; F-IV-3; exosomatic ways and means, F-III-4; vehicles, C-II-6, dynamic, D-I-7; dynamic process, F-I-16; mental adaptations, D-I-4 (1915); variation, D-I-2; section (of part of human behavior), F-II-7; selection, D-I-2; common application of ideas, F-II-7; sociation, F-II-10.

product, mechanism, medium, culture as — product, A-12, F-I-16; mechanism, F-III-4; medium, G-2; employed by man, D-I-15; all that man has produced, F-I-3, F-I-14.

products of human activity — products, A-3, A-7, A-14, B-18, B-19, D-I-9. D-II-12, F-I-9, F-I-10; immaterial products, F-I-3; physical products, F-I-3; man-made products, D-I-6; results of human effort, D-I-9; results of behavior, D-5, F-I-15; results of experience, F-I-8; results (products), F-I-9, F-I-10; precipitate (product), F-I-13; artifacts, A-14, B-6, D-II-12, E-4, G-5; possessions, B-7; amulets, F-

III-4; books, A-15; buildings, A-15; consumers' goods, A-13; goods, B-6, F-I-8; implements, A-13 instruments, A-II, D-I-6, D-I-7; inventions, E-3, E-9; materials, F-II-7; objects, A-6, A-18, C-I-18, F-I-14; ornaments, F-III-4; paintings, A-15; shelter, F-I-8; tools, C-I-5a, C-I-18, D-I-6, F-I-2, F-I-3, F-I-8, F-III-3, F-III-4; utensils, F-III-3, F-III-4; weapons, F-I-8.

psychoanalytic elements — impulses, D-IV-1; substitutes, D-IV-1; sublimations, D-IV-1; reaction-formations, D-IV-1; distorted satisfaction, D-IV-1.

responses (see *behavior*)

sanction — C-I-18.

skills (see *techniques, skills, and abilities*)

social — social, A-3, A-8, A-13, A-16, A-18, B-1, B-4, B-6, B-7, B-9, B-11, B-12, B-13. B-14, B-15, C-I-1, C-I-4, C-I-6, D-I-15, D-I-16, D-I-17, D-II-4, D-II-5, D-III-3, E-2, E-3, E-7, F-I-4, F-I-6, F-I-8, F-I-12, F-I-13, F-I-16, F-II-1, F-lI-7, G-2; social group, A-8, B-22, C-I-2, D-II-5, E-7; social groupings, A-13; socially, A-8, A-17, B-2, B-3, D-II-2, F-I-19; social categories, E-7; social class, B-22 (see also *group references*).

social heritage or tradition — social heritage, B-1, B-6, B-7, B-11, B-12, B-13, B-16; social heredity, B-9, B-15; socially inherited, B-2, B-3, B-6; social inheritance, B-14; inherits, B-4, B-13, B-19; tradition, A-8, B-14, B-18, C-1-2, C-I-6, D-II-5; traditional, B-10, D-I-10, D-I-13, D-III-3; cultural tradition, B-22, E-4; social tradition, B-8; racial temperament, B-1; social legacy, A-10a, B-20; ready-made, C-I-12; received, C-I-5; experience, D-I-6; cumulative, D-I-6; accumulated treasury, A-15, B-13, F-I-15.

social institutions — institutions, A-6, A-16, C-II-2, D-I-16, D-II-5, E-3, F-I-8, F-I-14, F-III-3; institutional, D-IV-2; constitutional charters, A-13; religion, A-15; religious order, A-3; property system, A-2; marriage, A-2; social order, A-3.

societal — societal problems, D-1-8, D-I-10, D-I-13; societal behavior, D-I-6 (see also *group reference*).

society (see *group reference*)

sum (see *totality, culture as comprehensive*)

symbols — symbols, C-I-5a, C-I-6, D-I-6, F-I-3, F-II-4, F-III-1, F-III-2, F-III-3; symboling, F-III-4; symbolic action, F-II-9; symbolic systems. D-I-6; symbolic behavior, F-I-12; speech-symbols, A-6; sign configuration, G-6.

systems — systems, A-11, A-15, B-21, C-II-6, D-I-7, E-1, E-3, E-6, F-I-19, F-II-8; systems of thought, A-8; systems of knowledge, D-II-12 (see also *patterns, systems, and organization*).

techniques, skills, and abilities — techniques, A-6, A16, A-17, A-18, B-11, D-II-8; mental, moral, and mechanical technique, D-I-1; adjustment technique, D-I-6; moral technique, D-I-1; mechanical technique, D-I-1; technical processes, B-6; equipment of technique, D-I-1; technologies, D-I-6; methods of handling problems, etc., D-I-5; method of communication, B-11; skills, A-11, B-22, D-I-7; capabilities, A-1, B-8, C-I-4; mental ability, F-III-4; higher human faculties, C-II-1; use of tools, B-11; use of artifacts, D-II-12; common use, F-II-7; language uses, A-9; practical arts, A-8, F-I-8; industries, A-2, A-5, A-12; crafts, A-13; labor, A-20.

thinking (see *ideas and cognitive processes*)

thought (see *ideas and cognitive processes*)

time and historical derivation — time, D-I-12, F-I-8; point in time, D-I-13; period of time, B-10, D-I-1; given time, C-I-11; present, C-I-2, F-II-4; past, B-4a, C-I-2, C-I-3, F-II-4; past behavior, F-I-15; historically, C-I-10, C-I-11, C-II-4, E-6, F-II-8; historical life, B-1; history, B-17.

totality, culture as comprehensive — total, A-3, A-10, A-19, A-20, B-1, B-7, B-9, B-20, C-I-2, C-I-5, C-I-9, D-I-I, D-I-17, D-lI-8. D-II-10, F-I-2, F-I-3, F-I-7, F-I-8, F-I-20, F-II-4, F-II-7; totality, A-9, A-17, C-I-17, E-9; sum, A-3, A-5, A-10, A-10a, B-1, B-7, C-I-1, C-I-5, D-I-2, D-I-4 (1915), D-II-5. D-II-8, D-II-10, D-IV-1, D-IV-2, F-I-2, F-I-3, F-I-7, F-I-8, F-II-4; summation, E-9, F-II-6; synthesis, D-I-4 (1915); complex whole, A-1, A-4, A-11, A-14, B-11, D-I-7; integral whole, A-13; whole complex, B-10; all (social activities), A-2; accumulated treasury, A-15; body, A-19, B-14, F-I-19; embodiment, D-II-5; mass, A-17, D-I-5; aggregate, C-I-1, E-8; assemblage, B-2; outfit, F-I-2; texture, B-2; set, C-I-12; fund, B-13; congeries, C-II-6; collection, C-I-8; interactional fields, E-8.

tradition (see *social heritage or tradition*)

traits — traits, A-9; D-I-14, E-3, F-II-8; non-material traits, A-9, D-III-2, E-3; material traits, A-9, D-III-2 E-3.

transmission, non-genetic — transmission, A-17, B-5, B-14, B-16, B-17, B-.8, C-I-8, D-I-2, D-I-6, D-I-14, D-II-2, D-II-4, E-5, F-I-15; group-transmitted, E-9; socially transmitted, D-II-14, D-II-16, F-I-19, F-II-10; transferable, A-6; communication, B-11, F-I-6, F-I-11; communicated, B-11, F-II-4, F-II-5; communicable intelligence, G-2; communicative interaction, F-III-5; pass from individual to individual, F-II-9; passed down (or on), C-I-6, D-I-5, D-II-7, F-I-2, F-I-3 F-I-14.

values, ideals, tastes, and preferences — values, A-17, A-19, E-6, C-I-5a, C-II-6, D-II-7; material values, C-II-2; social values, C-II-2; intellectual ideals, C-II-3, C-II-4; social ideals, C-II-3, C-II-4; artistic ideals, C-II-3, C-II-4; aesthetic tastes, B-22; meanings, C-II-6; preference, D-I-14; norms, A-10a, C-II-6; judgments, F-I-8; spiritual element, B-3.

ways and life-ways — ways, A-8, A-15, B-7, C-I-2, C-I-3, C-I-15, C-I-17, D-I-10, D-I-12, D-I-14, F-IV-5, exosomatic ways and means, F-III-4; scheme for living, D-I-14; design of the human maze, D-II-3; way of life, A-19, B-12, B-20, C-I-4, C-I-8, C-I-9, C-I-13, C-I-14, C-I-16, C-I-17, C-I-19, D-I-3, E-8; ways of thought, A-20; ways of doing, thinking, feeling, C-I-5a; common sense, eidos, implicit dominant ontology, F-II-7; forms of behavior, C-I-18; mode of life, C-I-1; modes of behavior, C-I-5, D-II-14; modes of conduct, C-I-17; modes of operation, F-I-6; modes of thought, F-I-14, F-III-5; modes of action, F-I-14; folkways, C-I-3, D-I-5; maniere de vivre, C-I-18a.

Words Not Included In Index B

abstraction — D-II-16.

complex — association complex of ideas, F-II-2.

conscious — conscious activity, F-I-7.

effort — effort at adjustment, D-I-9.

energy — dissipation of energy, C-II-1; surplus human energy, C-II-1.

explicit — explicit, C-I-11; explicit design for living, E-7.

feature — feature, C-I-16.

human — human nature, A-11.

man — man, A-1, A-14, B-8, etc., etc. (unmeaningful element); mankind, men, social men, A-11, A-17, D-I-7.

motor — motor reactions, A-17.

overt — overt behavior patterns, C-I-6.

phase — crystallized phase, A-6.

probable — probable behaviors, E.8.

profess — ideals, C-II-3, C-II-4.

strive — strive for ideals, C-II-3.

super-individual — super-individual, F-I-19.

non-automatic — non-automatic, B-18.

non-genetic — non-genetic efforts, F-I-9, F-I-11; non-genetically, F-IV-3.

non-instinctive — non-instinctive, B-18; non-instinctive activities, E-9.

non-mechanical — non-mechanical, F-I-11.

objective — objective, D-I-7; objective external situations, F-IV-5; objective ideas, F-II-7.

oral — oral form of culture, G2

organism — social organism, F-II-1.

organismic — organismic efforts, F-I-9.

Part Three - Some Statements about Culture

Grouping of Statements about Culture

Group *A.* The Nature of Culture
Group *B.* The Components of Culture
Group *C.* Properties of Culture
Group *D.* Culture and Psychology
Group *E.* Culture and Language
Group *F.* Relation of Culture to Society, Individuals, Environment, and Artifacts

Introduction

THE following excerpts [1] will repeat some of the ideas that have already emerged in the more formal definitions. However, some new and important points will also appear, and these quotations are placed, for the most part, within a fuller context of the writer's thinking. Parts II and III supplement each other significantly, though the assignment of a statement to one part or the other was in some cases arbitrary'. This Part will also serve the function of a thesaurus of representative or significant statements on cultural theory.

In Part II we have made some progress toward factoring out the notions subsumed under the label "culture" and relating them to each other. The word "culture," like the pictures of the Thematic Apperception Test, invites projection. The sheer enthusiasm for such an idea that is "in the air" not only makes projection easier but gives an intensity to the development which makes the process easy to delineate. We shall therefore m Part III present primarily passages where writers have taken "culture" as a cue to, almost, free association and trace the projections of various interpreters upon the concept.

[1] We have eliminated authors' footnotes except where directly germane to the theoretical issues we are concerned with.

Group A: The Nature of Culture

1. *Ogburn, 1922: 6, 13.*
  ...The terms, the superorganic, social heritage, and culture, have all been used interchangeably....
  ...The factor, social heritage, and the factor, the biological nature of man, make a resultant, behavior in culture. From the point of view of analysis, it is a case of a third variable determined by the two other variables. There may of course be still other variables, as for instance, climate, or natural environment. But for the present, the analysis, concerns the two variables, the psychological nature of man and culture.
2. *Ellwood, 1927a: 9.*
  [Culture includes] on the one hand, the whole of man's material civilization, tools, weapons, clothing, shelter, machines, and even systems of industry; and, on the other hand all of non-material or spiritual civilization, such as language, literature, art, religion, ritual, morality, law, and government.
3. *Bose, 1929: 7-8, 24.*
  But in another branch of the science, emphasis is laid upon the life-activities of nun instead of his physical characters. Just ns in studying an animal species we might pay more attention to its life and habits instead of anatomical characters, so in that branch of the science named Cultural Anthropology, we consider what the ruling forces of man's life are, in what way he proceeds to meet them, how human behaviour differs from animal behaviour, what are the causes of difference, if they throw any light upon unknown specific characters, how such characters have evolved in relation to environment and so on. Much of the data of Cultural Anthropology is accordingly furnished by human behaviour. We shall presently see that Anthropology cannot use every aspect of human behaviour on account of limiting conditions present in the data. It is concerned more with the crystalised products of human behaviour, which can be passed on from one individual to another. Culture in Anthropology is specially designed to indicate this particular product of crystallisation....

There are certain modes of behaviour which are found to be common among groups of men. These modes of behaviour are associated with social and political organization, law, with some object like a material object or social institution, etc. These objects and the associated types of behaviour, forming distinct and isolable units, are called cultural traits. The assemblage of cultural traits is known as culture. Culture is also to be viewed as an adaptive measure.

4, *Radcliffe-Brown, 1930: 3, 3-4.*

I shall confine myself, then, in this address, to the science called, somewhat clumsily. Social Anthropology, which has for its task to formulate the general laws of the phenomena that we include under the term culture or civilization. It deals with man's life in society, with social and political organization, law, morals, religion, technology, art, language, and in general with all social institutions, customs, and beliefs in exactly the same way that chemistry deals with chemical phenomena....

The readiest way in which to understand the nature of culture and realize its function in human life, its biological function we may perhaps say. is to consider it as a mode or process of social integration. By any culture or civilization a certain number, larger or smaller, of human beings are united together into a more or less complex system of social groups by which the social relations of individuals to one another are determined. In any given culture we denote this system of grouping as the social structure....

The function of any element of culture, a rule of morality or etiquette, a legal obligation, a religious belief or ritual can only be discovered by considering what part it plays in the social integration of the people in whose culture it is found.

5. *Wallis, 1930: 9, 13, 32, II, 33.*

(P. 9): [Culture] may be defined as the artificial objects, institutions, and modes of life or of thought which are not peculiarly individual but which characterize a group; it is "that complex whole..." [repeating Tylor]. (P. 13): Culture is the life of a people as typified in contacts, institutions, and equipment. It includes characteristic concepts and behavior, customs and traditions. (P. 32): Culture, then, means all those things, institutions, material objects, typical reactions to situations, which characterize a people and distinguish them from other peoples. (P. 11): A culture is a functioning dynamic unit...the...traits...[of which] are interdependent. (P. 33): A culture is more than the sum of the things which compose it.

6. *Murdock, 1932: 213.*

Four factors...have been advanced...as explanations of the fact that man alone of all living creatures possesses culture — namely, habit-forming capacity', social life, intelligence, and language. These factors may be likened to the four legs of a stool, raising human behavior from the floor, the organic level or hereditary basis of all behavior, to the superorganic level, represented by the seat of the stool. No other animal is securely seated on such a four-legged stool.

7. *Forde, 1934: 463, 469-70.*

Neither the world distributions of the various economies, nor their development and relative importance among particular peoples, can be regarded as simple functions of physical conditions and natural resources. Between the physical environment and human activity there is always a middle term, a collection of specific objectives and values, a body of knowledge and belief: in other words, a cultural pattern. That the culture itself is not static, that it is adaptable and modifiable in relation to physical conditions, must not be allowed to obscure the fact that adaptation proceeds by discoveries and inventions which are themselves in no sense inevitable and which are, in any individual community, nearly all of them acquisitions or impositions from without....

...That complex of activities in any human society which we call its culture is a going concern. It has its own momentum, its dogmas. Its habits, its efficiencies and its weaknesses. The elements which go to make it are of very different antiquity; some are old and moribund, but others as old may be vigorous; some borrowings or developments of yesterday are already almost forgotten, others have become strongly entrenched. To appreciate the quality of a particular culture at a particular time; to understand why one new custom or technique is adopted and another rejected, despite persistent external efforts at introduction; to get behind the general and abstract terms which label such somewhat arbitrarily divided categories of activity and interest as arts and crafts, social organization, religion, and so forth; and to see the culture as a living whole — for all these purposes it is necessary to inquire minutely into the relations bet\veen the multifarious activities of a community and to discover where and how they buttress or conflict with one another. Nothing that happens, whether it is the mere whittling of a child's toy or the concentration of energy on some major economy, operates in isolation or fails to react in some degree on many other activities. The careful exploration of what have been called "functional," or "dynamic," relations within a society may disclose much that was unexpected in the processes of interaction between one aspect of culture and another.

8. *Schapera, 1935: 319.*

...For culture is not merely a system of formal practices and beliefs. It is made up essentially of individual reactions to and variations from a traditionally standardized pattern; and indeed no culture can ever be understood unless special attention is paid to this range of individual manifestations.

9. *Faris, 1937: 23.*

Language is communication and is the product of interaction in a society. Grammars are not contrived, vocabularies were not invented, and the semantic changes in language take place without the awareness of those in whose mouths the process is going on. This is a super-individual phenomenon and so also are other characteristic aspects of human life, such as changes in fashions or alterations of the mores.

Herbert Spencer called these collective phenomena superorganic; Durkheim referred to them as *faits sociaux;* Sumner spoke of them as folkways; while anthropologists usually employ the word "culture."

10. *Mumford, 1938: 492.*

Culture in all its forms: culture as the care of the earth: culture as the disciplined seizure and use of energy toward the economic satisfaction of man's wants: culture as the nurture of the body, as the begetting and bearing of children, as the cultivation of each human being's fullest capacities as a sentient, feeling, thinking, acting personality: culture as the transmission of power into polity, of experience into science and philosophy, of life into the unity and significance of art: of the whole into the tissue of values that men are willing to die for rather than forswear — religion...

11. *Firth, 1939: 18-19.*

Most modern authors are agreed, whether explicitly or not, upon certain very general assumptions about the nature of the material they study. They consider the acts of individuals not in isolation but as members of society and call the sum total of these modes of behavior "culture." They are impressed also by the dynamic interrelationship of items of a culture, each item tending to vary according to the nature of the others. They recognize too that in every culture there are certain features common to all: groups such as the family, institutions such as marriage, and complex forms of practice and belief which can be aggregated under the name of religion. On the basis of this they argue for the existence of universally comparable factors and processes, the description and explanation of which can be given in sociological laws or general principles of culture.

12. *von Wiese, 1939: 593.*

Culture is above all not "an order of phenomena," and is not to be found in the worlds of perceptible or conceived things. It does not belong to the world of substance; it is a part of the world of values, of which it is a formal category...Culture is no more a thing-concept than "plus," "higher" or "better."

12a. *Murdock, 1940: 364-69.*

1. *Culture Is Learned.* Culture is not instinctive, or innate, or transmitted biologically, but is composed of habits, i.e., learned tendencies to react, acquired by each individual through his own life experience after birth. This assumption, of course, is shared by all anthropologists outside of the totalitarian stares, but it has a corollary which is not always so clearly recognized. If culture is learned, it must obey the laws of learning, which the psychologists have by now worked out in considerable detail. The principles of learning are known to be essentially the same, not only for all mankind but also for m.ost mammalian species. Hence, we should expect all cultures, being learned, to reveal certain uniformities reflecting this universal common factor.

2. *Culture Is Inculcated.* All animals are capable of learning, but man alone seems able, in any considerable measure, to pass on his acquired habits to his offspring. We can housebreak a dog, teach him tricks, and implant in him other germs of culture, but he will not transmit them to his puppies. They will receive only the biological inheritance of their species, to which they in turn will add habits on the basis of their own experience. The factor of language presumably accounts for man's preeminence in this respect. At any rate, many of the habits learned by human beings are transmitted from parent to child over successive generations, and, through repeated inculcation, acquire that {persistency over time, that relative independence of individual bearers, which justifies classifying them collectively as "culture." This assumption, too, is generally accepted by anthropologists, but again there is an underestimated corollary. If culture is inculcated, then all cultures should show certain common effects of the inculcation process. Inculcation involves not only the imparting of techniques and knowledge but also the disciplining of the child's animal impulses to adjust him to social life. That there are regularities in behavior reflecting the ways in which these impulses are thwarted and redirected during the forma-

tive years of life, seems clear from the evidence of psychoanalysis, e.g., the apparent universality of intra-family incest taboos.

3, *Culture Is Social.* Habits of the cultural order are not only inculcated and thus transmitted over time; they are also social, that is, shared by human beings living in organized aggregates or societies and kept relatively uniform by social pressure. They are, in short, group habits. The habits which the members of a social group share with one another constitute the culture of that group. This assumption is accepted by most anthropologists, but not by all. Lowie, for example, insists that "a culture is invariably an artificial unit segregated for purposes of expediency...There is only one natural unit for the ethnologist — the culture of all humanity at all periods and in all places..." The author finds it quite impossible to accept this statement. To him, the collective or shared habits of a social group — no matter whether it be a family, a village, a class, or a tribe — constitute, not "an artificial unit" but a natural unit — a culture or subculture. To deny this is, in his opinion, to repudiate the most substantial contribution which sociology has made to anthropology. If culture is social, then the fate of a culture depends on the fate of the society which bears it, and all cultures which have survived to be studied should reveal certain similarities; because they have all had to provide for societal survival. Among these cultural universals, we can probably list such things as sentiments of group cohesion, mechanisms of social control, organization for defense against hostile neighbors, and provision for the perpetuation of the population.

4. *Culture Is Ideational.* To a considerable extent, the group habits of which culture consists are conceptualized (or verbalized) as ideal norms or patterns of behavior. There are, of course, exceptions; grammatical rules, for example, though they represent collective linguistic habits and are thus cultural, are only in small part consciously formulated. Nevertheless, as every field ethnographer knows, most people show in marked degree an awareness of their own cultural norms, an ability to differentiate them from purely individual habits, and a facility in conceptualizing and reporting them in detail, including the circumstances where each is considered appropriate and the sanctions to be expected for nonconformity. Within limits, therefore, it is useful to conceive of culture as ideational, and of an element of culture as a traditionally accepted idea, held by the members of a group or subgroup, that a particular kind of behavior (overt, verbal, or implicit) should conform to an established precedent. These ideal norms should not be confused with actual behavior. In any particular instance, an individual behaves in response to the state of his organism (his drives) at the moment, and to his perception of the total situation in which he finds himself. In so doing, he naturally tends to follow his established habits, including his culture, but either his impulses or the nature of the circumstances may lead him to deviate therefrom to a greater or lesser degree. Behavior, therefore, does not automatically follow culture, which is only one of its determinants. There are norms of behavior, of course, as well as of culture, but, unlike the latter, they can be established only by statistical means. Confusion often arises between anthropologists and sociologists on this point. The former, until recently, have been primarily preoccupied with ideal norms or patterns, whereas sociologists, belonging to the same society as both their subjects and their audience, assume general familiarity with the culture and commonly report only the statistical norms of actual behavior. A typical community study like *Middletown* and an ethnographic monograph, though often compared, are thus in reality poles apart. To the extent that culture is ideational, we may conclude, all cultures should reveal certain similarities, flowing from the universal laws governing the symbolic mental processes, e.g., the world-wide parallels in the principles of magic.

5. *Culture Is Gratifying.* Culture always, and necessarily, satisfies basic biological needs and secondary needs derived therefrom. Its elements are tested habitual techniques for gratifying human impulses in man's interaction with the external world of nature and fellow man. This assumption is an inescapable conclusion from modern stimulus-response psychology. Culture consists of habits, and psychology has demonstrated that habits persist only so long as they bring satisfaction. Gratification reinforces habits, strengthens and perpetuates them, while lack of gratification inevitably results in their extinction or disappearance. Elements of culture, therefore, can continue to exist only when they yield to the individuals of a society a margin of satisfaction, a favorable balance of pleasure over pain. Malinowski has been insisting on this point for years, but the majority or anthropologists have either rejected the assumption or have paid it but inadequate lip service. To them, the fact that culture persists has seemed to raise no problem; it has been blithely taken for granted. Psychologists, however, have seen the problem, and have given it a definitive answer, which anthropologists can ignore at their peril. If culture is gratifying, widespread similarities should exist in all cultures, owing to the fact that basic human impulses, which are universally the same, demand similar forms of satisfaction. The "universal culture pattern" propounded by Wissler would seem to rest on this foundation.

6. *Culture Is Adaptive.* Culture changes; and the process of change appears to be an adaptive one» comparable to evolution in the organic realm but of a different order. Cultures tend, through periods of time, to become adjusted to the geographic environment, as the anthropogeographers have shown, although environmental influences are no longer conceived as determinative of cultural development. Cultures also adapt, through borrowing and organization, to the social environment of neighboring peoples. Finally, cultures unquestionably tend to become adjusted to the biological and psychological demands of the human organism. As life conditions change, traditional forms cease to provide a margin of satisfaction and are eliminated; new needs arise or are perceived, and new cultural adjustments are made to them. The assumption that culture is adaptive by no means commits one to an idea of progress, or to a theory of evolutionary stages of development, or to a rigid determinism of any sort. On the contrary-, one can agree with Opler, who has pointed out on the basis of his Apache material, that different cultural forms may represent adjustments to like problems, and similar cultural forms to different problems. It is probable, nevertheless, that a certain proportion of the parallels in different cultures represent independent adjustments to comparable conditions.

The conception of cultural change as an adaptive process seems to many anthropologists inconsistent with, and contradictory to, the conception of cultural change as an historical process. To the author, there seems nothing inconsistent or antagonistic in the two positions — the "functional" and the "historical," as they are commonly labeled. On the contrary, he believes that both are correct, that they supplement one another, and that the best anthropological work emerges when the two are used in conjunction. Culture history is a succession of unique events, in which later events are conditioned by earlier ones. From the point of view of culture, the events which affect later ones in the same historical sequences are often, if not usually, accidental, since they have their origin outside the continuum of culture. They include natural events, like floods and droughts; biological events, like epidemics and deaths; and psychological events, like emotional outbursts and inventive intuitions. Such changes alter a society's life conditions. They create new needs and render old cultural forms unsatisfactory, stimulating trial and error behavior and cultural innovations. Perhaps the most significant events, however, are historical contacts with peoples of differing cultures, for men tend first to ransack the cultural resources of their neighbors for solutions to their problems of living, and rely only secondarily upon their own inventive ingenuity. Full recognition of the historical character of culture, and especially of the role of diffusion, is thus a prime prerequisite if a search for cross-cultural generalizations is to have any prospect of success. It is necessary to insist, however, that historical events, like geographic factors, exert only a conditioning rather than a determining influence as the course of culture. Man adjusts to them, and draws selectively upon them to solve his problems and satisfy his needs.

7. *Culture Is Integrative.* As one product of the adaptive process, the elements of a given culture tend to form a consistent and integrated whole. We use the word "tend" advisedly, for we do not accept the position of certain extreme functionalists that cultures actually are integrated systems, with their several parts in perfect equilibrium. We adhere, rather, to the position of Sumner that the folkways are "subject to a strain of consistency to each other," but that actual integration is never achieved for the obvious reason that historical events are constantly exerting a disturbing influence. Integration takes time — there is always what Ogburn has called a "cultural lag" — and long before one process has been completed, many others have been initiated. In our own culture, for example, the changes wrought in habits of work, recreation, sex, and religion through the introduction of the automobile are probably still incomplete. If culture is integrative, then correspondences or correlations between similar traits should repeatedly occur in unrelated cultures. Lowie, for example, has pointed out a number of such correlations.

13. *Dennes, 1942: 164.-65.*

Following the lead of eminent historians, anthropologists, psychologists, and philosophers, I have now directed your attention to eight phases or characteristics of group living which have been taken by them as definitive of the term culture, or of the term civilization, when those terms are used descriptively. Some scholars, as we have seen, use the name culture for the "simpler" phases, civilization for the more complex; others exactly reverse this practice; and still others use the two terms virtually as synonyms. We may observe at this point that none of these eight descriptive notions restricts culture or civilization to any particular pattern of organization. For example, a highly aristocratic or a highly democratic pattern of social living might, either of them, conspicuously exemplify — or fail to exemplify — what is meant by culture or civilization in any of the eight senses. We must note, also, that there are *indefinitely many* other types, phases, and products of social living which can be distinguished and studied, and taken as criteria of civilization; — how many (and which) a man will deal with will be determined by his interests and capacities and by the problems that are felt as pressing at the time. The eight descriptive notions I have selected and brought to your attention are, to resume:

1. Material culture.
2. Culture, that is, material culture conjoined with art, ritual, laws.
3. "Genuine culture" (in Sapir's phrase) — a firm integration and mutually reinforcing development of all the factors specified as constituting culture in sense 2.
4. Civilization as culture (or "genuine culture") *mediated by history and science.*
5. Civilization as tribal or national culture so mediated by history and science as to lead to the recognition of the equal humanity of other nations.
6. Civilization as that special development of sense 5 which is essentially characterized by the employment of intelligence to discern the dominant tendencies of change in men's ways of living together, to predict future changes in these respects, and to accommodate men to (and even facilitate) such change.
7. Civilization as values realized, and particular civilizations as the patterns of social living more or less conducive to, or adequate to, the enactment and experience of values.
8. Civilization as an active process of growth in communication and appreciation.

14. *Roheim, 1943: 81-82.*

...When looking at the situation from a remote, biological point of view I wrote of culture as a neurosis, my critics objected. Attempting to reply to this criticism I now defined culture with greater precision as a psychic defense system. Since this view has also been questioned, I have taken up the question again in the present book and tried to analyze culture in some of its aspects which are most ego-syntonic, most useful and therefore appear to be remote from defense mechanisms. The result of this investigation is to confirm me in the view that defence systems against anxiety are the stuff that culture is made of and that therefore specific cultures are structurally similar to specific neuroses. This view of psychoanalytical anthropology was really the starting point of the whole problem. However other processes must follow the formation of these neurosis-systems to produce sublimations and culture. The psyche as we know it is formed by the introjection of primary objects (super-ego) and the first contact with environment (ego). Society itself is knitted together by projection of these primarily introjected objects or concepts followed by a series of subsequent introjections and projections.

15. *Kluckhohn and Kelly, 1945a: 93-94.*

The philosopher: ...where is the locus of culture — in society or in the individual?

Third anthropologist: Asking the question that way poses a false dilemma. Remember that "culture" is an abstraction. Hence culture as a concrete, observable entity does not exist anywhere — unless you wish to say that it exists in the "minds" of the men who make the abstractions, and this is hardly a problem which need trouble us as scientists. The objects and events from which we make our abstractions do have an observable existence. But culture is like a map. Just as a map isn't the territory but an abstract representation of the territory so also a culture is an abstract description of trends toward uniformity in the words, acts, and artifacts of human groups. The data, then, from which we come to know culture are not derived from an abstraction such as "society" but from directly observable behavior and behavioral products. Note, however, that "culture" may be said to be "supra-individual" in at least two non-mystical, perfectly empirical senses:

1. Objects as well as individuals show the influence of culture.
2. The continuity of culture seldom depends upon the continued existence of any particular individuals.

16. *Kluckhohn and Kelly, 1945b: 33-35.*

...there are four variables in the determination of human action: nun's biological equipment, his social environment, his physical environment, and his culture. Let us designate those as a, b, c, and d. But a given system of designs for living is clearly the product of a, b, c, *and* d. In other words, it is quite clearly different from "d" alone, so let us call it "x." It would seem, then, that anthropologists have used the same term "culture" to cover both "d" and "x." This is enough to make a logician's hair stand on end.

Third anthropologist: Perhaps, in practice, the confusion has been mitigated by the tendency to use "culture" for the analytical abstraction "d" and "a culture" for the generalizing abstraction "x." But it is all too true that anthropologists and other scholars have frequently treated "d" (the explanatory concept) and "x" (the descriptive concept) as synonyms or equivalents. Having given a sound abstract description of "group habits," the anthropologist then unthinkingly employs this ("x") as an explanatory concept, forgetting that "x" must be regarded as the joint product of "d" and three other determiners.

"X" is much closer to observable "reality" than "d." "D" is, if you will, only an hypothesis — though a highly useful hypothesis'. "X," however, is an abstract representation of central tendencies in observed facts. Let me trivc you an example. Some peoples call their mothers and their mothers' sisters by the same kin term, and they tend to make few distinctions in the ways in which they behave toward their mothers and toward their mothers' sisters. Other peoples apply different terms of address and of reference to these two classes of relatives and perhaps also differentiate between the younger and the older sisters of the mother. With such usages, in most instances, go variations in behavior. Rigorous abstract description of all these patterns does not require the invocation of hypotheses. But we do not know, and perhaps never can know, in an ultimate and complete sense, why these two examples of differing behavior exist. The concept "culture" does however help to understand how it is that at a given point in time two different peoples, living in the same natural environment, having the same "economic" system, can nevertheless have different usages in this respect.

In sum, when a culture is *described,* this is merely the conceptualization — highly convenient for certain purposes — of certain trends toward uniformity in the behavior of the people making up a certain group. No pretense is made at a total "explanation" of all this behavior. Just to approach such an understanding would require the collaboration of a variety of specialists in biology, medicine, and many other subjects. The primary utility of "culture" as an explanatory concept is in illuminating the *differences* between behavioral trends as located in space and time.

17. *Bidney, 1947: 395-96.*

According to the polaristic position adopted here, *culture is to be understood primarily as a regulative process initiated by man for the development arid organization of his determinate, substantive potentialities.* There is no pre-cultural human nature from which the variety of cultural forms may be deduced *a priori,* since the cultural process is a spontaneous expression of human nature and is coeval with man's existence. Nevertheless, human nature is logically and genetically prior to culture since we must postulate human agents with psychobiological powers and impulses capable of initiating the cultural process as a means of adjusting to their environment and as a form of symbolic expression. In other words, the determinate nature of man is manifested functionally through culture but is not reducible to culture. Thus one need not say with Ortega y Gassett, "Man has no nature; he has history." There is no necessity in fact or logic for choosing between nature and history. Man has a substantive ontological nature which may be investigated by the methods of natural science as well as a cultural history which may be studied by the methods of social science and by logical analysis. Adequate self-knowledge requires a comprehension of both nature and history. The theory of the polarity of nature and culture would do justice to both factors by allowing for the ontological conditions [1] of the historical, cultural process.

18. *Hinshaw and Spuhler, 1948: 17.*

In an attempt to resolve certain conflicting philosophies of culture, Bidney has suggested that the "idealistic" and "realistic" conceptions of culture are not in conflict, that they can be unified. In discussing this contention he defines five fallacies. He makes commission of these fallacies contrary to achievement of conceptual unification. While we feel that the definition of such fallacies is an important methodological service, we believe that Bidney has not made sufficiently clear what some might call the purposes or what we have called the levels of his analysis. We do not wish to challenge his substantive contributions; rather we wish to have his methodological remarks clarified.

On the scientific (perceptual) level of inquiry, the subject matter of cultural anthropology is necessarily parcelled by confining attention to a (more or less) definite group of abstractions. We would insist that those anthropologists who have confined attention to a "realist" set of abstractions, and those who have been concerned with an "idealist" set of abstractions, have both made significant and useful contributions to anthropology on the scientific level. The disadvantage of exclusive attention to a parcelled group of abstractions, however well-founded, is that, by the nature of the subject matter, one has neglected a remainder of that subject matter. Insofar as the excluded data are important to the subject matter, this particular methodology or mode of thought is not fitted to deal, in an adequate way, with the larger problems in question. Since, in practice, the working anthropologist cannot proceed without making a classification of his subject matter, it is of great importance to pay constant attention to the modes of abstraction.

It is here that the philosophy of anthropology finds its role essential to the progress of the subject. And this task, the authors contend, can be carried out solely within the perceptual or scientific level.

19. *Kroeber, 1948a: 8-9, 253.*

Culture, then, is all those things about nun that are more than just biological or organic, and are also more than merely psychological. It presupposes bodies and personalities, as it presupposes men associated in groups, and it rests upon them; but culture is something more than a sum of psychosomatic qualities and actions. It is more than these in that its phenomena cannot be wholly understood in terms of biology and psychology. Neither of these sciences claims to be able to explain why there are axes and property laws and etiquettes and prayers in the world, why they function and perpetuate as they do, and least of all why these cultural things take the particular and highly variable forms or expressions under which they appear. Culture thus is at one and the same time the totality of products of social men, and a tremendous force affecting all human beings, socially and individually. And in this special but broad sense, culture is universal for man...

The terms "social inheritance" or "tradition" put the emphasis on how culture is acquired rather than on what it consists of. Yet a naming of all the kinds of things that we receive by tradition — speech, knowledge, activities, rules, and the rest — runs into quite an enumeration. We have already seen...that things so diverse as hoeing corn, singing the blues, wearing a shirt, speaking English, and being a Baptist are involved. Perhaps a shorter way of designating the content of culture is the negative way of telling what is excluded from it. Put this way around, culture might be defined as all the activities and non-physical products of human personalities that are not automatically reflex or instinctive. That in turn means, in biological and psychological parlance, that culture consists of conditioned or learned activities (plus the manufactured results of these); and the idea of learning brings us back again to what is socially transmitted, what is received from tradition, what "is acquired by man as a member of societies." So perhaps *how it comes to be* is really more distinctive of culture than what it *is*. It certainly is more easily expressed specifically. .

20. *Bidney, 1949: 470.*

Modern ethnology has shown that all historical societies have had cultures or traditional ways of behavior and thought in conformity with which they have patterned their lives. And so valuable have these diverse ways of living appeared to the members of early human society that they have tended to ascribe a divine origin to their accepted traditions and have encouraged their children to conform to their folkways and mores as matters of faith which were above question. With the growth of experience and the development of critical thought, first individuals and then groups began to question some elements of the traditional thoughtways and practices and thereby provided a stimulus for cultural change and development.

21. *Radcliffe-Brown 1949: 510-11.*

The word "culture" has many different meanings. As a psychologist I would define culture in accordance with its dictionary meaning in English, as the process by which a human individual acquires, through contact with other individuals, or from such things as books and works of art, habits, capabilities, ideas, beliefs, knowledge, skills, tastes, and sentiments; and, by an extension common in the English language, the products of that process in the individual. As an Englishman I learned Latin and French and therefore some knowledge of Latin and French are part of my culture. The culture process in this sense can be studied by the psychologist, and in fact the theory of learning is such a study.

...The sociologist is obviously obliged to study the cultural traditions of all kinds that are found in a society of which he is making a study. Cultural tradition is a social process of interaction of persons within a social structure.

22. *Zipf, 1949: 276.*

Culture is relative to a given social group at a given time: that is it consists of *n* different social signals that are correlated with *m* different social responses...

Comment

Five of this group of statements attempt to list the factors that make culture: Ogburn, (1) 1922; Murdock, (6) 1932; Murdock, (12a) 1940; Dennes, (13) 1942; Kluckhohn and Kelly, (16) 1945a. Dennes stands somewhat apart from the others. He thoughtfully lists eight "phases or characteristics" which have been taken to be definitive of the terms culture or civilization — eight senses in which they have been used. This is in a way an essay similar in goal to our present one — indeed, nearer to it in general outcome than might be anticipated from a philosopher as against a pair of anthropologists.

Of the others, Ogburn is earliest and, no doubt for that reason, simplest. He recognizes two factors, social heritage and biological nature of man, whose resultant is cultural behavior. Murdock, ten years later, admits four factors that raise human behavior from the organic, hereditary level to the super-organic level. These four are habit-forming capacity, social life, intelligence, and language. Only the fourth would today be generally accepted as one of the pillars on which culture rests. Habits, society, and intelligence are now universally attributed to sub-human as well as to human beings, in kind at any rate, though often less in degree. It is only by construing "habits" as customs, and "intelligence" as symbol-using imagination, that these two factors would today be retained as criteria; and as for "social life" — how get around the cultureless ants? It would appear that .Murdock started out to give "explanations" of the factors that make culture a uniquely human attribute, but that in part he substituted faculties which are indeed associated in man with culture but are not differential criteria of it. [3] In his 1940 statement (12a), however, he is clear on this distinction, and indeed his position as developed here is quite close to our own.

Kluckhohn and Kelly also name four factors ("variables") determinative of "human action": biological equipment, physical environment, social environment, and culture. They complain, however, or have one of the characters in their dialogue complain, that anthropologists use the same word culture for the product of these four factors and for the fourth factor — a procedure logically hair-raising.

The one of the present authors not involved in the 1945 dialogue is less troubled logically. It is a given culture that is the product, antecedent culture that always enters into it as a factor. He sees cultural causality as inevitably circular; equally so whether culture be viewed impersonally and historically or as something existing only in, through, or by persons. In the latter case the persons are inevitably influenced by existing and previous culture. The two-term formula is: culture > (persons assumed) > culture; the three term: culture > persons > culture. Each formula has its proper uses, and particular risks. The culture > culture formula eliminates the personalities that in a long-range historical or mass situation can contribute little but may rather clog or distract from understanding. The risk in exclusive use of this formula is that it may lead to assumption of culture as a wholly autonomous system, with immanent, preordained causation. The culture-persons-culture formula obviously is most useful in short-term, close-up, fine-view analyses. Its risk is the temptation to escape from circularity of reasoning by short-circuiting into a simplistic two-term formula of persons > culture or culture > personalities.

Three British social anthropologists, (7) Forde, 1934, (11) Firth, 1939, and (21) Radcliffe-Brown, 1949, stress the dynamic interrelations of activities within a culture. In addition, Radcliffe-Brown as usual narrows the concept of culture as much as possible: culture is the *process* by which language, beliefs, usages, etc., are handed on (similar to statements in [19] Kroeber, 1948!); and, says Radcliffe-Brown, cultural tradition is a *social* process of interaction of *persons* within a *social* structure. This seems to leave culture a mere derivative by-product of society, a position shared with Radcliffe-Brown by some sociologists, but by few if any anthropologists; who, if they insist on deriving culture, nowadays try to derive it out of personality, or at least from the interaction of personalities as opposed to society as such.

Radcliffe-Brown's earlier position in (4), 1930, emphasizes that the nature and function of culture in general are a mode of *social integration*, and he repeats this for the function of elements of culture. The focus of interest here is slightly different from that of 1949, but the subordination of culture to society is about the same.

Firth in (11), 1939, adduces a second property of culture: it contains *universally comparable* factors and processes. These can be described and explained in "social laws or general principles of culture."

In (12) von Wiese, 1939, and (17, 20) Bidney, 1947, 1949, we feel modern repercussions of the old nature-spirit duality, even though Bidney expressly criticizes the idealistic concept of culture. Von Wiese holds that culture is not in the world of substance but is part of the world of values, of which it is a category. It is not a thing concept, it is not even an order of phenomena. Bidney is less vehement. He sees culture as a *regulative* process *initiated* by man *for* the *development* and organization of his determinate, substantive *potentialities.* We have italicized the words in this statement which seem to us as construable of idealistic if not teleological implications. Again, man is said to have a substantive ontological nature open to investigation by natural science, as well as a culture history open to investigation by social science and logical analysis. To us — subject to correction — this smacks of the Natur-Geist opposition of Kantian, post-Kantian, and perhaps Neo-Kantian idealism. In an important footnote which we have retained, Bidney says that he is speaking of the metacultural presuppositions of any culture; that the problem was soundly appraised by Dilthey, Ortega, and Cassirer; and that his disagreement is only with their Neo-Kantian epistemology.

Hinshaw and Spuhler, (18) 1948, seem to sense something of the same point we are making, when they reply to Bidney that the task of anthropology can be carried out only within the perceptual or scientific level. We too hold that everything about culture. including its values and creativities, is within nature and interpretable by natural science.

A few more isolated statements are worth mentioning.

Schapera (8), 1935. emphasizes the need, for understanding culture, of attending to the range of individual variations from the traditionally standardized pattern. There is no quarreling with this. It is much like insisting that a mean plus variability has more significance than the mean alone. At the same time much depends on the focus. If interest lies primarily in persons, the standardized pattern need only be defined, and examination can concern itself with the range of variation. If interest is in cultural forms as such and their interrelations, individual variability becomes of secondary moment.

Bose (3), 1929, strikes a somewhat new note with his statement that while cultural anthropology draws its data from human behavior, it specializes on those *crystallized* products of behavior which can be passed on between individuals. "Crystallized" here appears to mean the same as standardized to Schapera.

Roheim (14), 1943, in holding that defense systems against anxiety are the stuff that culture is made of, and that therefore specific cultures are structurally [why structurally?] similar to specific neuroses, is virtually adhering to Freud's *Totem and Taboo* theory of the origin of culture in a slightly new dress.

On the other hand, we agree with the dictum of Fails (9), 1957, that Spencer's superorganic, Durkheim's *faits sociaux,* Sumner's folkways, and the anthropologists' culture refer to essentially the same collective phenomena.

Wallis (5), 1930. ambles through several points on culture, all of which are unexceptionable, but which do not add up to a definition nor even quite to a condensed theory.

[1] [Bidney's footnote] There is an important distinction to be made between the ontological conditions of the cultural process and the ontological presuppositions of given systems of culture. Sorokin, for example, in his *Social and Cultural Dynamics,* and Northrop in his *The Meeting of East and West* have discussed the views of reality inherent in diverse cultural systems. *In this paper, my concern is with the meta-cultural presuppositions of any system of culture whatsoever.* The problem, it seems to me, was soundly appraised by Dilthey, Ortega y Gasset, and Cassirer; my disagreement is solely with their Neo-Kantian epistemology.

[2] As regards habits this is explicitly recognized by Murdock. Cf. III-b-3, below.

Group B: The Components of Culture

1. *Bose, 1929: 25.*

The stuff of which culture is composed is capable of analysis into the following categories: Speech -Material traits Art Mythology Knowledge Religion Family and Social systems Property Government and War (Wissler), Any of these components of culture does not by itself, however, form an independent unit, but is closely bound up with the rest through many tics of association.

2. *Menghin, 1931: 614.*

Die Kultur lässt sich noch weiter einteilen, natürlich wiederum nur rein begreiflich, denn tatsächlich treten uns, wie schon in der Einleitung gesagt wurde, die verschiedenen Kultursachgebiete konkret so gut wie immer in vermengtem Zustande entgegen. Die Systemarik der Kultur, als der verhälmismässig reinsten Objektivarion des Geistigen, schliesst sich am besten den Grundsstrebungen an, die an der Menschheit beobachtet werden können. Dies sind nach meiner Auffassung das Streben nach Erhaltung, Geltung und Einsicht. Das erste erfüllt die materielle, das zweite die soziale, das dritte die geistige Kultur. Dabei ist aber nicht zu übersehen, dass in der Wurzel jedes dieser Sachgebiete geistiger Natur ist, da es ja einer Strebung entspringt. Der Unterschied, der die Bezeichnungen rechtfertigt, beruht lediglich in der Art und Stärke der Stoffgebundenheit. Man kann diese drei Sachgebiete weiter gliedern. Doch soll hier nur die geistige Kultur nähere Behandlung erfarhren. Sie zerfällt in Kunst, Wissenschaft, und Sitte.

3. *Murdock, 1932: 204-05.*

Habit alone, however, is far from explaining culture. Many cultureless animals possess a considerable habit-forming capacity, and some of the mammals are in this respect not radically inferior to man. Social scientists agree, therefore, that culture depends on life in societies as well as on habit. Individual habits die with their owners, but it is a characteristic of culture that it persists though its individual bearers are mortal. Culture consists of habits, to be sure, but they differ from individual habits by the fact that they are shared or possessed in common by the various members of a society, thus acquiring a certain independence and a measure of immortality. Habits of the cultural order have been called "group habits." To the average man they are known as "customs," and anthropologists sometimes speak of the "science of custom."

The process of custom forming (as Chapin...correctly states) is similar to that of habit forming, and the same psychological laws are involved. When activities dictated by habit are performed by a large number of individuals in company and simultaneously, the individual habit is converted into mass phenomenon or custom.

To the anthropologist, group habits or customs are commonly known as "culture traits," defined by Willey as "basically, habits carried in the individual nervous systems." The sociologists, on the other hand, almost universally speak of them as "folkways." General agreement prevails, therefore, that the constituent elements of culture, the proper data of the science of culture, are group habits. Only the terms employed are at variance.

Of the several terms, "folkway" possesses certain manifest advantages, "Custom" lacks precision. Moreover, though it represents adequately enough such explicit group habits as words, forms of salutation, and burial practices, it scarcely suffices for implicit common responses, mental habits, or ideas, such as religious and magical concepts, which are equally a part of culture. The term "culture trait," though it covers both of these types of group behavior, is also used to include material objects or artifacts, which are not group habits, indeed not habits at all but facts of a totally different order. Artifacts are not themselves primary data of culture, as is shown by the recognized distinction between their dissemination by trade and the process of cultural diffusion proper.

4. *Boas, 1948: 4-5.* [1]

Aspects of culture: Man and nature. Culture itself is many-sided. It includes the multitude of relations between man and nature; the procuring and preservation of food; the securing of shelter; the ways in which the objects of nature are used as implements and utensils; and all the various ways in which man utilizes or controls, or is controlled by, his natural environment: animals, plants, the inorganic world, the seasons, and wind and weather.

Man and man. A second large group of cultural phenomena relate to the interrelation between members of a single society and between those belonging to different societies. The bonds of family, or tribe, and of a variety of social groups are included in it, as well as the gradation of rank and influence; the relation of sexes and of old and young; and in more complex societies the whole political and religious organization. Here belong also the relations of social groups in war and peace.

Subjective aspects. A third group consists of the subjective reactions of man to all the manifestations of life contained in the first two groups. These are of intellectual and emotional nature and may be expressed in thought and feeling as well as in action. They include all rational attitudes and those valuations which we include under the terms of ethics, esthetics, and religion.

5. *Murdoch, 1941: 143.*

The elements of which a culture is composed, though all alike are traditional, habitual and socially shared, may be conveniently divided into techniques, relationships, and ideas. Techniques relate the members of a society to the external world of nature...Relationships...are the interpersonal habitual responses of the members of a society...ideas consist not of habits of overt behavior but of patterned verbal habits, often subvocal but capable of expression in speech. These include technological and scientific knowledge, beliefs of all kinds, and a conceptual formulation of normal behavior in both techniques and relationships and of the sanctions for deviation therefrom.

6. *Firth, 1944: 20.*

Social anthropology is a scientific study of human culture. Its interest is in the variety of men's rules, conduct, and beliefs in different types of society and in the uniformity (as for instance in basic family organization) which underlies all societies. It is not concerned only with the different forms of customs all over the world, but also with the meaning these customs have for the people who practise them. Values are part of its material for examination...

7. *White, 1941: 165.*

Culture is the name of the means, the equipment, employed by man and by man alone in this struggle. Concretely and specifically, culture is made up of tools, utensils, traditional habits, customs, sentiments, and ideas. The cultural behavior of man is distinguished from the non-cultural behavior of the lower animals and of man himself considered *as an animal* as distinguished from man *as a human being* — by the use of *symbols*. A symbol may be defined as a thing whose meaning is determined by those who use it. Only man has the ability' to use symbols. The exercise of this faculty has created for this species a kind of environment not possessed by any other species: a cultural environment. Culture is a traditional organization of objects (tools, and things made with tools), ideas (knowledge, lore, belief), sentiments (attitude toward milk, homicide, mothers-in-law, etc.) and use of symbols. The function of culture is to regulate the adjustment of man as an animal species to his natural habitat.

Comment

A few statements as to the components of culture are enumerative, somewhat like Tylor's original definition of culture (Part II-A-1), without straining to be absolutely inclusive. Such is White's 1947 list (7): tools, utensils, traditional habits, customs, sentiments, ideas. The context shows that White is concerned with the nature and function of culture, and his enumeration is illustrative rather than exhaustive. Bose (1), 1929 takes over Wissler's universal pattern (with one minor change). He merely says that culture can be analyzed into these nine categories, and is express that these are not independent units in their own right. Wissler's classificatory attempt — with his sub-classes it is about a page long and looks much like a Table of Contents — has never been seriously used, developed, or challenged. It is evident that anthropologists have been reluctant to classify culture into its topical parts. They have sensed that the categories are not logically definite, but are subjectively fluid and serve no end beyond that of convenience, and thus would shift according to interest and context.

Sorokin (1947, ch. 17, 18) calls the divisions, segments, or categories of culture, such as those of Wissler and Bose, "cultural systems," which, with cultural congeries, underlie his Ideational, Idealistic, and Sensate super systems of culture. He recognizes five "pure" cultural systems: (1), language; (2), science, evidently including technology; (3), religion; (4), fine arts; (5), ethics or law and morals. [2] Of "mixed" or derivative systems, there are three most notable ones: philosophy, economics, politics. Philosophy, for instance, is a compound of science, religion, and ethics.

Except for Wissler's one fling at the universal pattern of culture, which was enumerative and which he did not follow up, anthropologists have fought shy of trying to make formal classification of the components of culture. [3] Being mostly preoccupied with dealing with cultures substantively, such classification has evidently seemed to them a matter mainly of pragmatic convenience, and they have dealt with it in an *ad hoc* manner, in contrast with Sorokin, whose logical and systematizing bent is much more developed than theirs — more than that of most sociologists, in fact.

Menghin (2: 1931) Strivings: Fulfilled by:	Subsistence Material Culture	Recognition (Geltung) Social Culture	Insight (Einsicht) Geistige Kultur
Boas (4: 1938) Aspects of Culture, Relations of:	Man to Nature Food, shelter, implements, control of nature	Man to Man	Subjective Aspects of two preceding, intellectual and emotional, including actions: rational attitudes, and valuations
Murdock (5: 1941) Culture composed of:	Techniques Relating society to nature	(Social) Relationships Interpersonal habitual responses	Ideas: patterned verbal and sub-vocal habits. Knowledge (including technology), beliefs, formulations of normal behavior
Weber (1920; Part I, § 5, above)	Civilizational Process: Science, technology	Social Process Including economics, government	Cultural Movement: Religion, philosophy, arts
MacIver (1942, *Social Causation*)	Technological Order ("Civilization" in 1931): Technology, including economics, government — viz., "Apparatus" of living	Social Order	Cultural Order Religion, philosophy, arts, traditions, codes, mores, play; viz., "Modes of living"
Thurnwald (1950, *passim*)	Civilization Dexterities, skills, technology, knowledge. Accumulative. Its sequence is progress	(Gesellungsleben)	Culture Bound to societies; perishable. Uses civilization as means
Kroeber (1951, in press)	Reality Culture	(Social Culture)	Value culture Includes pure science

There is however one tripartite classification of culture which appears several times — in substance though not in the same nomenclature — in the foregoing statements: those by Menghin (2), 1931, Boas (4), 1938, Murdock (5), 1941. [4] Under this viewpoint, the major domains of culture are: (1) the relation of man to nature, subsistence concerns, techniques, "material" culture; (2) the more or less fixed interrelations of men due to desire for status and resulting in social culture; (3) subjective aspects, ideas, attitudes and values and actions due to them, insight, "spiritual" culture. We have already touched on one aspect of this ideology in Part One, Section 4, 5, in discussing distinctions attempted, in Germany and the United States, between "civilization" and "culture." The addition of social relations, process, or culture yields the trichotomy now being considered.

As a matter of fact Alfred Weber in 1912 appears to have been the first to make the dichotomy in the present specific sense, and to have expanded it to the trichotomy in 1920. In America, MacIver (1931, 1942) and Merton (1936) seem to have been the first to see its significance. It thus appears that this three-way distinction was first made in Germany and for a while remained a sociological one, anthropologists coming to recognize it later, but again first in Germany and second in the United States. In so far as the trichotomy developed out of one of the several culture-civilization distinctions, it could not well have originated in England or France, where we have seen that use of the word culture was loner respectively resisted and refused.

At any rate, this three-fold segmentation of culture has now sufficient usage to suggest that it possesses a certain utility. We therefore tabulate the principal instances of its employment as a convenient way of illustrating the substantial uniformity of authors' conceptions, underneath considerable difference of terms used, as well as some minor variations of what is included in each category.

F. Kluckhohn [5] has recently developed a classification of cultural orientations which includes the following categories: Innate Predispositions, Man's Relation to Nature, Time Dimensions, Personality, Modality of Relationship (Man's Relation to Other Men.)

[1] Boas in *The Mind of Primitive Man,* revised edition of 1938, opens his Chapter 9 on page 159 with t definition of culture based on his 1930 one (which we have already cited in Part II-A-7) but expanded, and then in a sense effaced by a second paragraph which grants most the components of culture to animals other than man. The two paragraphs read:

"Culture may be defined as the totality of the mental and physical reactions and activities that characterise the behavior of the individuals composing a social group collectively and individually in relation to their natural environment, to other groups, to members of the group itself and of each individual to himself. It also includes the products of these activities and their role in the life of the groups. The mere enumeration of these various aspects of life, however, does not constitute culture. It is more, for its elements are not independent, they have a structure.

The activities enumerated here are not by any means the sole property of man, for the life of animals is also regulated by their relations to nature, to other animals and by the interrelation of the individuals composing the same species or social group."

Apart from its non-limitation to man, this statement by Boas is strongly behavioral: culture consists of psychosomatic reactions and activities. Beyond these activities, culture includes their products (presumably artifacts, material culture) and possesses structure. Not mentioned are the rational attitudes and ethical, aesthetic, and religious valuations mentioned in statement (4) in the text above.

[2] In Sorokin, 1950, p. 197, philosophy seems to be added as a pure system, "applied technology" to have taken its place among the derivative ones.

[3] Murdock, 1945, constitutes, in part, a follow-up of Wissler.

[4] Tessman, 1930, in listing culture items of East Peruvian tribes, groups them under the headings of material, social, and spiritual culture, corresponding to Menghin's divisions.

[5] F. Kluckhohn, 1950, esp. pp. 378-82.

Group C: Distinctive Properties of Culture

1. *Case, 1927: 920.*

Culture consists essentially in the external storage, interchange, and transmission of an accumulating fund of personal and social experience by means of tools and symbols...Culture is the unique, distinctive, and exclusive possession of man, explainable thus far only in terms of itself.

2. *Ellwood, 1921b: 13.*

The process by which the spiritual element in man is gradually transforming not only the material environment, but man himself...[It is] culture which has made and will make our human world.

3. *Bose, 1929: 32-33.*

Beneath the outer framework of culture, there lies a body of beliefs and sentiments which are responsible for the particular manifestation of a culture. They do not form part of any specific trait, but working beneath many traits, they give to each culture a character of its own....

Such a body of ideas and sentiments grows out of life's philosophy and is consequently conditioned by the needs and aspirations of each particular age.

4. *Faris, 1931: 5, 278.*

The following...are presented as postulates...

The reality of culture. The collective habits have produced uniformities of speech, thought, and conduct which form a body of phenomena with laws of its own.

The priority of culture. With respect to the members of a group, the cultural habits and forms are pre-existing, so that the most important aspects of a given person are to be traced back to influences existing in the culture into which he comes.

The inertia of culture. Slow unnoticed changes in a culture may be noted but these are relatively unimportant. Culture tends to produce itself indefinitely.

Culture is a phenomenon of nature. Language, manners, morals, and social organization grow up within the ongoing activity in the effort of a group to maintain itself, to secure food, and to rear children....

5. *Goldenweiser, 1937: 45-46.*

In summary it might then be said that culture is historical or cumulative, that it is communicated through education, deliberate and non-deliberate, that its content is encased in patterns (that is, standardized procedures or idea systems), that it is dogmatic as to its content and resentful of differences, that its contribution to the individual is absorbed largely unconsciously, leading to a subsequent development of emotional reinforcements, and that the raising of these into consciousness is less likely to lead to insight and objective analysis than to explanations ad hoc, either in the light of the established status quo, or of a moral reference more or less subjective, or of an artificial reasonableness or rationality which is read into it; also, finally, that culture in its application and initial absorption is local

6. *Opler, 1944: 452.*

The capacity for culture is a function of an accent on plasticity, on the development of general adaptability instead of specific structures, on the reduction of the importance of instinct. The inauguration of culture was heralded, we may believe, by the invention of tools and symbols. The tools, crude enough at first, were extraorganic means of doing what man had been forced to accomplish by the power of his own body to that moment. The symbols (generally understood vocal labels for familiar objects and processes) made possible communication (speech, language) and the conservation of whatever gains accumulated from tool-making and experience. Thus tools and symbols (or invention and communication, to phrase it in terms of process) can be considered the building blocks of culture.

7. *Herskovits, 1948: 625.*

Culture (1) is learned; (2) derives from the biological, environmental, psychological, and historical components of human existence; (3) is structured; (4) is divided into aspects; (5) is dynamic; (6) is variable; (7) exhibits regularities that permit its analysis by the methods of science; (8) is the instrument whereby the individual adjusts to his total setting, and gains the means for creative expression.

8. *White, 1949a: 374.*

...articulate speech is the most important and characteristic form of symbolic behavior. Man alone is capable of symbolic behavior by virtue of unique properties of his nervous system, which, however, cannot yet be described except in terms of gross anatomy — exceptionally large forebrain, both relatively and absolutely; an increase in quantity of brain has eventuated in a qualitatively new kind of behavior.

Tradition — the non-biological transmission of behavior patterns from one generation to the next — is found to a limited extent in some of the lower animal species. But in man, thanks particularly to articulate speech, the transmission of experience in the form of material objects, patterns of behavior, ideas, and sentiments or attitudes becomes easy, varied, and extensive; in short, the culture of one generation and age is passed on to the next. And, in addition to this lineal transmission of culture, it is transmitted laterally, by diffusion, to contemporary neighboring groups. Culture is cumulative as well as continuous; new elements are added through invention and discovery. It is also progressive in that more effective means of adjustment with and control over environment are achieved from time to time.

Culture thus becomes a continuum of extrasomatic elements. It moves in accordance with its own principles, its own laws; it is a thing *sui generis.* Its elements interact with one another, forming new combinations and syntheses. New elements are introduced into the stream from time to time, and old elements drop out.

9. *Osgood, 1951: 206, 207, 210, 211, 213.*

...Culture consists of all ideas concerning human beings which have been communicated to one's mind and of which one is conscious.

...Culture consists of all ideas of the manufactures, behavior, and ideas of the aggregate of human beings which have been directly observed or communicated to one's mind and of which one is conscious.

...Thus we can say that the manufactures and behavior of the aggregate of human beings which have been directly observed are the percepta of culture, while the ideas of the aggregate of human beings which have been communicated are the concepta of culture.

...Material culture consists of all ideas of the manufactures of the aggregate of human beings which have been directly observed and of which one is conscious.

...Social culture consists of all ideas of the behavior of the aggregate of human beings which have been directly observed and of which one is conscious.

...Mental culture consists of all ideas (i.e., an ego's) of the ideas (i.e., concepta) of the aggregate of human beings which have been communicated to one's mind and of which one is conscious. By disregarding epistemological considerations, one can greatly simplify this definition to read: .Mental culture consists of the ideas of the aggregate of human beings.

Comment

The statements that seem to fall under this head cover the period 1927-1951. They tend to be enumerative. In this quality they resemble the broad descriptive definitions of II-A, though these attempt to list constituents of culture rather than its properties. The majority of these enumerative descriptions date from before 1934. We can thus probably conclude that as definitions became more cardinal, enumeration tended to become transferred from definition to less concentrated statement about culture.

As might be expected, the properties mentioned run rather miscellaneous, only a few being noted by as many as three or four of the nine authors cited. Now and then an author stands wholly alone in emphasizing a quality, as Ellwood in bringing in spirituality' with a hopefully ameliorative tone, or Goldenweiser in dilating on the affect of hidden *a prioris* when brought to consciousness. Case's statement contains an allusive metaphor in "external storage." On account of the variety of properties mentioned, a discussion of them would be lengthy. Accordingly we content ourselves with a condensed presentation of the properties, grouped as far as possible, to serve as a summary.

Summary of Properties

External (to body), extraorganic, extrasomatic (1, 6, 8)
Symbolism (1, 6, 8)
Communicated (6, 9), by speech (8), transmitted (8), learned (7), by education (5), prior to individual and influencing him (4)
Education deliberate and non-deliberate (5), individual absorption also unconscious (5)
Accumulating, cumulative (1, 5, 8), gains conserved (6)
Aggregate of human beings (9)
Historical (5), continuous (8)

Human only (1), unique property of nervous system (8), *sui generis* (8)
Spiritual (2)
Ideas (9), percepts and concepts (9)
Uniformities with laws (4), regularities promoting scientific analysis (7), own principles and laws (8)
Real (4), phenomenon of nature (4)
Explicable only in terms of self (1)

Inertia, tending to indefinite reproduction (4)
Plastic (6), variable, dynamic (7), new combinations (8)
Localized (5), each culture underlain by particular beliefs and sentiments (3)
General adaptability instead of specific structures and instincts (6)

Means for creative expression (7)
Invention (6, 8), tools (6), manufacture (9)

Instrument of adjustment to environment (7, 8), effort at group maintenance (4)

Transforms natural environment (2)

Patterned, standardized (5), structured (7)
Dogmatic with emotional reinforcement (5), if made conscious, resentful and leading to moral judgments or false rationalizing (5)
Conscious (9)

Group D: Culture and Psychology

1. *Marett, 1920: 11-12* (cf. footnote 6).

It is quite legitimate to regard culture, or social tradition, in an abstract way as a tissue of externalities, as a robe of many colours woven on the loom of time by the human spirit for its own shielding or adorning. Moreover, for certain purposes which in their entirety may be termed sociological, it is actually convenient thus to concentrate attention on the outer garb. In this case, indeed, the garb may well at first sight seem to count for everything; for certainly a man naked of all culture would be no better than a forked radish. Nevertheless, folklore cannot out of deference to sociological considerations afford to commit the fallacy of identifying the clothes worn with their live wearer....Hence I would maintain that in the hierarchy of the sciences psychology is superior to sociology, for the reason that as the study of the soul it brings us more closely into touch with the nature of reality than does the study of the social body....

...Tylor called our science the science of culture, and it is a good name. But let us not forget that culture stands at once for a body and a life, and that the body is a function of the life, nor the life of the body.

2. *Freud, 1927: 62-63.*

...order and cleanliness are essentially cultural demands, although the necessity of them for survival is not particularly apparent, any more than their suitability as sources of pleasure. At this point we must be struck for the first time with the similarity between the process of cultural development and that of the libidinal development in an individual. Other instincts have to he induced to change the conditions of their gratification, to find it along other paths, a process which is usually identical with what we know so well as sublimation (of the aim of an instinct), but which can sometimes be differentiated from this. Sublimation of instinct is an especially conspicuous feature of cultural evolution; this it is that makes it possible for the higher mental operations, scientific, artistic, ideological activities, to play such an important part in civilized life. If one were to yield to a first impression, one would be tempted to say that sublimation is a fate which has been forced upon instincts by culture alone. But it is better to reflect over this a while longer. Thirdly and lastly, and this seems most important of all, it is impossible to ignore the extent to which civilization is built up on renunciation of instinctual gratifications, the degree to which the existence of civilization presupposes the non-gratification [suppression, repression or something else?] of powerful instinctual urgencies. This "cultural privation" dominates the whole field of social relations between human beings; we know already that it is the cause of the antagonism against which all civilization has to fight.

3. *Redfield, 1928: 292.*

The barrios have, indeed, obviously different cultures, or, what is the same thing, different personalities....

4. *Benedict, 1932: 23, 24.*

Cultural configurations stand to the understanding of group behavior in the relation that personality types stand to the understanding of individual behavior....

...It is recognized that the organization of the total personality is crucial in the understanding or even in the mere description of individual behavior. If this is true in individual psychology where individual differentiation must be limited always by the cultural forms and by the short span of a human lifetime, it is even more imperative in social psychology where the limitations of rime and of conformity are transcended. The degree of integration that may be attained is of course incomparably greater than can ever be found in individual psychology. Cultures from this point of view are individual psychology thrown large upon the screen, given gigantic proportions and a long time span.

This is a reading of cultural from individual psychology, but it is not open to the objections that always have to be pressed against such versions as Frazer's or Lévy-Bruhl's. The difficulty with the reading of husband's prerogatives from jealousy, and secret societies from the exclusiveness of age- and sex-groups, is that it ignores the crucial point, which is not the occurrence of the trait but the social choice that elected its institutionalization in that culture. The formula is always helpless before the opposite situation. In the reading of cultural configurations as I have presented it in this discussion, it is this selective choice of the society which is the crux of the process. It is probable that there is potentially about the same range of individual temperaments and gifts, but from the point of view of the individual on the threshold of that society, each culture has already chosen certain of these traits to make its own and certain to ignore. The central fact is that the history' of each trait is understandable exactly in terms of its having passed through this needle's eye of social acceptance.

5. *Goldenweiser, 1933: 59.*

...If we had the knowledge and patience to analyse a culture retrospectively, every element of it would be found to have had its beginning in the creative act of an individual mind. There is, of course, no other source for culture to come from, for what culture is made of is but the raw stuff of experience, whether material or spiritual, transformed into culture by the creativeness of man. An analysis of culture, if fully carried out, leads back to the individual mind.

The content of any particular mind, on the other hand, comes from culture. No individual can ever originate his culture — it comes to him from without, in the process of education.

In its constituent elements culture is psychological and, in the last analysis, comes from the individual. But as an integral entity culture is cumulative, historical, extra-individual. It comes to the individual as part of his objective experience, just as do his experiences with nature, and, like these, it is absorbed by him, thus becoming part of his psychic content.

6. *Roheim, 1934: 216.*

Thus we are led logically to assume that individual cultures can be derived from typical infantile traumata, and that culture in general (everything which differentiates man from the lower animals) is a consequence of infantile experience.

7. *Roheim, 1934: 169, 171, 235-236.*

I believe that every culture, or at least every primitive culture, can be reduced to a formula like a neurosis or a dream.

If we assume that differences in the treatment of children determine differences in culture, we must also suppose that the origin of culture in general, that is, the emergence of mankind was itself determined by traumata of ontogenesis to be found in the parent-child relation among the anthropoids or pre-human beings from whom we are descended. Analysis teaches us that super-ego and character, the moral attitudes that are independent of reality, of the current situation, result from infantile experience. The possession of these moral attitudes is specifically human; it separates man from his pre-human forbears.

*The prolongation of the period of infancy is the cause of a trauma that is common to all mankind. Differentiation in the erotic play activities in different hordes has modified it and so produced the typical traumata arid the specific cultures of different groups...*Although neurosis is a super-culture, an exaggeration of what is specifically human, analysis adds to the cultural capacity of the patient; for those archaic features of quick discharge which arise as a compensation to the over-culture disappear during its course. Rut in general we have no cause to deny the hostility of analysis to culture. Culture involves neurosis, which we try to cure. Culture involves superego, which we seek to weaken. Culture involves the retention of the infantile situation, from which we endeavour to free our patients.

8. *Sapir (1934) 1949: 591-92.*

What is the genesis of our duality of interest in the facts of behavior? Why is it necessary to discover the contrast, real or fictitious, between culture and personality, or, to speak more accurately, between a segment of behavior seen as cultural pattern and a segment of behavior interpreted as having a person-defining value? Why cannot our interest in behavior maintain the undifferentiated character which it possessed in early childhood? The answer, presumably, is that each type of interest is necessary for the psychic preservation of the individual in an environment which experience makes increasingly complex and unassimilable on its own simple terms. The interests connected by the terms culture and personality are necessary for intelligent and helpful growth because each is based on a distinctive kind of imaginative participation by the observer in the life around him. The observer may dramatize such behavior as he takes note of in terms of a set of values, a conscience which is beyond self and to which he must conform, actually or imaginatively, if he is to preserve his place in the world of authority or impersonal social necessity. Or, on the other hand, he may feel the behavior as self-expressive, as defining the reality of individual consciousness against the mass of environing social determinants. Observations coming within the framework of the former of these two kinds of participation constitute our knowledge of culture. Those which come within the framework of the latter constitute our knowledge of personality. One is as subjective or objective as the other, for both are essentially modes of projection of personal experience into the analysis of social phenomena. Culture may be psychoanalytically reinterpreted as the supposedly impersonal aspect of those values and definitions which come to the child with the irresistible authority of the father, mother, or other individuals of their class. The child does not feel itself to be contributing to culture through his personal interaction but is the passive recipient of values which lies completely beyond his control and which have a necessity and excellence that he dare not question. We may therefore venture to surmise that one's earliest configurations of experience have more of the character of what is later to be rationalized as culture than of what the psychologist is likely to abstract as personality. We have all had the disillusioning experience of revising our father and mother images down from the institutional plane to the purely personal one. The discovery of the world of personality is apparently dependent upon the ability of the individual to become aware of and to attach value to his resistance to authority. It could probably be shown that naturally conservative people find it difficult to take personality valuations seriously, while temperamental radicals tend to be impatient with a purely cultural analysis of human behavior.

9. *Opler, 1935: 145, 152-53.*

Now this cultural factor is the chief concern and object of study of the anthropologist, and he is adverse, naturally, to seeing it disqualified at the outset. He is then further disturbed to see the totality of culture explained as a sublimation, as a channelization of the repressed element of the Oedipus complex into more acceptable avenues. As has been pointed out, in this view totemism is the "first religion" and the ritual extension of the act of parricide; exogamy is also derived from the aftermath of the parricide and is connected with totemism. Art develops as a vehicle of ritualism. The parricide is the "criminal act with which so many things began, social organization, moral restrictions and religion." A. L. Kroeber has pointedly remarked the discouraging implications of such a view for anthropology when he comments, "...the symbols into which the 'libido' converts itself, are phylogenetically transmitted and appear socially.... Now if the psychoanalysts are right, nearly all ethnology and culture history are waste of effort, except insofar as they contribute new raw materials...."

Thus the ego is the expression of the psychological sustenance drawn from the total culture by the individual. There are those whose contacts are rich, varied, and balanced. There are those whose experiences have proved poor, stultifying, and unsatisfying. But whatever we attain, whatever we become, it is only a small part of what the total culture has to offer; above the slight shadow any of us casts, looms the greater image of the world of ideas, attainments, and ideals from which we draw our aspirations. This is the measuring stick by which our individual statures must be evaluated. This is the glass through which our neighbors watch us. This is the judge before whom we must pass before we dare breathe, "Well done," of our works. This is the total culture of the anthropologist and the ego-ideal of Freud.

Now we are prepared to understand what Freud means when he says: "The tension between the demands of conscience and the actual attainments of the ego is experienced as a sense of guilt. Social feelings rest on the foundation of identification with others, on the basis of an ego-ideal in common with them." What we have in common with fellowmen whose judgments mean much to us is culture, a community of understandings, artifacts, concepts, and ethics. The individual ego approaches, resembles, and utilizes this, or failing to do so. it suffers the condemnation of its fellows and withdraws in guilty self-approach.

The difference between the anthropologist and psychoanalyst in respect to the offices of the id, ego, and ego-ideal as thus defined, is hardly more than terminological.

The psychoanalyst says: "Whereas the ego is essentially the representative of the external world, of reality, the super-ego stands in contrast to it as the representative of the internal world, of the id."

The anthropologist would phrase the matter just a little differently. He would say: "That is a statement demonstrating remarkable insight, Dr. Freud. We anthropologists have been much impressed with its truth. We too have noted that culture (ego-ideal) tends to express the deep-seated wishes (id). Man's whole world of supernaturalism, for instance, is largely a response to wish-fulfillment. The much tried individual (ego) is constantly in the position of attempting to accommodate the ideal, fictitious world that culture deems should be, with the realities of living."

10. *Seligman, 1936: 113.*

...A mosaic, as we all know, may be of any degree of elaboration, and this holds equally of the cultures we study. A mosaic may exhibit well-defined patterns, or it may be a mere scatter of different coloured *tesserae;* moreover, the *tesserae* are held together by a matrix, and I believe that in studying so-called patterns of culture attention should equally be paid to an element comparable to the matrix of a mosaic. If I may be allowed to develop my metaphor, this matrix or cementing substance will in the first place consist of some of the deeper or fundamental attitudes of the human psyche, including, perhaps, ethnic elements and possibly fixations resulting from infantile experiences, if these are sufficiently general to affect the majority of children of a social group.

11. *Faris, 1937: 278.*

It is assumed that culture and personality are correlative terms; that to know the culture of a people is to know the types of personalities to be found within it; and that to know the personalities is to understand the culture. These two products of human life are twinborn. Culture is the collective side of personality; personality, the subjective aspect of culture. Society with its usages and personalities with their variations are but two ways of looking at human life.

It is further assumed that these two concepts are not to be thought of as arranged in a causal sequence. Personalities do not cause culture, nor does culture produce personality. Interaction, interstimulation, interlearning are continuous, and personalities are always affecting culture, and culture is always modifying personality. It would appear that society does not mold the individual, tor molding is too passive a term. Individuals do not produce a culture, for collective life has its own laws and its own procedure. Society and the individual, culture and personality: both are useful and necessary abstractions made sometimes at will, forced sometimes upon the student as he tried to understand the phenomena before him.

And yet a sequence is assumed, if not causal, at least temporal. All culture can be assumed to arise out of a former culture or some blend or combination of more than one. Similarly, all personal ties are organized from the contact with other personalities and cultural forms. But in any particular instance, in the consideration of any one individual personality, it is here assumed that a personality arises subsequently to a specific cultural system. The priority of culture seems to be not only a demonstrable fact; it is a heuristic principle of great utility.

12. *Nadel, 1937a: 280-81.*

...The present discussion attempts to demonstrate that we have to reverse the argument; that we must define (at least in the first instance) the observable psychological trends in culture as an expression of dominating "contents," rational interests, and concrete purpose-directed activity....

The "pattern" of a culture thus appears as a co-ordination of social activity of primarily sociological, i.e., rational ("purposive-rational," as Max Weber would say) nature. The rational interdependence of culture facts reveals the agency of certain obtaining social conditions and concrete dominant interests. In certain cases we may be able to trace these determining conditions and interests still further, down to objective "absolute" needs and necessities: to physical facts and psycho-physical or biological factors. In other cases there may be no such solution, and functional interpretation will then be definitely relieved by the descriptive statement of history (in the narrow sense), by the "uniqueness of events" of which we spoke in the beginning, and by the arbitrariness of the "illogical" phenomena of culture (Pareto). It is implied in the nature of this purpose-directed integration of society that it tends to penetrate into every detail of culture: religion, education, recreation, and art will reflect the dominating interests of a culture as much as the institutions which serve these interests more directly. Here, for the complex wheels-within-wheels-mechanism, of culture in which each element is conditioned as well as conditioning, directed as well as directing. Dr. Benedict's formulation of the "consolidations" of culture in "obedience to (dominating) purposes." holds true in a new and, I believe, logically more correct sense. Evidently, this consolidation can only work and become effective through concrete mental processes. Expressed in terms of mental organization, functional integration of culture means logical connection and relation (of which purposive relation is only one category), working with "assumption," "premises," and syllogistic schemata. In its collectivity it coincides with Mr. Bateson's logical *structure* or *eidos* (or rather with one side of this slightly ambiguous concept).

13. *Nadel, 1937b: 421-23, 433.*

As this article is to describe an attempt to include psychology in anthropological field work a few words must be said first in justification of this attempt to examine, over and above the concrete realities of culture, the psychological factors "behind" culture...

The anthropological analysis defines the constitution and structure of a culture (including the institutionalized activities which involve psychological factors); the psychological experiment is to define, independently, the psychological organization of the human substratum of the culture...

We have been able, by means of the experiment, to isolate psychological organization from the body of culture, and we have demonstrated that an essential correspondence obtains between the two systems or phenomena.

14. *Woodard, 1938: 649.*

From the angle of contained imperatives, the culture, like the individual, must have an integration. A rational, and thereby a complete, integration is not possible until much experience has been accumulated. Hence, in both cases, the first integration cannot escape being an incomplete, inconsistent, and emotional one. As an emotional integration, it resists the necessary transitional break-ups incident to achieving; a mature and rational integration, and, as an incomplete and inconsistent pattern, it achieves general workability of a sort by compartmentalization, rationalization, the development of subintegrations, and the achievement of only accommodative mechanisms *between* these, rather than reaching the full adjustment of a single, all inclusive integration. Precisely this same mechanism produces the three subintegrations within the personality (Super-ego, Ego, and Id) and the three divisions of culture (Control, Inductive, and Aesthetic-expressive culture) and the various merely accommodative mechanisms between them. Blocking at the hands of the dominant subintegration; exaggerated pressure from the blocked impulse; defensive overprotection and repression; further exaggeration and consolidation of the repressed elements; still further over-protestation, consolidation, and protective severity: this is the contained process which forges the threefold structure both of personality and of culture. Make it only a little more severe than usual and it is the vicious circle of neuroticism and psychotic dissociation (social disorganization and revolution at the social level) expressed in its broadest terms.

15. *Kardiner, 1939: 84-85.*

Cultures have been described by analogies with the variations found in human character, drawn either from psychopathology, from literary or from mythological sources. Thus cultures have been described as "paranoid," "introverted," or "extroverted"; cultures have been named after literary figures like "Faust," or after Greek deities like "Apollo" or "Dionysus." The effort in all these cases is to convey some general impression of the predominant direction of life goals, of moral values, or of a psychological technique.

Such designations as these cannot claim any great accuracy. No culture is exclusively extroverted or introverted. No culture is predominantly "paranoid." These epithets rely on very vague connotations. The term "paranoid" may refer to megalomania, to persecution, or merely to anxiety, and the reader's selection of one of these depends on his conception of "paranoid." The term "extrovert" likewise can mean any number of things: uninhibited, interested in activity, interested in the outer world; "introverted" may mean inhibited, introspective, interested in fantasy, etc. The designation "Faustian" or "Dionysian" is different in kind from the preceding ones. Here a culture is described in accordance with a characterological type in which the characteristic dominant objectives or values or ideologies are taken as guides to the adaptation of a group.

All these focal ideas are open to the same objection, because they destroy the boundaries between individual and institution. The basic fallacy involved is that, according to any contemporary psychology, variations in human character are created by habitual methods of reacting to external conditions. The character trait may be a reaction formation, a compensation or flight, the nature of which can be decided only from the disciplines or reality situations in the culture. From this point of view, if a group is paranoid, one ought to be able to track down those institutional forces with which all constituents make contact and which terminate in this common trait. However, to regard character as an irreducible racial or cultural idiosyncrasy is at once to use a psychological designation and at the same time to deny the validity of psychological derivation of character.

16. *Mandelbaum, 1941: 238.*

A graduated weighting of patterns, a hierarchy of values, is characteristic of the phenomena we call cultural as well as of the behavior we term personal. The shape of a culture, when we probe into its essential nature, begins to look more and more like the structure of a personality....

17. *Roheim, 1941: 3-4, 23.*

The theory of a collective unconscious would be an assumption we might be compelled to make if we had no other way to explain the phenomenon of human culture. I believe, however, that psychoanalysis has another contribution to offer and that this second suggestion is safer and easier to prove. The second suggestion is that the specific features of mankind were developed in the same way as they are acquired to-day in every human individual as a sublimation or reaction-formation to infantile conflicts. This is what I have called the ontogenetic theory of cultures. I found a society in which the infant was exposed to libidinal trauma on the part of the mother and have shown that this predominantly male society was based on the repression of that trauma. In the same way I have shown that in a matrilineal society the libidinal trauma consisted in the father playing at devouring the child's genital and that this society was based on the fiction that there are no fathers.

If we remember some significant passages in Freud's writings, we notice that Freud also holds this second view of culture. If culture consists in the sum total of efforts which we make to avoid being unhappy, this amounts to an individualistic and therefore, from the psycho-analytic point of view, to the ontogenetic explanation of culture. If culture is based on the renunciation of instinctual gratification, this means that it is based on the super-ego and hence also explained by the fact that we acquire a super-ego.

Of if we take Freud's papers in which he explains not culture as a whole, but certain elements of culture, we find that these interpretations are individualistic and psychological, and not based on a hypothetical phylogenesis. Finally, if we consider especially the interpretations given by Melanie Klein and in general by the English school of psycho-analysts, it is quite evident that all these interpretations of individual evolution also imply an interpretation of human culture as based on the infantile situation. Thus, if Melanie Klein regards symbolism as a necessary consequence of the infant's aggressive trends and the mechanisms mobilized against these trends and also as the basic elements in the subject's relation to the outside world and in sublimation, this implies an explanation of culture in terms of the infantile situation. If demons are explained as projections of the super-ego, if the functions of a medicine man are explained by the assumption that the help of an external object is sought against the introjected object, or if introversion or extraversion in an individual or a group are due to the flight of the internal or external object, these and many others are obviously explanations based on the infantile situation...

1. Culture or sublimations in a group are evolved through the same process as in the individual.
2. Cultural areas are conditioned by the typical infantile situation in each area.
3. Human culture as a whole is the consequence of our prolonged infancy.
4. Typically human forms of adjustment are derived from the infantile situation.
5. Our conquest of nature is due to the synthetic function of the ego.
6. Psycho-analytic interpretations of culture should always be ego plus id interpretations.
7. The interpretation of cultural elements through individual analysis is probably correct, but should be combined with the analysis of anthropological data.

18. *Roheim, 1942: 151.*

Ever since the first attempts were made to apply psychoanalysis to cultural phenomena the structural similarity of culture and neurosis or "psychical system formation" has been tacitly assumed. No psychoanalyst would be likely to contradict Freud's famous threefold comparison of paranoia to philosophy, of compulsion neurosis to religion (ritual) and of hysteria to art. By comparing three of the most important aspects of culture to three types of neurosis Freud has implicitly compared culture itself to neurosis in general. Furthermore, if we consider the whole literature on "applied analysis" we see in every case a cultural element of some kind is explained on basis of the same mechanisms that underlie the various kinds of neurosis.

19. *Kluckhohn and Mowrer, 1944: 7-8.*

The cultural facet of the environment of any society is a signally important determinant both of the content and of the structure of the personalities of members of that society. The culture very largely determines what is learned: available skills, standards of value, and basic orientations to such universal problems as death. Culture likewise structures the conditions under which learning takes place: whether from parents or parent surrogates or from siblings or from those in the learner's own age grade, whether learning is gradually and gently acquired or suddenly demanded, whether renunciations are harshly enforced or reassuringly rewarded. To say that "culture determines" is, of course, a highly abstract way of speaking. In the behavioral world what we actually see is parents and other older and more experienced persons teaching younger and less experienced persons. We assume that biology sets the basic processes which determine how man learns, but culture, as the transmitted experiences of preceding generations (both technological and moral) very largely determines what man learns (as a member of a society rather than as an individual who has his own private experiences). Culture even determines to a considerable extent how the teaching that is essential to this learning shall be carried out.

20. *Beaglehole and Beaglehole, 1946: 15.*

The culture of each individual overlaps to a greater or less degree with the culture of each and every other individual making up the group in question. This overlapping makes up a world of generally understood feelings, thoughts, actions, and values. In other words, it makes up the culture of the people. One of the jobs of the social scientist is to study this culture as thus defined. But in doing so, he must abstract and generalize from the private experience of as many informants as he is able to study. The result can only be an abstraction. It can only be a valid abstraction if a sensitive member of the group feels a fair amount of familiarity as he reads the words which define these abstractions.

Depending both on the skill of the investigators and on the relative amount of integration of the culture (that is, the preponderance of common symbols over private symbols in the culture), the informed reader is likely to say, "Yes, this *is* so," or "Yes, that *may* be so, but it is outside the context of my own experience." Because of our feeling that Kowhai Maori culture today suffers from a lack of integration (a feeling that we will try to document later on in this report), we expect disagreement of the "Yes, but..." type with some of our analyses and statements. Such disagreements would not necessarily imply that our study was subjective and perhaps prejudiced. They would indicate only that in trying to see Kowhai Maori culture as a going concern we have inevitably neglected to explore all the private worlds of all the Maoris living in Kowhai. A moment's reflection will doubtless convince the general reader of the impossibility of ever presenting an absolutely true and absolutely objective account of Kowhai Maori life.

21. *Leighton, 1949: 76.*

There exist psychological uniformities common to all tribes, nations, and "races" of human beings. Each psychological uniformity has a range through which it varies; some variants are characteristic of particular groups of people and as such form a part of their culture.

22. *Merton, 1949: 379*

Despite her consistent concern with "culture," for example, Horney does not explore differences in the impact of this culture upon fanner, worker and businessman, upon lower-, middle-, and upper-class individuals, upon members of various ethnic and racial groups, etc. As a result, the role of "inconsistencies in culture" is not located in its differential impact upon diversely situated groups. Culture becomes a kind of blanket covering all members of the society equally, apart from their idiosyncratic differences in life-history. It is a primary assumption of our typology that these responses occur with different frequency within various sub-groups in our society' precisely because members of these groups or strata are differentially subject to cultural stimulation and social restraints. This sociological orientation will be found in the writings of Dollard and, less systematically, in the work of Fromm, Kardiner, and Lasswell.

Comment

[1]

These excerpts are largely variations upon two themes: the relationship of the abstraction, culture, to concrete individuals and certain similarities between personalities and cultures.

The variations on the first theme consist partly in general discussions of the origins of culture in the individual psyche, partly in attempts to provide a specific theory through psychoanalytic principles.

Marett (1) (cf. also III-f-21) strikes a chord which has been developed by many later writers, perhaps most subtly and effectively by Sapir (cf. also III-f-7). A somewhat crude paraphrase of this position might run as follows: "Let us not be so seduced by captivating abstractions that we lose sight of the experiencing organism in all his complexity and variability. We must not dehumanize the science of man by concentrating exclusively upon 'the outer garb.' What we in fact observe and we ourselves experience is not culture but an intricate flux that is influenced, channeled but never completely contained within cultural forms. Actual living always has an affective tone, and each human being has a uniqueness that is partly the product of his own special biological nature, partly the resultant of his own private life history up to that point. Abstractions may be useful but they must not be confused with 'reality.'" Goldenweiser's (5) main point is an extension of this argument: culture change could not occur were it not for the creative activity of concrete individuals.

It is perfectly true, as Nadel (12) insists, that culture not only "conditions" individuals but is also "conditioned" by them. There is certainly a ceaseless interplay between the tendencies toward standardization that inhere in cultural norms and the tendencies toward variation that inhere in the processes of biological heredity and biological development. However, any argument over "primacy" is as bootless as any other question cast in the chicken or the egg formula. To be sure, there were presumably human or at least humanoid organisms before there was culture. But as far as the phenomena with which anthropologists and psychologists can actually deal, the issue of "primacy" resolves itself into a selection between problems and between equally legitimate frames of reference.

Study of what Nadel calls "the psychological factors behind culture" is clearly essential to a satisfactory theory of the cultural phenomenon. For historical accident, environmental pressures, and seemingly immanent causation, though all important, are not adequate to explain fully the observed facts of cultural differentiation. Unless we are to assume that each distinct culture was divinely revealed to its carriers, we must have recourse to psychology as part of the process.

Thus far only the psychoanalysts have proposed somewhat systematic theories. How helpful the suggestions of Freud, Roheim, and Kardiner are is highly arguable. Freud's "Just So Stories" are contradicted, at least in detail, by much anthropological evidence. It also appears to most anthropologists that he has exaggerated "cultural privation" at the expense of the many ways in which cultures reward and gratify those who participate in them. Insofar as Freud was merely saying that family life and social life in general were possible only at the price of surrendering many "instinctual gratifications" to the control of cultural norms, few anthropologists would gainsay him. Many would likewise agree that culture is to a large degree a "sublimation" — i.e., a redirecting of bodily energies from such immediate satisfactions as sex and aggression (Roheim, 18).

Freud developed a putative explanation of culture in general but hardly of the variations between cultures. Roheim (6, 7, 17), however, has offered such a theory. [2] This briefly is that the distinctiveness of each culture is to be understood in terms of the infantile traumata maximized by the child-training practices of that culture. The institutions of the adult culture are, as it were, reaction-formations against the specific "instinctual deprivations" emphasized in what Herskovits calls the process of "enculturation." Obviously, this cannot serve as an explanation of the *origins* of the special features of each culture. Roheim (cf. also III-a-14) would have to resort to historical accident for that. His theory may be useful in understanding the perpetuation of a set of culture patterns. At any rate, it is a testable hypothesis, and unpublished research by John .M. Whiting and others is directed toward determining what degree of validity this theory possesses.

On the whole, the last few years have seen considerable improvements in communication between psychoanalysts and anthropologists and a re-casting of certain central propositions on both sides in forms more nearly acceptable to each of the two groups. [3] Thus Roheim in his last book says:

...the theory of cultural conditioning cannot account for certain parallelisms in widely divergent cultures...the psychic unity of mankind is more than a working hypothesis...cross-cultural parallels, although *they may have an additional context-determined meaning,* have an underlying meaning that is independent of the social system or culture or basic institutions and is based on the nature of the primary process. There is such a thing as a potentially universal symbolism. The latent content is universal, but the symbol itself may become verbalized by a certain individual or many individuals in many parts of the world and then accepted by others on basis of the universal latent content...those who condition are subject to the same biological laws as are the others whom they are conditioning. (1950, 5, 435, 488, 489; italics Roheim's).

In the Roheim Festschrift Hartmann, Kris, and Loewenstein observe:

The comparative study of culture includes the question as to variant and invariant traits of "human nature..." The "biological" is neither limited to the innate nor identical with invariant traits in man. There is obviously a vast area in which the same statements are part of both biological and sociological sets of assumptions...The biological approach thus indicates a framework within which the fact that man is the social animal becomes meaningful. Once this has become clarified it becomes evident that the study of human behavior can, and in many cases must, be viewed from both sides: we can characterize the relationship between mother and child as a biological relationship or we can characterize it as a social one: the fact that both concatenations are overlapping constitutes the human...Both psychoanalysts and anthropologists are interested in the same processes, but they are partly using data of different kinds... (1951, 6, 10).

Everyone will agree that human biology and those aspects of human psychology which arise from biological potentialities set limiting frames for cultures (Leighton, 21; Seligman, 10). How the selections that are possible within these frames are arrived at by different peoples each in a somewhat distinctive way — this is one of the largest questions in culture theory and one which has hardly gone beyond the phase of speculation and reasoning by analogy and the illustrative example. It does seem certain that simplistic "functional" explanations will help us only a little.

Neither a society nor an individual will survive unless behavior makes a certain minimum of sense in terms of environment demands. But how is one to account thus for the enormously diverse conceptions of time found in the cultures of the world? The ancient Egyptians were pioneers in astronomical and calendrical investigations. This makes good "functional" sense, for Egyptian agriculture was tied to the periodicities in the inundations of the Nile. Why, however, is the dominant theme in Egyptian thought, as we have recently been assured by Frankfort, [4] the conviction that the universe is static and that only the changeless is ultimately significant? Did the Judaic conception of sin originate in the Near East because this had unusual survival or adjustive value under the circumstances of life in this area?

It seems more likely that conceptions of time and of the good life were largely determined by the accidents of history operating through psychological mechanisms as yet unknown but including the genius and temperament of individuals who happened to be born at a crucial period arid born to key positions in the social structure. Societies make what, for want of a more accurate word, we may call "choices." Such decisions are of special importance when a new culture is being created or when an old one has become relatively loose and malleable under extreme stress. But with societies as with individuals any crucial "choice" is to greater or lesser degree a determiner of later ones. Once a group starts down one road, the paths that would have opened up on another route that was "objectively" available will not be traversed; even if they should be, the territory will be reacted to, not freshly, but in a fashion colored and shaped by the experience upon the first road. The principle of "limitation of possibilities" is operative.

The functionalist assumption that culture is solely the result of response to physiological drives and needs as modified by acquired drives reduces culture change to the tautology of "culture begets or determines culture." Undoubtedly the systemic quality of each culture does tend to give cultures the property or at least appearance of immanence or orthogenesis. Some culture change may well be predetermined once the culture has assumed its fundamental organization. Much more, however, culture change seems to be due to the ceaseless feedback between factors of idiosyncratic and universal human motivation, on the one hand, and factors of universal and special situation, on the other. Unfortunately, we lack conceptual instruments for dealing with such systems of organized complexity. [5]

Nevertheless we can consistently and explicitly recognize the interdependence of cultural and psychological phenomena. While anthropologists will always resist the tendency of some psychologists to reduce culture to psychology (as in the Katz and Schanck definition, D-IV-2), they increasingly acknowledge that psychologists and anthropologists inevitably start from the same data. More strictly, they start from data of the same order, namely human behavior. They may start from the same particular data, but often do not, because their interests and problems usually differ. More concretely: a psychologist seldom starts with a custom considered as such, anthropologists hardly from acts of learning or remembering as such. To the psychologist a fresco of Giotto is primarily a datum on a certain creative personality. To the anthropologist the fresco is a datum on art style of a certain period in Italy and on culture content (costume, house types, other artifacts, etc.). In Sapir's (8) words, a segment of behavior may be seen either as cultural pattern or as having a person-defining value.

Moreover — and this brings us to the second major theme of this group of extracts — culture and personality are not only abstractions from data of the same order; they have intrinsic similarities. Certain definitions of culture state that it is a "mental" phenomenon, and many definitions of personality start from the same premise. Both personalities and cultures appear to acquire their distinctiveness at least as much from organization as from content (Woodward, 14). More and more personality psychologists and anthropologists have had recourse to such ideas as "themes," and "configurations," "orientations," and "implicit logics" in constructing their conceptual models. As Mandelbaum (16) says: "The shape of a culture, when we probe into its essential nature, begins to look more and more like the structure of a personality."

Benedict's famous parallels were of a slightly different order — between personality *types* and cultural *types*. Yet she seemed to many of her readers to be saying: culture is personality writ large; personality is culture writ small. The equation of culture with the personality of a society (Redfield, 3) or of personality as the subjective side of culture (Faris, 11) represents an unfortunate over-simplification. The former analogy leads to the brink of the "group-mind" fallacy. The latter is false because culture is far from being the only constituent of personality; a unique biological heredity and idiosyncratic life history also enter in.

The parallels nevertheless remain arresting. Of cultures as well as of personalities one can properly say: "This culture is in some respects like all other cultures, in other respects like some other cultures only, in a few respects completely individual." A personality can participate much more nearly in the whole of a culture than in the whole of a society. The fact that students of personality and students of culture have more in common than either have with students of societies as such is attested by some interesting contrasts in disciplinary affiliations.

Superficially, sociologists and cultural anthropologists appear to be studying much the same things. Yet the record shows more instances of cooperation and intellectual sympathy between sociologists and social psychologists than between anthropologists and sociologists. Anthropologists have more often been affiliated with students of personality (clinical psychologists, psychiatrists, psychoanalysts) and have had deeper influence upon the thinking of these groups. Probably the fundamental difference is that social psychologists and contemporary American sociologists are more obsessed with the quantitative and more ready to pull their data out of context, while the other two groups insist upon the relevance of form, of features of order and arrangement which are not (at least as yet) measurable. It will, however, be germane to our analysis of the relationships between culture and psychology to examine a little further the factors that have brought students of personality and students of culture together.

Just as the anthropologist attempts to get a picture of the whole of a culture, so the clinical type of psychologist tries to envisage the whole of a personality. In both cases this entails, for the rime being at least, some deficiency in workmanship as well as loss of rigor. The anthropologist cannot have enough specialized knowledge to describe music, basketry, and kinship with equal expertness. Nor can the psychologist be equally well trained in mental and projective tests, depth interviewing, and techniques of the personal document. Nevertheless holistic, controlled impressionism has certain merits, at any rate for heuristic purposes in this particular stage of the development of the human sciences.

One may take as an extreme case the relationship between psychoanalysis and anthropology. For all of the extravagant dogmatism and *mystique* of much psychoanalytic writing, the anthropologist sensed that here at least he was getting what he had long been demanding from academic psychology: a theory of raw human nature. The basic assumptions of the theory might turn out to be false in general or in derail. The anthropologist was positive that the theory was culture-bound to an important degree, though the evidence of the past twenty years indicates that many anthropologists exaggerated the extent of the distortion they thought produced by bourgeois Viennese culture and by late nineteenth-century science. At all events, psychoanalysis provided anthropology with a general theory of psychological process that was susceptible of cross-cultural testing by empirical means and with clues that might be investigated as to the psychological causes of cultural phenomena.

Moreover, there were experiential factors that drew the psychoanalysts and the anthropologists together. Psychiatrists of all persuasions were showing that there was meaning in the most apparently chaotic and non-adaptive acts of the mentally ill. This struck an answering chord with the anthropologist, for he was engaged in demonstrating the fact that the seemingly bizarre patterns of non-Western cultures performed the same basic functions as did our familiar customs. The same amnesty that the psychoanalyst grants to incestuous dreams the anthropologist had learned to accede to strange cultures. That is, both insisted that the queerest behavior had significance in the economy of the individual or of the society. There was no implication of moral approval, necessarily, on the part of either psychiatrist or anthropologist. Both merely agreed that behavior could not be legislated out of existence unless psychologically satisfying and socially acceptable substitutes were discovered. The essential scientific task was that of gaining maximal understanding of underlying determinants.

Finally, the dominant experience of cultural anthropologists had been as "unscientific" — in the narrow sense of that term — as that of the psychoanalysts. Most cultural anthropologists are as innocent of statistics as the psychoanalysts; both groups operate with procedures that are essentially "clinical." Ordinarily the anthropologist working under field conditions has as little chance to do controlled experiments as has the psychoanalyst who sees his patient for an hour a day in the consulting room. The skilled of both professions do make predictions of a crude order and test them by subsequent observation. But these observations do not lend themselves to presentation in neat graphs and "t" distributions. Indeed both groups would maintain, without disparaging the indispensable importance of statistics for other purposes, that some of their main problems involve matters of form, position, and arrangement more than of the incidence and clusterings of random variations. Such problems may find an eventual solution in terms of matrix algebra or some other form of topological mathematics but, in the nature of the case, not in an applied mathematics based on probability theory. Probably in all culture, as well as in that aspect known as linguistics, the crucial issue is not that of size or frequency but of what point in what pattern. One may compare the principle of the circle which does not depend upon measurement as such but upon a fixed patterning, even though measurements are necessary to draw any particular circle to specification.

And so the anthropologist, however skeptical he may be of certain psychoanalytic dogmas, tends to feel in some measure at home m psychoanalytic psychology. He recognizes certain similarities which confront him in describing and interpreting a culture with those met by a psychoanalyst in diagnosing a personality; the relationships between forms and meanings, between content and organization, between stability and change.

Culture is not merely a "tissue of externalities" (Marett, 1). It is "built into" the personality and as such is part, though only part, of the personality'. From many different private versions of a given aspect of a culture as manifested by so many different unique personalities, the anthropologist constructs the ideal type of that aspect which he, perfectly legitimately, incorporates in his conceptual model of the total culture. This is the "supposedly impersonal aspects of values and definitions" which worries Sapir (8). But almost all anthropologists today are fully aware that as culture influences the concrete act of the individual actor it is not "impersonal" at all. Concretely, culture is internalized. This is the basis of those resemblances between culture and super-ego [6] to which Opler (9) and others have drawn attention. To a considerable degree (though not completely) anthropological culture, psychoanalytic super-ego, and indeed the conscience collective of Durkheim are all constructs from the same data and have many overlapping theoretical implications.

There is no genuine problem as to the "inwardness" or "outwardness" of culture. It is "outward" and "impersonal" as an abstraction, a logical construct; it is very much "inward" and affective as internalized in a particular individual. One must merely take care not to confuse these two frames of reference. It is highly convenient to construct an abstract conceptual model of a culture. But this does not mean that culture is a force like Newtonian gravity "acting at a distance." Culture is a precipitate of history but, as internalized in concrete organisms, very much active in the present. One might almost say that a culture is to a society as the memory is to a person. The past is present through memory and through the structuring of the present which previous events have produced.

Culture is manifested in and through personalities. Personality shapes and changes culture but is in turn shaped by culture. Culture exists to the extent to which the "private worlds" of which Sapir (8) and the Beagleholes (20) write overlap. In a complex stratified and segmented society like our own these "private worlds" overlap for the majority of the total population only upon the broadest of issues. Generalized American culture, as Merton (22) says, has a "differential impact upon diversely situated groups."

The exploration of the mutual interrelations between culture and psychology must continue. However, we may conclude with Stern (1949, 34:) that:

There has been considerable unrewarding controversy...around the contrast of culture as a thing in itself, and culture as an activity of persons participating in it. Actually both approaches are valid, and are required to supplement each other for a rounded understanding of cultural behavior.

Both culture and personality are inferential constructs that start (but select) from behavior or products of behavior. Symbolization (in a very broad sense) seems to be central to both models, and such symbolization is carried on at various levels of awareness and with varying degrees of compulsiveness. In the past culture has tended to emphasize explicitness of both design and content, personality theory implicitness and "internality." Now culture theory seems to be working "downward" toward the implicit and "internal," personality theory "upward" to explicit forms. Hence the two bodies of theory converge more and more but will not, we think, fuse completely.

[1] This comment must be linked to that in the comment on III-f, subsection entitled, "Culture and Individuals."
[2] Cf. also Seligman (10).
[3] Cf. Kluckhohn and Morgan, 1951.
[4] Frankfort, 1948.
[5] Cf. Weaver, 1948.
[6] A case can also be made for comparing culture at least as closely to another concept of Freud's, that of the ego ideal. However, this would involve us in through the structuring of the present which previous events have produced a highly technical consideration of psychoanalytic terminology.

Group E: Culture and Language

1. *Boas, 1911: 67-68.*

It would seem that the obstacles to generalized thought inherent in the form of a language are of minor importance only, and that presumably the language alone would not prevent a people from advancing to more generalized forms of thinking if the general state of their culture should require expression of such thought; that under these conditions the language would be molded rather by the cultural state. It does not seem likely, therefore, that there is any direct relation between the culture of a tribe and the language they speak, except in so far as the form of the language will be molded by the state of culture, but not in so far as a certain state of culture is conditioned by morphological traits of the language....

Of greater positive importance is the question of the relation of the unconscious character of linguistic phenomena to the more conscious ethnological phenomena. It seems to my mind that this contrast is only apparent, and that the very fact of the unconsciousness of linguistic processes helps us to gain a clearer understanding of the ethnological phenomena, a point the importance of which cannot be underrated. It has been mentioned before that in all languages certain classifications of concepts occur. To mention only a few: we find objects classified according to sex, or as animate and inanimate, or according to form. We find actions determined according to time and place, etc. The behavior of primitive man makes it perfectly clear that all these concepts, although they are in constant use, have never risen into consciousness, and that consequently their origin must be sought, not in rational, but in entirely unconscious, we may perhaps say instinctive, processes of the mind. They must be due to a grouping of sense-impressions and of concepts which is not in any sense of the term voluntary, but which develops from quite different psychological causes. It would seem that the essential difference between linguistic phenomena and other ethnological phenomena is, that the linguistic classifications never rise into consciousness, while in other ethnological phenomena, although the same unconscious origin prevails, these often rise into consciousness, and thus give rise to secondary reasoning and to re-interpretations. It would, for instance, seem very plausible that the fundamental religious notions — like the idea of the voluntary power of inanimate objects, or of the anthropomorphic character of animals, or of the existence of powers that are superior to the mental and physical powers of man — are in their origin just as little conscious as are the fundamental ideas of language. While, however, the use of language is so automatic that the opportunity never arises for the fundamental notions to emerge into consciousness, this happens very frequently in all phenomena relating to religion. It would seem that there is no tribe in the world in which the religious activities have not come to be a subject of thought. While the religious activities may have been performed before the reason for performing them had become a subject of thought, they attained at an early time such importance that man asked himself the reason why he performed these actions. With this moment speculation in regard to religious activities arose, and the whole series of secondary explanations which form so vast a field of ethnological phenomena came into existence.

2. Sapir, 1912: 239-41 (1949: 100-02)

...Perhaps the whole problem of the relation between culture and environment generally, on the one hand, and language, on the other, may be furthered somewhat by a consideration simply of the rate of change or development of both. Linguistic features are necessarily less capable of rising into the consciousness of the speakers than traits of culture. Without here attempting to go into an analysis of this psychological difference between the two sets of phenomena, it would seem to follow that changes in culture are the result, to at least a considerable extent, of conscious processes or of processes more easily made conscious, whereas those of language are to be explained, if explained at all, as due to the more minute action of psychological factors beyond the control of will or reflection. If this be true, and there seems every reason to believe that it is, we must conclude that cultural change and linguistic change do not move along parallel lines and hence do not tend to stand in a close causal relation. This point of view makes it quite legitimate to grant, if necessary, the existence at some primitive stage in the past of a more definite association between environment and linguistic form than can now be posited anywhere, for the different character and rate of change in linguistic and cultural phenomena, conditioned by the very nature or those phenomena, would m the long run very materially disturb and ultimately entirely eliminate such an association....

To some extent culture and language may then be conceived of as in a constant state of interaction and definite association for a considerable lapse of time. This state of correlation, however, cannot continue indefinitely. With gradual change of group psychology, and physical environment more or less profound changes must be effected in the form and content of both language and culture. Language and culture, however, are obviously not the direct expressions of racial psychology and physical environment, but depend for their existence and continuance primarily on the forces of tradition. Hence, despite necessary modifications in either with lapse of time, a conservative tendency will always make itself felt as a check to those tendencies that make for change. And here we come to the crux of the matter. Cultural elements, as more definitely serving the immediate needs of society and entering more clearly into consciousness, will not only change more rapidly than those of language, but the form itself of culture, giving each element its relative significance, will be continually shaping itself anew. Linguistic elements, on the other hand, while they may and do readily change in themselves, do not so easily lend themselves to regroupings, owing to the subconscious character of grammatical classification. A grammatical system as such tends to persist indefinitely. In other words, the conservative tendency makes itself felt more profoundly in the formal groundwork of language than in that of culture. One necessary consequence of this is that the forms of language will in course of time cease to symbolize those of culture, and this is our main thesis. Another consequence is that the forms of language may be thought to more accurately reflect those of a remotely past statue of culture than the present ones of culture itself. It is not claimed that a stage is ever reached at which language and culture stand in no sort of relation to each other, but simply that the relative rates of change of the two differ so materially as to make it practically impossible to detect the relationship.

3. *Sapir, 1924b: 152-53 (1949, 155-56)*

...If the Eskimo and the Hottentot have no adequate notion of what we mean by causation, does it follow that their languages are incapable of expressing the causative relation? Certainly not. In English, in German, and in Greek we have certain formal linguistic devices for passing from the primary act or state to its causative correspondent, e.g., English *to fall, to fell,* "to cause to fall"; wide, *to widen;* German *hangen*, "to hang, be suspended"; *hängen*, "to hang, cause to be suspended"; Greek *pherō*, "to carry'"; *phoreō*, "to cause to carry'." Now this ability' to feel and express the causative relation is by no manner of means dependent on an ability to conceive of causality as much. The latter ability is conscious and intellectual in character; it is laborious, like most conscious processes, and it is late in developing. The former ability is unconscious and nonintellectual in character, ercerciscs itself with great rapidity and with the utmost ease, and develops early in the life of the race and of the individual. We have therefore no theoretical difficulty in finding that conceptions and relations which primitive folk are quite unable to master on the conscious plane are being unconsciously expressed in their languages — and, frequently, with the utmost nicety. As a matter of fact, the causative relation, which is expressed only fragmentarily in our modern European languages, is in many primitive languages rendered with an absolutely philosophic relentlessness. In Nootka, an Indian language of Vancouver Island, there is no verb or verb form which has not its precise causative counterpart.

Needless to say, I have chosen the concept of causality solely for the sake of illustration, not because I attach an especial linguistic importance to it. Every language, we may conclude, possesses a complete and psychologically satisfying formal orientation, but this orientation is only felt in the unconscious of its speakers — is not actually, that is, consciously, known by them.

Our current psychology does not seem altogether adequate to explain the formation and transmission of such submerged formal systems as are disclosed to us in the languages of the world....

4. *Trubetzkoy (1929), 1949: xxv.*

. . une étude attentive des langues orientée vers la logique interne de leur évolution nous apprend qu'une telle logique existe et qu'on peut établir route une série de lois purement linguistiques indépendantes des facteurs extralinguistiques, tels que la "civilisation," etc. Mais ces lois ne nous diront rien du tout, ni sur le "progres" ni sur la "regression."...Les divers aspects de la civilisation et de la vie des peuples évoluent aussi suivant leur logique interne, et leurs propres lois n'ont, elles aussi, rien de commun avec le "progrès"...Dans l'histoire littéraire, les formalistes se sont enfin mis à étudier les lois immanentes, et cela nous permet d'entrevoir le sens et la logique interne de l'évolution littéraire. Toutes les sciences traitant de l'évolution sont tellcment négligées du point de vue méthodologique que maintenant le "problème du jour" consiste à rectifier la méthode de chacune d'elles séparément. Le temps de la synthèse n'est pas encore venu. Néanmoins on ne peut douter qu'il existe un certain parallélisme dans l'évolution des différents aspects de la civilisation; donc il doit exister certaines lois qui déterminent ce parallélisme.... Une discipline spéciale devra surgir qui aura uniquement en vue l'étude synthétique du parallélisme dans l'évolution des divers aspects de la vie sociale. Tout cela peut aussi s'appliquer aux problèmes de la langue.... Ainsi, au bout du compte, on a le droit de se demander, non seulement pourquoi une langue donnée, avant choisie une certaine voie, a évolué de telle manière et non d'une autre, mais aussi pourquoi une langue donnée, appartenant à un peuple donné, a choisi precisément cette voie l'évolution et non une autre: par example le tchèque: la conservation de la quantité vocalique, et le polonais: la conservation de la mouillure des consonnes....

5. *Sapir, 1929: 211-14 (1949: 164-66).*

...Of all forms of culture, it seems that language is that one which develops its fundamental patterns with relatively the n.ost complete detachment from other types of cultural patterning. Linguistics may thus hope to become something of a guide to the understanding of the "psychological geography" of culture in the large. In ordinary life the basic symbolisms of behavior are densely overlaid by cross-functional patterns of a bewildering variety. It is because every isolated act in human behavior is the meeting point of many distinct configurations that it is so difficult for most of us to arrive at the notion of contextual and non-contextual form in behavior. Linguistics would seem to have a very peculiar value for configurative studies because the patterning of language is to a very appreciable extent self-contained and not significantly at the mercy of intercrossing patterns of a nonlinguistic type....

...The regularity and typicality of linguistic processes leads to a quasi-romantic feeling of contrast with the apparently free and undetermined behavior of human beings studied from the standpoint of culture. But the regularity of sound change is only superficially analogous to a biological automatism. It is precisely because language is as strictly socialized a type of human behavior as anything else in culture and yet betrays in its outlines and tendencies such regularities as only the natural scientist is in the habit of formulating, that linguistics is of strategic importance for the methodology of social science. Behind the apparent lawlessness of social phenomena there is a regularity of configuration and tendency which is just as real as the regularity of physical processes in a mechanical world, though it is a regularity of infinitely less apparent rigidity and of another mode of apprehension on our part. Language is primarily a cultural or social product and must be understood as such. Its regularity and formal development rest on considerations of a biological and psychological nature, to be sure. But this regularity and our underlying unconsciousness of its typical forms do not make of linguistics a mere adjunct to either biology or psychology. Better than any other social science, linguistics shows by its data and methods, necessarily more easily defined than the data and methods of any other type of discipline dealing with socialized behavior, the possibility of a truly scientific study of society' which does not ape the methods nor attempt to adopt unrevised the concepts of the natural sciences....

6. *Bloomfield, 1945: 625.*

Every language serves as the bearer of a culture. If you speak a language you take part, in some degree, in the way of living represented by that language. Each system of culture has its own way of looking at things and people and of dealing with them. To the extent that you have learned to speak and understand a foreign tongue, to that extent you have learned to respond with a different selection and emphasis to the world around you, and for your relations with people you have gained a new system of sensibilities, considerations, conventions, and restraints. All this has come to you in part unnoticed and in part through incidents which you remember, some of them painful and some pleasurable. If the culture is remote from your own, many of its habits differ very widely from those of your community. No exception is to be iiir.de here for the peoples whom we are inclined to describe as savage or primitive; for science and mechanical invention, in which we excel them, represent only one phase of culture, and the sensitivity of these peoples, though different, is no less than our own.

7. *Voegelin and Harris, 1945: 456-457.*

Language is part of culture. Everyone acknowledges this theoretically and then tends to treat the two separately in actual work because the techniques of gathering data and making analyses are not the same for both. The result of this practical divorce of linguistic work from cultural investigation often means that the final linguistic statements and the final cultural statements are incomplete; or statements covering the ethno-linguistic situation as a whole are neglected.

8. *Voegelin and Harris, 1947: 588, 590-92, 593.*

The data of linguistics and of cultural anthropology are largely the same.

Human behavior, as well as (or rather, which includes) behavior between humans, is never purely verbal; nor, in the general case, is it non-verbal. Linguistics characteristically study only that part of a situation which we here call verbal. Cultural anthropologists often segregate the non-verbal from the verbal, relegating the latter to special chapters or volumes (such as folklore), as contrasted with chapters devoted to various aspects of material culture, such as house types; one might infer from some ethnographies that houses are built in sullen silence....

The techniques of linguistics and of cultural anthropology are in general different.

Linguistic techniques enable a worker to state the parts of the whole (for any one language), and to find the distribution of the parts within the whole. This provides criteria of relevance: it is possible to distinguish sharply between what is and what is not linguistic. Such criteria are lacking in ethnographies where culture traits are none too clearly distinguished from culture complexes and where a given segment of behavior may be regarded by one worker as an expression of culture, by another as an expression of personality; another segment of behavior, thought to be entirely physiological (as morning sickness in pregnancy), may later be shown to be stimulated by cultural expectation. Accordingly, neither the historian treating of past cultures, nor the anthropologist dealing with present cultures is ever half as comfortable as is the linguist in excluding any datum as irrelevant...

Cultural anthropology is dependent upon comparative considerations for finding its elements; linguistics is not. Linguistic analysis provides an exhaustive list of its elements (thus, there are between a dozen and a score or two of phonemes for any given language); cultural analysis does not.

9. *Greenberg, 1948: 140-46.*

The special position of linguistics arises from its two-fold nature: as a part of the sciences of culture by virtue of its inclusion in the mass of socially transmitted tradition of human groups, and as a part of the nascent subject of semiotics, the science of sign behavior in general. That language should be included in both of these more general sciences is no more contradictory than, for example, the double status of physical anthropology with its simultaneous affiliation with a physiologically oriented zoology and with anthropology, the general study of man approached both physically and culturally. Since linguistics faces in these two directions, it should be aware of the implications for itself both of the semiotician's discussions of language and of the general science of culture. Linguists have, on the whole, been more aware of their affiliations with cultural anthropology than with semiotics, a state of affairs which is understandable in view of the recency of the semiotician's interest in the general features of language....

...Careful compilation of a lexicon is...a field in which the linguist and ethnologist can fruitfully collaborate. To the ethnologist, the semantics of the language of the people in whom he is interested is a subject of considerable interest since it presents him with a practically exhaustive classification of the objects in the cultural universe of the speakers. For certain morphemes whose *designata* are not sensually perceivable events in the space-time of the investigator the linguistic approach is crucial. That this has been realized in general by ethnologists is evidenced by the liberal use of native terms which characterize magical and other ideological components of culture, a practice which has resulted in the borrowing via the ethnographic literature of such words as *mana* and *taboo* into the European languages.

The lexicon of a language holds as it were a mirror to the rest of culture, and the accuracy of this mirror image sets a series of problems in principle capable of empirical solution. In certain instances, notably that of kinship terminology, this problem is a familiar one, and has occasioned a number of specific investigations. On the whole, however, the ethnographic problems presented by this aspect of language remain for the future....

The unit of the descriptive linguist is a speech community, taken more or less widely, as indicated by such rough terms as language, dialect, or sub-dialect. The definition of this community is often undertaken in the introductory portion of a linguistic description where the people are named, and population figures and geographical distributions are given. In his choice of a unit of description the linguist resembles the cultural anthropologist who describes cultural norms valid for a circumscribed group of people, a tribe, community, or nation. Such a treatment disregards — and justifiably so for the purpose in hand — relations in two directions, one towards the individual, and the other in the direction of the exact determination of the membership in this community and the relationship of its membership to others whose speech show some degree of similarity to its own. This superorganic approach to linguistics I call cultural, as opposed to individual and social. Thus far...our discussion has been of cultural linguistics in the syntactic, semantic, and pragmatic phases....

Social linguistics, often called ethnolinguistics, involves in its synchronic aspect, a whole series of significant problems regarding correlations between population groupings as determined by linguistic criteria and those based on biologic, economic, political, geographical, and other non-linguistic factors....

Social diachronic studies or historical ethnolinguistics is the phase of the inter-relationships of ethnology and linguistics of which there has probably been the greatest awareness. The correlations between linguistic groupings of people and those derived on other bases, notably physical and cultural, is a standard problem in historic research. Examples of historical ethnolinguistic approaches are the tracing of former population distributions through linguistic groupings, the estimate of chronologic remoteness or recency of the cultural identity of groups on the basis of degree of linguistic divergence, the reconstruction of a partial cultural inventory of a proto-speech community on the basis of a reconstructed vocabulary, acculturational studies of the influence of one culture on another by the study of loan-words, and diffusionist studies of single elements of culture in which points of primary or secondary diffusion can be traced by a consideration of the form of the words which often point unequivocally to a particular language as the source.

It is perhaps worthwhile to note the extent to which our analysis of language is also applicable to culture traits in general. Obviously the distinction between synchronic and diachronic is relevant and it is possible to study cultures either descriptively or historically. The distinction between the cultural, the social, and the individual approaches is also valid. If we adopt Linton's convenient concept of status, then the behavior patterns themselves are the results of cultural analysis, while the manner of selection of individuals for given statuses, whether achieved or ascribed, together with factors of sex, age, geographical locations, etc., are social as here defined. The study of personality variations in the carrying out of the patterns is part of the individual approach.

10. *Hoijer, 1948: 335.*

Culture, to employ Tylor's well-known definition, is "that complex whole which includes knowledge, beliefs, art, morals, law, custom, and any other capabilities and habits acquired by man as a member of society." It is clear that language is a pan of culture: it is one of the many "capabilities acquired by man as a member ot society."

Despite this obvious inclusion of language in the total fabric of culture, we often find the two contrasted in such a way as to imply that there is little in common between them. Thus, anthropologists frequently make the point that peoples sharing substantially the same culture speak languages belonging to disparate stocks, and, contrariwise, that peoples whose languages are related may have very different cultures. In the American Southwest, for example, the cultures of the several Pueblo groups, from Hopi in the west to Taos in the east, are remarkably alike. Puebloan languages, however, belong to four distinct stocks: Shoshonean, Zunian, Keresan, and Tanoan. The reverse situation — peoples speaking related languages but belonging to different culture areas — is illustrated by the Athapaskan-speaking groups in North America. Here we find languages clearly and unmistakably related, spoken by peoples of the Mackenzie area, the California area, and the area of the Southwest, three very different cultural regions.

The fact that linguistic and culture areas do not often coincide in no way denies the proposition that language is part and parcel of the cultural tradition. Culture areas result from the fact that some traits of culture are easily borrowed by one group from neighboring groups. In essence, then, the similarities in culture which mark societies in the same culture area result from contact and borrowing, and are limited to those features of culture which are easily transmitted from one group to another.

Language areas, on the other hand, are regions occupied by peoples speaking cognate languages. The similarities in language between such peoples are due, not to contact and borrowing, but to a common linguistic tradition. Traits of language are not readily borrowed and we should not expect to find linguistic traits among those cultural features shared by peoples in the same culture area.

If whole cultures could be grouped genetically as we now group languages into stocks and families, the culture areas so formed would be essentially coincident with language areas. This is difficult to do, since much of culture does not lend itself to the precise comparison necessary to the establishment of genetic relations.

11. *Voegelin, 1949: 36, 45.*

A *culture whole* is to ethnology what a single natural language is to linguistics. In the earlier ethnological and sociological theory a *culture whole* was merely a point of departure. [1] Nowadays a given *culture whole* is held as a constant against which a particular analysis or theory is tested; in a somewhat parallel way, *the linguistic structure* of a given natural language may be said to be what emerges after certain operations are followed.

Some writers jump from this parallel way of delimiting a single cultural community or a single speech community to either or both of the following conclusions: (1) that language is a part of culture, which is debatable; (2) that the techniques for analysis of language and culture are the same or closely similar — this is surely an error. [2] It is obvious that one does not find culture in a limbo, since all human communities consist of human animals which talk; but culture can be, and as a matter of fact, is characteristically studied in considerable isolation; so also in even greater isolation, the human animal is studied in physical anthropology, and not *what* the human animal talks about, but rather the *structure* of his talk is studied in linguistics. *What* he talks about is called (by philosophers and semanticists) *meaning;* but for most anthropologists *what* he talks about is *culture...*

If language were merely a part of culture, primates should be able to learn parts of human language as they actually do learn parts of human culture when prodded by primatologists. No sub-human animal ever learns any part of human languages — not even parrots. The fact that *Polly wants a cracker* is not taken by the parrot as part of a language is shown by the refusal of the bird to use part of the utterance as a frame (*Polly wants a...*) with substitutions in the frame. (For the three dots, a speaker of a language would be able to say *cracker* or *nut* or *banana* or anything else wanted.) As George Herzog has phrased this, imitative utterances of subhuman animals are limited to one morpheme; to the parrot, then, *Polly wants a cracker* is an unchangeable unit. From this point of view, we can generalize: an inescapable feature of all natural human languages is that they are capable of multi-morpheme utterances.

12. *Silva-Fuenzalida, 1949: 446.*

...When we hear the statement that "language is a part of culture," it is in fact meant that utterances are correctly understood only if they are symbols of cultural phenomena. This implies that since experience is communicated by means of language, a person speaking any language participates to some degree in the ways of lire represented by that language. These verbal symbols are not loosely joined, but co-ordinated by means of a system that expresses their mutual relations. Language is thus the regular organization of series of symbols, whose meanings have to be learned as any other phenomenon. The implication of this is that as each culture has its own way of looking at things and at people and its own way of dealing with them, the enculturation of an individual to a foreign body of customs will only be possible as he learns to speak and understand the foreign language and to respond with new selection and emphasis to the world around him — a selection and emphasis presented to him by this new culture.

13. *Hockert, 1950: 113.*

Two recent remarks concerning the relation of language to culture call forth this brief protest. C. F. Voegelin (1949) labels "debatable" the usually accepted contention that language is part of culture. Silva-Fuenzalida (1949) does not debate the claim, but certainly misunderstands it; he says language is part of culture because "utterances are correctly understood only if they are symbols of cultural phenomena."

Voegelin's claim is flatly false; Fuenzalida's misunderstanding is unhappily confusing. We may state succinctly what it means to say that language is part of culture, and prove in a few words why it is true...That our speech habits are thus acquired has been proved time and again: bring an X-baby into a Y-speaking environment and there raise him, and he will grow up speaking Y, not X. Therefore language is part of culture.

Since linguistics is the study of language and cultural anthropology the study of (human) culture, it follows that linguistics is a branch of cultural anthropology. It also follows that every linguist is an anthropologist. But it does not follow, by any means, that every linguist *knows* that he is an anthropologist, or that a linguist necessarily knows something about phases of culture other than language, or, for that matter, that every cultural anthropologist knows that language is culture and that linguistics is a branch of his own field, even if one to which he chooses to pay no particular attention. The historical fact is that there have been two distinct traditions, with differing terminologies, different great names and landmarks, differing levels of achievement, differing chief problems and direction of interest. Only two men (to exclude those now living) have so far achieved reputations in both fields, and of those two, Boas as anthropologist far outshadows Boas as linguist, Sapir as linguist probably somewhat outshadows Sapir as culturalist.

It is probably because of the separateness of the two traditions that we have the unfortunate habit of speaking of "language *and* culture." We ought to speak of "language *in* culture" or of "language and *the rest* of culture." From the fact that language is part of culture does not follow that we have, as yet, anything very significant to say about "language in culture" or the interrelationships between "language and the rest of culture."

14. *Buswell, 1950: 285.*

Surely it is not amiss to consider *a* language, as related to the body of science called linguistics, in the same sense as *a* culture, as related to ethnology. This Voegelin does, with the perfectly logical result that he can now speak analytically of language *and* culture *in terms of this abstract comparison*. That the relationship of language to culture is debatable, is then the only reasonable way to state it, but only in the sense that "the *structure* of [man's] talk is studied in linguistics." And "... for most anthropologists *what* he talks about is culture." (Voegelin, ms. in press, Proceedings, XXIX International Congress of Americanists).

15. *Voegelin, 1950, 432.*

Speaking only in terms of scientific usage, can it be agreed that linguistics and culture and physical anthropology are coordinate? The content descriptions of general courses in anthropology departments often specify these three main divisions of anthropology just as the content description of a general biology course might specify botany and zoology and bacteriology as the three main divisions of biology. Because bacteria are classified as plants, and other microorganisms as animals, while viruses remain unclassified in this respect, perhaps a biologist would not object to saying that bacteriology adjoins zoology as well as botany, thus paralleling the position of culture: adjacent to linguistics on the one hand, and to physical anthropology on the other — assuming, of course, that phenotypic as well as genotypic traits are included in physical anthropology. Whatever the majority opinion may be on the relationship of language to culture, linguistic analysis characteristically proceeds without reference to the culture of speakers — even when data on the culture of speakers are available. If most anthropologists really do think that linguistics is part of culture, then it is a very dispensable part; it does not keep the majority from classifying the archaeological remains of particular preliterate peoples as the culture of the people in question — despite the fact that their culture must, by definition, be presented without any linguistic data at all.

It is relatively easy to abstract linguistics from culture and to define linguistics without reference to culture, as I have done; it is much more difficult to abstract culture and define culture or covert culture without reference to language.

16. *Olmsted, 1950: 7-8.*

There is a good deal in [the 1949] article of Voegelin's that ought to evoke comment. First, the fact that great apes can learn to drive a car but not to speak is significant, but it in no way proves that language is not a part of culture. If this be the test of whether something is a part of culture, then surely Tylor's or Herskovits' definitions of culture (to name only a couple of widely accepted ones) will straightway be shot to pieces as we amass a colossal list of things that apes cannot be taught to master.

That linguistic and ethnological techniques are not strictly comparable is one claim; that culture traits and phonemes are not comparable is another. Probably few students would disagree with the later claim. For the phoneme is not a piece of raw data as are most generally recognized culture traits; a phoneme is something inferred from raw data, a construct shown to have crucial linguistic value within the structure of the language under study. The linguist, in determining the phonemes of a language, applies certain standard techniques that enable him to discover and describe the linguistically important sound-units. He then may go on to compare one structure with another, always being sure that he knows the relation of any of the phonemic units to the whole. The culture trait (or anything like it) does not as yet have the same status in ethnology. What is of crucial importance in one culture may be ancillary in another. It is this lack of a handy label indicating the structural value of data that lies at the roots of the deficiencies of such a comparative project as the Cross-cultural Survey. As Voegelin (1949) points out, the status of phonemes is something inherent in the linguistic structure being studied, and, theoretically, a linguist who knew the techniques, even if he had never studied another language, could study any language and come up with the phonemes in a way that would satisfy any other competent linguist. However, the anthropologist, lacking any such standard procedure for determining the relative ethnological value of each "culture trait," must needs call on his knowledge of other cultures in order to investigate, in a specific culture, what has been found to be crucial in other cultures. In this sense the ethnologist is dependent on comparative techniques for the examination of any given culture, while the linguist is not.
17. *Taylor, 1950: 559-60.*

In all fairness to C. F. Voegelin, it may be questioned whether the phrase "language and culture" is any more vicious than, for example, "culture and society." Certainly, non-human societies without culture exist; whereas language and culture (or the rest of culture) are not found apart. But within the human species, society, language, and culture are concomitant; and it is hard to see how one is any less acquired or learned than the other.

Nevertheless, there is an important difference between language and the other universal aspects of culture: the latter lean heavily on precept — that is to say, on language — for their practice and transmission, whereas the rudiments of the former can be passed on only by example and imitation. Not until the child has gained some control of speech, by a process comparable to that by which a kitten learns to kill mice, can its enculturation progress far in other directions — this time by the instrumentality of language itself, and hence by a process unknown on the sub-human level.

Language has often been called the vehicle of culture; and there would seem to be no particular vice in distinguishing a conveyance from that which it conveys, even when in practice the two may be inseparable.

Comment

It is remarkable how fitfully anthropologists and linguists have discussed the relation of culture and language.

We have found no passages explicitly dealing with the subject in Jespersen's, Sapir's, or Bloomfield's books called *Language.*

In 1911 Boas (1) pointed out that linguistic phenomena are unconscious and automatic, but cultural phenomena more conscious. This distinction has become widely accepted. Boas went on, however, to suggest that cultural phenomena, such as fundamental religious notions (animism, supernaturalism, etc.) may in their origin have been equally unconscious, but have secondarily became a subject of thought and been rationalized into consciousness, whereas the use of language remained automatic. This second suggestion seems to have been developed little further, either by Boas or others. [3]

Sapir (2) in 1912 made much the same point as Boas: culture changes result from processes easily made conscious, linguistic changes are due to minute factors beyond the control of will or reflection. Sapir in his turn adds a second suggestion — which also appears not to have been developed — that with time the interaction of culture and language became lessened because their rates of change were different. Cultural elements serve immediate needs, and cultural forms reshape themselves, but linguistic elements do not easily regroup because their classification is subconscious.

A dozen years later, Sapir (3) returned to the issue with the point that consistent grammatical expression of causality may occur in languages whose associated cultures possess no adequate explicit notions of causality. Languages often contain "submerged formal systems" whose psychology is unclear and not closely related to conscious thought. This issue was subsequently revived in an opposite sense by Whorf and by Lee in their met-alinguistic papers.

Trubetzkoy (4) in 1929 touched on the theme of the relation — "purely linguistic laws independent of extra-linguistic factors such as civilization." But he also submitted the claim that linguistics ought ultimately be able to give the reasons why particular languages followed one line of development and not others.

Sapir (5) returned to the subject in 1929. Language patterns develop in relative self-containment and detachment from "other types of cultural patterning." Linguistics thus has a peculiar value for configurative studies, including Gestalt psychology. It shows the possibilities open to the social sciences when they do not ape the methods or adopt the unrevised methods of natural science.

It is evident that up to this point there was fundamental consensus that language showed in a somewhat accentuated degree certain features, such as consistency and unconsciousness of patterning, which occurred also in lesser measure in non-linguistic culture.

Then there appears to have been a lull until 1945, when two papers, by Bloomfield (6) and by Voegelin and Harris (7) reopened the subject: "Every language serves as the bearer of a culture" and "Language is part of culture." These were followed by interrelated statements (8-16) by Voegelin and Harris, Greenberg, Hoijer, Voegelin (11, 15), Silva-Fuenzalida, Hockett, Buswell, Olmsted, and Taylor. Voegelin partly reversed his former position with Harris, at least to the extent of speaking of language as not "merely a part of culture" (11) and suggesting that they are "coordinate" (15); and was bluntly contradicted by Hockett (13). As of early 1951, the discussion is still in progress, and promises to be fruitful of increased sharpening of concepts. Greenberg's appraisal is particularly broad: he specifically considers semiotic aspects, and he recognizes cultural or superorganic, social, and individual approaches or emphases as valid in linguistics as well as in cultural anthropology. His mention of language and "the rest of culture" is typical of the position, with various shadings, of most of the participants in the discussion. It is evident that culture has been used in two senses, each usually implicit in its context and validated there: culture including language, and culture excluding language. It is also clear that language is the most easily separable part or aspect of total culture, that its processes are the most distinctive, and that the methods of linguistics are also the most distinctive as well as the best defined in the social sciences. What the "cultural" equivalent of phonemes, or the linguistic equivalent of "cultural traits," may be has not yet become apparent: it may be unanswerable until the question is reformulated. Similar obscurities remain unresolved as to the conceptual relation or non-relation of cultural and organic concepts (culture trait, culture whole, species, genus, or family, ecological assemblage or faunistic area). Underlying the problem, and in a sense constituting it, is the fact, as Voegelin (15) says, that it is obviously easier to abstract linguistics from the remainder of culture and define it separately than the reverse.

Group F: Relation of Culture to Society, Individuals, Environment, and Artifacts

1. *Wissler, 1916: 200-01.*

...when we are dealing with phenomena that belong to original nature, we are quite right in using psychological and biological methods; but the moment we step over into cultural phenomena we must recognize its [sic] historical nature.... We often read that if cultural phenomena can be reduced to terms of association of ideas, motor elements, etc., there remains but to apply psychological principles to it [sic] to reveal its causes. This is a vain hope. All the knowledge of the mechanism of association in the world will not tell us why any particular association is made by a particular individual, will not explain the invention of the bow, the origin of exogamy, or of any other trait of culture except in terms that are equally applicable to all.

2. *Marett, 1920: 11-13* (cf. d-1).

It is quite legitimate to regard culture, or social tradition, in an abstract way as a tissue of externalities, as a robe of many colors woven on the loom of time.... Moreover, for certain purposes, which in their entirety may be called sociological, it is actually convenient thus to concentrate on the outer garb. In this case, indeed, the garb may well at first sight seem to count for everything, for certainly a man naked of all culture would be no better than a forked radish...Human history [nevertheless] is no Madame Tussaud's show of decorated dummies. It is instinct with purposive movement through and through...

According to the needs of the work lying nearest to our hand, let us play the sociologist or the psychologist, without prejudice as regards ultimate explanations. On one point only I would insist, namely that the living must be studied in its own right and not by means of methods borrowed from the study of the lifeless. If a purely sociological treatment contemplates man as if there were no life in him, there will likewise be no life in it. The nemesis of a deterministic attitude towards history is a deadly dullness.

3. *Ogburn, 1922: 48.*

Kroeber has recently made an attempt to show that the subject matter of sociology is culture, apparently relatively free from any consideration of the organic factor. His attempt is quite bold considering the agreement existing as to the nature of society and the acceptance of society as the subject matter of sociology, and is also significant because of his logical and consistent analysis which sets forth the importance of culture as a subject of science. Briefly, his thesis flows from his classification of sciences according to planes, the inorganic, the vital organic, the mental organic, and the superorganic.

4. *Case, 1924a: 106.*

Environment and race...may be regarded as in a sense original, with culture emerging from [their] interaction.... The factor thus derived from the two preceding becomes itself an active member of a triumvirate of forces, whose interaction constitutes the process known as...social evolution or "civilization."

5. *Kroeber, 1928: 331 (1931: 476).*

The kite, the manner of manipulating the marbles, the cut of a garment, the tipping of the hat, remain as cultural facts after every physiological and psychological consideration of the individuals involved has been exhausted.

6. *Sapir, 1931: 658 (1949: 365).*

The word custom is used to apply to the totality of behavior patterns which are carried by tradition and lodged in the group, as contrasted with the more random personal activities of the individual.... Custom is a variable common sense concept which has served as the matrix for the development of the more refined and technical anthropological concept of culture. It is not as purely denotative and objective a term as culture and has a slightly more affective quality indicated by the fact that one uses it more easily to refer to geographically remote, to primitive or to bygone societies than to one's own.

7. *Sapir (1932), 1919: 515-516.*

The so-called culture of a group of human beings, as it is ordinarily treated by the cultural anthropologist, is essentially a systematic list of all the socially inherited patterns of behavior which may be illustrated in the actual behavior of all or most of the individuals of the group. The true locus, however, of these processes which, when abstracted into a totality, constitute culture is not in a theoretical community of human beings known as society for the term "society" is itself a cultural construct which is employed by individuals who stand in significant relations to each other in order to help them in the interpretation of certain aspects of their behavior. The true locus of culture is in the interactions of specific individuals and, on the subjective side, in the world of meanings which each one of these individuals may unconsciously abstract for himself from his participation in these interactions. Every individual is, then, in a very real sense, a representative of at least one subculture which may be abstracted from the generalized culture of the group of which he is a member. Frequently, if not typically, he is a representative of more than one subculture, and the degree to which the socialized behavior of an' given individual can be identified with or abstracted from the typical or generalized culture of a single group varies enormously from person to person.

It is impossible to think of any cultural pattern or set of cultural patterns which can, in the literal sense of the word, be referred to society as such. There are no facts of political organization or family life or religious belief or magical procedure or technology or aesthetic endeavor which are coterminous with society or with any mechanically or sociologically defined segment of society....

...The concept of culture, as it is handled by the cultural anthropologist, is necessarily something of a statistical fiction and it is easy to see that the social psychologist and the psychiatrist must eventually induce him to carefully reconsider his terms. It is not the concept of culture which is subtly misleading but the metaphysical locus to which culture is generally assigned.

7a. *Winston, 1933: 5-7.*

Societal life is both social and cultural in nature. The social and the cultural are intimately related; nevertheless they are not the same. Inasmuch as it is necessary for the purposes of this book to grasp the significance of both approaches, separately and together, the distinction between the two may be analyzed briefly.

Artificial attempts to distinguish between fields on the basis of word-splitting are not unknown phenomena in the realm of the sciences, physical or social. It is not the intention to add one more literary discussion to the fairly large accumulation along this line. It is, however, necessary for the purposes of the adequate presentation of the cultural approach to differentiate, in so far as differentiation is possible or necessary between the social and the cultural. Instances common to everyday life afford materials for exemplification. The social interaction which takes place between two individuals comes under the category of the social, in so far as it pertains to their reactions to one another as individuals. But where their behavior is affected by the patterned ways of behavior existent in the society of which they are a part, their own *social* behavior is influenced by a *cultural* factor. The introduction, the tipping of the hat and other formalized rules of politeness, the methods of courtship and the channeled ways of behavior toward each other of man and wife, are all examples of patterned ways of behaving. The interaction is social but it is affected by the cultural; it may largely coincide or, as in the case of antisocial behavior, it may veer away from the patterned ways of behavior laid down by a given society.

Turning to group behavior, we may take the play groups of children. Children play the world over. The chemical, the physical, the biological, the individual, and the social components in play may be separately studied. But when the play life follows a definite pattern, it has become culturally conditioned. The play of children with other children, a psychosocial phenomenon, is affected by the culturally imposed types of play, whether it be in New Guinea or in New Mexico.

The interactions of individuals with others, of individuals with groups, or of group upon group are exemplifications of social interaction. But interaction in society takes place within a cultural framework. This cultural framework influences human behavior and at the same time is to be distinguished sharply from it, in order to analyze completely and more objectively the functions and structure of society...

...Even in the social field there is still prevalent the error of considering behavior as altogether a matter of social relationships. There is a cultural milieu within which social relationships always take place. This cultural milieu, while it has been built up as a result of societal life, has become, *from the standpoint of the present*, the framework within which present social relationships occur and are influenced. The relationships between husband and wife, between employer and employee, among members of a club or members of a church, are social or psychosocial. These relationships are affected by the particular patterns of behavior developed in a given society. The relationships not only involve social interaction; they also involve patterned ways of behaving. Thus it is that, with the same biological processes, the same chemical processes, the apparently same inherited psychological traits, the apparently same type of interaction, i.e., that of a man and a woman, the courtship and marriage systems, differ in all parts of the world, and in differing affect differently the behavior of men and women in, say, the United States, Siam, Sweden, and Spain. There are no laws in the physical sciences, there are no explanations in the social sciences on the purely social level to explain the differing habits of peoples, so far as these habits are wide-spread and not individual peculiarities. Failure to recognize these facts leads to an inadequate explanation of human behavior.

8. *Goldenweiser, 1933: 63.*

...Man, being part of culture, is also part of society, the carrier of culture.

9. *Forde, 1934: 466.*

The differences in character and content between particular cultures have, as has been said, often been ascribed to one or more of a number of general factors, and especially to differences of race and physical environment, or to differences in the alleged state of social or even psychological evolution. No one of these general factors can alone explain anything, nor can their significance be analyzed in isolation; for they do not operate singly or in a vacuum. They fail both singly and collectively because they ignore the fact that the culture of every single human community has had a specific history.

10. *Ford, 1937: 226.*

Culture is concerned primarily with the way people act. The actions, then, of manufacture, use, and nature of material objects constitute the data of material culture. In their relation to culture, artifacts and materials are to be classed in the same category as the substances, such as minerals, flora, and fauna, which compose the environment in which people live. Artifacts themselves are not cultural data, although, to be sure, they are often the concrete manifestations of human actions and cultural processes. The cultural actions of a people cannot even be inferred from them without extreme caution, for a number of reasons. Chief among these are the following: (1) instead of being a product of the culture the artifact may have been imported; (2) the process of manufacture is frequently not implicit in the artifact itself; and (3) the use or function of the artifact is not deducible from the object alone.

11. *Murdock, 1937: xi.*

Patterned or cultural behavior does not, however, exhaust the data available to the student of society. Realizing that culture is merely an abstraction from observed likenesses in the behavior of individuals organized in groups, the authors of several of the articles, especially those dealing with aspects of modern society, find themselves interested in the culture-bearing groups, sub-groups, and individuals themselves. To them sociology is not merely the science of culture; it is also the science of society. While it is perfectly legitimate conceptually to exclude all data save cultural patterns, and while this particular procedure has proved extremely fruitful in the hands of anthropologists and others, this does not appear to exhaust all possibilities of social science. In this respect our authors find themselves in disagreement with certain American sociologists who, discouraged by the apparently chaotic situation within their own discipline, have turned in desperation to cultural anthropology and have imported into sociology a whole series of anthropological concepts: diffusion, invention, culture area, etc. Applying these to phenomena in our own culture, they believe they have achieved an objectivity which their colleagues have missed. The followers of Sumner and Keller, who have been "cultural sociologists" for a much longer rime — who have, indeed, always been such — do not, however, see any impelling reason why the sociologist should thus arbitrarily limit his field.

12. *Parsons, 1937: 762-63.*

On an analytical basis it is possible to see emerging out of the study as a whole a division into three great classes of theoretical systems. They may be spoken of as the systems of nature, action and culture...The culture systems are distinguished from both the others in that they are *both* non-spatial and atemporal. They consist, as Professor Whitehead says, of *eternal* objects, in the strict sense of the term eternal, of objects not of indefinite duration but to which the category of time is not applicable. They are not involved in "process."

13. *Plant, 1937: 13, fn. 4.*

The terms environment, milieu, and cultural pattern are used interchangeably in this volume.

14. *Bierstedt, 1938: 211.*

The social group is the culture, artifacts and traits are its attributes.

[This bases on the passage from Wallis cited as III-*a*-5. Bierstedt asks: What is this "more than the sum" of Wallis? And answers: This "more," the functioning dynamic unit, is the people who possess a certain complex of traits.... The nucleus around which these traits are grouped is the people who have them. Then follows the statement above.]

15. *Kardiner, 1939: 7.*

When we have collected, described, and catalogued all its institutions, we have the description of a culture. At this point we find Linton's differentiation between a society and a culture very useful: a society is a permanent collection of human beings; the institutions by which they live together are their culture.

16. *Rouse, 1939: 16, 18, 19.*

...culture cannot be inherent in the artifacts. It must be something in the relationship between the artifacts and the aborigines who made and used them. It is a pattern of significance which the artifacts have, not the artifacts themselves.

Culture, then, is merely a single one of a group of factors which influence the artisan's procedure in making an artifact.... Culture may be the most important of the interplaying factors. Nevertheless, it would not seem justifiable to consider the artifacts themselves to be equivalent to culture.

The types and modes, then, express the cultural significance possessed by the Fort Liberté artifacts. In effect, they separate the cultural factors which produced the artifacts from the non-cultural factors which are inherent in the artifacts.

17. *Radcliffe-Brown, 1940: 2.*

Let us consider what are the concrete, observable facts with which the social anthropologist is concerned. If we set out to study, for example, the aboriginal inhabitants of a part of Australia, we find a certain number of individual human beings in a certain natural environment. We can observe the acts of behaviour of these Individuals, including, of course, their acts of speech, and the material products of past actions. We do not observe a "culture," since that word denotes, not any concrete reality, but an abstraction, and as it is commonly used a vague abstraction. But direct observation does reveal to us that these human beings are connected by a complex network of social relations. I used the term "social structure" to denote this network of actually existing relations. It is this that I regard it as my business to study if I am working, not as an ethnologist or psychologist, but as a social anthropologist. I do not mean that the study of social structure is the whole of social anthropology, but I do regard it as being in a very important sense the most fundamental part of the science.

18. *Kluckhohn and Kelly, 1945b: 29.*

...human action is framed by four universal dimensions: (1) physical heredity as manifested in the human organism, (2) the external non-human environment, (3) the social environment, (4) a precipitate from past events which has partially taken its character at any given moment as a consequence of the first three dimensions as they existed when those events occurred, partially as a consequence of the selective force of an historical pre-cipitate (culture) that already existed when a given past event occurred.

19. *Kluckhohn and Kelly, 1945b: 35.*

...to have the maximum usefulness, the term [culture] should be applicable to social units both larger and smaller than those to which the term "society" is normally applied. Thus, we need to speak of "Mohammedan culture" in spite of the fact that various peoples which share this to greater or lesser extent interact with each other much less intensively than they do with other societies which do not possess Mohammedan culture. Also, it is useful to speak of the culture of cliques and of relatively impermanent social units such as, for example, members of summer camps. Often it may be desirable to refer to these "cultures" by qualified terms such as "subcultures" or "cultural variants." Nevertheless, such abstractions are inescapably "culture" in the generic sense.

19a. *Kluckhohn, 1945a: 631-633.*

The third abstraction (social) arises out of the fact that human beings must adjust to other human beings as well as to impersonal forces and objects. To some extent these adjustments are implemented and limited only by the presence or absence of other human beings in specified numbers, at particular points, and of specified age, sex, size, and intelligence, relative to the actors whose action is being "explained." Insofar as the human environment of action does not go beyond such inevitables of the interaction of human beings with each other, it may be called "the social environment." It is imperative, however, to isolate a fourth dimension (the cultural) before we can adequately deal with the total environment of human action. This fourth abstraction arises from the observed fact that any given human interaction can take place in a variety of ways so far as the limitations and facilitations of the biological and impersonal environmental conditions are concerned. Some human interactions, indeed, do seem to be subject only to the constraints supplied by the field of biological and physical forces. Such interactions may be designated as "social" without further qualification. However, careful observations or the words and deeds of human beings make it certain that many of their acts are not a consequence simply of physical and biological potentialities and limitations. If the latter were the case, the possible variations within a defined field of biological and physical forces would be random. The variations within different human groups which have some historical continuity tend beyond all possible doubt to cluster around certain norms. These norms are demonstrably different as between groups which have different historical continuities. These observed stylizations of action which are characteristic of human groups are the basis for isolating the fourth, or cultural, dimension to action.

The concrete social (*i.e.,* interactive) behavior observed among human beings must in most cases be assumed to be the combined product of biological and cultural "forces." Often, then, the "social" and the "cultural" are inextricably intermingled in observable acts. However, some social acts are not culturally patterned. This is one reason for including a distinct "social" dimension. Another arises out of one certainly valid aspect of Durkheim's position. If we postulate that all ongoing human behavior must be in some sense adaptive and/or adjustive, we must posit social collectivities as the referents of some behavior systems, for these cannot be "explained" as meeting needs (biological or "psychological") of isolated human organisms. In other words, "society," like "culture," is an "emergent" with properties not altogether derivable from a summation of even the fullest kind of knowledge of the parts. Indeed — to go back to the framework of "determination" — it seems likely that culture itself may be altered by social as well as by biological and natural environmental forces. A plurality of individuals (of such and such numbers, etc.) continuously interacting together, produces something new which is a resultant not merely of previously existing cultural patterns and a given impersonal environmental situation but also of the sheer fact of social interaction. Suppose that two random samples, of, say, 5000 and 500 persons from a society possessing a relatively homogeneous culture are set down on islands of identical ecological environment (but of areas varying proportionally with the sizes of the two groups). After a few generations (or a shorter interval) one could anticipate that two quite distinct cultures would have evolved - partly as a result of "historical accidents" but also as accommodations to the contrasting number of actual and potential face-to-face relationships. Patterns for human adjustment which were suitable to a society of 500 would not work equally well in the society of 5000 and vice versa. Thus we must regard the environment of interaction (abstracted from the cultural patterning which prevails in it) as one of the determiners of alterations in the system of designs for living (culture).

20. *Fortes, 1949a: 57-58.*

The qualitative aspect of social facts is what is commonly called culture. The concept "structure" is, I think, most appropriately applied to those features of social events and organizations which are actually or ideally susceptible of quantitative description and analysis. The constant elements most usually recognized in any social event by ethnographers are its cultural components; its structural aspect, being variable, is often overlooked. It should be emphasized that I am not suggesting a division of the facts of social life into two classes; I am referring to the data of observation. "Culture" and "structure" denote complementary ways of analysing the same facts. In the present stage of social anthropology all analysis of structure is necessarily hybrid, involving descriptions of culture as well as presentation of structure...

21. *Murdock, 1949b: 82-83.*

Since it is mainly through face-to-face relations that a person's behavior is influenced by his fellows — motivated, cued, rewarded, and punished — the community is the primary seat of social control. Here it is that deviation is penalized and conformity rewarded. It is noteworthy that ostracism from the community is widely regarded as the direst of punishments and that its threat serves as the ultimate inducement to cultural conformity. Through the operation of social sanctions, ideas and behavior tend to become relatively stereotyped within a community, and a local culture develops. Indeed the community seems to be the most typical social group to support a total culture. This, incidentally, provides the theoretical justification for "community studies," a field in which anthropologists, sociologists, and social psychologists alike have shown a marked interest in recent decades.

Under conditions of relative isolation, each community has a culture of its own. The degree to which this is shared by neighboring local groups depends largely upon the means and extent of inter-communication. Ease of communication and geographical mobility may produce considerable cultural similarity over wide areas, as, for example, in the United States today, and may even generate important social cleavages which cut across local groupings, as in the case of social classes. For most of the peoples of the earth, however, the community has been both the primary unit of social participation and the distinctive culture-bearing group.

22. *Radcliffe-Brown, 1949: 321, 322.*

Malinowski produced a variant, in which culture is substituted for society, and seven "basic biological needs" are substituted for the desires, interests and motives of the earlier writers....

[The] theory of society in terms of structures and process, interconnected by function, has nothing in common with the theory of culture as derived from individual biological needs.

23. *Nadel, 1951: 29, 79-80.*

Is there any behavior of man which is not "in society?" The (somewhat conventional) phraseology we used before, when we spoke of "man in the group," seems to suggest that there is such behaviour. But since man does not exist without the group (omitting Robinson Crusoes, "wolf-children," and other dubious anomalies), this addition would seem to be either misleading or redundant. It is, however, not quite that. The qualification has meaning in that it distinguishes between forms of acting and behaving which are part of the existence of the group and those which, though occurring in the group, are not of it. The distinction is essentially one between recurrent and unique behaviour. The forms of behaviour, then, with which we are primarily concerned are recurrent, regular, coherent, and predictable. The subject matter of our enquiry is *standardized behaviour patterns;* their integrated totality is *culture.*

In this sense, then, social facts are two-dimensional. Like any two-dimensional entity, they can be projected on to one or the other co-ordinate, and so viewed under one or the other aspect. If we wish to find names also for the dimensions themselves, they seem suggested by the familiar words *Society* and *Culture.* Society, as I see it, means the totality of social facts projected on to the dimension of relationships and groupings; culture, the same totality in the dimension of action. This is not merely playing with words. In recent anthropological literature, in fact, the terms "society" and "culture" are accepted as referring to somewhat different things, or, more precisely, to different ways of looking at the same thing. And indeed, the very existence of these two words would seem to support our two-dimensional schema: categorizing thought, as expressed in language, has been led towards the same twoness-in-oneness. "

The consistent distinction between these two concepts entails considerable linguistic difficulties. Mostly, when we speak of "culture" and "society" we mean a totality of facts viewed in both dimensions; the adjective "social" especially, for example, in the familiar phrase "social facts," or in the less familiar one, "things social" (which is my translation of Durkheim's *choses sociales*), has always this double connotation. Nor do we possess a convenient term summarizing this twofold reality as such save the clumsy word socio-cultural. I can, therefore, only hope that the sense in which the terms social and cultural, society and culture, will subsequently be used will become clear from their context.

Now, anthropologists sometimes assign to the two "dimensions" a different degree of concreteness and reality. Radcliffe-Brown, for example, regards only social relations as real and concrete, and culture as a mere abstraction; while Malinowski's whole work seems to imply that culture is the only reality and the only realm of concrete facts. Understood in so absolute a sense, both views are misconceptions. Social relations and the groupings into which they merge are as much of an abstraction as is culture. Both, too, are abstractions evolved from the same observational data — individuals in co-activity; but they are not, I think, abstractions of the same level.

Comment

Superficially this seems like a residual group, but it centers on the relation of culture to society and extends from that on the one hand to relation to the individuals who compose society and on the other to the environment that surrounds it.

Culture and Society. The statements on the culture-society relation begin in 1932 with a passage from a famous article by Sapir (7). The definitions in Part Two that most consistently deal with this relation of society and culture constitute our group C-1, which see culture as the way of life, or sum of the ways of doing.

by a society or group. [1] These way-of-life definitions begin only three years before the statements we have grouped into Section f. In the same year of 1929 Bernhard Stem published his important article explicitly distinguishing society from culture and pointing out conceptual deficiencies due to the ambiguity of using "social" to cover phenomena of both society and culture. It is evident that for a decade or more previously there had been half-conscious uneasinesses and stirrings against the conceptual haziness and undifferentiation of social and cultural phenomena; [2] but the explicit partition appears not to have come until 1929. Once it had been effected, it was natural that it should soon be reflected in discursive statements as well as in formal definitions.

Sapir, however, differed from the others here considered in that while he began with an interest in culture (including language) as such, and came to add a powerful interest in individual personality, [3] he was never interested in society, just as he remained cold to non-holistic or non-personality psychology. In our citation (7), he disposes of society as a cultural construct employed by individuals in significant relations to each other in order to help them in the interpretation of certain aspects of their behavior. The true locus of culture he places in the interactions of individuals, and subjectively in the meanings which individuals may abstract from their participation in the interactions. This leaves to the individual the primacy as regards significance; to culture, something; to society, almost nothing. Sapir goes on to say that it is impossible to think or any cultural pattern which can literally be referred to society as such. These drastic statements have had surprisingly little notice taken of them by social scientists.

Winston (7a) was exceptionally clear at an early period in distinguishing between the social and the cultural but seems to have had little influence on later writers, though he was a direct influence on Kluckhohn and Kelly (19) and Kluckhohn (19a).

Goldenweiser (8) a year later than Sapir speaks of society as the carrier of culture. Murdock (11), 1937, calls culture patterned behavior and has some anthropologists confining themselves to it, legitimately enough, in distinction from society. He approves less of those sociologists who "in desperation" have applied culture and other anthropological concepts to our own society. The Sumner-Keller school, however, he maintains have always been "cultural sociologists" — which last, at least, seems indubitable to the present authors.

Bierstedt (14), 1938, a year later misfired completely in saying that the social group is the culture, artifacts and traits its attributes. This comes down to saying that what has the culture therefore is the culture. The route by which Bierstedt arrives at this position is equally hazy. Starting from Wallis's remark about culture (already cited in a-5) that culture is more than the sum of its parts, Bierstedt confuses this "sum" with "the functioning dynamic unit" through which culture comes to be, and decides this is society. This is equivalent to saying that the locus of a thing is the thing itself! Beyond which is the question already raised by Sapir in (7) whether the locus of culture really is in society as such or in individuals. It is hard to understand these strange lungings of Bierstedt except as motivated by an anxiety at the spread of the concept of culture.

Bierstedt bases on Wallis (j-5), 1930, as a springboard to leap to his startling conclusion that the social group is the culture. One could of course also go on to regard the society as being individuals, the social organization and social relations constituting merely their attributes; then, to assert that individual organisms are organized groups of cells with biochemical interactions, with psychosomatic behavior as attributes thereof; and so on. This sort of reduction is evidently self-defeating.

Another year later we find Kardiner (15) implicitly equating culture with institutions, which might pass as an off-hand, by-the-way definition; but then going on to imply that it was Linton who discovered the distinction between culture and society! It was perhaps from Linton that Kardiner learned of the distinction.

Still another year, 1940, brings us to Radcliffe-Brown (17) and one of his several attempts not indeed to deny culture but to belittle it, to make it unimportant as compared with social structure. As against observable human beings and their observable behavior, including speech and artifacts as products of past behavior, he says that culture is not observable "since that word [culture] denotes, not any concrete reality, but an abstraction" — and "as commonly used a vague abstraction." But "direct observation does reveal" that "human beings are connected by a complex network of social relations" which may be called "social structure." The study of this social structure is "the most fundamental part" of the science of social anthropology. This conclusion seems indeed to follow from Radcliffe-Brown's premises that (1) culture is only a vague abstraction and that (2) social anthropology is the scientific part of anthropology, ethnology consisting merely of antiquarian non-structured facts or of speculative sequences of such facts. The partiality of the second of these premises is sufficiently evident to require no refutation at this date. The first premise does need correction, because while it is true that culture must be regarded as an abstraction in that its recognition involves more than sense impressions, [4] the same is of course true of social relations or structure. A kinship relation or an incest barrier is no more "observable" than a myth or a property' valuation: social structure is inferred or abstracted from behavior no more and no less than are customs. Radcliffe-Brown slides over this identical conceptual status, partly by first labeling culture as vague, and partly by then immediately saying that the complex network of social relations is "revealed" by "direct observation"; whereas of course it is revealed by direct observation plus inquiry and inference that generalize and abstract, exactly as customs and beliefs are revealed. Certainly no complex network of structure, social or otherwise, is ascertainable by direct sensory observation. Radcliffe-Brown has cajoled himself into the belief that his social structure rests on a legitimate foundation of observable reality that the vague and spuriously abstract thing called culture lacks. Viewed historically even in 1940, and of course more so today, Radcliffe-Brown is conducting a rearguard action against the advance of the concept of culture.

Radcliffe-Brown's 1949 statement (22) is essentially contrastive of his own position with Malinowski's. It is true that the two have little in common but use of function: Malinowski does deal with culture and his explanatory biological or psychosomatic needs reside in individual men, not in society. Radcliffe-Brown deals with society in terms of its structure, process, and function.

Fortes (20), 1949, makes a curious distinction between culture and structure. Culture is the qualitative aspect of "social facts"; structure, those analyzed quantitatively (!). Most often recognized are the constant elements that constitute culture; the structural aspect is "variable and often overlooked." Culture and structure are not classes of social facts but complementary ways of analyzing them. — This is a most puzzling statement. Culture and structure are obviously not complementary concepts. There is no apparent reason why qualities should be permanent and structure variable. The two terms are evidently being used by Fortes with some unusual or private meaning; or at least one of them is. Can it be that he means by culture what it generally means, or at least its forms, norms, and values, and that his "structure" designates the individual and personal variability in social adherence to cultural norms? This would make an intelligible concept; but what has it to do with "structure"? [5]

Nadel (23), 1951, another British social anthropologist, voices a position not far from our own. To paraphrase; society' and culture are different abstractions from data of the same order; society emphasizes "the dimension of relationships and groupings"; a culture is a system of patterns of behavior modalities. We would only make explicit two small reservations. First, the patterns *for* such relationships and groupings are cultural. Second, the anthropologist abstracts not only from "action" (including, of course, verbal acts) but also from the products of patterned action (i.e., artifacts).

Kluckhohn and Kelly (19), 1945, take for granted the correspondence of societies and cultures and point our that just as there are societies greater and smaller than the customary units of tribes, communities, and nations, so cultures also range in size from that of Mohammedanism down to the sub-cultures of say cliques or summer camps. [6] Murdock, however (21), 1949, is inclined to regard the community as the seat of social control and as therefore the "most typical" social group to support a total culture. By community he seems to mean the group in which interpersonal relations are still largely, or at least potentially, face-to-face. This is true for tribes, is only partly true for peasant-like communities, and mostly does not apply in modern urbanized or semi-urbanized nations. Even in peasant communities the army, the church, taxes, trials, railroads, and posts, at least part of fashions, news, and sentiments exist on a national and not at all primarily on a face-to-face scale. The church edifice and the pastor may be closely linked into the communal setup, but dogma, ritual, the forms of marriage, the selection of the priest are at least nationwide and often super-nationwide. Undoubtedly greater intimacy, warmth, and holistic integration attach to the community, in the sense of the Toennies Gemeinschaft, than to any Gesellschaft organization. On the other hand, cultural totalities of national and supernational scope can contain a far greater variety of content and attain to achievements of more profundity and intensity. There may well have existed more cultures limited to' tribes, in the history of mankind, than those of national size. Also no doubt most nations are, historically, confluences of communities, and communities continue to persist in them. Yet it is also obvious that in societies like our own or the Russian, or even in the Roman Empire or in Egypt of four thousand years ago, the total culture was of an intricacy, richness, and effectiveness that could not possibly have been supported by any face-to-race community.

Parsons' position (12), 1937, is expressed so that it might logically be considered either here or in the culture-individual discussion that follows. Of Parsons' great theoretical "systems of nature, action, and culture" we take the middle one to mean "social action," or what others would call society or organized interpersonal relations viewed as an" activity which possesses structure. This conception of society is Parsons' special contribution to social theory, but, in the framework of our present monograph that deals with culture, his concept of society, however important, is obviously of only marginal concern. .More relevant is his assertion that culture systems are distinguished from natural and action systems in being non-spatial and atemporal, consisting of "eternal objects" to which the category of time is not applicable, and which are not involved in process. We take it that this means that the essential things in culture are its forms and that these can be viewed timelessly. For instance a religion or an aesthetic product or a language can be examined in terms of itself for its qualities or values or the integration of these; or several religions, arts, or languages can be compared for their relative development of qualities. This we agree to; but we also hold that it is not the only or necessary way in which culture can be approached. Particular cultures do occur in particular places and at particular rimes, and their interconnection in space and rime and content and form can be studied as well as their abstracted forms alone. That is indeed what culture history is.

We suspect that the real crux of Parsons' statement lies in his assertion that culture systems are not involved in *process.* To this we would subscribe: culture is obviously not only a way of behavior but also a product of human beings. Its cause in the modern sense of the word, equivalent to the Aristotelian efficient cause, is the actions of men — human behavior, in contemporary phraseology. No amount of analysis or comparison of cultural forms *per se* will yield understanding of the specific *causes* of the particular forms. Aristotle would have called the forms of cultural phenomena, or at any rate the relationships of such forms, their formal causes. These are not productive of what we call process; though they are involved in it. Existing culture is undoubtedly determinative of subsequent culture in that it normally enters into its constitution to a high degree. It is thus an almost inescapable precondition as well as constituent of any arising culture. In Aristotelian parlance earlier culture could quite properly be called the material cause of subsequent culture. But that again is not "cause" in the modern scientific sense: it is only conditioning material on which human activity — itself largely determined by previous human activity' conditioned by culture — impinges and operates as efficient agent. We thus agree with Parsons that if process in culture means its continuing concrete causation, this does not reside in the culture itself but in the actions or behavior of men.

How far it is proper and useful to designate this behavior as specifically "social" action, and to put it into a "system" contrasted with that of nature is another matter. Human behavior is rooted in organic structure and function, which can surely not be left out of "nature": human action is by no means all social or concerned wholly with interrelations of persons. And on the other hand, even after we have admitted that culture as such is not concrete cause, we have only to abstract in imagination out from almost any situation of social action all the present and past culture that is actually involved in it, is phenomenally enmeshed with it, to realize how relatively barren of significance the remainder of pure social action would mostly be. Culture can be conceded to be literally a product, and yet the claim be maintained that cultureless social action, like a human nature not steeped in culture, would be phenomenally a fiction and operationally nearly empty.

Parsons' more recent position as evidenced in his 1949 definition (II-B-19) has moved in the anthropological direction. However, a still more recent work [7] shows a strong disposition to restrict culture to values or to "symbol systems." He, together with Edward Shils (also a sociologist), agrees that there is no such thing as either personality." or social system without culture. But he maintains that personalities and social systems are "concrete systems," whereas he regards culture as an organization of symbols in abstraction from "the other components of action, specifically the motivational and non-symbolic situational components."

Our own view is that "social system" or "social structure," "personality," and "culture" are all abstractions on about the same level. To a large degree, as we have indicated earlier, they all depart from the same order of data, and the distinction rests primarily in the focus of interest and type of question asked (i.e., "frame of reference"). If one thinks of "a society" (*not* a "social system" or a "social structure") as a specific group of individuals who interact with each other more than with "outsiders," [8] then, of course, "a society" is more concrete than "a culture." It is also possible and legitimate to distinguish "the social" from "the cultural" by pointing to facts that are not culturally patterned but which yet influence social (i.e., interactive) life. One may instance such phenomena as population density, the location of a group, and others (cf. III-*f*-19 and III-*f*-19a). Finally, a plurality of individuals in more or less continuous interaction produces something new which is a product of that interaction and not merely a perpetuation of pre-existing cultural patterns. *Cultural* factors influence the greater part of social behavior but social factors in their turn modify culture and create new culture.

In Parsons' new book *The Social System* one also sees the tendency, shared by certain other American sociologists and many British social anthropologists, to restrict culture to normative, idea, and symbolic elements. It will be well to quote at some length: [9]

Culture...consists...in patterned or ordered systems of symbols which are objects of the orientation of action, internalized components of the personalities of individualized actors and institutionalized patterns of social systems....

...cultural elements are elements of patterned order which mediate and regulate communications and other aspects of the mutuality of orientations in interaction processes. There is, as we have insisted, always a normative aspect in the relation of culture to the motivational components of action; the culture provides standards of selective orientation and ordering.

The most fundamental starting point for the classification of cultural elements is that of the three basic "functional" problem-contexts of action-orientation in general, the cognitive, the cathectic and the evaluative. It is fundamental to the very conception of action that there must be pattern-complexes differentiated with respect to each of these major problem contexts. These considerations provide the basis for the initial classification of cultural pattern types, namely belief systems, systems of expressive symbols, and systems of value-orientation, (p. 317)

In some fundamental respects (emphasis upon patterning, symbols, internalization of culture on the part of individuals), we are completely happy with this statement. Earlier in the same work (p. 15) Parsons also says that culture is transmitted, learned, and shared and that it is "on the one hand the product of, on the other hand a determinant of, systems of human social interaction." These are points with which anthropologists would agree. We can also accept Parsons' distinction of culture from social system as resting, amoncr other things, on the fact that culture is transmissible. It is also clear in this book that Parsons treats the cultural dimension as an independent one in his general theory.

Our incomplete satisfaction with Parsons probably arises from the fact that his scheme is centered so completely upon "action." This leaves little place for certain traditional topics of anthropological enquiry: archaeology, historical anthropology in general, diffusion, certain aspects of culture change, and the like. What anthropologists call "material culture" he deals with as "cultural objects" and "cultural possessions," nor, again, does his approach encompass certain aspects of the study of the products of human behavior with which anthropologists have long been concerned. Finally, his version of the theory of action is, in our view, overly complex for the present state of the sciences of man. His intricate system of categories cuts across and, we feel, dismembers the concept of culture. In particular, we are resistant to his absorbing into "social systems" abstracted elements which we think are better viewed as part of the totality of culture.

Raymond Firth has just published a remarkably clear and cogent statement:

In the description and analysis of the group life of human beings the most general terms used are society, culture, and community. Each is commonly used to express the idea of a totality. As abstractions they can give only a selected few of the qualities of the subject-matter they are meant to represent. Naturally, then, the definition of them has tended to mark contrasted rather than shared qualities. The types of contrast made familiar by German sociologists have drawn a distinction between the more purposeful associations serving individual ends and those arising from less-well-defined principles of aggregation. This has value as an analytical device, to classify social relationships. But at the broadest level, to cover almost the complete range of association, this mutual exclusiveness is misplaced. The terms represent different facets or components in basic human situations. If, for instance, society is taken to be an organized set of individuals with a given way of life, culture is that way of life. If society is taken to be an aggregate of social relations, then culture is the content of those relations. Society emphasizes the human component, the aggregate of the people and the relations between them. Culture emphasizes the component of accumulated resources, immaterial as well as material, which the people inherit, employ, transmute, add to, and transmit. Having substance, if in part only ideational, this component acts as a regulator to action. From the behavioural aspect, culture is all learned behaviour which has been socially acquired. It includes the residual effects of social action. It is necessarily also an incentive to action. The term community emphasizes the space-time component, the aspect of living together. It involves a recognition, derived from experience and observation, that there must be minimum conditions of agreement on common aims, and inevitably some common ways of behaving, thinking, and feeling. Society, culture, community, then involve one another — though when they are conceived as major isolates for concrete study their boundaries do not necessarily coincide. (1951, 27-28)

To sum up: the simple, biological analogy of "organism and environment" is inadequate because man is a culture-bearing animal. Some sort of three-way paradigm is necessary since we have: (a) individuals, (b) the situations in which they find themselves, and (c) the modes or ways in which they are oriented to these situations. In terms of the intellectual division of labor which has generally been adhered to during this century the study of individual organisms and their motivations has been the province of psychology and biology. Insofar as sociology has had a distinct conceptual field, it has been that of investigation of the situation. Cultural anthropology has been dealing with the modes of orientation to the situation. How the individual is oriented to his situation is in the concrete sense "within" the actor but not in the analytic sense, for modal orientations cannot, by definition, be derived from observing and questioning a single individual — they are culture. It is clear that these three points of the triangle are statements of foci in a broader frame of reference; they are not independent but each has implications for the other. For example, culture is not motivation but it affects motivation and likewise is part of the individual's "definition of the situation."

Culture and Individuals. This is a briefer [10] group than the preceding.

Wissler (1), 1916, is of importance because he was trained in psychology and was one of the first anthropologists to consider relations with psychology. He makes the simple and definite and incontestable point that no amount of psychology as such will give historical answers such as why inventions and organizations or changes of culture were made when, where, and by whom they were made.

Marett (2), 1920, (cf. also d~i), accepts a parallelism of sociology and psychology, but warns against a sociological treatment of man and history done as if there were no life in the subject matter: such treatment is dead and dull. No one will dissent from this. Marett's remark about human history being "instinct with purposive movement through and through" is evidently intended as a reminder that history deals with live men who strove and tried. It is probably not to be construed as a claim that history itself, as an entity, has an immanent or God-implanted purpose.

Ogburn (3), 1922, is commenting on Kroeber's then recent first attempt to distinguish planes of phenomena reducing to each other m one direction only, but also containing each an autonomous component or at least aspect. It so happened that Kroeber at that time did not name a social level, but passed directly from the cultural ("superorganic") to the mental and thence to the organic and inorganic planes of phenomena. In fact, with all endeavor at "splitting" he was not yet conceptually separating cultural and social phenomena, being still caught in the then prevalent ambiguity of meaning of the word "social." Ogburn had been influenced by personal contact with Boas and was sympathetic to the recognition of culture, but considered Kroeber's attempt "bold." It was certainly only half thought through.

The citation from Kroeber himself nearly a decade later (5), 1931, merely affirms the existence of cultural facts over and beyond their physiological and psychological aspects. It is worth remarking that a specifically social aspect is still not mentioned: the social facies was being included either in the psychological or the cultural.

Culture and Environment. Environment as a causative factor has been less in evidence in recent thinking than in the eighteenth and nineteenth centuries, but has of course never been ruled out. We may begin with the latest statement, that of Kluckhohn and Kelly (19), 1945, which recognizes "four universal dimensions" framing human action. They are: organic heredity, non-human environment, social environment, and a historical precipitate which includes the effects of the three foregoing as well as its own selectivity. In more usual but looser terminology, these four dimensions are race, environment, society', and culture.

Case (4), 1924, already recognizes three of these four "dimensions": race and environment interacting to produce culture, and this interacting with them to produce — a tautological anticlimax — "social evolution or civilization." Progress thus gets itself smuggled in. Yet, from a sociologist, the omission of society is remarkable.

Daryll Forde (9), 1934, attributes culture (not human action as in Kluckhohn and Kelly's case) to the four factors of race, physical environment, society, and psychology. However, his point is not so much to distinguish these as to point out the fallacy of using any of them alone as an explanation, because all cultures have had specific, individual histories.

Plant's statement that he is using "environment, milieu, and cultural pattern" interchangeably could hardly have been made in other than a specifically psychological work. It is only in the fact of their all being impingements on the individual psyche that these three are alike.

Culture and Artifacts. Clellan Ford (10), 1937, and Rouse (16), 1939, both of Yale, one with a psychological, the other with an archaeological approach, agree that artifacts are not culture. This is a position implied in some of the definitions cited in Part Two — those which emphasize ideas, ideals, behavior; though contrariwise artifacts are undoubtedly implied in many other definitions, and are explicitly mentioned in several, such as A14, B-6, D-II-12, E-4, G-5. Ford's position is that culture is concerned with the way people act. How people make and use artifacts is part of culture; the artifacts themselves are cultural data but not culture. Artifacts stand in the same category of relationship to culture as does environment. Rouse words it a little differently. "Culture cannot be inherent in" artifacts. It is the relationship between artifact and user, the pattern of significance of artifacts, that is cultural, not the artifacts as such.

Culture and Customs. Sapir (5), 1931, "who apparently never gave a full-length formal definition of culture, [11] wrote one of his many profoundly illuminating articles in the Encyclopedia of Social Sciences on "Custom." It is, he says, a common sense concept that has served as the matrix for the development of the concept of culture, and remains somewhat more connotive, subjective, and affect-laden. The authors feel this to be a pregnant remark, which, if consistently kept in mind by all of us, would have obviated many deviations and missteps in the understanding of culture.

Sapir does define custom in this article. He says it is "the totality of behavior patterns which are carried by tradition and lodged in the group, as contrasted with the more random personal activities of the individual." We feel that this definition is both common-sense and precise: it hits the nail on the head.

[1] The group, society', community, etc., also appear frequently in the class A or descriptive definitions, bat more incidentally. The C-I class really *rests* on the distinction: culture is the way of a society.

[2] As there had to be, once Tylor as far back as 1871 had given formal definition of culture that concluded with the phrase "of man as a member of society."

[3] It is interesting, however, that in 1931 (*f*-6) Sapir sees the behavior patterns "lodged" in the group and "carried by tradition" — not by the individuals of the group.

[4] Specifically, a selection of aspects of sense impressions that have a common feature. This is, of course, the differentia of abstraction (etymologically: "drawing away from").

[5] As a pupil of Radcliffe-Brown, and as editor of the 1949 volume of studies presented to Radcliffe-Brown, in the pages immediately preceding our citation from his own essay in that book. Fortes questions the validity of another distinction made by Radcliffe-Brown in his 1940 article (beyond the distinction just discussed by us), namely between "structure as an actually existing concrete reality" and general or normal "structural form." Fortes, like ourselves, challenges the dictum that structure is immediately visible in concrete reality, pointing out, again like ourselves, that it is discovered by comparison, induction, and analysis, in other words, "by abstraction from concrete reality" (1949, p. 56). It is in going on from this finding that Fortes sets up his new differentiation of culture from quantitatively viewed "structure," as a suggested replacement of Radcliffe-Brown's.

[6] See also Kroeber, 1951b, p. 282.

[7] Parsons, *et al.,* 1951.

[8] This may mean the people of another community (locality differentiation), another tribe or nation ("political" differentiation), people of another speech (linguistic differentiation), or any combination of these criteria. The size of unit taken as "a society" can properly vary with the problem. But frequency of interaction is always closely correlated with in-group, out-group reeling, though this correlation may have negative as well as positive aspects.

[9] The ensuing definition is not included in Part Two because we found it necessary to close our survey of definitions with works published in 1950.

[10] The ensuing discussion should be linked with that in the comment on III-*d.*

[11] His B-2, B-3, G-1 in Part Two are brief as well as incidental.

Addenda

The two following passages are added to extend completeness of documentation. They were received when the manuscript was already in the hands of the editor and hence the comments and subsequent tabulations have not been revised to include them. But they bear, clearly enough, upon central issues touched upon many times in the course of this work.

a) *Evans-Pritchard, 1951: 17-18.*

Among the older anthropological writers, Morgan, Spencer, and Durkheim conceived the aim of what we now call social anthropology to be the classification and functional analysis of social structures. This point of view has persisted among Durkheim's followers in France. It is also well represented in British anthropology today and in the tradition of formal sociology in Germany. Tylor, on the other hand, and others who leant towards ethnology, conceived its aim to be the classification and analysis of cultures, and this has been the dominant viewpoint in American anthropology for a long time, partly, I think, because the fractionized and disintegrated Indian societies on which their research has been concentrated lend themselves more easily to studies of culture than of social structure; partly because the absence of a tradition of intensive field work through the native languages and for long periods of time, such as we have in England, also tends towards studies of custom or culture rather than of social relations; and partly for other reasons.

When a social anthropologist describes a primitive society the distinction between society and culture is obscured by the fact that he describes the reality, the raw behaviour, in which both are contained. He tells you, for example, the precise manner in which a man shows respect to his ancestors; but when he comes to interpret the behaviour he has to make abstractions from it in the light of the particular problems he is investigating. If these are problems of social structure he pays attention to the social relationships of the persons concerned in the whole procedure rather than to the details of its cultural expression.

Thus one, or a partial, interpretation of ancestor worship might be to show how it is consistent with family or kinship structure. The cultural, or customary, actions which a man performs when showing respect to his ancestors, the facts, for instance, that he makes a sacrifice and that what he sacrifices is a cow or an ox, require a different kind of interpretation, and this may be partly both psychological and historical.

This methodological distinction is most evident when comparative studies are undertaken, for to attempt both kinds of interpretation at the same time is then almost certain to lead to confusion. In comparative studies what one compares are not things in themselves but certain particular characteristics of them. If one wishes to make a sociopolitical comparison of ancestor cults in a number of different societies, what one compares are sets of structural relations between persons. One necessarily starts, therefore, by abstracting these relations in each society from their particular modes of cultural expression. Otherwise one will not be able to make the comparison. What one is doing is to set apart problems of a certain kind for purposes or research. In doing this, one is not making a distinction between different kinds of things — society and culture are not entities — but between different kinds of abstraction.

b) *Infield, 1951: 512-13.*

It would seem that the first step in this direction would have to be a sociological definition of culture. Such a definition would have to specify the functional interrelations between the mode of interaction, or as Lewin would call it the "structural configuration of socio-dynamic properties," and both the aggregate of acquired meanings on the one side as well as the needs of individuals on the other. In this sense, it could be possibly formulated as follows: Culture is an acquired aggregate of meanings attached to and implemented in material and non-material objects which decisively influence the manner in which human beings tend to interact so as to satisfy their needs.

By "aggregate of acquired meanings" we understand something equivalent to what constitutes culture in the eyes of anthropology. The "whole of material and non-material values together with the vehicles of their implementation," as anthropology likes to define It, is a somewhat static complex. By substituting for values the term "meanings" we at once open the possibility of relating the cultural element to what interests the sociologist most: the mode of sociation. In this way, a place is also accorded to that factor which the natural science point of view tends to neglect, the active element in human nature. Acquired meanings are both those accumulated and transmitted by former generations, the social heritage, as well as those which the present generation makes actively its own, the cultural activities of the present. In this manner, the nature of the acquired meanings has a direct functional relation to the mode of social interaction. In its turn, the mode of social interaction is functionally related to and oriented toward the satisfaction of needs of the interacting individuals. Actually, like any true functional interrelation, the one presented in our definition can be analyzed by starting from any of its terms. Taking its starting point, for instance, from the acquired meanings, the analysis can show how, by way of the mode of social interaction, they affect the nature of the needs. Or, by starting from the needs — taking them generally as being of the kind that can be satisfied by acting mainly for oneself or of the kind that can be satisfied by acting mainly together with others — it can be shown how they influence the mode of social interaction which in turn determines the selection, acceptance, and cultivation of specific meanings attached to material and non-material objects. Finally, the analysis can set out from the mode of social interaction and show how this interaction forms, so to speak, a relay system between meanings and needs. Wherever we start from, it is clear that the sociologically relevant character of a given group's culture can be understood fully only if the analysis is capable of accounting not only for the main terms of the culture but for the functional interrelation of these terms as well.

Index to Authors in Part Three

Part Four - Summary and Conclusions

A: Summary

Word and Concept

THE history of the concept of culture as used today in science is the story of the emergence of an idea that was gradually strained out of the several connotations of an existing word. The word culture, in turn, goes back to classical or perhaps pre-classical Latin with the meaning or cultivation or nurture, as it still persists in terms like agriculture, horticulture, cult, cultus, and in recent formations like bee culture, oyster culture, pearl culture, bacillus cultures. The application of culture to human societies and history was late apparently post-1750 — and for some reason was characteristic of the German language and at first confined to it.

The Romance languages, and English in their wake, long used civilization instead of culture to denote social cultivation, improvement, refinement, or progress. This term goes. back to Latin civis, civilis, civitas, civiUtas, whose core of reference is political and urban: the citizen in an organized state as against the tribesman. The term civilization does not occur in classical Latin, but seems to be a Renaissance Romance formation, probably French and derived from the verb civiliser, meaning to achieve or impart refined manners, urbanization, and improvement. An Italian near-counterpart civiltà is as early as Dante; and Samuel Johnson still preferred civility to civilization.

Thus both terms, culture and civilization, began by definitely containing the idea of betterment, of improvement toward perfection. They still retain this meaning today, in many usages, both popular and intellectual. However, in science as of 1952, the word culture has acquired also a new and specific sense (sometimes shared with civilization), which can fairly be described as the one scientific denotation that it possesses. This meaning is that of a set of attributes and products of human societies, and therewith of mankind, which are extrasomatic and transmissible by mechanisms other than biological heredity, and are as essentially lacking in sub-human species as they are characteristic of the human species as it is aggregated in its societies. This concept of culture (and/or civilization) did not exist anywhere in 1750. By 1850 it was de facto being held in some quarters in Germany, though never quite explicitly, and with considerable persisting wavering between the emerging meaning and the older one of cultivating or improvement. In 1871 the first formal or explicit definition of the new concept which we have been able to find was given by the anthropologist Tylor. This history of the emergence of the concept within its existing terminological matrix is still far from clear in detail, but its main course can be traced.

The Middle Ages looked backward toward perfection as established at the beginning of Time. Truth was already revealed, human wisdom long since added to it; there was no place left for progress. The Renaissance felt Itself achieving great things, but could hardly as yet formulate how these achievements differed from those of the past. Toward 1700 the idea began to dawn in western Europe that perhaps "the Moderns" were equalling or surpassing "the Ancients." To this daring idea several factors probably contributed: the channeling, constricting, and polishing of language, manners, and customs under the leadership of France; the positive achievements of science from Copernicus to Newton; the surge of a philosophy finally conscious of new problems; an upswing of population and wealth; and no doubt other influences. By about 1750 not only was the fact of modern progress generally accepted, but the cause of it had become clear to the times: it was the liberation of reason, the prevalence of rational enlightenment.

Philosophy of History

In 1765 Voltaire established the term "the philosophy of history." An earlier and longer work by him on the generalized history of mankind, dating from 1756, was the famous *Essai sur les Moeurs et l'Esprit des Nations*. This title pointed the two paths that led out from Voltaire. One emphasized the *spirit* of peoples and led to a sort of philosophical commentary or reflections on human history. In this tradition were the Swiss Iselin's 1768 *History of Humanity;* Condorcet's *Sketch of a Historic Survey of the Progress of the Human Spirit*, posthumous in

1801, and the final if belated culmination of the movement in Hegel's *Philosophy of History,* also posthumous in 1837. In all these the effort was to seize the spirit or essence, the esprit or Geist, of human progressive history. It is history as distilled deductively by principles; documentation is secondary; and the course of thought shears away from comparative recognition of many cultures or civilizations, whose inherent plurality and diversity tend to interfere with formulations that are at once compact and broad.

Use of Culture in Germany

The second path emphasized the "moeurs," *customs,* which are variable, particular, plural, and empirical rather than rational. Custom, as Sapir says, [1] is indeed a common-sense concept that has served as a matrix for the development of the scientific concept of culture. The best-known early exponents of this line of inquiry are Adelung, 1782, Herder, 17841791, Jcnisch, 1 80 1. The movement was essentially German; and the weighting was definitely historic and even in parts ethnographic rather than philosophical, though aiming to cover the entire human species throughout its duration. The titles of the works of the three authors mentioned all contain the term History and the term Humanity (or Human Race). Adelung uses Culture in his title, Jenisch in a subtitle. Herder puts Philosophy into his title, but speaks constantly of culture, humanity, and tradition as near-equivalents. Culture is defined as a progressive cultivation of faculties by Herder, as an amelioration or refinement by Adelung. But in context of usage, many statements by both authors when they use "culture" have a modern ring — not because Adelung and Herder had really attained to the modern scientifically generalized concept of culture, but because their approach was historical, pluralistic, relativistic, and yet aiming to cover the totality of the known world of custom and ideology'. The first use of "history of culture" is by Adelung, of "culture history" by Hegewisch, 1788.

The Adelung-Herder movement experienced a sort of revival a half-century later at the hands of Klemm, who began publishing a many-volumed General Culture History in 1843, and a General Science of Culture in 1854. Klemm's ability to generalize, let alone theorize, was limited. He was interested in information and he was industrious. He has far less sweep and empathy than Adelung and Herder. He describes instead of narrating; history begins to dissolve into ethnography in his hands. Vet his use of the term culture shows the drift of the rimes. The sense of "cultivating" has receded. There is a great deal about stages of culture. And there are a number of passages in which the word culture can be without strain construed in its modern scientific meaning — though we probably cannot be completely sure that in any of these passages Klemm did so construe it, because he seems never to have given a definition of the term. He probably had attained — at times at least — to the implicit recognition of the scientific concept; he certainly stood at its threshold. After him, beginning with Burckhardt, 1860, and going on through a series of historians, philosophers, anthropologists, and others — Hellwald, Lippert, Rickert, Frobenius, Lamprecht, Bierkandt, and Simmel — there is no longer any question of wide German recognition of the scientific concept of culture, whether defined or not.

Spread of the Concept and Resistances

Even more important, however, is the spread of the concept from Germany to other countries. Danilevsky's "culture-historical types" of 1869 are major cultures or civilizations as surely as are Spengler's and Toynbee's. Tylor explicity acknowledged his use of and obligation to Klemm. In his 1865 Researches he had occasionally ventured on the term culture, though he mostly used civilization. But in 1871 he boldly called his major book Primitive Culture and in its opening sentence gave the first, formal, explicit definition of culture. This may be set down as the recordable date of birth of the scientific concept, though the procreation had been German.

Still, in the retrospect of eighty years, it is remarkable how slowly Tylor's formulation and term were accepted. Two years before, Matthew Arnold had defined culture as the pursuit of perfection, characterized by sweetness and light. A generation or two later, a hundred speakers of English would still have accepted Arnold's definition to one that even knew of Tylor's, directly or at second-hand. The Oxford Dictionary referred to Arnold in 1893, to Tylor not until the 1933 Supplement. [2] The first though still imperfect penetration of the scientific or Tylorian concept of culture into the world of dictionaries was in the Webster of 1929; and its earliest adequate recognition we have found in any general English dictionary is of 1947.

All in all, British scientists and intellectuals have been more resistitve than American ones to acceptance of the term culture as long as they could get by with either society or civilization. Thus the phrase social anthropology was coined in England and is still used there when Americans would more often say cultural anthropology. Toynbee deals with societies and civilizations, very rarely with cultures. The resistance appears to be stylistic, a matter of idiom, of distaste for a word usage first established in another language. Americans scrupled much less to borrow from the Germans.

France has been even more resistive than England. Civilization, with its implications of advancement and urbanization, is still the preferred French noun used for culture, though the adjective "cultural" has more standing. In many situations the indeterminate word "social" continues to do service in France today for the concepts of the both the social and the cultural, much as in Durkheim's day. It is not clear to what degree this old-fashioned and ambiguous terminology is a minor symptom or a contributing factor of a certain backwardness in spots of contemporary French theoretical thinking in the social and cultural field.

Outside these two countries acceptance of the term culture is universal and understanding of the concept wide: in Russia, other Slavic lands, Scandinavia, Holland, Latin America much as in Germany and the United States.

Culture and Civilization

Much as Tylor for a time wavered between culture and civilization and perhaps finally chose the former as somewhat less burdened with connotation of high degree of advancement, the two terms have continued to be near-synonyms to many students writing in English, both British and American. The concepts attached to the two words in usage have been close enough to make choice between them to a large extent a matter of preferential taste.

In German, however, three separate attempts have been made to contrast culture and civilization. The first of these, whose beginnings are attributed to Wilhelm von Humboldt, and which was carried on by Lippert and Barth, makes culture concerned with the technological-economic activities or the "material" sphere, but civilization, with spiritual ennoblement or enriching. This view found temporary reflection in American sociology in Lester Ward and Albion Small around 1900.

Next, Spengler used civilization to denote the final, petrifying, non-creative phase which was the old age or winter of his unique monadal, fate-charged cultures. This usage had wide temporary repercussions in Germany, but few echoes outside.

Finally there is the Alfred Weber reaction of 1920 to Spengler, still maintained by Thurnwald as of 1950, identifying civilization with the objective technological and informational activities of society, but culture with subjective religion, philosophy, and art. Civilization is accumulative and irreversible; the cultural component is highly variable, unique, non-additive. This view has found somewhat modified reflection in MacIver, Odum, and Merton among American sociologists.

The tenacity of these several German efforts to drive through to a distinction between culture and civilization is as marked as their variety of position. It seems almost as if, there being two words close in sense, a compulsion arose to identify them with contrasting aspects of the major meaning which they shared.

Culture as an Emergent or Level

Once culture had been recognized as a distinctive product of men living in societies, or as a peculiar, coherent, and continuous set of attributes of human behavior, it was probably only a question of time until the claim was advanced that culture constituted a separate "level," "dimension," or "aspect" of phenomena, analogous to the distinctive organization or patterning characteristic of organic phenomena in addition to their physicochemical basis. C. Lloyd Morgan's *Emergent Evolution* of 1923 is perhaps the best-known work developing the principle of emergence, though wholly without reference to culture. Alexander's *Space, Time and Deity* — issued in 1920 — is the first book on the subject by a philosopher and has publication priority over Morgan but was evidently influenced by him. The autonomy of the cultural level was apparently first advanced by Frobenius as earnas 1898 in *Ursprung der Afrikanischen Kulturen und Naturwissenschaftliche Kulturlehre,* and restated in *Paideuma,* 1921. It was of course completely assumed and asserted by Spengler in 1918. It is advocated by Kroeber in *The Superorganic* in 1917: even to a diagram showing superposed divergent or emergent levels. More recently, Warden among psychologists, and White [3] among anthropologists, have concerned themselves with culture as an emergent. [3a]

As between all levels, it is the lower ones that set the frame in which phenomena of superior level operate. The "laws" or forces of the lower level do not per se "produce" the upper-level phenomena; at any rate, these cannot be wholly derived from below; there is always a specific residuum, a sum of the parts, a combination or organization, that is of and in the level being considered. Thus organic processes of events conform wholly to physico-chemical process, but cannot be non-residually resolved into them. Lower-level factors adequately explain certain constants and uniformities in upper-level phenomena. but they do not wholly explain, nor even describe, the distinctive properties specific to phenomena of the upper level.

Culture constitutes the topmost phenomenal level yet recognized — or for that matter, now imaginable — in the realm of nature. This of course does not compel the prediction that emergence into our consciousness of a new and higher level is precluded.

The danger in the construal of culture as an emergent level evidently lies in the consequent tendency to reify or hypostasize culture, to view it as a distinctive substance or actual superorganism, and then to assume that it moves through autonomous, immanent forces. Spengler certainly believed this; so did Frobenius, at least at times; and Kroeber has been flatly charged with the same errors by Boas, Benedict, and Bidney, besides incurring opposition to the concept of the superorganic from Sapir and Goldenweiser. Too few anthropologists have, however, participated in the discussion of this phenomenological set of problems to render it clear whether recognition of a cultural level or aspect necessarily compels the reification of culture as a substance containing its own self-moving forces, or whether it is possible to take the first step and refrain from the second. To put it differently, is the value of recognition of a cultural level essentially methodological and operational, or is it misleading because it must lead to substantification and stark autonomy? Sociologists have been of little help on this point because their specific approach being through the social aspects of phenomena, they tend to treat the cultural aspects as an extension or secondary, so that the problem is marginal to them. Philosophers on the whole have shown no great interest in the issue. This very fact, however, suggests that the recognition of levels does not necessarily have ontological implication, but is essentially an operational view arising within empirical scientific practice. [4]

Definitions of Culture

In Part II we have cited one hundred sixty-four [4a] definitions of culture. The occurrence of these in time is interesting — as indeed the distribution of all cultural phenomena in cither space or time always reveals significance.

Our earliest definition, Tylor's of 1871, seems not to have been followed by any other for thirty-two years. Between 1900 and 19 19 (actually 1903 and 1916), we have found only six; but for 1920 to 1950, one hundred fifty-seven. In other words, the distribution is: in the first three-fifths of our eighty years, less than four per cent; in the last two-fifths, ninety-six per cent. The long wait after Tylor is particularly striking. The word culture was by then being bandied about by all kinds of German thinkers; and one has only to turn the leaves of the 1888-98 Old Series of the *American Anthropologist* to find the term penetrating even to titles of articles — in 1895, Mason on *Similarities in Culture;* in 1896, Fewkes on *Prehistoric Culture of Tusayan;* in 1898, McGee on *Piratical Acculturation.* The point is that the word culture was being used without definition.

Before and After 1920

The few twentieth-century definitions earlier than 1920 are also interesting, both with reference to the profession of the authors and to the class to which we have assigned the definitions.

1871	Tylor	Anthropologist	A-1, Enumerative	1915	Ostwald	Chemist	F-IV-2, Residual
1903	Ward	Sociologist	F-II-1, Ideas	1916	Wissler	Anthropologist	D-II-1, Learning
1905	Small	Sociologist	D-I-1, Adjustment	1916	Wissler	Anthropologist	F-II-2, Ideas.
1907	Ostwald	Chemist	F-IV-1, Residual				

For the period 1920-50 we submit a tabular list of definition groups or classes arranged in the chronological order of their earliest post1920 definition, with mention of the author of this first post1920 one, and citation of the number of definitions in each group during each of the three decades 1920-50. .

It is evident that once a post1920 definition with a certain new emphasis has been made, others in the same group follow pretty steadily, in fact usually increase in numbers. For the three decades (1940-50 comprising eleven instead of ten years) the total definitions are 22, 35, 100.

In contrast, the time gap between the seven pre-1920 definitions and the first post-1920 ones (within the same emphasis groups) runs from nine to forty-nine years and averages twenty-eight years. The length of this interval inevitably raises the question whether an isolated statement, so far ahead as this of all the rest in its group, can have been actuated by the same motivations as these; that is, whether in spite of formal or verbal resemblance to them, it actually "meant" the same — whether it was aimed at the same sense or was a chance shot.

For instance, when the chemist Ostwald in 1907 and 1915 defined culture as that which man alone among animals possesses, his statement is evidently *not* part of the same *specific* current of thought that led the sociologist Blumenthal to say in 1941 that culture is all non-genetically produced means of adjustment (F-IV-1, 2, 3).

Definitions in Part Two

Pre-1920 Definition	First post-1920 Definition	By	Definition group, Emphasis on	Number of Definitions 1920-29	1930-39	1940-50	Total[*]
A. Beginning 1920-29							
(1871)	1920	Wissler	Enumeration, A	5	5	9	20
—	1921	Park-Burgess, Sapir	Tradition, Heritage, B	6	5	12	23
—	1921	Sapir	Incomplete, G	2	2	3	7
(1916)	1925†	Hart-Pantzer	Learning, D-II	1	—	(13)	(15)
(1903)	1927	Sumner-Keller	Adjustment, D-I	2	5	9	17
—	1927	Willey	Product, F-I	3	6	12	21
—	1929	Wissler	Rule, Way, C-I	1	4	15	20
—	1929	Willey	Patterning, E	1	1	7	9
—	pre-1930	Tozzer	Habit, D-III	1	1	1	4
B. Beginning after 1930							
—	1934	Roheim	Purely Psychological, D-IV	—	2	1	2
—	1935	Carver	Ideals and Behavior, C-II	—	2	4	6
(1903; 1916)	1937	Schmidt, Blumenthal	Ideas, F-II	—	2	6	10
C. Beginning after 1940							
(1907, 1915)	1941	Blumenthal	Residual, F-IV	—	—	3	5
(1916)	1941**	Miller-Dollard	Learning, D-II	(1)	—	13	15
—	1942	Bain	Symbols, F-III	—	—	5	5

[*] Includes all definitions from Tylor's onward,
[**] Repeated, because of long interval 19:5 to 1941.

Ostwald was not thinking of adjustment, nor of its means; and he accepted culture as a property or result, rather than inquiring into the process that produced it.

Again, Small's 1905 statement (D-I-1) centers on attainment or promotion of ends, individual or social; which is characteristic of the psychologizing sociology of his day — vaguely psychologizing it seems in the retrospect of a half-century. But, beginning with Sumner and Keller in 1917, the emphasis comes to rest on a new basis, which instead of being limited to the subjectively psychological, is concerned with adaptation to total environment.

Similarly, in the emphasis-on-ideas group F-II, Ward's 1903 statement refers to ideas, but the central concept is that culture is a social structure or organism; to which there is then appended the supplementary remark "and ideas are its germs" — whatever "germs" may mean in this context. Wissler, thirteen years later, when he says that culture is a definite association complex of ideas, is undoubtedly trying to give a specific psychological definition; especially as his own training was largely psychological. Still, Wissler did not pursue this approach — in fact abandoned it for others. So it is as much as twenty-one yean after Wissler that a continuing stream of definitions with idea emphasis (F-II-4 to 9, nine in number including variants) first begins to be produced, from 1937 to 1949. The half-dozen authors involved in this continuity evidently in part influenced one another, in part were responding to the times.

The Place of Tylor and Wissler

The case of Tylor as a precursor is somewhat special. It was almost a half-century — from 1871 to 1920 — before his earliest of all definitions had a successor in the enumeratively descriptive class "A." As usual, Wissler was first, after Tylor; anthropologists predominate among the successors; and Tylor's influence is traceable, sometimes even in rums of wording, to as late as Kroeber, Herskovits, and Thurnwald, 1948-50. The reason for this continuity is not only that Tylor possessed unusual insight and wisdom, but that he was deliberately establishing a science by defining its subject matter. That he made this definition the first sentence of a book shows that he was conscious of his procedure.

Yet why Tylor was so long in being followed even by Wissler remains a problem. The reasons evidently were multiple. First, Tylor was introducing a new meaning from a foreign language for an established English word, and English idiom was resistant. Then, concurrently, the older English sense of the word culture was being given an ultra-humanistic sharpening by Matthew Arnold; and as against this literary significance, with its highly charged connotation in a country where higher education was classical, a contrary effort in an incipient science had little force. In fact, the names of Lang and Frazer suggest how little extricated from belles lettres the new science of anthropology remained in Britain for more than a generation after Tylor. Then, the whole orientation of the evolutionary school, whose productivity began just ten years before 1871 and of which Tylor himself formed part, and which led anthropology out of the fringe of philosophy, history, geography, biology, and medicine into an autonomous activity with problems of its own — the orientation of this evolutionary school was toward origins, stages, progress and survivals, and spontaneous or rational operations of the human mind. Culture entered consideration chiefly as an assemblage of odd customs and strange beliefs used to substantiate the broad principles advanced as to origins and progress. In short, the assumptions as well as the findings of the "evolutionists" were schematic and, except for Tylor, the men themselves remained uninterested in culture as a concept.

Finally, it is probable that the influence of Boas was a factor. As we have seen, American anthropologists were using both the concept, and the word culture fairly freely in the eighteen-nineties, perhaps already in the eighties beginning with the establishment of the Bureau of Ethnology. Boas, coming from Germany in the eighties, was certainly familiar with both idea and word. However, Boas was interested in dealing with culture, not in systematically theorizing about it. He gave his first definition of it at the age of seventy-two, in an encyclopedia article on the scope of anthropology. His first book, issued when he was fifty-three, was called *The Mind of Primitive Man;* his last, a selection from his articles and papers, chosen by himself at the age of eighty-two, he named *Race, Language, and Culture.* So far as there is a central theme in both works, it is that one cannot infer or deduce between environment, race, language, and culture; that spontaneous or inherent developments cannot be proved and must not be assumed, and that so far as they tend to occur they are generic and subject to variation or even suppression; that as regards human groups different influences can produce similar effects, and that causes are multiple and must be independently ascertained in each case with due regard to the specificity of its history. The upshot was a far more critical approach than had been displayed by any predecessor, and results that were positive as regards many particular problems, but as regards generalities were largely methodological or negative. Boas was interested in the complex interactions of culture, language, race, and environment; he was much less interested in the nature and specific properties of culture. As Boas in one way or another influenced almost all his successors in American anthropology, the result was that directly he contributed little to Tylor's attempt to isolate and clarify the concept of culture as such, and that indirectly he hindered its progress by diverting attention to other problems.

This interpretation is strengthened by the fact that Wissler, whose anthropological training stemmed from Boas, but who broke personally with him about 1906, by 1916 had offered two definitions of culture (D-II-1, F-II-2) and was the first to follow with definitions of different emphasis (A-2, C-I-1) in 1920 and 1929. Wissler was lunging rather than consistent in these tries. But it is evident that he was concerned with the problem of what culture was and what characterized it, more than Boas ever was; and the parting of the personal ways of the two men may have freed Wissler for this interest. As in so much of his other work, he was somewhat casual, imprecise, and perhaps unintense in his attack on the problem; but he possessed an exploratory and pioneering mind. Of Wissler's four definitions which we cite, all are the first of their class except for the precedence of one by Tylor.

The Course of Post-1920 Definitions

Let us revert to our tabulation. After the Enumerative class (A) of definitions launched by Tylor and revived by Wissler, the next to be initiated was the Historical one which emphasized Tradition or Social Heritage (B). Tradition" goes back to Herder, who consistently used the term alongside Cultur and Humanitaet, almost as a synonym. Social Heritage of course *is* culture — the matrix in which culture as a technical term of science grew up, according to Sapir. Sapir himself and Park and Burgess lead off the chain in 1921; eight of the first ten definitions, to 1917, are by anthropologists, and seven of the remaining thirteen.

Passing over the Incomplete Definitions (G), and for a moment those that emphasize Learning (D-II), we come to those stressing Adjustment or Problem Solving (D-I). Here Small had pointed the way as early as 1903 with his stress on "ends," and it was the sociologist Keller, editing and continuing Sumner's work in 1927, that established Adjustment (or Adaptation in 1915) as a factor in culture. This is a characteristic sociological type of definition. Only four of the seventeen examples found by us emanate from anthropologists: in 1942, Clellan Ford, who was trained also in sociology and psychology at Yale, and who varied adaptations to problem-solutions; in 1946, Kluckhohn and Leighton; in 1949 Turney-High with maintenance of "equilibrium as a psychological organism" as a variant of adaptation; and in 1950 the British anthropologist, Piddington.

Our group next in time, beginning in 1928, with emphasis on culture as a Product or Artifact (F-I), is again dominantly the result of sociological thinking. Apart from the pre-historian Menghin's statement of 1934 that culture is the objectified, materialized result (Ergebnis) of spiritual activity, there are only four definitions by anthropologists — the last four, from 1948 to 1950.

A year later, in 1929, Wissler initiated the Rule or Way type of conceiving of culture (C-I). With "way" close to custom, and again to tradition or heritage, one might expect this formulation to come mainly from anthropologists. It does: they made or participated in thirteen of the twenty statements assembled. [5]

Patterning or Organization as an emphasized factor in culture (E) might be looked for as also an anthropological view, in view of Benedict's influence; but it is not so in origin. Willey, Dollard, and Ogburn and Nimkoff are the only representatives from 1929 to 1940. However, the emphasis is not yet sharp. The word pattern [6] is not used; correlation, interrelation, interdependence, system do occur. With 1941 the anthropologists join in. Redfield speaks of "organization," Linton of "organized" and of "configuration," Kluckhohn and Kelly of a "system of designs for living." The word "patterned" appears only since 1948, with Gillin and Tumey-High. We believe, as intimated in our Comment on group E, that the concept is likely to have greater weighting in the future, whatever the terms may be that will be used to designate it.

From 1930 to 1934 no new types of definitions were launched. In 1935 Carver, an economist, made a statement that does not fit any of our groups too well but is perhaps nearest our Ideals-plus-Behavior class C-II. Two eminent sociologists, Thomas and Sorokin, and the philosopher Bidney, have produced the remaining five statements which we have collated. "Behavior" is of course a mechanistically-charged term given its wide vogue in post-World-War-I psychology. The older anthropologists spoke of activities, reactions, or practices. Values or norms, on the other hand, have probably long been a covert constituent of conceptions of culture, which have only recently begun to be acknowledged.

In 1937 the anthropologist Pater Schmidt and the sociologist Blumenthal independently revived an interest in ideas as a characteristic component of culture (group F-II) which had lain dormant since the sociologist Ward in 1003 and the anthropologist Wissler in 1916. All the remaining statements of the class, except one by the philosopher Feibleman and one by the sociologist Becker, are from anthropologists.

Interest in culture being learned (D-II) has two roots. One is old, and rests on the recognition that culture is non-instinctive, noncrenetic, acquired by social process, whether that process be called tradition, imitation, or education. This is reflected, as early as 1871, in Tylor's "acquired by man as a member of society." The second interest is much more recent, and is a reflection of emphasis on learning theory in modern psychology. While all culture is learned, most cultureless animals also learn, so that learning alone can never suffice either to define or to explain culture. The mention of learning by anthropologists like Benedict, Opler, Hoebel, Slotkin, and Kluckhohn thus evidences the growing rapport between anthropology and psychology.

In the tabulation we have ventured to group this class as essentially post1940 and beginning with Miller and Dollard in 1941. This implies that we construe the Hart and Pantzer 1925 definition as historically premature to the main current, like the 19 16 Wissler one. Actually. Wissler says "acquired by learning;" Hart and Pantzer mention imitation, tuition, social acquisition, and transmission; but in both cases the point is the fact of acquisition (as against innateness), rather than the precise manner of acquisition. On the contrary. Miller and Dollard in 1941 dwell on the stimulus-response and cue-reward underlay of the manner of acquisition and do not even mention learning as such; which first reappears with Kluckhohn in 1942.

Our F-III group emphasizing Symbolization dates only from 1942. We may have missed some extant statements that belong here. Certainly there is as of 1951 a wide recognition among philosophers, linguists, anthropologists, psychologists, and sociologists that the existence of culture rests indispensably upon the development in early man of the faculty for symbolizing, generalizing, and imaginative substitution. Another decade ought therefore to see a heavier accentuation of this factor in our thinking about culture.

Rank Order of Elements Entering Into Post-1930 Definitions

Let us now consider conceptual elements from the point of view of entrance into definitions in any explicit form rather than from the exclusive point of view of emphasis. We shall include only those elements which occur most frequently or which (as just indicated above) seem to have special importance in more recent developments of the concept. The rank order for the pre-1940 decade is as follows:

Group reference ("social" etc.) 23	Ideas 8
Historical product ("heritage," "tradition," etc.) 18	Carriers of culture ("individuals," "persons," etc.) 7
Totality 16	Group product 5
Behavior ("acts," etc.) 12	Values and ideals 4
Non-genetic transmission 11	Learning 3
Patterned ("system," "organized," etc.) 11	Way or mode 3
Adjustive-adaptive ("gratification," etc.) 10	

The same breakdown of elements entering explicitly into definitions of the 1941-50 (inclusive) period gives:

Group reference 43	Adjustive-adaptive 23	Ideas 13
Behavior 35	Carriers of Culture 22	Group product 13
Non-genetic 32	Learning 22	Values and ideals 12
Way or mode 26	Totality 20	
Patterned 24	Historical product 15	

These counts are only rough [8] because in some cases words or phrases had to be interpreted, perhaps arbitrarily. Nevertheless, a fairly trustworthy picture emerges of constancies and variations during these two decades. Of the one hundred thirteen definitions here considered, thirty-three fall into the first decade and eighty into the second. In both groups the attribution of culture to a group or social group is the single element most often given explicit mention. However, it occurs in about two-thirds of the earlier definitions and in only about half of the more recent ones. The historical dimension drops from second place in the rank order to tenth, appearing in less than a fifth of the definitions of the last decade. Totality drops almost but not quite as sharply proportionately but perhaps here much of the same notion is expressed by "system" (and other words and phrases subsumed under "patterned.") Similarly, perhaps "non-genetic" (which climbs to third place in the second list) conveys part of what was previously designated as "historical" or "traditional." The two most striking shifts are with respect to "learning" and "way or mode." The former is largely to be attributed to a contemporary intellectual fashion. If culture was considered a social heritage and non-genetically transmitted (as it was in a high proportion of the 1931-40 definitions), it clearly had to be learned. The real difference

Probably rests in the greater emphasis upon earning as a special kind of psychological process and upon individual learning. The trend toward thinking of culture as a distinctive mode of living, on the other hand, is genuinely new.

Making allowance for changes in the favorite words of intellectuals from one decade to the next, we feel that this examination indicates more constancy than variation in the central notions attaching to the concept of culture. There are interesting differences in emphasis and shading, but the conceptual core has altered significantly only in the direction of stressing the "style of life" or "over-all pattern" idea.

Number of Elements Entering Into Single Definitions

In another conceptual respect, however, there appears a real trend — namely, toward creating more sophisticated definitions that include a larger number of criteria.

	1931-1940	1941-1950
Based on one criterion [1]	2	3
Based on two criteria	9	4
Based on three criteria	12	22
Based on four criteria	7	27
Based on five criteria	3	16
Based on six criteria	–	6
Based on more than six criteria	–	2

Final Comments on Definitions

Society being presupposed by culture, it is not surprising that reference to the group appears in so many of our definitions of culture. Sometimes the reference is to human society generally, or "the social;" more often, to a society or group or community or segment within the human species; sometimes the members of the society or the fact of "sharing" are emphasized.

Fairly frequent explicit reference to human culture — or for that matter the culture of any one society — as constituting a sum or whole or total, in distinction from particular customs, ways, patterns, ideas, or such, is probably also expectable. It may have been reenforced by realization of the variably composite origin of the content of most or all cultures.

Custom is most frequently mentioned in the broad type of definition — weighted for inclusiveness rather than sharpness — that originated with Tylor and was continued by Boas and Dixon. However, the concept is retained also in a series of recent definitions by students under specific psychological influencing: Linton, Dollard, Gillin, Thomas, LaPiere.

The use of the word pattern was almost certainly furthered by the title of Benedict's famous book of 1934. At the same time, pattern is conceptually not very far from way, just as this overlaps with custom. Part of the recent drift toward pattern thus appears to be linguistic fashion. However, the connotation of selectivity seems to be sharper in the term pattern. And the idea of selection becomes explicit in various recent definitions. "Selectivity" and "a distinctive way of life" are obviously very close. "A selective orientation toward experience characteristic of a group" would almost serve as a definition of culture.

A historically accumulating social heritage transmitted from the past by tradition is mentioned in thirty-three cases. None of the group-A definitions, those in the Tylor tradition, are here included: it is evident that they view culture as a momentary dynamic cross-section rather than as something perpetually moving in time. There are also no "product" definitions of class F-1 formally represented in the heritage group. Terms like products, creation, formation, precipitate are ambiguous as between preponderance of dynamic or historic connotation.

Traditional heritage roots in custom and way, bat with more or less implication or sometimes consciousness of the mechanism of transmission and acquisition. When emphasis shifts from the long-range process and from its result in culture, to a close-up view of the mechanism operative in the ultimate participating individual, the interest has become psychological and new terms appear: acquired, non-genetic, learning. These are primarily post1935, mostly post-1940, and at least in part represent specific influence of psychological thinking on anthropology and sociology.

The same may be said of the largish group of definitions which mention behavior, response, and stimulus. These were probably touched off by Linton's, Mead's, and Thomas' statements of 1936 and 1937. One of the few previous mentions of behavior is by Wallis in 1930, in his lengthy, piecemeal adumbration of a definition, and there it is by no means emphasized. Wallis also uses reactions, along with Boas, 1930; and Dixon, 1928, activities. These three seem to antedate formal psychological influencing.

Even Linton, Mead, and Thomas, who certainly were psychology-conscious by 193637, qualify behavior, when they mention it, so that its emphasis seems subsidiary and incidental, compared with that of the remainder of the phrase. Their wordings are, respectively, "pattern of habitual behavior;" "complex of traditional behavior;" "values...[i.e.] institutions, customs, attitudes, behavior."

Whether behavior is to be included in culture remains a matter of dispute. The behavior in question is of course the concrete behavior of individual human beings, not any collective abstraction. The two present authors incline strongly to exclude behavior as such from culture. This is on two grounds. First, there also is human behavior not determined by culture, so that behavior as such cannot be used as a differentiating criterion of culture. Second, culture being basically a form or pattern or design or way, it is an abstraction from concrete human behavior, but is not itself behavior. Behavior is of course a pre-condition of culture; just as the locus or residence of culture can only be in the human individuals from whose behavior it is inferred or formulated. It seems to us that the inclusion of behavior in culture is due to confusion between what is a pre-condition of culture and what constitutes culture. Since behavior is the first-hand and outright material of the science of psychology, and culture is not — being of concern only secondarily, as an influence on this material — it is natural that psychologists and psychologizing sociologists should see behavior as primary in their own field, and then extend this view farther to apply to the field of culture also. Linton seems to be the only anthropologist who has made culture consist of responses and behavior (C-I-9, 1945a); and this he did in a work written in an explicit context of psychology, whereas in another essay of the same year (C-I-8, 1945b) he sees culture as a way of life, a collection of ideas and habits. As a matter of fact, Linton wavers somewhat even in his psychological book. The core of his briefer statement there is that culture is "organized repetitive responses;" the core of his longer formulation is that culture is "the configuration of learned behavior." Since a configuration is a pattern or form or design or way, the emphasis here is really no longer on the behavior but on a form abstracted from it. [10]

Bidney, whose specialty is the application of philosophical method to anthropology, has culture (C-II-3) consist both of acquired or cultivated behavior and of ideals (or patterns of ideals). This seemingly paradoxical combination rests upon the assumption of a polarity which leaves room for creativity and expression - Bidney is an avowed humanist - and is meant to allow the reconciliation of materialistic and idealistic interpretations of culture. Sidney's argument in reiterated support of this position must be read in the originals to do him justice. We content ourselves with pointing out the uniqueness of his view. No one among anthropologists has shared it; in fact they seem to have sheered off from "ideals" up to date, though "values" are increasingly mentioned.

The degree to which even lip-service to values has been avoided until recently, especially by anthropologists, [11] is striking. Thomas explicitly read values into social study in the *Polish Peasant* thirty years ago. The hesitation of anthropologists can perhaps be laid to the natural history tradition which persists in out science for both better and worse. The present writers are both convinced that the study of culture must include the explicit and systematic study of values and value-systems viewed as observable, describable, and comparable phenomena of nature.

The remaining conceptual elements which we have encountered occur rather scatteringly in the definitions: adjustment; efforts, problems, and purpose; artifacts and material products; even environment. None of these appears to have forged completely into common consensus among scientists as an essential ingredient or property of culture. The same is true of symbols (mediation, understanding, communication).

All in all, it is clear that anthropologists have been concrete rather than theoretical minded about culture. Their definitions of it have tended either to be descriptively and enumeratively inclusive like Tylor's original one; or to hug the original concept of custom or near-derivatives of it like ways or products. Although more occupied than sociologists with the past and with changes in time, they have mostly not stressed seriously the influence of the past on culture or its accumulative character — formally perhaps less so than the sociologists. Heritage and tradition, it is true, do involve the past; but their focus is on the reception by the present, not on the perduring influence of the past as such. At two important points the sociologists have in general anticipated the anthropologists: recognition of values as an essential element, and of the crucial role of symbolism. Learning, responses. and behavior have come into the consideration of culture through direct or indirect influencing from psychology. Of these, learning, which extends to cultureless animals, is obviously too undifferentiated a process to serve as a diagnostic criterion for culture; and behavior seems rather — as we have also already said — to be that within whose mass culture exists and from which it is conceptually extricated or abstracted.

The proportion of definitions of culture by non-anthropologists in the pre-1930 period is striking. This is partly a reflection of the relative lack of interest of anthropologists in theory, partly a result of the enormous influence of Tylor's definition. This is not altogether remarkable when one considers how much Tylor packed into his definition. Take, for example, the phrase "acquired by man as a member of society." This, in effect, links heritage, learning, and society. It also implies that culture is impossible without the biologically inherited potentialities of a particular kind or mammal.

We do not propose to add a one hundred and sixty-fifth formal definition. Our monograph is a critical review of definitions and a general discussion of culture theory. We think it is premature to attempt encapsulation in a brief abstract statement which would include or imply all of the elements that seem to us to be involved. Enumerative definitions are objectionable because never complete. Without pretending to "define," however, we think it proper to say at the end of this summary discussion of definitions that we believe each of our principal groups of definitions points to something legitimate and important. In other words, we think culture is a product; is historical; includes ideas, patterns, and values; is selective; is learned; is based upon symbols; and is an abstraction from behavior and the products of behavior.

This catalogue does not, of course, exhaust the meaningful and valid propositions which can be uttered about culture. Lest silence on our part at this point be misinterpreted, it is perhaps as well to restate here some few central generalizations already made by us or quoted from others.

All cultures are largely made up of overt, patterned ways of behaving, feeling, and reacting. But cultures likewise include a characteristic set of unstated premises and categories ("implicit culture") which vary greatly between societies. Thus one group unconsciously and habitually assumes that every chain of actions has a goal and that when this goal is reached tension will be reduced or disappear. To another group, thinking based upon this assumption is by no means automatic. They see life not primarily as a series of purposive sequences but more as made up of disparate experiences which may be satisfying in and of themselves, rather than as means to ends.

Culture not only markedly influences how individuals behave toward other individuals but equally what is expected from them. Any culture is a system of expectancies: what kinds of behavior the individual anticipates being rewarded or punished for; what constitute rewards and punishments; what types of activity are held to be inherently gratifying or frustrating. For this and for other reasons (e.g., the strongly affective nature of most cultural learning) the individual is seldom emotionally neutral to those sectors of his culture which touch him directly. Culture patterns are *felt,* emotionally adhered to or rejected.

As Harris has recently remarked, "the 'whole' culture is a composite of varying and overlapping subcultures." [12] Sub-cultures may be regional, economic, status, occupational, clique groups — or varying combinations of these factors. Some sub-cultures seem to be primarily traceable to the temperamental similarities of the participating individuals. Each individual selects from and to greater or lesser degree systematizes what he experiences of the total culture in the course of his formal and informal education throughout life:

Sapir speaks of "the world of meanings which each one of these individuals may unconsciously abstract for himself from his participation in these interactions."...In some cases, as in social organization or linguistic usage and vocabulary, the individual carries out only a part of the socially observed pattern..., and we cannot say that his selection of behavior is the same as the social pattern. In other cases, as in grammatical structure, the individual's behavior is virtually the same as that which is described for the society as a whole...Sapir shows how the speaker of a particular language uses the particular pattern of that language no matter what he is saying...the social pattern (i.e., the behavior of the other individuals in society) provides experience and a model which is available to each individual when he acts. Just how he will use this model depends on his history and situation: often enough he will simply imitate it, but not always. [13]

Statements about Culture

Our quoted Statements about culture in Part III are longer but fewer than the Definitions of Part II. We did include every definition we found, including even some incomplete ones. That is why they increased geometrically through recent decades: more were attempted with growing conceptual recognition of culture. Of "statements," however, we included only the more significant or interesting or historically relevant ones. Their number could easily have been doubled or trebled. On the whole the six groups or classes into which we have divided the statements show about the same incidence in time. Only the relation of culture to language (group *e*) was discussed at these separate periods: 1911-12; 1924-29; 1945-50; but different problems were being argued in these three periods.

When all returns were in, we discovered that the three of our cited statements which antedate 1920 were all made by anthropologists who were admitted leaders of the profession: Boas, Sapir, Wissler.

Throughout, anthropologists constitute somewhat over half of those cited.

[1] Part Three-*f*-5.
[2] While Tylor long failed to influence the humanists and dictionary makers (Part One. 13, 14) with his definition and use of the word culture, he did quickly influence some of the men who were shaping anthropology. General A. Lane-Fox Pitt-Rivers in two papers read in 1874 and 1875 uses the term freely, wholly with Tylor's meaning, and without defining it, that is, as if its sense were known to his audiences. See "Principles of Classification," pp. 1, 2, 3 and "On the Evolution of Culture" pp. 21, 23, 24 (3 times), 26 (twice), 31 (twice), 44; these page references being to the 1906 reprint by the Clarendon Press, Oxford, under the title: *The Evolution of Culture and other Essays,* edited by J. L. Myres (in which the places of original publication are cited).

[3] White's general theory of culture has been discussed at length by one of us a few years ago (Kroeber, 1948b). With minor reservations the other author of the present monograph is in complete agreement with this critique.

[3a] See also Znaniecki, 1952, which appeared while the present monograph was in galley proof.

[4] For a more extended discussion of "levels," see Kroeber, 1949.

[4a] Actually, if additional definitions in Part Three, in footnotes, and in quotations throughout the monograph are counted, there are probably close to three hundred "definitions" in these pages. However, sampling indicates that the main conclusions we draw from the one hundred and sixty-four would not be substantially altered if we had retabulated to include every possible "definition."

[5] An additional definition of this type, discovered too late to include in Part II, is by the classical scholar and student of comparative religion. H. J. Rose. It is only a year later than Wissler: "Throughout, the word 'culture' is used in the sense of German Kultur, which it translates. That is, it signifies any way of life distinctively human, however far from civilization or refinement." (Translator's preface to Schmidt, 1930, p. ix).

[6] It does occur in Winston, 1933 (F-I-4).

[7] Excludes Residual Category and Incomplete Definitions (both those in G and a few in the earlier sections which were obviously not intended by their authors as full definitions).

[8] A finer but more complicated analysis can be based upon tabulating the actual words used (as listed in Index B of Part II).

[9] The criteria included here go beyond the thirteen in the two previous lists. They take account of such additional elements as "symbols," "habits," and the like. An enumeration is counted as one element, but, in addition, such elements as "ideas" and "values" are counted separately.

[10] Harris (1951: 314) has put it well: "What the anthropologist constructs are cultural patterns. Wh.it members of the society observe, or impose upon others, are culturally patterned behaviors." Lasswell (1935: 136) hinted at much the same idea in saying: "When an act conforms to culture it is conduct; otherwise it is behavior."

[11] As far back as 1921 the sociologists Park and Burgess (II-B-1) emphasized the social meaning component of the social heritage, but anthropologists have been as backward in recognizing meaning (other than for traits) as they have been slow to admit values.

[12] Harris, 1951, p. 323.

[13] Harris, 1951, pp. 316, 320.

B: General Features of Culture

As the statements quoted have been dis. cussed in some detail in the Comments on the six groups, it seems unnecessary to re-review these Comments further here.

It does remain to us, however, to discuss systematically, if briefly, certain general features or broad aspects of culture which have entered to only a limited degree or indirectly into the Definitions and the Statements we have assembled. These aspects of culture may be conveniently grouped under the headings Integration, Historicity, Uniformity, Causality, Significance and Values, and Relativism.

Integration

As of 1951, there seems to be general agreement that every culture possesses a considerable degree of integration of both its content and its forms, more or less parallel to the tendency toward solidarity possessed by societies; but that the integration is never perfect or complete, Malinowski and the functionalists having overstated the case, as well as Spengler and Benedict with their selected examples. Institutions can certainly clash as well as the interests of individuals. In any given situation, the proper question is not. Is integration perfect? But, what integration is there?

It is also plain that while a bro.id, synthetic interpretation is almost always more satisfactory than an endlessly atomistic one, a validly broad interpretation can be built up only from a mass of precise knowledge minutely analyzed. Nor does it follow that it has been only unimaginative "museum moles" and poor stay-at-homes debarred from contact with strange living; cultures who have done "atomistic" work. Very little reliable culture history would ever have been reconstructed without the willingness to take the pains to master detail with precision. This is no different from functionally integrative studies: both approaches have validity in proportion as they are substantiated with accurate evidence. That some intellects and temperaments find one approach more congenial than the other, means merely that interests are differently weighted. A significant historical interpretation is just as synthesizing as a functional interpretation. The principal difference is that the historical interpretation uses one additional dimension of reference, the dynamic dimension of time. Two synchronous, connected activities in one culture, or two successive, altered forms of the same activity in one culture a generation or century apart, both possess interrelation or integration with each other. The particular significance of the relations may be different; but it would be erroneous to suppose that the degree of connection was intrinsically greater in one case than in the other.

Historicity

This brings us to the question of how far anthropology or the study of culture is, should be, or must be historical or non-historical. There is general agreement that every culture is a precipitate of history. In more than one sense "history is a sieve,"

In the early "classical" days' of anthropology, beginning with Bachofen, Morgan, Tylor, Maine, and their contemporaries, the question did not arise, because their "evolutionistic" philosophies of developmental stages, essentially deductive and speculative however much buttressed by selected evidence, posed as being historical or at least as surrogate-historical in realms on which documentary historical evidence was lacking.

In the eighteen-eighties and nineties there began two reactions against this school: by Ratzel and by Boas. Ratzel was and remained a geographer sufficiently entangled in environmental determinism that he never got wholly mobilized for systematic historical aims. Boas also began as a geographer (after training in physics) but passed rapidly over into ethnology, becoming an anti-environmentalist, and insisted on full respect being given historical context. In fact, he insisted that his approach was historical. It certainly was anti-speculative; but a certain "bashfulness," as Ackerknecht recently has aptly called it in a paper before the New York Academy of Sciences, prevented Boas from undertaking historical formulations of serious scope.

A third effort in the direction of historical interpretation of culture occurred around the turn of the century in Germany. It seems to have been first presented in 1898 by Frobenius, who however was unstable as a theoretician and vacillated between historical, organicist, and mystic positions. Graebner, Foy, and Ankermann m 1904 developed Frobenius's suggestions into the Culture-sphere principle; which assumed a half-dozen separate original cultures, each with its characteristic inventory of distinctive traits, and whose persistences, spreads, and minglings might still be unraveled by dissection of surviving cultures. After initial criticism. Father Schmidt adopted this scheme and carried it farther under the name of "the" Culture-historical .Method. The method was indeed historical in so far as it reconstructed the past, but it was also schematic, and therewith anti-historical, in that the factors into which the early history of culture was resolved were selected arbitrarily or dogmatically, and received their validation only secondarily during the resolution. By about 191 5, repercussions of this German-Austrian movement had reached Britain and resulted in the formulation of a simplified one-factor version by Rivers, Elliott Smith, and Perry: the "Heliolithic" theory of transport by treasure-seeking Phoenicians of higher culture as first developed in Egypt.

The excesses of these currents gave vigor, soon after 1920, to the anti-historical positions of Malinowski and Radcliffe-Brown, which, for a while at least, were almost equally extreme. Actually, the two had little in common, as Radcliffe-Brown subsequently pointed out, besides an anti-historical slant and the attributed name of "functionalism." Malinowski was holistically interested in culture, Radcliffe-Brown in social structure. The latter's approach aimed to be and was comparative; Malinowski compared very little, but tended to proceed directly from the functional exposition of one culture to formulation of the principles of all culture. The result was a Malinowskian theory of culture in many ways parallel to standard "economic theory" — a set of permanent, autonomous principles whose acceptance tended to make observed historical change seem superficial and unimportant in comparison.

It was in reaction partly to this functionalist view, and partly to Boas's combination of professed historical method with skepticism of specific historical interpretations, that Kroeber, about 1930, began to argue that cultural phenomena were on the whole more amenable to historical than to strictly scientific treatment. This position has also been long maintained by Radin, and with reference to "social anthropology" was reaffirmed by Evans-Pritchard in 1950.

Kroeber's view rests upon Windelband's distinction of science, in the strict sense of the word, as being generalizing or nomothetic, but of history as particularizing or idiosyncratic in aim. Rickert, another Neo-Kantian, attributed this difference to the kind of phenomena dealt with, the subject matter of science being nature, whereas that of history was what it had been customary to call "Geist" but what really was culture. Nature and culture each had their appropriate intellectual treatment, he argued, respectively in scientific and in historical method. Kroeber modified the Rickert position by connecting it with the recognition of "levels" of conceptualization ("emergence") of phenomena, as already discussed, and by rejecting an all-or-none dichotomy between science and history. This gradualist view left to cultural history an identity of procedure with the admittedly historical sciences that flourish on sub-cultural levels — paleontology and phylogenetic biology, geology, and astronomy. On the other hand, the possibility of scientific uniformities or laws on the sociocultural level was also not precluded. Cultural phenomena simply were more resistive to exact generalizations than were physical ones, but also more charged with individuality and unique values. Physical science "dissolves" its data out of their phenomenality, resolves them into processes involving causality which are not attached to particular time or place. A historical approach (as distinct from conventional "History") preserves not only the time and place of occurrence of its phenomena but also their qualitative reality. It "interprets" by putting data into an ever-widening context. Such context includes time as an implicit potential, but is not primarily characterized by being temporal. In the absence of chronological evidence a historical interpretation can still develop a context of space, quality-, and meaning, and can be descriptively or "synchronically historical" — as even a professional historian of human events may pause in his narrative for the depiction of a cross-sectional moment — may indeed succeed in delineating more clearly the significant structural relations of his phenomena by now and then abstracting from their time relations.

It is an evident implication of this theory that a historical approach tends to find the aimed-at context primarily on the level of its own phenomena: the context of cultural data is a wider cultural frame, with all culture as its limit. The "scientific" approach on the contrary, aiming at process, can better hope to determine cause, which may be attainable only contingently or implicitly by historical method. The "scientific" approach has achieved this end by translevel reduction of phenomena — reduction, for instance, of cultural facts to causes resident on a social, psychological, or biological level. At any rate, the possibility of exact and valid and repeatable findings of the nature of "laws" in regard to culture is not precluded, in this epistemological theory, but is explicitly admitted. It is merely that the processes underlying phenomena of the topmost level can be of so many levels that their determination might be expected to be difficult and slow — as indeed it has actually been to date.

Accordingly there is no claim in this position that one approach is the better or more proper. The historical and the scientific methods simply are different. They point at different ends and achieve them by different means. It is merely an empirical fact that thus far more reasonably adequate and usable historic findings than systematic processual ones appear to have been made on cultural data. It is not at all certain that this condition will continue. Indeed Murdock's (1950) book on social structure and Horton's (1943) monograph on alcoholism already constitute two impressive attempts at demonstrating correlations that are more functional than historical. It is certainly more desirable to have both approaches actively cultivated than one alone.

It cannot be said that the foregoing point of view has been widely accepted by anthropologists and sociologists. It could hardly be held while the theory of levels remained generally unaccepted, and as long as the method of physics [1] continues to be regarded as the model of method for all science, the only conceded alternative being an outright approach through art toward the "aesthetic component" of the universe.

Students of human life who pride themselves on being "scientific" and upon their rigor [2] still tend, consciously or unconsciously, to hold the view of "science" set forth in Karl Pearson's famous *Grammar*. In other words, they not only take physics as their model but specifically nineteenth-century physics. Here problems of measurable incidence and intensity predominate. Such problems also have their importance in anthropology, but the most difficult and most essential questions about culture cannot be answered in these terms. As W. M. Wheeler is said to have remarked, "Form is the secretion of culture." Form is a matter of ordering, of arrangement, of emphasis. Measurement in and of itself will seldom provide a valid description of distinctive form. Exactly the same measurable entities may be present in precisely the same quantities, but if the sequences or arrangements of these entities differ, the configurations may have vastly different properties. Linguistics, which is, on the whole, the most rigorous and precise of the cultural sciences, has achieved its success much more by configurational analysis than by counting.

Experimental psychology (with the partial exception of the Gestalt variety) and various social sciences have made of statistics a main methodological instrument. A statistic founded upon the logic of probability has been and will continue to be of great use to cultural anthropology. But, again, the main unresolved problems of culture theory will never be resolved by statistical techniques precisely because cultural behavior is patterned and never randomly distributed. Mathematical help may come from matrix algebra or some form of topological mathematics. [3]

None of this argument is intended to deprecate the significance of the mathematical and quantitative dimensions in science generally and in anthropology in particular. Quite the contrary. Our point is two-fold: the specific mathematic applied must be that suited to the nature of the problem; there are places where presently available quantitative measures are essential and places where they are irrelevant and actually misleading.

Ethnographers have been rightly criticized for writing "The Hopi do (or believe) thus and so" without stating whether this generalization is based upon ten observations or a hundred or upon the statement of one informant or of ten informants representing a good range of the status positions in that society. No scientist can evade the problems of sampling, of the representativeness of his materials for the universe he has chosen to study. However, sampling has certain special aspects as far as cultural data are concerned. If an ethnographer asks ten adult middle-class Americans in ten different regions "Do men rise when ladies enter the room on a somewhat formal occasion?" and gets the same reply from all his informants, it is of no earthly use for him — so far as establishment of the normative middle-class pattern is concerned — to pull a random sample of a few thousand from the .million American men in this class.

Confusion both on the part of some anthropologists and of certain critics of anthropological work has arisen from lack of explicit clarity as to what is encompassed by culture. Some anthropologists have described cultures as if culture included *only* a group's patterns *for* living, their conceptions of how specified sorts of people ought to behave under specified conditions. Critics of Ruth Benedict, for example, have assumed that she was making generalizations as to how Zuñis in fact do behave whereas, for the most part, she is talking of their "ideals" for behavior (though she doesn't make this altogether clear). In our opinion, as we have indicated earlier, culture includes *both* modalities [4] of actual behavior and a group's conscious, partly conscious, and unconscious designs for living. More precisely, there are at least three different classes of data: (1) a people's notions of the way things ought to be; (2) their *conceptions* of the way their group actually behaves; (3) what does in fact occur, as objectively determined. The anthropologist gets the first class of data by interviewing and by observing manifestations of approval and disapproval. He gets the second class from interviewing. The third is established by observation, including photography and other mechanical means of recording. All three classes of data constitute the materials from which the anthropologist abstracts his conceptual model of the culture. [5] Culture is not a point but a complex of interrelated things.

Uniformities

Most anthropologists would agree that no constant elemental units like atoms, cells, or genes have as yet been satisfactorily established within culture in general. Many would insist that within one aspect of culture, namely language, such constant elemental units have been isolated: phonemes, [6] and morphemes. It is arguable whether such units are, in principle, discoverable in sectors of culture less automatic than speech and less closely tied (in some ways) to biological fact. We shall present both sides of this argument, for on this one point we ourselves are not in complete agreement. [7]

One of us feels that it is highly unlikely that any such constant elemental units will be discovered. Their place is on lower, more basic levels of organization of phenomena. Here and there suggestions have been ventured that there are such basic elements: the culture trait, for instance, or the small community of face-to-face relations. But no such hints have been systematically developed by their proponents, let alone accepted by others. Culture traits can obviously be divided and subdivided and re-subdivided at will, according to occasion or need. Or, for that matter, they are often combined into larger complexes which are still treatable, in *ad hoc* situations, as unitary traits, and are in fact ordinarily spoken of as traits in such situations. The face-to-face community, of course, is not actually a unit of culture but the supposed unit of *social* reference or frame for what might be called a minimal culture. At that, even such a social unit has in most cases no sharply defined actual limits.

As for the larger groups of phenomena like religion that make up "the universal pattern" — or even subdivisions of these such as "crisis rites" or "fasting" — these are recurrent indeed, but they are not uniform. Any one can make a definition that will separate magic from religion; but no one has yet found a definition that all other students accept: the phenomenal contents of the concepts of religion and magic simply intergrade too much. This is true even though almost everyone would agree in differentiating large masses of specific phenomena as respectively religious and magical — supplicating a powerful but unseen deity in the heavens, for instance, as against sticking a pin into an effigy. In short, concepts like religion and magic have an undoubted heuristic utility in given situations. But they are altogether too fluid in conceptual range for use either as strict categories or as units from which larger concepts can be built up. After all, they are in origin common-sense concepts like boy, youth, man, old man, which neither physiologists nor psychologists will wholly discard, but which they will also not attempt to include among the elementary units and basic concepts upon which they rear their sciences.

This conclusion is akin to what Boas said about social-science methodology in 1930: "The analysis of the phenomena is our prime object. Generalizations will be more significant the closer we adhere to definite forms. The attempts to reduce all social phenomena to a closed system of laws applicable to every society and explaining its structure and history do not seem a promising undertaking." [8] Significance of generalizations is proportional to definiteness of the forms and concepts analyzed out of phenomena — in this seems to reside the weakness of the uniformities in culture heretofore suggested; they are *indefinite.*

A case on the other side is put as follows by Julian Steward in his important piper: *Cultural Causality and Law: A Trial Formulation of the Development of Early Civilizations.* [9]

It is not necessary that any formulation of cultural regularities provide an ultimate explanation of culture change. In the physical and biological sciences, formulations are merely approximations of observed regularities, and they are valid as working hypotheses despite their failure to deal with ultimate realities. So long as a cultural law formulates recurrences of similar inter-relationships of phenomena, it expresses cause and effect in the same way that the law of gravity formulates but does not ultimately explain the attraction between masses of manor. Moreover, like the law of gravity, which has been greatly modified by the theory of relativity, any formulation of cultural data may be useful as a working hypothesis, even though further research requires that it be qualified or reformulated.

Cultural regularities may be formulated on different levels, each in its own terms. At present, the greatest possibilities lie in the purely cultural or superorganic level, for anthropology's traditional primary concern with culture has provided far more data of this kind. Moreover, the greater part of culture history is susceptible to treatment only in superorganic terms. Both sequential or diachronic formulations and synchronic formulations are superorganic, and they may be functional to the extent that the data permit. Redfield's tentative formulation that urban culture contrasts with folk culture in being more individualized, secularized, heterogeneous, and disorganized is synchronic superorganic, and functional. .Morgan's evolutionary schemes and White's formulation concerning the relationship of energy to cultural development are sequential and somewhat functional. Neither type, however, is wholly one or the other. A time-dimension is implied in Redfield's formulation, and synchronic, functional relationships are implied in White's....

The present statement of scientific purpose and methodology rests on a conception of culture that needs clarification. If the more important institutions of culture can be isolated from their unique setting so as to be typed, classified, and related to recurring antecedents or functional correlates, it follows that it is possible to consider the institutions in question as the basic or constant ones, whereas the features that lend uniqueness are the secondary or variable ones. For example, the American high civilizations had agriculture, social classes, and a priest-temple-idol cult. As types, these institutions are abstractions of what was actually present in each area, and they do not take into account the particular crops grown, the precise patterning of the social classes, or the conceptualization of deities, details of ritual, and other religious features of each culture center.

To amplify and generalize what Steward has said, there are admittedly few, if any absolute uniformities in culture content unless one states the content in extremely general form — e.g., clothing, shelter, incest taboos, and the like. But, after all, the content of different atoms and of different cells is by no means identical. These are constant elemental units of *form.* The same may be said for linguistic units like the phoneme. One of us suspects that there are a number, perhaps a considerable number, of categories and of structural principles found in all cultures. Fortes [10] speaks of kinship as "an irreducible principle of Tale social organization." It probably is an irreducible principle of all cultures, however much its elaboration and emphasis upon it may vary. When Fortes [11] also says that "Every social system presupposes such basic moral axioms," he is likewise pointing to a constant elemental unit of each and every culture. These considerations will later be elaborated in our discussion of Values and Relativism below. It is clear that such problems are still on the frontier of anthropological inquiry because the anthropologists of this century have only begun to face them systematically.

We cannot better close this section then by quoting an extremely thoughtful passage from Fortes: [12]

What lies behind all this? What makes kinship an irreducible principle of Tale social organization? ...We know from comparative studies that kinship bears a similar stress (though its scope is often more limited) in the social organization of peoples with far more highly differentiated social systems than that of the Tallensi.

The usual solution to this question, explicitly stated by Malinowski, Firth, and others, and implicit in the descriptive work of most social scientists who write on kinship, puts the emphasis on the facts of sex, procreation, and the rearing of offspring. There is obvious truth in this view. But like all attempts to explain one order of organic events by invoking a simpler order of events necessarily involved in the first, it borders on over-simplification. It is like trying to explain human thinking by the anatomy of the brain, or modern capitalist economy by the need for food and shelter. Such explanations, which indicate the necessary pre-conditions of phenomena, are apt to short-circuit the real work of science, which is the elucidation of the sufficient causal or functional determinants involved in the observed data of behaviour. They are particularly specious in social science. It is easy and tempting to jump from one level of organization to another in the continuum of body, mind, and society when analysis at one level seems to lead no farther. As regards primitive kinship institutions, the facts of sex, procreation, and the rearing of offspring constitute only the universal raw material of kinship systems. Our study has shown that economic techniques and religious values nave as close a connexion with the Tale lineage system, for example, as the reproductive needs of the society. Indeed, comparative and historical research leaves no doubt that radical changes in the economic organization or the religious values of a society like that of the Tallensi might rapidly undermine the lineage structure; but some form of family organization will persist and take care of the reproductive needs of the society. The postulate we have cited overlooks the fact that kinship covers a greater field of social relations than the family.

The problem we have raised cannot be solved in the context of an analytical study of one society; it requires a great deal of comparative research. We can, however, justifiably suggest an hypothesis on the basis of our limited inquiry. One of the striking things about Tale kinship institutions is the socially acknowledged sanctions behind them. When we ask why the natives so seldom, on the whole, transgress the norms of conduct attached to kinship ties, we inevitably come back either to the ancestor cult or to moral axioms regarded as self-evident by the Tallensi. To study Tale kinship institutions apart from the religious and moral ideas and values of the natives would be as one-sided as to leave out the facts of sex and procreation. On the other hand, our analysis has shown that it is equally impossible to understand Tale religious beliefs and moral norms, apart from the context of kinship. A very close functional interdependence exists between these two categories of social facts. The relevant connecting link, for our present problem, is the axiom, implicit in all Tale kinship institutions, that kinship relations are essentially moral relations, binding in their own right. Every social system presupposes such basic moral axioms. They are implicit in the categories of values and of behaviour which we sum up in concepts such as rights, dunes, justice, amity, respect, wrong, sin. Such concepts occur in every known human society, though the kind of behaviour and the content of the values covered by them vary enormously. Modern research in psychology and sociology makes it clear that these axioms are rooted in the direct experience of the inevitability of interdependence between men in society. Utter moral isolation for the individual is not only the negation of society but the negation of humanity itself.

Causality

So far as cultural phenomena are emergents, their causes would originate at depths of different level, and hence would be intricate [13] and hard to ascertain. This holds true of the forms of civilization as well as of social events — of both culture and history in the ordinary sense. There are first the factors of natural environment, both inorganic and organic, and persistent as well as catastrophic. Harder to trace are internal organic factors, the genetic or racial heredity of societies. While these causes clearly are far less important than used to be assumed, it would be dogmatic to rule them out altogether. There is also the possibility that the congenitally specific abilities of gifted individuals traceably influence the culture of the societies of which they are members. Then there are strictly social factors: the size, location, and increase rate of societies or populations considered as influences affecting their cultures. And finally there are cultural factors already existent at any given period of time that can be dealt with; that is, in our explanations of any particular cultural situation, the just enumerated non-cultural causes must always necessarily be viewed as impinging on an already existing cultural condition which must also be taken into account, though it is itself in turn the product in part of preceding conditions. Though any culture can variably be construed as being at once adaptive, selective, and accumulative, it never starts from zero, but always has a long history. The antecedent conditions enter in varying degrees, according to their nearness and other circumstances, into the state of culture being examined; but they always enter with strength.

This variety of factors acting upon culture accounts for its causality being complex and difficult. It is also why, viewed in the totality of its manifestations, culture is so variable, and why it generally impresses us as plastic and changeable. It is true that cultures have also sometimes been described as possessed of inertia. Yet this is mostly in distant perspective, when the constant innumerable minor variations are lost to view and the basic structural patterns consequently emerge more saliently.

Further, it would seem that a full and open-minded examination of what brought about any given cultural condition would regularly reveal some degree of circular causality. This is both because of the degree to which

131

antecedent conditions of culture necessarily enter into it, and because of the relations of culture and persons. It is people that produce or establish culture; but they establish it partly in perpetuation and partly in modification of a form of existing culture which has made them what they are. The more or less altered culture which they produce, in turn largely influences the content of subsequent personalities; and so on. This perpetual circularity or continued interaction was first recognized among students of culture; but in the past two or three decades, psychiatrists and psychologists also became increasingly aware of the influence of culture on personalities.

This awareness of interrelation has constituted an advance, but has also brought about some forced causalities and exaggerations, particularly by those using psychoanalytic explanations. Thus the influence of toilet and other childhood training has quite evidently been overemphasized, that a particular kind of training should have specific consequences is to be expected. But to derive the prevailing cast of whole national civilizations from such minute causes is one-sided and highly improbable. Again, it is legitimate to think that any established culture will tend to be accompanied by a modal personality type. But there is then a temptation to portray the development of individuals of this type as if it were this development that produced the particular quality of content of the culture; which is equivalent to dogmatically selecting one of two circularly interacting sets of factors as the determinative one.

Rather contrary is the habit of many anthropologists of treating cultural facts in certain situations without reference to the people producing these facts. For instance, archaeologists ascertain much of the content and patterning of cultures, and the interrelations of these cultures, without even a chance, ordinarily, of knowing anything about the people through whose actions these cultures existed, let alone their individual personalities. It is true that this deficiency constitutes a limitation of the scope of archaeological interpretation, but it certainly does not invalidate the soundness or significance of archaeological study within its scope. In the same way linguists consider their prime business to be determination of the content and patterns of languages and the growth and changes of these, mainly irrespective of the speakers either as individuals or as personality types. Culture history, again, largely dispenses with the personalities involved in its processes and events; in part because they can no longer be known, for the rest, because as particular individuals they possess only minor relevance. Similarly, ethnography can be adequately pursued as a study of the classification, interrelations, and history of cultural forms and culture-wholes as such; what it gains from the addition of personalities is chiefly fullness, texture, color, and warmth of presentation.

It is clear from these several cases that culture can be historically and scientifically investigated without introduction of personality factors. In fact, the question may fairly be raised whether ordinarily its study — as culture — does not tend to be more effective if it is abstracted from individual or personality factors, through eliminating these or holding or assuming them as constant.

It is, of course, equally legitimate to be interested in the interrelations of culture and personality. And there is no question that there is then an added appeal of "livingness of problem; and understanding thus arrived at ought to possess the greatest ultimate depth. At present, however, the well-tried and mainly impersonal methods of pure culture studies still seem more efficiently productive for the understanding of culture process than the newer efforts to penetrate deeper by dealing simultaneously with the two variables of personality and culture — each so highly variable in itself.

What the joint cultural-psychological approach can hope to do better than the pure-cultural one, is to penetrate farther into causality. This follows from the fact of the immediate causation of cultural phenomena necessarily residing in persons, as stated above. What needs to be guarded against, however, is confusion between recognition of the area in which causes must reside and determination of the specific causes of specific phenomena. It cannot be said that as yet the causal explanation of cultural phenomena in terms of either psychoanalysis or personality psychology has yielded very clear results. Some of the efforts in this direction certainly are premature and forced, and none, to date, seem to have the clear-cut definiteness of result that have come to be expected as characteristic of good archeology, culture history, and linguistics.

Finally, the question may be suggested — though the present is not the occasion to pursue it fully — whether certain personality-and-culture studies may be actuated less by desire to penetrate into culture more deeply than by impulses to get rid of culture by resolving or explaining it away. This last would be a perfectly legitimate end if it were admitted.

Let us return, however, to causality once more. In a sense we are less optimistic than was Tylor eighty years ago when he wrote:

Rudimentary as the science of culture still is, the symptoms are becoming very strong that even what seem its most spontaneous and motiveless phenomena will, nevertheless, be shown to come within the range of distinct cause and effect as certainly as the facts of mechanics. (1871, 17)

For reasons indicated above and elsewhere in this study, we do not anticipate the discovery of cultural laws that will conform to the type of those of classical mechanics, though "statistical laws" - significant statistical distributions - not only are discoverable in culture and language but have been operated with for some two decades. [14]

Nevertheless, cultural anthropologists, like all scientists, are searching for minimal causal chains in the body of phenomena they investigate. It seems likely at present that these will be reached — or at any rate first reached — by paths and methods quite different from those of the physical sciences of the nineteenth century The ceaseless feedback between culture and personality and the other complexities that have been discussed also make any route through reductionism seem a very distant one indeed.

The best hope in the foreseeable future for parsimonious description and "explanation" of cultural phenomena seems to rest in the study of cultural forms and processes as such, largely — for these purposes — abstracted from individuals and from personalities. Particularly promising is the search for common denominators or pervasive general principles in cultures of which the culture carriers are often unaware or minimally aware. Various concepts [15] (Opler's "themes"; Herskovits' "focus"; Kroeber's "configurations of culture growth"; and Kluckhohn's "implicit culture") have been developed for this kind of analysis, and a refinement and elaboration of these and similar approaches may make some aspects of the behavior of individuals in a culture reducible to generalizations that can be stated with increased economy. The test of the validity of such "least common denominators" or "highest common factors" [16] will, of course, be the extent to which they not only make the phenomena more intelligible but also make possible reasonably accurate predictions of culture change under specified conditions.

One attempts to understand, explain, or predict a system by reference to a relatively few organizing principles of that system. The study of culture is the study of regularities. After field work the anthropologist's first task is the descriptive conceptualization of certain trends toward uniformity in aspects of the behavior of the people making up a certain group (cf. III-a-16). The anthropological picture of the explicit culture is largely as Firth (1939, IIIa-11) has suggested "the sum total of modes [17] of behavior." Now, however, anthropologists are trying to go deeper, to reduce the wide range of regularities in a culture to a relatively few "premises," "categories," and "thematic principles" of the inferred or implicit culture. [18] So far as fundamental postulates about structure are concerned, this approach resembles what factor analysts are trying to do. The methods, of course, are very different.

A model for the conceptually significant in these methods is subjected in the following excerpts from Jakobson and Lotz:

Where nature presents nothing but an indefinite number of contingent varieties, the intervention of culture extracts pairs of opposite terms. The gross sound matter knows no oppositions. It is the human thought, conscious or unconscious, which draws from it the binary oppositions. It abstracts them by eliminating the rest....A.s music lays upon sound under a graduated scale, similarly language lays upon it the dichotomal scale which is simply a corollary of the purely differential role played by phonemic entities...a strictly linguistic *analysis* which must specify all the underlying oppositions and their interrelations...Only in resolving the phonemes into their constituents and in identifying the ultimate entities (obtained, phonemics arrives at its basic concept...and thereby definitely breaks with the extrinsic picture of speech vividly summarized by L. Bloomfield: a *continuum* which can be viewed as consisting of any desired, and, through still finer analysis, infinitely increasing number of successive parts (Jakobson, 1949, 210, 211, 212)

Our basic assumption is that every language operates with a strictly limited number of underlying ultimate distinctions which form a set of binary oppositions. (Jakobson and Lotz, 1949, 151).

The fundamental oppositions in culture generally may turn out to be ternary or quaternary. Jakobson has indicated that language, though constructed around simple dichotomic oppositions, involves both an axis of successiveness and an axis of simultaneity which cuts its hierarchical structure even up to symbols. Certainly the analyses of Jakobson and Lotz involve complex multi-dimensional interrelationships. The resemblance of their graphic representations of French phonemic structure to similar drawings of the arrangements of atoms in organic molecules is striking.

The work of Jakobson and Lotz concerns only one aspect of culture, language. At present only the data of linguistics and of social organization are formulated with sufficient precision to permit of rigorous dissolution of elements into their constituent bundles of distinctive features. But there is abundant presumptive evidence that cultural categories are not a congeries; that there are principles which cut across. Aspects of given events are often clearly meaningful in various realms of culture: "economic," "social," "religious," and the like. The difficult thing is to work out a systematic way of making transformations between categories.

This direction is "so new — at least in its contemporary dress — and so basic to the anthropological attack upon cultural "causation" that the discussion must be extended a little. The prime search is, of course, for interrelationships between the patterned forms of the explicit and implicit culture.

The problem of pattern is the problem of symmetry, of constancies of form irrespective of wide variations in concrete details of actualization. So far as biological and physical possibilities are concerned, a given act can be carried out, an idea stated, or a specific artifact made in a number of different ways. However, in all societies the same mode of disposing; of many situations is repeated over and over. There is, as it were, an inhibition alike of the randomness of trial and error behavior, of the undifferentiated character of instinctive behavior, and of responses that are merely functional. A determinate organization prevails.

By patterning in its most general sense we mean the relation of units in a determinate system, interrelation of parts as dominated by the general character of wholes. Patterning means that, given certain points of reference, there are standards of selective awareness, of sequence, of emphasis. As the physical anthropologist H. L. Shapiro has remarked:

It is perhaps open to debate whether the variations should be regarded as deviations from a pattern, or the sequence be reversed and the pattern derived from the distribution of the variates. But by whichever end one grasps this apparent duality, the inevitable association of a central tendency with the deviations from it constitutes a fixed attribute of organic life. Indeed, in a highly generalized sense, the exposition of the central tendency and the understanding of individual variation furnish the several biological, and possibly all the natural sciences, with their basic problem. So pervasive is the phenomenon. it is difficult to conjure up any aspect of biological research that cannot ultimately be resolved into these fundamental terms.

The forms of the explicit culture are themselves patterned, as Sapir has said, "into a complex configuration of evaluations, inclusive and exclusive implications, priorities, and potentialities of realization" which cannot be understood solely from the descriptions given by even the most articulate of culture carriers. To use another analogy from music: the melodies (i.e., the patterns of the explicit culture) are rather easily heard by any listener, but it takes a more technical analysis to discover the key or mode in which a melody is written.

The forms of the explicit culture may be [18a] compared to the observable plan of a building. As Robert Lynd has said: "The significance of structure for a culture may be suggested by the analogy of a Gothic cathedral, in which each part contributes thrusts and weights relevant not only to itself alone but to the whole." Patterns are the framework, the girders of a culture. The forms of the implicit culture are more nearly analogous to the architect's conception of the total over-all effects he wishes to achieve. Different forms can be made from the same elements. It is as if one looks at a series of chairs which have identical proportions but which are of varying sizes, built of a dozen different kinds of wood, with minor ornamentations of distinct kinds. One sees the differences but recognizes a common element. Similarly, one may find in two individuals almost the same personality traits. Yet each has his own life style which differentiates the constellation of traits. So, also, a culture cannot be fully understood from the most complete description of its explicit surface. The organization of each culture has the same kind of uniqueness one finds in the organization of each personality.

Even a culture trait is an abstraction. A trait is an "ideal type" because no two pots are identical nor are two marriage ceremonies ever held in precisely the same way. But when we turn to those unconscious (i.e., unverbalized) predispositions toward the definition of the situation which members of a certain social tradition characteristically exhibit, we have to deal with second-order or analytical abstractions. The patterns of the implicit culture are not inductive generalizing abstractions but purely inferential constructs. They are *thematic principles* which the investigator introduces to explain connections among a wide range of culture content and form that are not obvious in the world of direct observation. The forms of the implicit culture start, of course, from a consideration of data and they must be validated by a return to the data, but they unquestionably rest upon systematic extrapolation. When describing implicit culture the anthropologist cannot hope to become a relatively objective, relatively passive instrument. His role is more active; he necessarily puts something into the data. Whereas the trustworthiness of an anthropologist's portrayal of explicit culture depends upon his receptivity, his completeness, and his detachment and upon the skill and care with which he makes his inductive generalizations, the validity of his conceptual model of the implicit culture stands or falls with the balance achieved between sensitivity of scientific imagination and comparative freedom from preconception.

Normative and behavioral patterns are specifically oriented. The forms of the implicit culture have a more generalized application but they are, to use Benedict's phrase, "unconscious canons of choice." The implicit culture consists in those cultural themes of which there is characteristically no sustained and systematic awareness [19] on the part of most members of a group.

The distinction between explicit and implicit culture is that of polar concepts, not of the all-or-none type. Reality, and not least cultural reality, appears to be a continuum rather than a set of neat, water-tight compartments. But we can seldom cope with the continuum as a whole, and the isolation and naming of certain contrastive sections of the continuum is highly useful. It follows, however, that the theoretical structure does not collapse with the production of doubtful or transitional cases. In a highly self-conscious culture like the American which makes a business of studying itself, the proportion of the culture which is literally implicit in the sense of never having been overtly stated by any member of the society may be small. Yet only a trifling percentage of Americans could state even those implicit premises of our culture which have been abstracted out by social scientists. In the case of the less self-conscious societies the unconscious assumptions bulk large. They are what Whorf has called "background phenomena." What he says of language applies to many other aspects of culture: "...our psychic make-up is somehow adjusted to disregard whole realms of phenomena that are so all-pervasive as to seem irrelevant to our daily lives and needs...the phenomena of a language are to its own speakers largely...outside the critical consciousness and control of the speaker...." This same point of view is often expressed by historians and others when they say: "The really important thing to know about a society is what it takes for granted." These "background phenomena" are of extraordinary importance in human action. Human behavior cannot be understood in terms of the organism-environment model unless this be made more complex. No socialized human being views his experience freshly. His very perceptions are screened and distorted by what he has consciously and unconsciously absorbed from his culture. Between the stimulus and the response there is always interposed an intervening variable, unseen but powerful. This consists in the person's total apperceptive mass which is made up. in large part of the more generalized cultural forms. [20]

Let us take an example. If one asks a Navaho Indian about witchcraft, experience shows that more than seventy per cent will give almost identical verbal responses. The replies will vary only in this fashion: "Who told you to talk to me about witchcraft?" "Who said that I knew anything about witchcraft?" "Why do you come to me to ask about this — who told you I knew about it?" Here one has a behavioral pattern of the explicit culture, for the structure consists in a determinate inter-digitation of linguistic symbols as a response to a verbal (and situational) stimulus.

Suppose, however, that we juxtapose this and other behavioral patterns which have no intrinsic interconnection. Unacculturated Navaho are uniformly careful to hide their faeces and to see to it that no other person obtains possession of their hair, nails, spit, or any other bodily part or product. They are likewise characteristically secretive about their personal names. All three of these patterns (as well as many others which might be mentioned) are manifestations of a *cultural enthymeme* (tacit premise) which may be intellectualized as "fear of the malevolent activities of other persons." Only most exceptionally would a Navaho make this abstract generalization, saying, in effect, "These are all ways of showing our anxiety about the activities of others." Nevertheless, this principle does order all sorts of concrete Navaho behavior and, although implicit, is as much a part of Navaho culture as the explicit acts and verbal symbols. It is the highest common factor in diverse explicit forms and contents. It is a principle which underlies the structure of the explicit culture, which "accounts for" a number of distinct factors. It is neither a generalization of aspects of behavior (behavioral pattern) nor of forms for behavior (normative pattern) — it is a generalization *from* behavior. It looks to an inner coherence in terms of structuralizing principles that are taken for granted by participants in this culture as prevailing in the world. Patterns are forms — the implicit culture consists in interrelationships between forms, that is, of qualities which can be predicated only of two or more forms taken together.

Just as the forms of the explicit culture are configurated in accord with the unconscious system of meanings abstracted by the anthropologist as cultural enthymemes, so the enthymemes may bear a relation to an oversummative principle. Every culture is a structure — not just a haphazard collection of all the different physically possible and functionally effective patterns of belief and action but an interdependent *system* with its forms segregated and arranged in a manner which is *felt* as appropriate. As Ruth Benedict has said, "Order is due to the circumstance that in these societies a principle has been set up according to which the assembled cultural mate-

135

rial is made over into consistent patterns in accordance with certain inner necessities that have developed with the group." This broadest kind of integrating principle in culture has often been referred to as *ethos*. Anthropologists are hardly ready as yet to deal with the ethos of a culture except by means of artistic insight. The work of Benedict and others is suggestive but raises many new problems beside those of rigor and standardized procedures. As Gurvitch [21] has said: "Une des caractéristiques essentielles des symbôles est qu'ils révèlent en voilant, et qu'ils voilent en révèlant."

Significance and Values [22]

We come now to those properties of culture which seem most distinctive of it and most important: its significance and its values. Perhaps we should have said "significance or values," for the two are difficult to keep separated and perhaps constitute no more than somewhat different aspects of the same thing.

First of all, significance does not mean merely ends. It is not teleological in the traditional sense. Significance and values are of the essence of the organization of culture. It is true that human endeavor is directed toward ends; but those ends are shaped by the values of culture; and the values are felt as intrinsic, not as means. And the values are variable and relative, not predetermined and eternal, though certain universals of human biology and of human social life appear to have brought about a few constants or near-constants that cut across cultural differences. Also the values are part of nature, not outside it. They are the

Products of men, of men having bodies and ving in societies, and are the structural essence of the culture of these societies of men. Finally, values and significances are "intangibles'' which are "subjective" in that they can)e internally experienced, but are also objective in their expressions, embodiments, or results.

Psychology deals with individual minds, and most values are the products of social living, become part of cultures, and are transmitted along with the rest of culture. It is true that each new or changed value takes its concrete origin (as do all aspects of culture) in the psychological processes of some particular individual. It is also true that each individual holds his own idiosyncratic form of the various cultural values he has internalized. Such matters are proper subjects of investigation for the psychologist, but values in general have a predominantly historical and sociocultural dimension. Psychology deals mainly with processes or mechanisms, and values are mental content. The processes by which individuals acquire, reject, or modify values are questions for psychological enquiry — or for collaboration between psychologists and anthropologists or sociologists. The main trend, however, is evidenced by the fact that social psychology, that bridge between psychology and sociology, recognizes a correspondence between values and attitudes, but has for the most part concerned itself, as social psychology, only with the attitudes and has abstracted from the values; much as individual psychology investigates the process of learning but not knowledge, that which is learned.

Values are primarily social and cultural: social in scope, parts of culture in substance and form. There are individual variants of cultural values and also certain highly personal goals and standards developed in the vicissitudes of private experience and reinforced by rewards in using them. But these latter are not ordinarily called values, and they must in any case be discriminated from collective values. Or, the place of a value in the lives of some persons may be quite different from that in the cultural scheme. Thus day-dreaming or autoerotic practices may come to acquire high value for an individual while being ignored, ridiculed, or condemned socioculturally. These statements must not be construed as implying that values have a substantive existence outside of individual minds, or that a collective mind containing them has any such substantive existence. The locus or place of residence of values or anything else cultural is in individual persons and nowhere else. But a value becomes a group value, as a habit becomes a custom or individuals a society, only with collective participation.

This collective quality of values accounts for their frequent anonymity, their seeming the spontaneous result of mass movement, as in morals, fashion responses, speech. Though the very first inception of any value or new part thereof must take place in an individual mind, nevertheless this attachment is mostly lost very quickly as socialization gets under way, and in many values has been long since forgotten. The strength of the value is, however, not impaired by this forgetting, but rather increased. The collectivization may also tend to decrease overt, explicit awareness of the value itself. It maintains its hold and strength, but covertly, as an implicit a priori, as a non-rational folkway, as a "configuration" rather than a "pattern" in Kluckhohn's 1941 distinction. [23] This means in turn that functioning with relation to the value or standard becomes automatic, as in correct speech; or compulsive as in manners and fashion; or endowed with high-potential emotional charge as often in morals and religion; in any event, not fully conscious and not fully rational or self-interested.

136

Values are important in that they provide foci for patterns of organization for the material of cultures. They give significance to our understanding of cultures. In fact values provide the only basis for the fully intelligible comprehension of culture, because the actual organization of all cultures is primarily in terms of their values. This becomes apparent as soon as one attempts to present the picture of a culture without reference to its values. The account becomes an unstructured, meaningless assemblage of items having relation to one another only through coexistence in locality and moment — an assemblage that might as profitably be arranged alphabetically as in any other order; a mere laundry list.

Equally revealing of the significance of values is an attempt to present the description of one culture through the medium or the value patterns of another. In such a presentation, the two cultures will of course come out alike in structure. But since some of the content of the culture being described will not fit the model of the other culture, it will either have to be omitted from the description, or it will stultify this model by not fitting it, or it will be distorted in order to make it seem to fit. This is exactly what happened while newly discovered languages were being described in terms of Latin grammar.

For the same reason one need not take too seriously the criticism sometimes made of ethnographers that they do not sufficiently distinguish the ideal culture from the actual culture of a society: that they should specify what exists only ideally, at all points specify the numbers of their witnesses, the personalities of their informants, and so on. These rules of technical procedure are sound enough, but they lose sight of the main issue, which is not validation of detail but sound conception of basic structure. This basic structure, and with it the significant functioning, are much more nearly given by the so-called ideal culture than by the actual one. This actual culture can indeed be so over-documented that the values and patterns are buried. It might even be said without undue exaggeration that — adequate information being assumed as available — the description of the ideal culture has more significance than the actual, if a choice has to be made. If the picture of the ideal culture is materially unsound or concocted, it will automatically raise doubts. But if the picture of the actual culture makes no point or meaning, it may be hard to inject more meaning from the statistical or personalized data available. In short, the "ideal" version of a culture is what gives orientation to the "actual" version.

Another way of saying this is that in the collection of information on a culture, the inquirer must proceed with empathy in order to perceive the cardinal values as points of crystallization. Of course this does not mean that inquiry should begin and end with empathy. Evidence and analysis of evidence are indispensable. But the very selection of evidence that will be significant is dependent on insight exercised during the process of evidence-collecting. What corresponds in whole-culture studies to the "hypothesis tested by evidence" in the experimental sciences is precisely a successful recognition of the value-laden patterns through which the culture is organized.

Values and significances are of course intangibles, viewed subjectively; but they find objective expression in observable forms of culture and their relations — or if one prefer to put it so, in patterned behavior and products of behavior.

It is this subjective side of values that led to their being long tabooed as improper for consideration by natural science. Instead, they were relegated to a special set of intellectual activities called "the humanities," included in the "spiritual science" of the Germans. Values were believed to be eternal because they were God-given, or divinely inspired, or at least discovered by that soul-part of man which partakes somewhat of divinity, as his body and other bodies and the tangibles of the world do not. A new and struggling science, as little advanced beyond physics, astronomy, anatomy, and the rudiments of physiology as Western science still was only two centuries ago, might cheerfully concede this reservation of the remote and unexplored territory of values to the philosophers and theologians and limit itself to what it could treat mechanistically. But a science of total nature cannot permanently cede anything which it can deal with by any of its procedures of analysis of phenomena and interpretation of evidence. The phenomena of culture are "as phenomenal" as those of physical or vital existence. And if it is true that values provide the organizing relations of culture, they must certainly be included in the investigation of culture.

How far values may ultimately prove to be measurable we do not know. It seems to us an idle question, as against the fact that they are, here and now, describable qualitatively, and are comparable, and their developments are traceable m some degree. Values are being dealt with, critically and analytically, not only be every sound social anthropologist, ethnographer, and archaeologist, but by the historians of the arts, of thought, of institutions, of civilization.

Anthropologists, up to this point, have probably devoted too little attention to the variability of cultural values and the existence of alternative value systems [24] within the same culture, as well the general relation of cul-

137

tural values to the individual. This regard for alternatives is necessary even in cultural studies per se because of the palimpsest nature of most cultures. As Spiro [25] has remarked:

The ideal norms that upper-middle class Americans are violating in their sexual behavior are not their norms, but the norms of their ancestors, or the norms of contemporary lower-middle class Americans.

There is a good case for the view that any complex stratified or segmented culture requires balance, counterpoint. an antagonistic equilibrium between values. Florence Kluckhohn [26] has put this argument well:

There is...too much stress — implied when not actually stated — upon the unitary character of value orientations. Variation for the same individual when he is playing different roles and variation between whole groups of persons within a single society are not adequately accounted for. More important still, the emphasis upon the unique of the variable value systems of different societies ignores the fact of the universality of human problems and the correlate fact that human societies have found for some problems approximately the same answers. Yet certainly it is only within a frame of reference which deals with universals that variation can be understood. Without this framework it is not possible to deal systematically with either the problem of similarity and difference as between the value systems of different societies or the questions of variant values within societies....

However important it is to know what is dominant in a society at a given time, we shall not go far toward the understanding of the dynamics of that society without paying careful heed to the variant orientations. That there be individuals and whole groups of individuals who live in accordance with patterns which express variant rather than the dominantly stressed orientations is, it is maintained, essential to the maintenance of the society. Variant values are therefore, not only permitted but actually required. It has been the mistake of many in the social sciences, and of many in the field of practical affairs as well, to treat all behavior and certain aspects of motivation which do not accord with the dominant values as deviant. It is urged that we cease to confuse the deviant who by his behavior calls down the sanctions of his group with the variant who is accepted and frequently required. This is especially true in a society such as ours, where beneath the surface of what has so often been called our compulsive conformity, there lies a wide range of variation.

In sum, we cannot emphasize too strongly the fact that if the essence of cultures be their patterned selectivity, the essence of this selectivity inheres in the cultural value system.

Values and Relativity

We know by experience that sincere comparison of cultures leads quickly to recognition of their "relativity." What this means is that cultures are differently weighted in their values, hence are differently structured, and differ both in part-functioning and in total functioning; and that true understanding of cultures therefore involves recognition of their particular value systems. Comparisons of cultures must not be simplistic in terms of an arbitrary or preconceived universal value system, but must be multiple, with each culture first understood in terms of its own particular value system and therefore its own idiosyncratic structure. After that, comparison can with gradually increasing reliability reveal to what degree values, significances, and qualities are common to the compared cultures, and to what degree distinctive. In proportion as common structures and qualities are discovered, the uniquenesses will mean more. And as the range of variability of differentiations becomes better known, it will add to the significance of more universal or common features — somewhat as knowledge of variability deepens significance of a statistical mean.

In attaining the recognition of the so-called relativity of culture, we have only begun to do what students of biology have achieved. The "natural classification" of animals and plants, which underlies and supplements evolutionary development, is basically relativistic. Biologists no longer group together plants by the simple but arbitrary factors of the number of their stamens and pistils, nor animals by the external property of living in sea, air, or land, but by degrees of resemblances in the totality of their structures. The relationship so established then proves usually also to correspond with the sequential developments of forms from one another. It is evident that the comparative study of cultures is aiming at something similar, a "natural history of culture"; and however imperfectly as yet, is beginning to attain it.

It will also be evident from' this parallel why so much of culture investigation has been and remains historical in the sense in which we have defined that word. "A culture described in terms of its own structure" is in itself idiographic rather than nomothetic. And if a natural classification implicitly contains an evolutionary development — that is, a history — in the case of life, there is some presupposition that the same will more or less hold for culture. We should not let the customary difference in appellations disturb us. Just as we are in culture de facto trying to work out a natural classification and a developmental history without usually calling them that, we may fairly say that the results attained in historical biology rest upon recognition of the "relativity" of organic structures.

We have already dwelt on the difficulties and slow progress made in determining the causes of cultural phenomena. An added reason for this condition will now be apparent. That is the fact that the comparison of structural patterns is in its nature directed toward what is significant in form rather than what is efficient in mechanism. This is of course even more true for cultural material, in which values are so conspicuously important, than for biological phenomena. And yet there is no reason why causation should not also be determinable in culture data, even if against greater difficulties — much as physiology flourishes successfully alongside comparative and evolutionary biology.

It is evident that as cultures are relativistically compared, both unique and common values appear, or, to speak less in extremes, values of lesser and greater frequency. Here an intellectual hazard may be predicted: an inclination to favor the commoner values as more nearly universal and therefore more "normal" or otherwise superior. This procedure may be anticipated because of the security sense promoted by refuge into absolutes or even majorities. Some attempts to escape from relativism are therefore expectable. The hazard lies in a premature plumping upon the commoner and nearer values and the forcing of these into false absolutes — a process of intellectual short-circuiting. The longer the quest for new absolute values can be postponed and the longer the analytic comparison of relative values can be prosecuted, the closer shall we come to reemerging with at least near-absolutes. There will be talk in those days, as we are beginning to hear it already, that the principle of relativism is breaking down, that its own negativism is defeating it. There have been, admittedly, extravagances and unsound vulgarizations of cultural relativity. Actually, objective relativistic differences between cultures are not breaking down but being fortified. And relativism is not a negative principle except to those who feel that the whole world has lost its values when comparison makes their own private values lose their false absoluteness. Relativism may seem i^ turn the world fluid; but so did the concepts of evolution and of relativity in physics seem to turn the world fluid when they were new. Like them, cultural and value relativism is a potent instrument of progress in deeper understanding — and not only of the world but of man in the world.

On the other hand, the inescapable fact of cultural relativism does not justify the conclusion that cultures are in all respects utterly disparate monads and hence strictly non-comparable entities. [27] If this were literally true, a comparative science of culture would be *ex hypothesi* impossible. It is, unfortunately the case that up to this point anthropology has not solved very satisfactorily the problem of describing cultures in such a way that objective comparison is possible. Most cultural monographs organize the data in terms of the categories of our own contemporary Western culture: economics, technology, social organization, and the like. Such an ordering, of course, I tears many of the facts from their own actual context and loads the analysis. The implicit assumption is that our categories are "given" by nature — an assumption contradicted most emphatically by these very investigations of different cultures. A smaller number of studies have attempted to present the information consistently in terms of the category system and whole way of thought of the culture being described. This approach obviously excludes the immediate possibility of a complete set of common terms of reference for comparison. Such a system of comparable concepts and terms remains to be worked out, and will probably be established only gradually.

In principle, however, there is a generalized framework that underlies the more apparent and striking facts of cultural relativity. All cultures constitute so many somewhat distinct answers to essentially the same questions posed by human biology and by the generalities of the human situation. These are the considerations explored by Wissler under the heading of "the universal culture pattern" and by Murdock under the rubric of "the least common denominators of cultures." Every society's patterns for living must provide approved and sanctioned ways for dealing with such universal circumstances as the existence of two sexes; the helplessness of infants; the need for satisfaction of the elementary biological requirements such as food, warmth, and sex; the presence of individuals of different ages and of differing physical and other capacities. The basic similarities in human biology the world over are vastly more massive than the variations. Equally, there are certain necessities in social life for this kind of animal regardless of where that life is carried on or in what culture. Cooperation to obtain subsistence and for other ends requires a certain minimum of reciprocal behavior, of a standard system of communication, and indeed of mutually accepted values. The facts of human biology and of human group living supply, therefore, certain invariant points of reference from which cross-cultural comparison can start without begging questions that are themselves at issue. As Wissler pointed out, the broad outlines of the ground plan of all cultures is and has to be about the same because men always and ever)' where are faced with certain una-voidable problems which arise out of the situation "given" by nature. Since most of the patterns of all cultures crystalize around the same foci, [28] there are significant respects in which each culture is not wholly isolated, self-contained, disparate but rather related to and comparable with all other cultures. [29]

Nor is the similarity between cultures, which in some ways transcends the fact of relativity, limited to the sheer forms of the universal culture pattern. There are at least some broad resemblances in content and specifi-cally in value content. Considering the exuberant variation of cultures in most respects, the circumstance that in some particulars almost identical values prevail throughout mankind is most arresting. No culture tolerates in-discriminate lying, stealing, or violence within the in-group. The essential universality of the incest taboo is well-known. No culture places a value upon suffering as an end in itself; as a means to the ends of the society (punishment, discipline, etc.), yes; as a means to the ends of the individual (purification, mystical exaltation, etc.), yes; but of and for itself, never. We know of no culture in either space or time, including the Soviet Russian, where the official ideology denies an after-life, where the fact of death is not ceremonialized. Yet the more su-perficial conception of cultural relativity would suggest that at least one culture would have adopted the simple expedient of disposing of corpses in the same way most cultures do dispose of dead animals — i.e., just throw-ing the body out far enough from habitations so that the odor is not troubling. When one first looks rather care-fully at the astonishing variety of cultural detail over the world one is tempted to conclude: human individuals have tried almost everything that is physically possible and nearly every individual habit has somewhere at some time been institutionalized in at least one culture. To a considerable degree this is a valid generalization — but not completely. In spite of loose talk (based upon an uncritical acceptance of an immature theory of cul-tural relativity) to the effect that the symptoms of mental disorder are completely relative to culture, the fact of the matter is that all cultures define as abnormal individuals who are permanently inaccessible to communica-tion or who fail to maintain some degree of control over their impulse life. Social life is impossible without communication, without some measure of order: the behavior of any "normal" individual must be predictable — within a certain range — by his fellows and interpretable by them.

To look freshly at values of the order just discussed is very difficult because they are commonplaces. And yet it is precisely because they are *common*places that they are interesting and important. Their vast theoretical significance rests in the fact that despite all the influences that predispose toward cultural variation (biological variation, difference in physical environments, and the processes of history) all of the very many different cul-tures known to us have converged upon these universals. It is perfectly true (and for certain types of enquiry important) that the value "thou shalt not kill thy fellow tribesman" is not concretely identical either in its cogni-tive or in its affective aspects for a Navaho, an Ashanti, and a Chukchee. Nevertheless the central conception is the same, and there is understanding between representatives of different cultures as to the general intent of the prohibition. A Navaho would be profoundly shocked if he were to discover that there were no sanctions against in-group murder among the Ashanti.

There is nothing supernatural or even mysterious about the existences of these universalities in culture con-tent. Human life is — and has to be — a moral life (up to a point) because it is a social life. It may safely be pre-sumed that human groups which failed to incorporate certain values into their nascent cultures or which abro-gated these values from their older tradition dissolved as societies or perished without record. Similarly, the biological sameness of the human animal (needs and potentialities) has also contributed to convergences.

The fact that a value is a universal does not, of course, make it an absolute. It is possible that changed circum-stances in the human situation may lead to the gradual disappearance of some of the present universals. How-ever, the mere existence of universals after so many millennia of culture history and in such diverse environ-ments suggests that they correspond to something extremely deep in man's nature and/or are necessary condi-tions to social life.

When one moves from the universals or virtual universals to values which merely are quite widespread, one would be on most shaky ground to infer "rightness" or "wrongness," "better" or "worse" from relative incidence. A value may have a very wide distribution in the world at a particular time just because of historical accidents such as the political and economic power of one nation at that time. Nations diffuse their culture into the areas their power reaches. Nevertheless this does not mean one must take all cultural values except universals as of necessarily equal validity. Slavery or cannibalism may have a place in certain cultures that is not evident to the ethnocentric Christian. Yet even if these culture patterns play an important part in the smooth functioning of these societies, they are still subject to a judgment which is alike moral and scientific. This judgement is not just a projection of values, local in time and space, that are associated with Western culture. Rather, it rests upon a *consensus gentium* and the best scientific evidence as to the nature of raw human nature — i.e., that human nature which all cultures mold and channel but never entirely remake. To say that certain aspects of Naziism were morally wrong [30] — is not parochial arrogance. It is — or can be — an assertion based both upon cross-cultural evidence as to the universalities in human needs, potentialities, and fulfillments and upon natural science knowledge with which the basic assumptions of any philosophy must be congruent.

Any science must be adequate to explain both the similarities and the differences in the phenomena with which it deals. Recent anthropology has focused its attention preponderantly upon the differences. They are there; they are very real and very important. Cultural relativism has been completely established and there must be no attempt to explain it away or to deprecate its importance because it is inconvenient, hard to take, hard to live with. Some values are almost purely cultural and draw their significance only from the matrix of that culture. Even the universal values have their special phrasings and emphases in accord with each distinct culture. And when a culture pattern, such as slavery, is derogated on the ground that it transgresses one of the more universal norms which in some sense and to some degree transcend cultural differences, one must still examine it not within a putatively absolutistic frame but in the light of cultural relativism.

At the same time one must never forget that cultural differences, real and important though they are, are still so many variations on themes supplied by raw human nature and by the limits and conditions of social life. In some ways culturally altered human nature is a comparatively superficial veneer. The common understandings between men of different cultures are very broad, very general, very easily obscured by language and many other observable symbols. True universals or near universals are apparently few in number. But they seem to be as deep-going as they are rare. Relativity exists only within a universal framework. Anthropology's facts attest that the phrase "a common humanity" is in no sense meaningless. This is also important.

Rapoport [31] has recently argued that objective relativism can lead to the development of truly explicit and truly universal standards in science and in values:

So it is incorrect to say that the scientific outlook is simply a by-product of a particular culture. It is rather the essence of a culture which has not yet been established — a *culture-studying* culture. Ironically, the anthropologists, who often are most emphatic in stating that no non-cultural standards of evaluation exist, are among the most active builders of this new culture-studying culture, whose standards transcend those of the cultures which anthropologists study and thus give them an opportunity to emancipate themselves from the limitations of the local standards. The anthropologist can remain the anthropologist both in New Guinea and in Middletown, in spite of the fact that he may have been born in Middletown or in New Guinea.

The moral attitudes contained in the scientific outlook have a different genesis from those contained in ordinary "unconscious" cultures. They are a result of a "freer choice," because they involve a deeper insight into the consequences of the choice.

In sum, cultures are distinct yet similar and comparable. As Steward has pointed out, the features that lend uniqueness are the secondary or variable ones. Two or more cultures can have a great deal of content — and even of patterning — in common and still there is distinctness; there are universals, but relativistic autonomy remains a valid principle. Both perspectives are true and important, and no false either-or antinomy must be posed between them. Once again there is a proper analogy between cultures and personalities. Each human being is unique in his concrete totality, and yet he resembles all other human beings in certain respects and some particular human beings a great deal. It is no more correct to limit each culture to its distinctive features and organization, abstracting out as "precultural" or as "conditions of culture" the likenesses that are universal, than to deny to each personality those aspects that derive from its cultural heritage and from participation in common humanity.

[1] And especially of nineteenth-century physics.
[2] Laboratory or experimental scientists strongly tend to take an attitude of superiority to historical problems — which, incidentally, they can't solve.
[3] Perhaps a completely new kind of mathematic is required. This seems to be the implication in Weaver, 1948. But some forms of algebra seem more appropriate to certain anthropological problems than probability statistics or the harmonic analysis used by Zipf and others. (Cf. the appendix by Weil to Part I of Lévi-Strauss, 1949.) mathematicians have commented orally to one of us that greater development of the mathematics of non-linear partial differential equations might aid materially in dealing with various perplexing questions in the behavioral and cultural sciences. The only contemporary statistical technique which seems to afford any promise of tiding in the determination of implicit culture is Lazarsfeld's latent structure analysis (see Chapters 10 and 11 in Stouffler, Gertman, Suchman, Lazars-

feld, et al. *Measurement and Prediction,* Vol. IV of *Studies in Social Psychology in World War II,* Princeton University Press, 1950).

[4] This implies, of course, an abstraction from concrete events — not the behavior itself.

[5] The problem considered in this paragraph is essentially that discussed by Ralph Linton under the rubric "real culture" and "culture construct." Our answer, of course, is not exactly the same as Linton's.

[6] Jakobson (1949, p. 213) remarks, "linguistic analysis with its concept of ultimate phonemic entities signally converges with modern physics which revealed the granular structure of matter as composed of elementary particles."

[7] Wiener (1948) and Levi-Strauss (1951) also present contrasting views on the possibilities of discovering lawful regularities in anthropological data. Wiener argues that (a) the obtainable statistical runs are not long enough; and (b) that observers modify the phenomena by their conscious study of them. Lévi-Strauss replies that linguistics at least can meet these two objections and suggests that certain aspects of social organization can also be studied in ways that obviate the difficulties. It may be added that Wiener has remarked in conversation with one of us that he is convinced of the practicability of devising new mathematical instruments which would permit of satisfactory treatment of social-science facts. Finally, note Murdock's (1949, p. 259) finding: "...cultural forms in the field of social organization reveal a degree of regularity and of conformity to scientific but not significantly inferior to that found in the so-called natural sciences."

[8] Reprinted in Boas, 1940, p. 268.

[9] Steward, 1949, pp. 5-7.

[10] Fortes, 1949b, p. 344.

[11] Fortes, 1949b, p. 346.

[12] Fortes, 1949b, pp. 344-46.

[13] Cf. Coulborn, 1952. p. 113: "The fantastically simple, monistic view of cause necessary to a thoroughgoing reductionism is none other than the cause which served the physical sciences from the seventeenth century to the nineteenth and was foisted upon other sciences by reason of the egregious success of the physical sciences in that period. Difficulties in nuclear physics and astrophysics have driven the physicists themselves out of that stronghold, and it might be supposed that the efforts of such a philosopher as Whitehead would have destroyed it completely. But this is not so: some non-physicists still lurk in it — a case of cultural lag! From Durkheim onward social scientists, latterly anthropologists, have argued vigorously against this opinion, some even wishing to establish a new monism contrary to it. But the truth is that cause actually operates in all sorts of ways: it can, as to certain particulars, be entirely on the cultural level, but, as to others, it operates both upwards and downwards, and perhaps round about, between the levels.... Aristotle's concept of formal cause is enlightening without being at the same time misleading, but his efficient cause — and this is surely generally agreed — is a harmful conception: any item in a causal structure can be regarded as efficient, for, if any item is missing, the event will be changed."

[14] As in the correlations of the Culture Element Survey of native western North America directed by one of the present authors, to mention but one example.

[15] Cf. Kluckhohn, 1951a.

[16] Although the approach is from a somewhat different direction and the terminology used is not the same, the point of view we express in these paragraphs seems thoroughly congruent with that expressed by Lévi-Strauss (1951). Compare: "...thus ascertain whether or not different types of communication systems in the same societies — that is, kinship and language — are or are not caused by identical unconscious structures" (p. 161). "We will be in a position to understand basic similarities between forms of social life, such as language, art, law, religion, that, on the surface, seem to differ greatly. At the same time, we will have the hone of overcoming the opposition between the collective nature of culture and its manifestations in the individual, since the so-called 'collective consciousness' would, in the final analysis, be no more than the expression, on the plane of individual thought and behavior, of certain time and space modalities of these universal laws which make up the unconscious activity of the mind" (p 163).

[17] Italics ours.

[18] For one try at this kind of analysis, see Kluckhohn, 1949b.

[18a] For some purposes a better simile is that of a large oriental rug. Here one can see before one the intricacy of patterns — the pattern of the whole rug and various patterns within this. The degree of intricacy of the patterns of the explicit culture tends to be proportional to the total content of that culture, as Kroeber has remarked: "Such a climax is likely to be defined by two characteristics: a larger content of culture; and a more developed or specialized organization of the content of the culture — in other words, more numerous elements and more sharply expressed and interrelated patterns. These two properties are likely to go hand in hand. A greater content calls for more definite organization; more organization makes possible the absorption of more content." (1936, p. 114.)

[19] "Awareness" has here the special and narrow sense of "manifested by habitual verbalization." The members of the group are of course aware in the sense that they make choices with these configurations as unconscious but de-

terminative backgrounds. Professor Jerome Bruner comments from the standpoint of a psychologist: "The process by which the implicit culture is 'acquired' by the individual (i.e., the way the person learns to respond in a manner congruent with expectation) is such that awareness and verbal formulation are intrinsically difficult. Even in laboratory situations where we set the subject the task of forming complex concepts, subjects *typically* begin to *respond* consistently in terms of a principle before they can verbalize (a) that they are operating on a principle, or (b) that the principle is thus-and-so. Culture learning, because so much of it takes place before very much verbal differentiation has occurred in the carrier and because it is learned along with the pattern of a language and as pan of the language, is bound to result in difficulties of awareness. Thoughtways inherent in a language are difficult to analyze by a person who speaks that language and no other since there is no basis for discriminating an implicit thoughtway save by comparing it with a different thoughtway in another language." (Letter to CK, September 7. 1951)

[20] A possible neurological basis of universals and of the culturally formed and tinged apperceptive mass has only recently been described.

[21] Gurvitch, 1950, p. 77.

[22] For a more extended treatment of values by one of us, see Kluckhohn 1951b.

[23] Cf. Kluckhohn, 1941; 1943.

[24] Cf. F. Kluckhohn, 1950.

[25] Spiro, 1951, p. 33.

[26] Kluckhohn, 1951, pp. 101, 108-09. Cf. also Goldschmidt's recent remark: "The existence of conflicting aims, and the conflict over the achievement of common aims, both of which are of greater importance to primitive social system than anthropologists have appreciated, and which have such far-reaching consequences for the nature of institutions..." (1951, p. 570)

[27] As a matter of fact, cultures may shire a large body of their content through historical connection and provable derivation and yet have arrived at pretty diverse value systems. If we could recover enough ancient and lost evidence, it is expectable that we would be driven to the admission that every culture shares some of its content, through derivation, with every other on earth. This historic interconnection leaves any monadal view or talk of the non-comparability of cultures without basis. Possessing co-ancestry, they must be comparable. All that the most confirmed relativists can properly claim b that to achieve the fullest understanding of any culture, we should not begin by applying to it the patterns and values of another culture. This eminently modest and reasonable principle of autonomy of comprehension, or reciprocity in understanding, does not assert that all the structure and all the values of any two cultures are utterly disparate — which would make them non-comparable and would be a manifestly extreme and improbable view. It affirms that there is comparability but that the structure-value system of one culture must not be imposed on another if sound understanding is the aim. Biologists have long taken this for granted about classes of organisms and yet have never stopped comparing them fruitfully. Only, their comparison means discovering likenesses and differences, not looking merely for likenesses or merely for differences.

[28] Cf. Aberle, et al., 1950.

[29] This paragraph summarizes the argument for similarity and comparability of culture on general grounds of logic and common observation. The argument of course becomes much stronger still as soon as the historic connections or interrelations of cultures are considered, as outlined in the preceding note. Really, comparability is not even questionable, and it has not been denied in practice except by occasional extreme dogmatists like Spengler. Indeed, it is precisely analytic comparison that first leads to recognition of differences of structure and values instead of naive assumption of essential uniformity, and therewith to relativism. But relativistically colored comparison does not aim merely at ever-accentuated differentiating, which would become sterile and self-defeating. We must repeat that true comparison deals impartially with likenesses and divergences as analysis reveals them.

[30] At very least, integratively and historically destructive.

[31] Rapoport, 1950, pp. 231-33.

C: Conclusion - A Final Review of the Conceptual Problem

ANTHROPOLOGISTS, like biologists somewhat earlier, were presented with a great array of structures and forms to describe. As the concept of culture was expanded, more and more things came to be described as their possible significance was grasped. The overwhelming bulk of published cultural anthropology consists in description. Slowly, this harvest of a rich diversity of examples has been conceptualized in a more refined manner. Starting with the premise that these descriptive materials were all relevant to a broad and previously neglected realm of phenomena, the concept of culture has been developed not so much through the introduction or strictly new ideas but through creating a new configuration of familiar notions: custom-tradition-organization-etc. In divorcing customs from the individuals who carried them out and in making customs the focus of their attention, anthropologists took an important step — a step that is perhaps still underestimated. When a time backbone was added to the notion of group variability in ways of doing things, not only group differences, but the notion of the historical derivation and development of these differences entered the picture. When the concept of "way" was made part of the configuration, this conceptualized the fact that not only discrete customs but also *organized* bodies of custom persisted and changed in time.

Various social theorists (Hegel, Weber, Comte, Marx, Huntington, and others) have tried to make particular forms the main dynamic in the historical process: ideas; religious beliefs and practices; forms of social organization; forms of technological control of the environment. One modern group would place forms of intra-family relationship in a central position. There has, of course, been some of this partisanship in anthropology: White and Childe who stress modes of technology; Laura Thompson and others who stress idea systems; British and American social anthropologists who make forms of social organization central; a few who have recently stressed the role of linguistic morphology. But if there be any single central tendency in the attempts to conceptualize culture over eighty years, it has been that of denying in principle a search for "*the*" factor. In the attempt to avoid simple determinisms, anthropologists have fairly consistently groped for a concept that would avoid commitment to any single dynamism for interpreting sociocultural life and would yet be broad and flexible enough to encompass all of the significant aspects in the "superorganic" life of human groups.

While in single definitions one can point to the splitters, the lumpers, the plumpers for one special feature, the over-all trend is certainly that indicated above. The majority emphasis, the steady emphasis has been upon working out a generalizing idea, a generative idea of the sort that Suzanne Langer [1] talks about:

The limits of thought ire not so much set from outside, by the fullness or poverty of experiences that meet the mind, as from within, by the power of conception, the wealth of formulative notions with which the mind meets experiences. Most new discoveries are suddenly-seen things that were always there. A new idea is a light that illuminates presences which simply had no form for us before the light fell on them. We turn the light here, there, and everywhere, and the limits of thought recede before it. A new science, a new art, or a young and vigorous system of philosophy, is generated by such a basic innovation. Such ideas as identity of manner and change of form, or as value, validity, virtue, or as outer world and inner consciousness, are not theories; they are the terms in which theories are conceived; they give rise to specific questions, and are articulated only in the form of these questions. Therefore one may call them generative ideas in the history of thought...

Again avoiding a new formal definition, we may say — extending a little what has already been stated in III-e-15 — that this central idea is now formulated by most social scientists approximately as follows:

Culture consists of. patterns, explicit and implicit, of and for behavior acquired and transmitted by symbols, constituting the distinctive achievement of human groups, including their embodiments in artifacts; the essential core of culture consists of traditional (i.e., historically derived and selected) ideas and especially their attached values; culture systems may, on the one hand, be considered as products of action, on the other as conditioning elements of further action.

The main respects in which, we suspect, this formula [2] will be modified and enlarged in the future are as regards (1) the interrelations of cultural forms: and (2) variability and the individual.

Perhaps a better way of putting the problem would be to say that as yet we have no full theory of culture. We have a fairly well-delineated concept, and it is possible to enumerate conceptual elements embraced within that master concept. But a concept, even an important one, does not constitute a theory. There is a theory of gravitation in which "gravity" is merely one term. Concepts have a way of coming to a dead end unless they are bound together in a testable theory. In anthropology at present we have plenty of definitions but too little theory.

The existence of a concept of culture apart from a general theory is with little doubt one factor which has influenced a few professional anthropologists toward shying away from the use of the concept. The position of Radcliffe-Brown and other British social anthropologists has been discussed. In this country, Chapple, Arensberg, and their followers have attempted to create a theory with biological and mathematical underpinnings, by-passing culture. We feel that their work, based upon careful measurements of interaction, has been limited by the fact that it is more readily productive to study culture in abstraction from concrete agents than to study social interaction segregated off from culture. But our point here is that they seem to have avoided the concept because it was not tied to other terms in generalized conceptual schemes such as have been constructed in biology and mathematics.

We suspect that a dynamic and generalized conceptual model in the area of culture will, develop largely as a result of further investigation or cultural forms and of individual variability.

The study of cultural structures, as opposed to content, has progressed markedly during the last generation. Sapir, drawing upon linguistics where sheer structure is often crucial, showed what a fertile field for analysis this was and how much that was not immediately apparent could be discovered. "Forms and significances which seem obvious to an outsider will be denied outright by those who carry out the patterns; outlines and implications that are perfectly clear to these may be absent to the eve of the onlooker." Benedict, building upon the clues offered by Sapir and others, demonstrated the dependence of concrete and manifest cultural forms upon deeper-lying, pervasive principles. Bateson explored the interrelationships of institutional, cognitive, and affective cultural structures. Kroeber attempted to trace the "behavior" of cultural configurations in time. Morris Opler indicated how masses of content data might be subsumed as expressive of a relatively small number of themes characteristic of each culture.

Examples could be multiplied. We now have, as already pointed out, adumbrations of a theory of cultural structure. This needs to be pulled together, pointed up, and deepened by both diachronic and synchronic studies. Steward has attempted to set up topological sequences of cultural forms recurring, putatively, because of environmental, demographic, and other constants. But we are still far from being able to state "the laws of cultural development." Analogies are dangerous, but it is tempting to suggest that the development of anthropology lags about a generation behind that of biology. Comparative morphology and evolutionary biology retain their importance in contemporary biology, but biochemistry and genetics are the most actively innovating fields. [3] We are still some distance from "cultural genetics."

The culture and personality approach can help bring us closer to a "cultural genetics." We think that those who have looked to the psychological level for explanations, whether following the lead of Boas or with subsequent importations from psychoanalysis and learning theory, are in a position to make significant contributions, provided they do not, in effect, try to "reduce" or "abolish" culture in the process.

There must be concurrent emphasis upon the variability of cultural forms as well as upon the variability of personalities within the group. In part, what seems to give structure to personality is the incorporation of cultural forms; underlying and expressing these are the basic meanings laid down beginning in early childhood. The formed cultural element must become as integral a part of the formulation of the concept "personality" as the idea of defense systems resulting from pressure on basic needs is part of it today. Investigators should make cross-cultural personality studies because thus they can compare individuals who have not only been exposed to different forms but to some of the same forms in different sequence.

Culture is an abstract description of *trends toward* uniformity in the words, acts, and artifacts of human groups. Like personality, culture might be conceived dynamically as the working out of the implications of certain genetic foci. Just as a personality system acquires early its characteristic bents so does a cultural one. There would appear to be a suggestive analogy between the weighting of themes on a projective test and the recurrence of the thematic principles of the implicit culture. The basic themes of a personality may be more unconscious, have a more dynamic role. The implicit configurations of a culture may be closer to conscious imagery and expressed in less disguised form through observable forms of behavior and expression.

However, the naive individual is unaware of the extent to which what he regards as his own personal habits are patterned (positively or negatively) along cultural lines. [4] This patterning is primarily that of the implicit culture. These underlying cultural forms often have extraordinary persistence even when shifts in culture content are major and rapid. "Plus ça change, plus c'est la meme chose." This has been repeatedly pointed out and documented by Boas, Kroeber, and Sapir (among others). Boas, for example, in his introduction to Benedict's *Patterns of Culture* remark's, "In comparison to changes of content of culture the configuration has often remarkable permanency," Kroeber in his 1928 discussion of the cultures of the American Southwest pointed out that "the container" of various distinctive cultures altered much less through time than the items, traits, and complexes that were "contained." Sapir has made a generalization with respect to the dynamism involved:

Whenever the human mind has worked collectively and unconsciously, it has striven for and often attained unique form. The important point is that the evolution of form has a drift in one direction, that it seeks poise, and that it rests, relatively speaking, when it has found this poise.

Since the unique cultural forms in accord with which individuals unconsciously pattern much of their behavior have, as it were, a logic of their own, [5] no psychological laws and no investigation of the culture-personality continuum which attempts to reduce culture to psychology will ever explain all of the broad principles of culture change. Maquet (1949, pp. 246-7) remarks:

Il est exact que les prémisses de culture ne sont pas des facteurs non-immanents. Cependent elles sont des facteurs sociaux, ou plus exactement socioculturels au sens où toute idée exprimée est un phénomène impossible sans societé. Par ailleurs - et ceci est plus important — ces prémisses culturelles, quoique de nature idéale, sont cependant des facteurs exterieurs par rapport aux divers domaines de la pensée.

As Sapir showed for language, [6] there are "configurational pressures" which bring about both parallel and differentiating changes. Every particular cultural structure through its emphases, its tendencies toward disequilibrium in certain sectors, its lack of development in particular areas, favors evolution in some directions and not in others. And, as Sapir further pointed out, "it is more than doubtful if the gradual unfolding of social patterns tends indefinitely to be controlled by function." [7]
Harris has well generalized Sapir's views as they relate to planned change:

Changes which are attempted at any one time will therefore be intimately connected with the cultural patterns existing at that time, and will lead to patterns which differ in certain directions rather than in others, and which are not entirely different and unrelated to the previous patterns. A more or less continuous and dircctioi.il shift, with observable regularities, is therefore often discernible in the history of cultural patterns taken by themselves, even though the *agency* of change is the reaction of the individual. (1951, 328; italics ours).

The polar case is, of course, that of fashion [8] or style. Here there seems to be an element of irreversibility or near irreversibility which few aspects of culture seem to possess. But there appears to be a degree of stylistic individuation or particularization in all forms of culture; sometimes this is deflected by external pressures or by strains in the total cultural system. In general, though, drift almost comes down to the matter of style, and each style has its fluctuations, its periodicities, or arrives at its inherent terminus ("pattern saturation").
The older biology also paid but little focused, systematic attention to individual variability. Darwin's *Origin of Species* is as full of reference to variations as it is to adaptations and heredity. But either it is particular, isolated variations that are cited and described, or the general fact of variability is assumed. To Darwin, variations go somewhere in making selective adaptation possible, but they come from nowhere, out of the blue. It was Mendel who first posed the question whether there was an order or form in which variations *came.* Darwin had focused on change in heredity and on selection-survival as its agency; but while his work reeks of the fact of variation, how variation operates remains out of the focus of the inquiry — which is why he could passively accept Lamarckianism. Similarly, in anthropology the notion of variability within the group is coming to be emphasized more and more, but is not yet sharply focused, at least not from the angle of culture — see Part Three, *d*, Comment. Linguistics, which is often a delicate indicator of cultural theory', is now stressing the phoneme — a range of variation of a pattern focus. The older anthropological approach, useful and sufficient in its day, has tended to obscure important issues that hinge upon the empirical fact of formal variability. Fulfilling cultural forms in individual behavior is not the easy achievement that is often tacitly assumed in anthropological literature. The individual's notions of "correct form" are often fuzzy. Even when they are more clear-cut, personal needs and drives frequently prevent more than a crude approximation. It is also probably difficult for both participant and investigator to project similarity into the behavior of others; the investigator misses the nuances.
The trend toward emphasizing variability is closely related to the growing emphasis on the individual in cultural studies. Not only is every individual different, but, concretely, the cultural forms differ too with the individuals who color them with their own needs and presses. Concretely, again, even the cultural heritage of each individual is unique, even though abstractly the total cultural heritage is available to all. Conversely, the same cultural forms are used as vehicles for very different sorts of personality projection. The same form can be used for an almost endless variety of purposes and for expressing an almost infinite shading of meanings. Certain socially accepted culture patterns receive their affective charge largely because they are circuitous outlets for feelings that cannot be more directly expressed Such forms as witchcraft, for example, are of about the same kind of significance in getting down to basic meanings as are significant responses on projective tests. Finally, a recent trend (as in the work of Morris) [9] has been to emphasize not just discrete cultural forms but formal types as models for personality development.

All of this is said not in the framework of the reductionism that pervades much of the culture and personality movement but because the study of culture itself would seem to require explicit provision in its central concept for the implications which cultural forms have for the individual and the variability of individuals. This point will be amplified in the next section.

We agree with L. L. Bernard [10] that:

...definition ranges all the way from the low level of accuracy of indicating (pointing out) an object or process through naming and describing it in a literary manner, to the various stages of symbolic condensation and functional conditioning, and ending in the formulation or an ideal hypothetical norm which is a sort of compromise between the generalization of inadequate experiental reality and a projected reality which is yet to be attained in its entirety.

"Culture" has now reached the state that Bernard calls that of "condensed representative abstract definition," [54] It remains for future work to produce a further symbolic condensation that will make adequate provision for the systemic nature of cultures ("interrelation of forms") and for individuals and their variabilities.

Review of Aspects of Our Own Position

We do not propose to attempt a summary of our "Summary," let alone of our many criticisms and appraisals of the discussions of others in the mam body of this work, plus our own, we hope, constructive points scattered through the body of the text. Yet, in the interests of clarity, it seems proper at this point to restate briefly our position on certain issues that are controversial at the moment, some of them perhaps needlessly so. The ensuing paragraphs are, therefore, highly selective and do not constitute a complete digest of our theory of culture but only of our stand on certain topics of special contemporary interest.

Culture is a general category of nature, and expressly of human nature. As such it is comparable to categories like energy, mass, evolution. As a general category it is both substantive (or classificatory) and explanatory. That is, it may be asked: to what main natural category is this or that phenomenon — or are these selected aspects of phenomena — to be ascribed? If the phenomenon is, for example, the religious system of the Haida, the answer is clearly "cultural," just as in the case of the reproductive cycle of the hamster the answer would be "biological." Or, the query may be: why do the Chinese avoid milk and milk products. The only possible shorthand answer is: because of their culture — which reply implicitly rejects an explanation in terms of heredity or present situation.

Substantively and descriptively, the totality of human culture includes the cultural phenomena of all peoples, times, and places insofar as these phenomena are known or knowable. Culture as a generalized explanatory category applies to all of these, though the totality constitutes an aggregation which does have in common the six general features just reviewed in B of Part Four. Cultural phenomena in general are also, of course, characterized by the fact that specific elements of each culture bear some relation both to the broad ground plan of all cultures *and* to the distinctive design of the specific culture to which the element belonged or belongs.

Literally, it might be contended that the totality of human culture is patterned only in the sense of a broad similarity at all times and places of some of its grand categories like transmissibility, and in the possession of the more or less universal values that have been discussed. Future work will show the extent to which the definition of these categories and values can be sharpened or to which they will shrink on comparison. But there is undoubtedly an element of patterning in the totality of human culture, whether this totality be regarded as the historical summation of individuated cultures, or as a context and implied standard of reference for particular cultural phenomena, or as a body of data useful in psychologically delimiting "raw human nature."

However, total culture is a generalization like "living matter" or total life on earth; and it is of the nature of generalizations that as such they cannot show the sharp patterning characteristic of particular phenomena, such as particular cultures constitute. In another sense, however, total culture can be seen as strongly patterned because, much like total life, it is not diffusely or amorphously uniform in its occurrence, but is expressed only through a great variety of highly patterned forms. This "culture in the partitive sense," [55] or particular cultures, as they are usually called, are, like particular forms of life, markedly idiosyncratic, and patterning is one of their most significant properties. It is patterning that gives to each culture — or species — its selective and distinctive life-way; to each culture its "selective orientation toward experience broadly characteristic of a group." [12a]

It is proper, then, to speak both of culture in general — whether in a descriptive or explanatory way — and of particular cultures. Moreover, the lines of demarcation of any cultural unit chosen for description and analysis are in large part a matter of level of abstraction and of convenience for the problem at hand. Occidental culture, Greco-Roman culture, nineteenth-century European culture, German culture, Swabian culture, the peasant culture of the Black Forest in 1900 — these are all equally legitimate abstractions if carefully defined. At one level "Mayan culture" is a useful concept; more microscopically, this entity dissolves into a series of rather differentiated, separate cultures. The same may be said of New Guinea Melanesian culture or cultures.

Culture is produced and changed, concretely, by individuals and each distinctive life-way is also the product of a group. Yet a culture is not necessarily tied throughout time to a particular society. Mohammedan culture, as we know it today, cuts across communities, societies, and nations. Roman society ceased to exist as such more than a millennium ago, but Roman culture was a vital force throughout the Middle Ages and, in certain aspects, is still "alive" today.

This is one of many reasons why culture must be regarded as an autonomous system or category and indeed — at least for certain purposes — can be treated quite frankly in relative abstraction from both personalities and societies. Culture is not a mystical "force" acting at a distance. *Concretely*, it is created by individual organisms and by organisms operating as a group. It is internalized in individuals and also becomes part of their environment through the medium of other individuals and of cultural products. Acts take place: (a) in time between persons, (b) in space in an environment partly made up of other persons. But because acts take place in time the past continues to influence the present. The history of each group leaves its precipitate — conveniently and, by now, traditionally called "culture" — which is present in person:;-, shaping their perceptions of events, other persons, and the environing situation in ways not wholly determined by biology and by environmental press. Culture is an intervening variable between human "organism" and "environment."

· As a matter of general theory, it must never be forgotten that there is a ceaseless interaction between personality (or individual variability) and culture; that only persons and not cultures interact in the concrete, directly observable world; and the like. All of this is manifestly true at the level of concrete events. Yet in science, abstractions at different levels are both permissible and desirable, so long as there remains awareness of the level of abstraction at which the investigator is operating. At the cultural level of abstraction it is perfectly proper to speak of relations between cultures, the mutual influencing of cultures, in the same way that, more concretely, we speak of relations between persons. Even fairly concretely, this is sometimes a better description. Take, as a simple example, the case of the modern scholar who learns about medieval North African culture from Ibn Khaldun. He does not interact with the person, Ibn Khaldun, nor the latter's Muslim contemporaries. The modern scholar really encounters, through a book, a different way of life which (as filtered through his personality and culture) he then reacts to and tends to diffuse into his own culture.

Those who still deny the autonomy (in some respects) of the cultural level are either stubborn reductionists who reject the validity of all emergent systems or such as find it impossible to deal satisfactorily with their own particular interests by a purely cultural approach. Dollard, [13] for example, in a well-known paper remarks:

...a very peculiar conception of the human animal emerges from the cultural way of viewing behavior. He appears as a bearer of culture, much as factory workers look like "hands" to their employer. What one sees from the cultural angle is a drama of life much like a puppet show in which "culture" is pulling the strings from behind the scenes. Men do not emerge in their full personal reality but they appear as actors of parts, as role-players, and the attention is never centered on them but only on their outline of behavior.

All of this is valid enough. But anthropologists .do not claim that culture provides a complete explanation of human behavior, merely that there is a cultural element in most human behavior, and that certain things in behavior make most sense when seen through culture. We would add that just as behavior in all its concreteness is a proper object of scientific enquiry, so culture and cultural process are, even when abstracted from behavior. Culture as an emergent and a culture as a system with its own properties are indeed more effectively studied in abstraction from personality and concrete individual variability, just as biology made notable progress without waiting for chemistry to solve all the problems of the underlying processes. To be sure, there is now biochemistry, and we have no doubt that there will eventually be a genuine cultural psychology or even cultural physiology: but we feel that the study of culture as such must not be abandoned for a perhaps premature synthesis or a disguised reductionism.

In general, approach from an underlying level may hope to explain the uniformities in phenomena of an upper level, but does not even attack the problem of their diversities. Granted that we know a great deal about the full biochemistry of the sex drive, we still know nothing of why a thousand human populations are likely to practice five hundred distinguishable kinds of marriage besides innumerable varieties of extra-marital sex behavior. Our experience to date makes it likely that there will always be irreducible residues which do make sense and do have meaning in terms of relations within their own level. It is in fact conceivable that as the body of reduced or trans-level understandings grows, our corpus of unreduced intra-level understandings will also continue to grow. Its simplicity is what renders reductionism attractive as a conceptual system. To believe that essential reduction has been accomplished is an illusion; [14] that it is about to be, is a wish fulfillment. Our fullest understanding of the world may well continue to be in pluralistic terms.

The realization of the pragmatic utility' and necessity of recognition of distinctive levels runs a risk of being pushed to a point of excess. In that event the aspects or properties of each level are exaggerated and transcendentalized into entities or kinds of realities in the substantive sense: life, mind, society, culture. Sometimes the motivation of such hypostasizing or reification is the ardor of a new attitude. Sometimes it is a hangover from old pre-scientific concepts like soul. The result is that radical innovators and die-hard reactionaries of the intellect may find themselves fellow-partisans against an orthodox bourgeoisie of reductionists and that the latter do not discriminate between their opponents.

Grace de Laguna has presented a balanced view which recognizes alike the existence of distinct realms of phenomena (the psychological and the cultural) and their interdependence:

It is as if the basic pattern of the culture must be reflected in the internal structure of each individual person; as if the individual were in some sense a microcosm and the culture to which he belongs a macrocosm. Each individual, like a Leibnizian monad, "reflects" the culture of his world from his own point of view and with varying degrees of clearness and confusion. The experienced ethnologist is now able to reconstruct a considerable part of the cultural system from any good informant, using not merely what the informant "knows," or can verbalize, but what he unwittingly reflects in his attitudes and modes of expressive response...observable differences are equally important and even more significant. The basic structure is rather to be found in the common ground of both their similarities and their differences, the trunk from which divergent personalities branch and by which they are all supported. (1949, 387-88)

From a mere insistence on the importance of recognizing culture as a distinct domain of phenomena, there has been considerable spilling-over to the further but hast)' and usually hazy attitude which sees culture as a special kind of entity or substance. Malinowski in the same essay credited culture with being "a reality sui generis" and yet saved his monism by deriving the manifestations of this same culture from physiological needs and psychological imperatives. Culture may be primarily intelligible in terms of itself, but it is never unresidually intelligible in terms of itself.

The efficient causes [15] of cultural phenomena unquestionably are men: individual personalities who are in interpersonal and social relations. This cannot be denied, and there, is neither use nor honesty in trying to whittle any of it away. But the manifestations of culture come characteristically in certain forms, patterns, or configurations, many of which are large, ramifying, and enduring. Now while persons undoubtedly make and produce these cultural forms, our knowledge of persons — and very largely also our knowledge of societies of persons — has failed conspicuously to explain the cultural *forms:* to derive specific cultural effects from specific psychic or social causes. In fact, psychological and social concepts or mechanisms are not even much good at *describing* cultural forms. [16] Such descriptions or characterizations begin to mean something only when they are made on the cultural level — in terms of intercultural relations and of cultural values.

Every anthropologist or historian concerned with culture realizes that cultural situations make more sense, reveal more meaning, in proportion as we know more of their cultural antecedents, or, generically, more total cultural context. In other words, cultural forms or patterns gain in intelligibility as they are set in relation to other cultural patterns.

We are convinced that the primary of patterns and pattern relation must be accepted in our intellectual operations with cultural data, possibly not forever, but at any rate in the present development of our learning and science. It is easy to cry for dynamic mechanisms, but they have been very hard to find. What the mechanisms or efficient causes residing in persons have explained in culture is on the one hand, certain kinds of cultural innovations; on the other hand, perhaps the broader recurrences, its rather hazily defined common denominators. All the characterized qualities of culture, all its variations and specificities, remain essentially unexplained by dynamic psychic mechanisms. [17]

The clearest case is furnished again by linguistics. Speech is a wholly human and wholly social phenomenon, but linguistics thrives by being completely anonymous and impersonal, with a minimum of reference to its carriers and their psychology, and by dealing with the relations of specific forms, without serious concern for their specific productive causes. The relation of *d, t, ts* in *deux, two, zwei* is a "law" in the sense of being a regularity of form, of consistent relation of pattern. But the linguist does not generally ask what made English have *t* where French has *d*. He could not give the answer and he knows he could not; and — if he has even thought about it — he probably suspects that no reductionist could give it either. The linguist may also be quite ready to concede that in his way the physicist is right if he claims that actually language is varying air vibrations made by the larynges and mouths of individuals of *Homo sapiens.* On the physicist's level language is that and remains that. The linguist wets something more significant than air waves out of his material because he does not try to explain it either through airwaves or through efficient causes residing: in persons, but by taking such causality for granted and concerning himself with the *interrelations* of linguistic *forms.*

Culture as a whole is more manifold and less channeled than its part, language. That perhaps is why students of culture have been less courageous or decisive in realizing that one of their most fertile procedures is essentially the same. Like language, culture exists only in and through human individuals and their psychosomatic properties; and like language it acquires a certain larger intelligibility' and systematic significance in the decree that it takes these persons for granted and proceeds to investigate the interrelations of superpersonal forms of culture. Culture may well yet reveal "laws" similar to the "laws" which the linguist calls sound shifts; only they will presumably be, like these, primarily relations of forms (synchronic or sequential), not laws of efficient causality. So far as these latter are determinable for culture, the prospect seems to be that they will continue to reside largely if not wholly in the psychic or psychosomatic level.

Until now anthropology has gone much farther in building up a theory for structures, personality theory farther in building up a theory of functions. In the past culture theory has tended to emphasize explicitness. In recent years culture theory has been working "downwards," personality theory "upwards." It may be that a single conceptual model, based not upon summary reductionism but upon gradual coalescence, may be created which is usable both for that portion of psychology that deals with the individual interacting with his fellows and with that part of anthropology which deals with the approximations of individuals to cultural forms and with the growth and change of cultures insofar as these arise from individual variation.

We recur, however, to our point that some aspects of cultural process not only can but can better be studied in abstraction from cultural agents. Cultures are systems (that is, are organized) because the variables are interdependent. [18] All systems appear to acquire certain properties that characterize the system *qua* system rather than the sum of isolable elements. Among these properties is that of directionality or "drift." There is a momentum quality to cultural systems. [19] The performance of a culturally patterned activity appears to carry with it implications for its own change which is by no means altogether random. Forms in general, as D'Arcy Thompson has shown, have momentum qualities. The existence of "drift" in one aspect of culture (linguistics) has been fairly well established. There is probably "cultural drift" in general. There may even be in some sense "cultural orthogenesis" within particular limited scopes; that is, the direction of at least some culture change is more predetermined by earlier forms of the culture than caused by environmental press and individual variability.

This is not to minimize the role of "accident" — the inability of our conceptual models to predict the entry of significant new factors that influence the body of phenomena under consideration. Just as mutations bring to the gene pool of a population previously non-operative elements, so invention, natural catastrophes or optima, perhaps gene mutations toward unusually endowed or specialized individuals, alter the course of cultures. [20] Nevertheless, in spite of all these "accidents," it is an empirical fact that there are significant freezings in the cultural process. It is these which anthropologists can most easily study. Anthropology, like Darwin's work, has been largely a matter of looking at acts in terms of their consequences rather than in terms of their "causes" — in the meaning of classical mechanics.

The logical construct, culture, is based upon the study of behavior and behavioral products. It returns to behavior and behavioral products in that the concept of culture makes more behavior intelligible and, to an appreciable extent, makes possible predictions about behavior in particular areas. But culture is not behavior [21] nor the investigation of behavior in all its concrete completeness. Part of culture consists in norms for or standards of behavior. Still another part consists in ideologies justifying or rationalizing certain selected ways of behavior. Finally, every culture includes broad general principles of selectivity [22] and ordering ("highest common factors") in terms of which patterns of and for and about behavior in very varied areas of culture content are reducible to parsimonious generalization.

Herewith we hope our basic theoretical position has been made clear. We are not too sure that we can properly classify ourselves as cultural realists, idealists, or nominalists. [23] We have been trying to make new wine: it may or may not decant usefully into eight-hundred-year old bottles. With all respect for the philosophical approach, we naturally cannot but hope that our views have a content broader than can be wholly subsumed by these categories. If we are asked: "How can a logical construct like culture explain anything.'" we would reply that other logical constructs and abstractions like "electromagnetic field" or "gene" — which no one has ever seen — have been found serviceable in scientific understanding. Analytic abstractions summarize an order of relationship between natural phenomena, and relations are as real as things. Whatever one or the other of us may have said in haste or error in the past, [24] in this monograph we have at any rate tried to honor the philosophical precept of not confusing substance with reality.

[1] Langer, 1948, p. 5.

[2] The word "formula" may well be objected to. Black is probably right when he writes: "Scientific method"...is a term of such controversial application that a definition universally acceptable can be expected to be platitudinous. A useful definition will be a controversial one, determined by a choice made, more or less wisely, in the hope of codifying and influencing scientific procedures.... The search for an immutable and determinate essence underlying the plenitude of historical process can result only in epigrammatic paradox.... The type of definition appropriate takes the form of a description of the constitutive factors, together with an indication of their relative weight or importance and their mutual relationships. (1949, 94)

[3] Certain outstanding biologists like Julian Huxley integrate the historical and experimental branches.

[4] Cf. Sapir, 1949 (originally 1927), p. 549 ff.

[5] This is the conclusion reached by Richardson and Kroeber (1940) as a result of their empirical and quantitative examination of women's dress fashions during three centuries:

  "We are now in position better to weigh the several possible causes of changes in variability. The primary factor would seem to be adherence to or departure from an ideal though unconscious pattern or formal clothing of women. The consistent conformity of variability to certain magnitudes of proportion — mostly a conformity of low variabilities to high magnitudes — leaves little room for any other conclusion...Social and political unsettlement as such might produce stylistic unsettlement and variability as such; but there is nothing to show that it would per se produce thick waists, ultra high or low ones, short and tight skirts. If there is a connection here, it seems that it must be through alteration of the basic semi-conscious pattern, through an urge to unsettle or disrupt this; and that when increased fashion variability occurs, it is as a direct function of pattern stress, and only indirectly, and less certainly, of sociopolitical instability. In short, generic historical causes tending toward social and cultural instability may produce instability in dress styles also; but their effect on style is expressed in stress upon the existent long-range basic pattern of dress, and the changes effected have meaning only in terms of the pattern." (1940, 147-48) The "unconscious" or "semi-conscious" patterns referred to would be aspects of what in the present monograph is designates as "implicit culture."

[6] Murdock (1949b, pp. 198-99) notes: "The phenomenon of linguistic drift exhibits numerous close parallels to the evolution of social organization, e.g., limitation in the possibilities of change, a strain toward consistency, shifts from one to another relatively stable equilibrium, compensatory internal readjustments, resistance to any influence from diffusion that is not in accord with the drift...The present study has led to the conclusion that social organization is a semi-independent system comparable in many respects to language, and similarly characterized by an internal dynamics of its own. It is not, however, quite such a closed system, for it demonstrably does change in response to external events, and in identifiable ways. Nevertheless, its own structure appears to act as a filter for the influences which affect it."

[7] Sapir, 1949, p. 341.

[8] Cf. Richardson and Kroeber, 1940.

[9] Morris, 1948.

[10] Bernard, 1941a, p. 510.

[11] Bernard, 1941a, p. 501.

[12] On "culture" and "a culture" and on explanatory and descriptive dimensions, see Kluckhohn and Kelly, 19451 and (945b. The term "partitive" comes from Taylor, 1948.

[12a] In correspondence with us Walter Taylor has made an interesting case for the view that holistic culture is "psychological" and only partitive culture is anthropological. He suggests that only particular cultures have structure — i.e. specific structures. Total human culture is additive or summative of many varieties — like the total class. Mammals. There is a Mammalian pattern, but of course there can't be a mammalian structure.

[13] Dollard, 1939, p. 52.

[14] On the difficulties and "illusion" of reduction in the natural sciences, cf. Nagel, 1949.

[15] We use this terminology here and elsewhere not because we subscribe whole-heartedly to the Aristotelian theory of causation but because those who attack culture as a "cause" or "explanation" are — whether they realize it or not — thinking in these or highly similar terms. We are aware that contemporary thought rejects the notion that a cause is connected with its effect as if by a sort of hidden string. We ourselves think of causality as interdependence or co-variance — if a, then b (under defined circumstances). Even this relationship, alike in most aspects of physical and social science, is not more than a statement of high probability: certain events or abstracted parts of events tend strongly to recur together. This is essentially Hume's interpretation of causality in terms of generality (cf. Reichenbach, 1951. csp. pp. 157-59)

[16] As shown by the fact that we have now in America a dozen or two of systematic books on social psychology which all deal with psycho-social mechanism and nearly all carefully refrain from dealing with the cultures produced by the mechanism.

[17] The problem may be that of Langmuir's "convergent and divergent phenomena." Cf. Langmuir, 1943.

[18] As L. J. Henderson used to say: "The interdependence of variables in a system is one of the widest inductions from experience that we possess; or, we may alternatively regard it as the definition of a system."

[19] Cf. Kroeber, 1944.

[20] Cf. Kluckhohn, 1945 b, pp. 161-64.

[21] Cf. Gide, "la rivalité du monde réel et de la représentation que nous nous en faisons,"

[22] Mauss, 1935, remains one of the most impressive examinations of selectivity. This study is not nearly as well known in the English-speaking world as it should be.

[23] Cf. Bidney, 1942, 1946, 1947; Spiro, 1951.

[24] Herskovits, 1951a, 1951b; Spiro, 1951.

References

Abel, T.
1930. Is a Cultural Sociology Possible? *American Journal of Sociology*, vol. 35, pp. 739-52.
Aberle, D. F., Cohen, A. K., Levy, M. J., Jr., and Sutton, F. X.
1950. The Functional Prerequisites of a Society. *Ethics*, vol. 60, no. 2, pp. 100-11
Adelung, J. C.
1781. Versuch einer Geschichte der Cultur des Menchlichen Geschlechts. Leipzig.
Angyal, A.
1941. Foundations for a Science of Personality. New York.
Arciniegas, G.
1947. La Civilisation en Amérique Latine. *Chemins du Monde*, no. 1 (Civilisation), pp. 143-50. Paris,
Arnold, M.
1869. Culture and Anarchy. New York.
Ashley-Montagu, M. F.
1951. Review of *Manhood of Humanity* by A. Korzybski. *Psychiatry*, vol. 14, pp. 251-52.
Bain, R.
1942. A Definition of Culture. Sociology and Social Research, vol. 27, pp. 87-94.
Bahth, P.
1922. Die Philosophic der Geschichte als Soziologie. I vols. Leipzig, (1st edition, 1897).
Beaglehole, E. and Beaglehole, P.
1946. Some Modern Maoris. New Zealand Council for Educational Research, Wellington.
Becker, H.
1950. Through Values to Social Interpretation. Durham.
Benedict, R.
1929. The Science of Custom. *Century Magazine*. (Reprinted in: V. F. Calverton, Editor, 1931. The Making of Man, pp. 805-17. New York.)
1932. Configurations of Culture in North America. *American Anthropologist*, vol. 34, no. 1, pp. 1-27.
1934. Patterns of Culture. Boston.
1947. Race, Science and Politics. (Rev. ed). New York.
Bennett, J. W. and Tumin, M. M.
1949. Social Life: Structure and Function. New York.
Bernard, L. L.
1926. The Interdependence of Factors Basic to the Evolution of Culture. *American Journal of Sociology*, vol. 32, pp. 127-205.
1930. Culture and Environment. *Social Forces*, vol. 8, pp. 327-34.
1931. Classification of Culture. *Sociology and Social Research*, vol. 25, pp. 209-29.
1941a. The Definition of Definition. *Social Forces*, vol. 19, no. 4, pp. 500-10.

1941b. Views on Definitions of Culture. Committee on Conceptual Integration. Mimeographed.
1942. An Introduction to Sociology. New York.
Bernheim, E.
1914. Lehrbuch der Historischen Methode. 6th ed. München. (The first edition was issued in 1889.)
Bidney, D.
1942. On the Philosophy of Culture In the Social Sciences. *Journal of Philosophy*, vol. 39, pp. 449-57
1946. The Concept of Cultural Crisis. *American Anthropologist*, vol. 48, no. 4, pt. 1, pp. 534-5.
1947. Human Nature and the Cultural Process. *American Anthropologist*, vol. 49, no. 3, pp. 375-99.
1949. The Philosophical Anthropology of Ernst Cassirer and its Significance in Relation to the History of Anthropological Thought. *The Philosophy of Ernst Cassirer* (Ed., P. A. Schilip), pp. 465-544. New York.
Bierstedt, R.
1936. The Concept of Culture. (Thesis for M.A., Columbia University.)
1938. The Meanings of Culture. *Philosophy of Science*, vol. 5, no. 2, pp. 204-16.
Binswanger, L.
1947. Ausgewählte Vorträge und Aufsätze zur phänomenologischen Anthropologie. Bern.
Black, M.
1949. The Definition of Scientific Method. *Science and Civilization* (Ed, R. C. Stauffer), pp. 67-95. Madison, Wisconsin.
Bloomfield L.
1945. About Foreign Language Teaching. Yale Review, vol. 34, pp. 615-41.
Blumenthal, A.
1937. The Best Definition of Culture. Marietta, Ohio.
1938a. The Importance of the Most Useful Definition of the Term Culture. Marietta, Ohio.
1938b. The Relations between Culture, Human Social Interactions, Personality, and History. Marietta, Ohio.
1941. Views on Definition of Culture. Committee on Conceptual Integration. Mimeographed.
Boas, F.
1911. The Mind of Primitive Man. New York. 1930. Anthropology. *Encyclopedia of the Social Sciences*, vol. 1, pp. 73-110. New York.
1938. The Mind of Primitive Man. (Rev. ed.) New York.
Boas, F. and others
1938. General Anthropology. Boston.
Bogardus, E. S.
1930. Tools in Sociology. *Sociology and Social Research*, vol. 14, pp. 332-41.
Bose, N. K.
1929. Cultural Anthropology. Calcutta.

Bayson, L.
1947. Science and Freedom. New York.
Burkitt, M. C.
1929. Archaeology. Encyclopedia Britannica (14th ed.). New York.
Burns, C D.
1929. Philosophy of Social Life: Part III, Culture and Institutions. *Journal of Philosophical Studies,* vol. 4, pp. 112-24.
Buswell, J. O., III
1950. Some Comments on Hockett's "Language 'and' Culture: A Protest." *American Anthropologist,* vol. 52, no. 2, pp. 284-86.
Carr, L.J.
1945. Situational Psychology. *American Journal of Sociology,* vol. 51, pp. 136-41.
Carver, T. N.
1935. The Essential Factors of Social Evolution. Cambridge.
Case, C.M.
1924a. Outlines of Introductory Sociology: A Textbook of Readings in Social Science. New York.
1924b. The Culture Concept in Social Science. *Journal of Applied Sociology,* vol. 8, pp. 146-55.
1927. Culture as a Distinctive Human Trait. *American Journal of Sociology,* vol. 31, pp. 906-20.
Cassirer, E.
1944. An Essay on Man. New Haven.
Chapin, F. S.
1925. A Theory of Synchronous Culture Cycles. *Social Forces,* vol. 3, pp. 596-604.
Chapple, E. D. and **Coon, C S.**
1947. Principles of Anthropology. New York.
Chase, S.
1948. The Proper Study of Mankind. New York.
Chugerman S.
1939, Lester F. Ward, the American Aristotle. Durham.
Coulburn, Rushton.
1952. Causes in Culture. *American Anthropologist,* vol. 54, pp. 112-116.
Coutu, W.
1949. Emergent Human Nature. New York.
Crozier, W. J. and **Wolf, E.**
1939. Specific Constants for Visual Excitation. *National Academy of Science, Proceedings,* vol. 25, no. 4, pp. 176-79.
Danilevsky, N. I.
1886. Rosiia i Evropa. *Zoria* (Dawn). German translation by Karl Nötzel, 1920, Russland und Europa. Stuttgart und Berlin.
Davis, A.
1948. Social-Class Influences upon Learning. Cambridge.
Davis, A. and **Dollard, J.**
1940. Children of Bondage, Washington.
Davis, K.
1949. Human Society. New York.
Dawson, C.

1928. The Age of the Gods: A Study in the Origins of Culture in Prehistoric Europe and the Ancient Elast. London.
Dennes, W. R.
1942. Conceptions of Civilization: Descriptive and Normative. *Civilization* (University of California Publications in Philosophy), vol. 23, pp. 166-90.
Dietschy, H.
1947. De Deux Aspects de la Civilisation. *Archives Suisses d'Anthropologie Générale,* vol. 12, pp. 116-31.
Dixon, R. B.
1918. The Building of Cultures. New York.
Dodd, S. C
1941. Views on Definitions of Culture. Committee on Conceptual Integration. Mimeographed.
Dollard, J.
1939. Culture, Society, Impulse, and Socialization. *American Journal of Sociology,* vol. 45, pp. 50-63.
Eliot, T. S.
1948. Notes Toward the Definition of Culture. London.
Ellis, H.
1923. The Dance of Life. New York.
Ellwood, C. A.
1927a. Cultural Evolution. New York.
1927b. Primitive Concepts and the Origin of Culture Patterns. *American Journal of Sociology,* vol. 33, pp. 1-13.
Eucken, R.
1878. Geschichte und Kritik de Grundbegriffe der Gegenwart. Leipzig.
Evans-Pritchard, E. E.
1950. Social Anthropology: Past and Present (The Marett Lecture). *Man,* vol. 50, pp. 118 24.
1951. Social Anthropology. London.
Fairchild H. P. (Editor)
1944. Dictionary of Sociology. New York.
Faris, E
1937. The Nature of Human Nature. New York.
Febvre, L. (Editor)
1930. Civilisation: Le Mot et I'ldée. Centre International de Synthèse. Première Semaine Internationale de Synthèse. Deuxième Fascicule. Paris.
Feibleman, J.
1946. The Theory of Human Culture. New York.
Firth, R.
1939 Primitive Polynesian Economy. London.
1944 The Future of Social Anthropology. Man, vol. 44, pp. 19-22.
1951 Elements of Social Organization. London.
Folsom, J.
1928. Culture and Social Progress. New York.
1931. Social Psychology. New York.
Ford, C. S.
1937. A Sample Comparative Analysis of Material Culture. *Studies in the Science of Society Presented to Albert Galloway Keller* (Ed., G. P. Murdock), pp. 223-46.
1939. Society, Culture, and the Human Organism. *Journal of General Psychology,* vol. 20, pp. 135-79

1942. Culture and Human Behavior. *Scientific Monthly,* vol. 55, pp. 546-57.

Ford, J. A.
1949. Cultural Dating of Prehistoric Sites in Vim Valley, Peru. *Anthropological Papers, American Museum of Natural History,* vol. 43.

Forde, C. D.
1934. Habitat, Economy and Society. London.

Fortes, M.
1949a. Time and Social Structure: An Ashanti Case Study. *Social Structure: Studies Presented to A. R. Radcliffe-Brown* (Ed., M. Fortes), pp. [54]-84.
1949b. The Web of Kinship Among the Tallensi. London.

Frank, L. K.
1931. The Concept of Inviolability in Culture. *American Journal of Sociology,* vol. 36, pp. 607-15.
1945. Society as the Patient. New Brunswick.

Frankfort, H. H.
1948. Ancient Egyptian Religion. New York,

Frazer, Sir James G.
1885. On Certain Burial Customs as Illustrative of the Primitive Theory of the Soul. *Journal of the Royal Anthropological Institute,* vol. xv, no. 1, pp. 64-104.

Freud, S.
1930. Civilization and Its Discontents (authorized translation by Joan Riviere). New York.
1946. An Autobiographical Study. London.

Funck-Brentano, C.
1947. Les Peuples se Civilisent Lentement. *Chemins du Monde,* no. 1 (Civilisation), pp. 64-67. Paris.

Gary, D. P.
1929. The Developing Study of Culture. *Trends in American Sociology* (Eds, G. A. Lundberg, R. Bain, and N. Anderson), pp. 172-220. New York.

Gillin, J. L. and **Gillin, J. P.**
1942. An Introduction to Sociology. New York.
1948. Cultural Sociology. New York.

Gillin, J. P.
1948. The Ways of Men. New York.

Goldenweiser, A. A.
1911. Early Civilization. New York.
1933. History, Psychology, and Culture. New York.
1937. Anthropology. New York.

Goldschmidt, W. R.
1951. Review of S. F. Nadel's *The Foundations of Social Anthropology. American Sociological Review,* vol. 16, no. 4, pp. 569-70.

Gorer, G.
1949. The People of Great Russia. London.

Greenberg, J. H.
1948. Linguistics and Ethnology. *Southwestern Journal of Anthropology,* vol. 4, pp. 140-47.

Groves, E. R.
1928. An Introduction to Sociology. New York.

Groves, E. R. and Moore, H. E.
1940. Introduction to Sociology. New York.

Gurvitch, G.
1950. La Vocation Actuelle de la Sociologie. Paris.

Haring, D. G.
1949. Is Culture Definable? *American Sociological Review,* vol. 14, pp. 26-32.

Harris, Z. S.
1951. Review of *Selected Writings of Edward Sapir in Language, Culture, and Personality* (edited by D. G. Mandelbaum). *Language,* vol. 17, no. 3, pp. 288-333.

Hart. H.
1941. Views on Definitions of Culture. Committee on Conceptual Integration. Mimeographed.

Hart, H. and **Pantzer, A.**
1925. Have Subhuman Animals Culture? *American Journal of Sociology,* vol. 30, pp. 703-09.

Hartmann, H., Kris, E., and **Loewenstein, R.**
1951. Some Psychoanalytic Comments on "Culture and Personality." In *Psychoanalysis and Culture* (edited by G. Wilbur and W. Muensterberger). New York.

Hegel, G. W. F.
1920. Vorlesungen über die Philosophie der Weltgeschichte. Leipzig.

Hegewisch, D. H.
1788. Aligemeine Uebersicht der teutschen Culturgeschichte.

Henry, J.
1949. Anthropology and Psychosomatics. *Psychosomatic Medicine,* vol. 11, pp. 216-23.

Herder, J. G. von
1887. Ideen zur Philosophie der Menschheit. *Saemmtliche Werke,* vols. 13 and 14 (Ed B. Suphan). Berlin.

Herrick, C. J.
1949. A Biological Survey of Integrative Levels. *Philosophy for the Future* (Eds., R. W. Sellars, V. J. McGill, and M. Farber), pp. 272-87. New York.

Herskovits, M. J.
1948. Man and his Works. New York.
1951a. On Cultural and Psychological Reality. *Social Psychology at the Crossroads* (Eds., J. H. Rohrer and M. Sherif), pp. 145-63. New York.
1951b. Tender and Tough-Minded Anthropology and the Study of Values in Culture. *Southwestern Journal of Anthropology,* vol. 7, no. I, pp. 22-31.

Herskovits, M. J. and **Willey, M. M.**
1923. The Cultural Approach to Sociology. *American Journal of Sociology,* vol. 29, pp. 188-99. (Reprinted in: J. Davis and H. E. Barnes, Editors, 1927. Readings in Sociology. New York.)

Hiller, E. T.
1933. Principles of Sociology. New York.

Hinshaw, V, Jr., and **Spuhler, J. N.**
1948. On Some Fallacies Derived in David Bidney's Philosophy of Culture. *Central States Bulletin* (American Anthropological Association), vol. 2, no. 2, pp. 12-18.

Hockett, C. F.

1950. Language "and" Culture: A Protest. *American Anthropologist,* vol. 52, no. i, p. 113.

Hoebel, E. A.
1949. Man in the Primitive World. New York.

Hoijer, H.
1948. Linguistic and cultural Change. *Language,* vol. 24, pp. 335-45

Honigsheim, P.
1945. Voltaire as Anthropologist. *American Anthropologist,* vol. 47, no. I, pp. 104-18.

Horton, D.
1943. The Functions of Alcohol in Primitive Societies; A Cross-Cultural Study. *Quarterly Journal of Studies on Alcohol,* vol. 4, no. 2, pp. 199-320.

Huizinga, J.
1936. In the Shadow of Tomorrow. London.
1945. Wenn die Waflen Schweigen. Basel.

Humboldt, Wilhelm von
1836-39. Ueber die Kawi-sprache auf der insel Java, nebst einer einleitung ueber die verschiedenheit des menschlichen sprachbaues und ihren einfluss auf die geistige entwickelung des menschengeschlechts. Berlin.

Huntington, E.
1945. Mainsprings of Civilization. New York.

Infield, H. F.
1951. Jewish Culture and the State of Israel. *American Sociological Review,* vol. 16, no. 4, pp. 506-13.

Irwing, K. F. von
1777-85 Erfahrungen und Untersuchungen über den Menschen. 4 vols. Berlin.

Iselin I.
1768. Ueber die Geschichte der Menschheit. 2nd ed. Zurich.

Jacobs, M. and Stern, B. J.
1947. Outline of Anthropology. New York.

Jakobson, R.
1949. On the Identification of Phonemic Entities. *Travaux du Cercle Linguistique de Copenhague,* vol. 5 (Recherches strucnirales), pp. 205-13.

Jacobson, R. and Lotz, J.
1949. Notes on the French Phonemic Pattern. *Word,* vol. 5, no. 2, pp. 151-58.

Jaeger, W.
1945. Paideia: The Ideals of Greek Culture (translated by G. Highet). (2nd ed.) New York.

Kant, I.
1787. Critik der reinen Vernunft. (2nd ed.) Riga.
1798. Anthropologie. (Vol. 7 of Reimer edition, 1907, of Kant's *Werke* has been used to cite from.) Berlin.
1896. Critique of Pure Reason (translated by F. M. Müller). New York.

Kardiner, A.
1939. The Individual and His Society. New York.

Katz, D. and Schanck, R. L.
1938, Social Psychology. New York.

Keith, Sir Arthur
1946. Essays on Human Evolution. London.

Keller, A. G.
1931. Societal Evolution. New York.

Klemm, G.
1843-52. Allgemeine Cultur-geschichte der Menschheit. 10 vols. Leipzig.
1854-55. Allgemeine Culturwissenschaft. 2 vols. Leipzig.

Klineberg, O.
1935. Race Differences. New York,
1940. Social Psychology. New York.

Kluckhohn, C.
1941. Patterning as Exemplified in Navaho Culture. *Language, Culture and Personality* (Eds, L. Spier, A. I. Hallowell, and S. S. Newman), pp. 109-30. Menasha, Wisconsin.
1942. Report to the Sub-sub-committee on Definitions of Culture. Committee on Conceptual Integration. Mimeographed.
1943. Covert Culture and Administrative Problems. *American Anthropologie,* vol. 45, no. 2, pp. 213-27.
1945a. Comment on C. J. Friedrich's "The Problem of Communication between Cultures Seen as Integrated Wholes." *Approaches to National Unity* (Eds., L. Bryson, L. Finkelstein, and R. M. MacIver), pp. 618-35. New York.
1945b. The Personal Document in Anthropological Science. *The Personal Document in History, Anthropology, and Sociology* (L. Gottschalk, C. Kluckhohn, and R. Angell), pp. 79-174. *Social Science Research Council, Bulletin* 53.
1949a. Mirror for Man. New York.
1949b, The Philosophy of the Navaho Indians. *Ideological Differences and World Order* (Ed„ F. S. C. Northrop), pp. 356-84. New Haven.
1951a. The Concept of Culture, *The Policy Sciences* (Eds., D. Lerner and H. D. Lasswell), pp. 86-101. Stanford, California.
1951b. Values and Value-Orientations in the Theory of Action. *Toward a General Theory of Action* (Eds., T. Parsons and E. Shils), pp. 388-433. Cambridge.

Kluckhohn, C. and Kelly, W. H.
1945a. The Concept of Culture. *The Science of Man in the World Crisis* (Ed., R. Linton), pp. 78-105. New York.
1945b. The Concept of Culture. Mimeographed. (Longer unpublished version of Kluckhohn and Kelly, 1945a.)

Kluckhohn, C. and Leighton, D.
1946. The Navaho. Cambridge.

Kluckhohn, C. and Morgan, W.
1951. Some Notes on Navaho Dreams. In: *Psychoanalysis and Culture* (edited by G. Wilbur and W. Muensterberger). New York.

Kluckhohn, C. and Mowrer, O. H.
1944. "Culture and Personality": A Conceptual Scheme. *American Anthropologist,* vol. 46, no. 1, pp. 1-29.

Kluckhohn, F. R.
1950. Dominant and Substitute Profiles of Cultural Orientations: Their Significance for the Analysis of Social Stratification. *Social Forces,* vol. 28, no. 4, pp. 376-93.

1951. Dominant and Variant Cultural Value Orientations. *The Social Welfare Forum*, pp. 97-113. New York.

Kroeber, A. L.
1917. The Superorganic. *American Anthropologist,* vol. 19, pp. 163-113.
1918. The Possibility of a Social Psychology. American Journal of Sociology, vol. 12, pp. 633-50.
1928. Sub-Human Culture Beginnings. *Quarterly Review of Biology,* vol. 3, pp. 325-42. (Reprinted in: A. L. Kroeber and T. T. Waterman, Editors. 1931. *Source Book in Anthropology,* pp. 472-89. New York.)
1936. "Area and Climax," *Culture Element Distribution* III. University of California Publications in American Archaeology and Ethnology, vol. 37, pp. 101-15.
1944. Configurations of Culture Growth. Berkeley.
1948a. Anthropology. New York.
1948b. White's View of Culture. *American Anthropologist,* vol. 50, no. 3, pt. I, pp. 405-15.
1949. The Concept of Culture in Science. Journal of General Education, vol. 3, pp. 182-88.
1951a. Configurations, Causes, and St. Augustine. American Anthropologist, vol. 53, no. 2, pp. 279-83.
1951b. Reality Culture and Value Culture. (No. 18 of 1952.)
1951. The Nature of Culture. In press. Chicago.

Kroner, R.
1928. Die Selbstverwirklichung des Geistes. Tübingen.

Krout. M. H.
1932. Cultures and Culture Change. *American Journal of Sociology,* vol. 38, pp. 253-63.

Laguna, G. A. de
1949. Culture and Rationality. *American Anthropologist,* vol. 51, no. 3, pp. 379-92.

Langer, S. K.
1942. Philosophy in a New Key. Cambridge. (The Mentor Book edition, 1948, has been used to cite from.)

Langmuir, I.
1943. Science, Common Sense, and Decency. *Science,* vol. 97, no. 2505, pp. 1-7.

LaPiere, R. T.
1946. Sociology. New York.

Lasswell, H. D.
1935. Collective Autism as a Consequence of Culture Contact. *Zeitschrift für Sozialforschung,* vol. 4, pp. 232-47.
1948. The Analysis of Political Behavior. London.

Lavisse, E.
1900-11. Histoire de France depuis les Origines jusqu'a la Revolution. 9 vols. Paris.

Leighton, A.
1949. Human Relations in a Changing World. New York.

Lévi-Strauss, C.
1949. Les Structures Élémentaires de la Parenté. Paris.
1951. Language and the Analysis of Social Laws. *American Anthropologist,* vol. 53, no. 2, pp. 155-63.

Linton, R.
1936. The Study of Man. New York.

1945a. The Cultural Background of Personality. New York,
1945b. Present World Conditions in Cultural Perspective. *The Science of Man in the World Crisis* (Ed., R. Linton), pp. 201-21. New York.

Lippert, J.
1931. The Evolution of Culture (translated by G. P. Murdock). New York.

Lowell, A. L.
1934. Culture. *At War with Academic Traditions in America,* pp. 115-24. Cambridge.

Lowie, R. H.
1917. Culture and Ethnology. New York.
1934. An Introduction to Cultural Anthropology. New York.
1937. The History of Ethnological Theory. New York.

Lundberg, G.
1939. Foundations of Sociology. New York.

Lynd, R. S.
1940. Knowledge for What? Princeton.

MacIver, R. M.
1926. The Modern State. Oxford.
1931. Society, Its Structure and Changes. New York.
1942. Social Causation. Boston.

Malinowski, B.
1931. Culture. *Encyclopedia of the Social Sciences,* vol. 4, pp. 621-46. New York.
1939. Review of Six Essays on Culture by Albert Blumenthal. *American Sociological Review,* vol. 4, pp. 588-92.
1944. A Scientific Theory of Culture. Chapel Hill, North Carolina.

Mandelbaum, D.
1941. Social Trends and Personal Pressures: The Growth of a Cultural Pattern. *Language, Culture, and Personality* (Eds., L. Spier, A. I. Hallowell, and S. S. Newman), pp. 219-38. Menasha, Wisconsin.

Maquet, J.
1949. Sociologie de la Connaissance. Louvain.

Marck, S.
1929. Die Dialektik in der Philosophie der Gegenwart. Tubingen.

Marett, R. R.
1912. Anthropology. London.
1920. Psychology and Folklore. New York.
1928. Man in the Making. Garden City, New York.

Mauss, M.
1935. Les Techniques du Corps. *Journal de Psychologie,* vol. 32, nos. 3-4, pp. 271-93. (Reprinted in: M. Mauss, 1950, *Sociologie et Anthropologie.* Paris.)

McKeon, R.
1950a. Conflicts of Values in a Community of Cultures. *Journal of Philosophy,* vol. 47, pp. 197-210.
1950b. Philosophy and the Diversity of Cultures. *Ethics,* vol. 60, pp. 233-60.

Mead, M.

1937. Cooperation and Competition among Primitive Peoples. New York.

Menghin, O.

1931. Weltgeschichte der Steinzeit. Vienna.

1934. Geist and Blut. Vienna.

Merton, R. K.

1936. Civilization and Culture. *Sociology and Social Research,* vol. 21, pp. 103-13.

1949. Social Theory and Social Structure. Glencoe, Illinois.

Miller, N. E. and **Dollard, J.**

1941. Social Learning and Imitation. New Haven.

Morris, C. W.

1946. Signs, Language and Behavior. New York.

1948. The Open Self. New York.

Meuhlmann, W. E.

1948. Geschichte der Anthropologie. Bonn.

Mumford, L.

1938. The Culture of Cities. New York.

Murdock, G. P.

1932. The Science of Culture. *American Anthropologist,* vol. 34, pp. 200-16.

1937. Editorial Preface to: *Studies in the Science of Society Presented to Albert Galloway Keller.* New Haven.

1940. The Cross-Cultural Survey. *American Sociological Review,* vol. 5, no. 3, pp. 361-70.

1941. Anthropology and Human Relations. *Sociometry,* vol. 4, pp. 140-50.

1945. The Common Denominator of Cultures. *The Science of Man in the World Crisis* (Ed., R. Linton), pp. 123-43. New York.

1949a. The Science of Human Learning, Society, Culture, and Personality. *Scientific Monthly,* vol. 69, pp. 377-82.

1949b. Social Structure. New York.

Murphy, G.

1947. Personality. New York.

Murray, R. W.

1943. Man's Unknown Ancestors. Milwaukee.

Myres, J. L.

1927. Political Ideas of the Greeks. New York.

Nadel, S. F.

1937a. The Typological Approach to Culture. *Character and Personality,* vol. 5, pp. 267-84.

1937b. Experiments on Culture Psychology. *Africa,* vol. 10, pp. 421-35.

1951. The Foundations of Social Anthropology. London.

Nagel, E.

1949. The Meaning of Reduction in the Natural Sciences. *Science and Civilization* (Ed., R. C Stauffer), pp. 99-135. Madison, Wisconsin.

Novikoff, A. B.

1945. The Concept of Integrative Levels and Biology. *Science,* vol. 101, pp. Z09-15.

Odum, H. W.

1947. Understanding Society. New York.

Ogburn, W. F.

1950. Social Change: With Respect to Culture and Original Nature. (Rev, ed.) New York (The first edition was issued in 1922.)

Ogburn, W. F. and **Nimkoff, M. F.**

1940. Sociology. Boston.

Olmsted, D. L.

1950. Ethnolinguistics So Far. *Studies in Linguistics: Occasional Papers,* vol. 2, pp. 1-16. Norman, Oklahoma.

Opler, M. E.

1935. The Psychoanalytic Treatment of Culture. *The Psychoanalytic Review,* vol. 22, pp. 138-57.

1944. Cultural and Organic Conceptions in Contemporary World History. *American Anthropologist,* vol. 46, no. 4, pp. 448-60.

1947. Theories of Culture and the Deviant. *Proceedings of the Spring Conference on Education and the Exceptional Child,* pp. 8-15. Mimeographed. The Woods Schools, Langhorne, Pennsylvania.

Oppenheimer, F.

1922. System der Soziologie. 3 vols, Jena,

Ortega y Gasset, J.

1933. The modern Theme (translated by J. Cleugh). London.

1944, The Mission of the University (translated by H. L. Nostrand). Princeton.

Osgood, C.

1940. Ingalik Material Culture. *Yale University Publications in Anthropology,* no. 22.

1942. The Ciboney Culture of Cayo Redondo, Cuba. *Yale University Publications in Anthropology,* no. 25.

1951. Culture: Its Empirical and Non-Empirical Character. *Southwestern Journal of Anthropology,* vol. 7, no. 2, pp. 202-14.

Ostwald, W.

1907. The Modern Theory of Energetics. *The Monist,* vol. 17, pp. 481-515.

1915. Principles of the Theory of Education. *Rice Institute (Texas) Pamphlet* 2, pp. 191-221.

Panunzio, C.

1939. Major Social Institutions: An Introduction. New York.

Park; R. E, and Burgess, E, W.

1921. Introduction to the Science of Sociology Chicago.

Parsons, T.

1937. The Structure of Social Action. New York.

1949. Essays in Sociological Theory. Glencoe, Illinois.

1951. The Social System. Glencoe, Illinois,

Parsons, T. (Editor)

1951. Toward a General Theory of Action. Cambridge,

Patten, S. N.

1916. Culture and War. New York.

Piddington, R.

1950. An Introduction to Social Anthropology. Edinburgh.

Pitt-Rivers, A. H. Lane-Fox

1906. The Evolution of Culture and Other Essays (Ed., J. L. Myres). Oxford.

Plant, J. S.
1937. Personality and Cultural Pattern. New York.
Powys, J. C.
1929. The Meaning of Culture. New York.
Price, M.T.
1930. The Concept *Culture Conflict:* In What Sense Valid? *Social Forces,* vol. 9, pp. 164-67.
Radcliffe-Brown, A. R.
1930. Applied Anthropology. *Report of Australian and New Zealand Association for the Advancement of Science,* pp. 1-14.
1940. On Social Structure. *Journal of the Royal Anthropological Institute of Great Britain and Ireland,* vol. 70, pp. 1-12.
1949. White's View of a Science of Culture. *American Anthropologist,* vol. 51, pp. 503-12.
Rapoport, A.
1950. Science and the Goals of Man. New York
Read, H.
1941. To Hell with Culture: Democratic Values are New Values, London.
Redfield, R.
Unpublished lectures. Quoted in Ogburn and Nimkoff, 1940.
1928. The Calpolli-Barrio in a Present-Day Mexican Pueblo. *American Anthropologist,* vol. 30, pp. 282-94.
1941. The Folk Culture of Yucatan. Chicago.
Reichenbach, H.
1951. The Rise of Scientific Philosophy. Berkeley.
Reuter, E. B.
1939 Race and Culture. *An Outline of the Principles of Sociology* (Ed., R. E. Park) New York.
Richardson, J. and **Kroeber, A. L.**
1940. Three Centuries of Women's Dress Fashions: A Quantitative Analysis. *University of California Anthropological Records,* vol. 5, no. 2.
Roberts, J. M.
1950. Three Navaho Households: A Comparative Study in Small Group Culture. *Peabody Museum of Harvard University, Papers,* vol. 40, no. 3.
Roheim, G.
1934. The Riddle of the Sphinx (translated by A. Money-Kyrle) . London .
1941. The Psycho-Analytic Interpretation of Culture. *The International Journal of Psycho-Analysis,* vol. 22, pp. 1-23.
1942. The Origin and Function of Culture. *The Psychoanalytic Review,* vol. 29, pp. 131-64.
1943. The Origin and Function of Culture. *Nervous and Mental Disease Monographs.* New York.
1950. Psychoanalysis and Anthropology. New York.
Rouse, I.
1939. Prehistory in Haiti. *Yale Publications in Anthropology,* no. 21.
Rückert, Heinrich.
1857. Lehrbuch der Weltgeschichte in Organischer Darstellung. 2 vols. Leipjug.

Sapir, E.
1912. Language and Environment. *American Anthropologist,* vol. 14, pp. 226-42. (Reprinted in Sapir, 1949, pp. 89-103.)
1921. Language. New York.
1924a. Culture, Genuine and Spurious. *American Journal of Sociology,* vol. 29, pp. 401-29. (Reprinted in Sapir, 1949, pp. 308-31.)
1924b. The Grammarian and His Language. *American Mercury,* vol. 1, no. 1, pp. 149-55. (Reprinted in Sapir, 1949, pp. 150-59).
1929. The Status of Linguistics as a Science. *Language,* vol. 5, pp. 207-14. (Reprinted in Sapir, 1949, pp. 160-66.)
1931. Custom. *Encyclopedia of the Social Sciences,* vol. 4, pp. 658-62. (Reprinted in Sapir, 1949, pp. 365-72.)
1932. Cultural Anthropology and Psychiatry. *Journal of Abnormal and Social Psychology,* vol. 27, pp. 229-42. (Reprinted in Sapir, 1949, pp. 509-21.)
1949. Selected Writings of Edward Sapir in Language, Culture, and Personality (Ed., D. G. Mandelbaum). Berkeley.
Schaeffle, A.
1875-78. Bau und Leben des socialen Körpers. 4 vols. Tübingen. 1881, 1896 (2 vols.).
Schapera, I.
1935. Field Methods in the Study of Modern Culture Contacts. *Africa,* vol. 8, pp. 315-28.
Schiller, J. C. F. von
1883. Saemmtliche Werke. 15 vols. Stuttgart.
Schmidt, H.
1922. Philosophisches Woerterbuch. (7th ed.) Leipzig.
Schmidt, W.
1931. The Origin and Growth of Religion, Facts and Theories (translated by H. J. Rose). London.
1937. Handbuch der Methode der Kulturhistorischen Ethnologic. Münster.
1939. The Culture Historical Method of Ethnology (translated by S. A. Sieber). New York.
Sears, P. B.
1940. Who Are These Americans? New York.
Seligman, C. G.
1936. Patterns of Culture. *Man,* vol. 36, pp. 113-15.
Sickel, K. E.
1933. J. C Adelung, seine Persönlichkeit und seine Geschichtsauffassung. Leipzig.
Siebert, O.
1905. Geschichte der deutschen Philosophie. Göttingen.
Simmons, L. W. (Editor)
1942. Sun Chief, the Autobiography of a Hopi Indian. New Haven.
Slotkin, J. S.
1950. Social Anthropology, the Science of Human Society and Culture. New York.
Small, A. W.
1905. General Sociology. Chicago.
Smith, R. G.

1929. The Concept of the Culture Area. *Social Forces,* vol. 7, pp. 421-32.

Silva-Fuenzalida, I.

1949. Ethnolinguistics and the Study of Culture. *American Anthropologist,* vol. 51, no. 3, pp. 446-56.

Sorokin, P. A.

1937-41. Social and Cultural Dynamics. 4 vols. New York.

1947. Society, Culture and Personality: Their Structure and Dynamics. New York.

1950. Social Philosophies of an Age of Crisis. Boston.

Spencer, H.

1895. Principles of Ethics. New York.

Spengler, O.

1918-22. Der Untergang des Abendlandes. Munich.

1926-28. The Decline of the West (translated by C. F. Atkinson). 2 vols. New York. (1939, 2 vols. in 1).

Spiro, M. E.

1951. Culture and Personality. *Psychiatry,* vol. 14, pp. 19-47.

Stauffer, R. C. (Editor)

1949. Science and Civilization. Madison, Wisconsin.

Stern, B, J.

1929. Concerning the Distinction between the Social and the Cultural. *Social Forces,* vol. 8, pp. 265-71.

1949 Some Aspects of Historical Materialism. *Philosophy for the Future* (Eds., R. W. Sellars, V. J. McFill, and M. Farber), pp. 340-57. New York.

Stevens, H. B.

1949. The Recovery of Culture. New York.

Steward, J. H.

1949. Cultural Causality and Law: A Trial Formulation of the Development of Early Civilization. *American Anthropologist,* vol. 51, no. 1, pp. 1-27.

1950. Area Research: Theory and Practice. *Social Science Research Council, Bulletin* 63.

Stoltenberg, H. L.

1937. Geschichte der deutschen Gruppwissenschaft (Soziologie) mit besonderer Beachtung ihres Wortschatzes. Leipzig.

Sumner, W. G.

1906. Folkways. Boston.

1934. Essays (Eds., A. G. Keller and M. R. Davie). New Haven.

Sumner, W. G. and Keller, A. G.

1927. The Science of Society. 4 vols. New Haven,

Sutherland, R. L. and Woodward, J. L.

1940. An Introduction to Sociology. 2nd ed. Chicago.

Taylor, D. M.

1950. Language and or in Culture. *American Anthropologist,* vol. 52, no. 4, pt. 1, pp. 559-60.

Taylor, W. W.

1948. A Study of Archaeology. *American Anthropological Association, Memoir* 69.

Tessman, G.

1930. Die Indianer Nordost Perus. Hamburg.

Thomas, W. I.

1937. Primitive Behavior. New York.

Thurnwald, R.

1950. Der Mensch geringer Nanirbeherrschung: scin Aufstieg zwischen Vernunft und Wahn. Berlin.

Titiev, M.

1949. Social Values and Personality Development. *Journal of Social Issues,* vol. 5, pp. 44-47.

Toennies, F.

1887. Gemeinschaft und Gesellschaft. Leipzig.

Tozzer, A.

N. D. Unpublished lectures.

1925. Social Origins and Social Continuities. New York.

Trubetzkoy, N. S.

1929. Principes de Phonologie (Ed. J. Cantineau). Paris.

Turney-High, H. H.

1949. General Anthropology. New York.

Tylor, E. B.

1870. Researches into the Early History and Development of Mankind. London.

1871. Primitive Culture. Boston.

Voegelin, C. F.

1949. Linguistics without Meaning and Culture without Words. *Word,* vol. 5, pp. 36-45.

1950. A "Testing Frame" for Language and Culture. *American Anthropologist,* vol. 52, no. 3, pp. 455-465.

Voegelin, C F. and Harris, Z. S.

1945. Linguistics in Ethnology. *Southwestern Journal of Anthropology,* vol. 1, pp. 455-65

1947. The Scope of Linguistics. *American Anthropologist,* vol. 49, no. 4, pt. 1, pp. 588-600.

Vogt, V. O.

1951. Cult and Culture. New York.

Wallas, G.

1911. Our Social Heritage. New Haven.

Wallis, W. D.

1929. Contemporary Society as a Culture Phenomenon. *Sociology and Social Research,* vol. 24, pp. 17-24.

1930. Culture and Progress. New York.

Ward, L. F.

1903. Pure Sociology. New York.

Warden, C. J.

1936. The Emergence of Human Culture. New York.

Weaver. W.

1948. Science and Complexity. *American Scientist,* vol. 36, pp. 536-44.

Weber, A.

1910. Prinzipielles zur Kultursoziologie. *Archiv für Sozialwissenschaft und Sozialpolitik,* vol. 47. pp. 1-49.

1927. Ideen zur Staats- und Kultursoziologie. Karlsruhe.

1931. Kultursoziologie. *Handwoerterbuch der Soziologie.* Stuttgart.

1935. Kulturgeschichte als Kultursoziologie. Leiden.

Wein, H.

1948. Von Descartes zur Heutigen Anthropologie. *Zeitschrift für Philosophische Forschung,* vol. 2, nos. 2-3, pp. 296-314.

White, L. A.
1940. The Symbol: The Origin and Basis of Human Behavior. *Philosophy of Science,* vol. 7, no. 4, pp. 451-63. 1943. Energy and the Evolution of Culture. *American Anthropologist,* vol. 45, no. 3, pt. 1. Pp. 335-56.
1947. Evolutionism and Anti-Evolutionism in American Anthropology. *Calcutta Review,* vol. 105, pp. 30-40.
1949a. Ethnological Theory. *Philosophy for the Future* (Eds., R. W. Sellars, V. J. McFill, and M. Farber), pp. 357-84. New York.
1949b. The Science of Culture. New York.
Whorf, B. L.
1949. Linguistics as an Exact Science. *Four Articles on Metalinguistics,* pp. 6-12. Foreign Service Institute, Washington. Department of State.
Wiener, N.
1948. Cybernetics. New York.
Wiese, L. Von
1932. Sociologie Relationnelle. *Revue Internationale de Sociologie,* vol. 40, pp. 23-56.
1939. Review of Six Essays on Culture by Albert Blumenthal. *American Sociological Review,* vol. 4, pp. 592-94.
Willey, M.
1927a. Society and Its Cultural Heritage. *An Introduction to Sociology* (Eds., J. Davis, H. E. Barnes and others), pp. 495-589.
1927b. Psychology and Culture. *Psychological Bulletin,* vol. 24, pp. 253-83.
1929 The Validity of the Culture Concept. *American Journal of Sociology,* vol. 35, pp. 204-19.
1931 Some Limitations of the Culture Area Concept. *Social Forces,* vol. 10, pp. 28-31.
Wilson, L. and Kols, W. L.
1949. Sociological Analysis. New York.
Winston, S.
1933. Culture and Human Behavior. New York.
Wissler, C.
1916. Psychological and Historical Interpretations for Culture. *Science,* vol. 43, pp. 193-201.
1920. Opportunities for Coordination in Anthropological and Psychological Research. *American Anthropologist,* vol. 22, pp. 1-12.
1923. Man and Culture. New York.
1929. An Introduction to Social Anthropology. New York.
Woodward, J. W.
1938. The Relation of Personality Structure to the Structure of Culture. *American Sociological Review,* vol. 3, pp. 637-51.
Woodger, J.
1937. The Axiomatic Method in Biology. Cambridge, England.
Wundt, W.
1910-20. Völkerpsychologie. 10 vols. Leipzig.
1912. Elemente der Völkerpsychologie. Leipzig.
Young, K.
1934. Introductory Sociology. New York.
1942. Sociology: A Study of Society and Culture New York.
1944. Social Psychology. (2nd ed.) New York.
Zipf, G. K.
1949. Human Behavior and the Principle of Least Effort. Cambridge.
Znaniecki, F.
1919. Cultural Reality. Chicago.
1952. Cultural Sciences. Their Origin and Development. Urbana, Illinois.

Appendices

Appendix A: Historical Notes on Ideological Aspects of the Concept of Culture in Germany and Russia

By Alfred G. Meyer

ONE reason why the German term "Kultur" could acquire a connotation different from that given it by contemporary American anthropology is the very trivial fact that the German language has another word which has often been used to denote "culture" in the anthropological sense. That word is "Volk," together with its derivatives, "Volkstum," "volkstuemlich," "voelkisch," and others. More often it is the plural, "Voelker," which has the meaning that "culture" has acquired in anthropology. "Volk," when used in the singular, often connotates the *German* people; [1] indeed, the adjective "voelkisch" acquired a distinctly jingoist character around the turn of the century, stressing the indigenous racial and cultural heritage rather than political allegiance. [2] But the plural, "Voelker" — often used in the combination "Voelker der Erde" — can often be translated as "cultures." "Voelkerkunde" and ethnography arc, as a rule, synonymous. [3] In both the German and the Russian tradition anthropology more often than not is physical anthropology, whereas social and cultural aspects are stressed by ethnography, hence "Voelkerkunde" is roughly equivalent to "cultural anthropology," As early as 1785 Meiners held that his comparative description of cultures might just as well be called "Voelkerkunde" or, more specifically, "Fruehvoelkerkunde." [4]

In this connection, it should be pointed out that the word "Voelker" is used more often to denote primitive cultures than advanced cultures. The plural of "Volk" thus came to denote cultures other than our own, specifically, non-European or non-Western cultures. [5]

Kultur theories can be explained to a considerable extent as an ideological expression of, or reaction to, Germany's political, social and economic backwardness in comparison with France and England. But the ideological reaction to this backwardness went into different and mutually hostile directions. For Kant and other representatives of eighteenth-century enlightenment in Germany, the enlightenment itself, the growth of rationalist and utilitarian philosophy, the flourishing of political and economic institutions, represented *Kultur,* and to emulate the achievements of *Kultur* was the task they set for Germany. *Kultur* thus had a universal, patently international flavor. Nonetheless individual nations or states could be regarded as the principal carriers of Kultur, and those nations were acclaimed as pathfinders and models for backward Germany. In this spirit, German radicals during the last decade of the eighteenth century supported revolutionary France and hailed Napoleon as the spreader of *Kultur* over all of Europe.

The other ideological strand tended to regard *Kultur* as a complex of qualities, achievements, and behavior patterns which were local or national in origin and significance, unique, non-transferable, non-repetitive, and therefore irrelevant for the outsider. Herder's relativism did much to pave the way for this conception of *Kultur.* The stress on such unique culture patterns as against the economic, political, scientific, or philosophical achievements of Western civilization can be regarded as an attempt to compensate for a deep-seated feeling of inferiority on the part of German intellectuals once they had come in contact with the advanced nations. Similarly, Russian cultural nationalism can easily be traced to such a feeling of inferiority; quite fittingly, Russian cultural nationalism developed in the measure as Russian contacts with the West intensified. These *Kultur* theories, then, are a typical ideological expression — though by no means the only one — of the rise of backward societies against the encroachments of the West on their traditional culture. *They consist in asserting the reality of something which is just about to be destroyed.*

This ideological reaction against the dynamics of westernization and industrialization need not, of course, be international only; it can be a purely domestic phenomenon. The tradition of enlightenment calls for support of those social strata in one's own country which are likely to further the spread of *Kultur;* conversely, Germans, in the name of *Kultur,* opposed the encroachments of Zivilisation, just as certain Americans, in the name of traditional American community ways, bewail urbanization, industrialization, and the curse of bigness. And in this fight for the preservation of the cultural heritage at home, the ideologist is often tempted to seek support for his denunciations of civilization in a glowing description of primitive but unspoiled cultures. Tacitus held up to his degenerate contemporaries the simple but upright life of the primitive cultures in Germany's forests; Rousseau similarly used the noble savage of the North American plains; Herder draws on an almost encyclopaedic knowledge of primitive cultures for the same reason; and one might even point out that Margaret Mead's studies of Samoan culture were undertaken in part in order to hold up a didactic mirror to modern man.

This is not, however, the original "domestic" significance of *Kultur* theories of this sort. Like theories of contact and popular sovereignty, *Kultur* theories were directed against the *ancien régime* and its absolutism; for they held, explicitly, that history was not made by states and dynasties, but by peoples. The difference between the two types of revolutionary ideologies is that the one conceives of "the people" as a political association; the other, as a natural community of culture. Both are liberal in their intent; but the one is rational, the other, romantic or even sentimental liberalism. One wants to go "forward" — if the word make any sense — to political democracy; the other, "back" to nature. [6]

Romantic liberalism and those *Kultur* theories which are within its tradition are therefore not only directed against absolutism, but also against the entire rational-utilitarian tradition of the Age of Enlightenment. It is therefore not at all astonishing that after the French Revolution, when rationalism, utilitarianism, and related theories were associated with Jacobinism, just as dialectical materialism is today associated with the Kremlin, the Romantic struggle against this tradition turned against the Revolution. The *Sturm und Drang* movement, of which Herder's preoccupation with primitive cultures is an intrinsic part, [7] had been a rebel ideology; Romanticism was clearly counter-revolutionary. Yet, *Kultur* theories of both the Kant and the Herder tradition were sufficiently identified with the idea of dissent or revolt that this identification alone might explain why the concept of *Kultur* was altogether eliminated from the dictionary of German social thought until after 1848, by which time its radical connotation had probably been forgotten entirely. [8] At the same time, it is quite possible to argue that the *Kultur* idea of Herder and his contemporaries too was directed against the French Revolution even before that revolution took place. Herder's history expressed dissatisfaction with the course or our own civilization. There is implicit in it a theory of the decline of the West and the ascendancy of unspoiled cultures like those of the Slavs. There is at times a mood of pessimism, a lamenting over the opportunities which the West has missed, and a warning of evil things to come. Thoughts like these were eagerly picked up by cultural nationalists in Russia. [9]

Russian social thought, one might rightfully claim, centered around problems of culture. Throughout the nineteenth century, the "problem of Russian history," i.e., the question concerning Russia's cultural characteristics, destiny, and mission, was one of the central themes with which all social thought, from Chaadaev to Stalin and Berdiaev, had to deal. Posing the problem of "Russia and the West," which was germane to this ever recurrent theme, gave a relativistic character to all Russian ideologies from the start. Similar to the divergent strands in German *Kultur* ideas, moreover, two schools of thought forked out in Russia as well, the Westerners — rationalists, utilitarian in orientation, mechanistic in method, who regarded Russia as an integral part (however backward) of Western civilization — and the Slavophiles, cultural nationalists, who asserted the distinctness and superiority of Russian or Slavic culture, the irrelevancy of European experience for Russia, and the inapplicability of historical laws of the West to Russian soil.

The ideological similarity or even identity of Russian cultural nationalism with German cultural nationalism is obscured by the fact that nineteenth-century Russian thought initially took its method and terminology largely from Hegel who spoke in terms of Geist, not of Kultur. It should not be forgotten, however, that Hegel's Weltgeist is supposed to manifest itself at different times and in different places within groups referred to as nations. Weltgeist thus institutionalized becomes Volksgeist, and the concrete investigation of any given Volksgeirt is nothing else than the Hegelian version of the comparative study of cultures of Herder and the historiography he represents. In spite of the idealistic phraseology which Hegel has carried *ad absurdum*, Hegel's concrete analyses of his own and other cultures are no less rich in material and insight than, for instance, Spengler's descriptions of those institutions, ideologies, and behavior patterns in which a culture's "soul" supposedly manifests itself.

Yet, the reemergence of the *Kultur* concept both in Germany and in Russia attests to the limitations of the Hegelian method and terminology. *Geist,* it appeared, was excessively laden with unstated methodological premises; culture served far better as a concept through which to view the social structure and institutions, behavior patterns, ideologies, and ethos of a given society in their totality and interdependence. Consequently, in the latter part of the century, when Klemm, Rickert, and others revived the *Kultur* concept in Germany, the concept of *kul'tura* enters the writings of Russian social scientists. Danilevskii's book, in which the term seems to have been used for the first time in Russia, is perhaps the most systematic statement of ideas latent in the entire Slavophile tradition. Marking the transition from cultural Slavophilism to political Pan-Slavism, it is the most significant statement of the secularization of Slavophile cultural and religious ideologies, and has fittingly been dubbed the "text book of Pan-Slavism."

In the last quarter of the nineteenth century, when Russian social thought flowered in unprecedented intensity and produced the most diverse schools, the term *kul'tura* was used in the moot diverse meanings.

Leontiev (1831-91) was greatly influenced by Danilevskii, though he insisted on identifying *kul'tura* with nations, similarly as Hegel had made nations the carriers of *Volksgeist.* Each nation thus has a culture of its own; and for Leontiev culture had primarily aesthetic significance.

Lavrov and Iuzhakov, both in the positivist tradition, spoke of culture in the sense of the statically given aspects of each society on which human intelligence and human labor works for progress or, in Lavrov's terminology, for civilization. For civilization, according to Lavrov, is "culture vitalized by the work of thought." [10] Attempting to define culture, Lavrov writes that each generation of mankind "receives from nature and history a totality of needs and appetites which are to a considerable extent conditioned by cultural habits and traditions. It satisfies these needs and appetites by the customs of life and the inherited social institutions, by its craft an (art is here used in the sense of know-how] and its routine technology. All that constitutes its culture, or the zoological element in the life of mankind." [11]

The culture of a society is the milieu given by history for the work of thought, and which conditions the *limits of possibilities* for that work in a given epoch with the same inevitability to which at all times the unchangeable law of nature sets limits to that work. Thought is the sole agent which communicates some *human* quality to social culture. The history of thought, conditioned by culture, in connection with the history of culture which changes under the influence of thought, — there you have the entire history of civilization. Into an intelligent history of mankind can go only such events as explain the history of culture and thought in their interaction." [12]

At another place he makes even clearer that progress is man's movement away from culture, to civilization. In a critical review of Mikhailovsky's theory of progress, Lavrov maintained that where there is no criticism as in that theory', there can be no progress at all "History would stop. The way I understand the word 'civilization' it would be inapplicable to such a society, *which would be leading a purely cultural life, the life of the highest vertebrates.*" [13]

Paul Miliukov appears to have taken the concept of culture in its broadest anthropological sense. His three-volume work, *Ocherki po istorii russkoi kul'tury* (Outline of a history of Russian culture), [14] deals with population, economic, political, and social institutions, religious life, education, nationalism, and public opinion.

As early as 1860, in an article entitled "Chto takoe antropologia?" (What is anthropology?), Lavrov had declared that anthropology should be the roof science integrating all our knowledge of man and society. But the conventional use of the word "anthropology'" in late nineteenth-century Russia tended to restrict its meaning to physical anthropology. It was at the suggestion of a professor of zoology, Anatol' Petrovich Bogdanov, that an anthropological section was added to the Society of Lovers of Natural Science (Obshchesrvo liubitelei estestvoznaiia) at the University of Moscow in 1864. And it was a natural scientist and geographer, Dmitri Nikolaevich Anuchin, who was the first to occupy the chair in anthropology established at Moscow University in 1876. He too regarded anthropology as a branch of the natural sciences and relegated social or cultural aspects to ethnography, which, for him, was a branch of historical science. [15]

Twentieth-century Russian thought has seen a curious revival of Danilevskiis ideas, not within the Soviet Union, to be sure, but among an émigré group calling itself the Eurasian movement. [16]

The beginning of the movement is marked by the publication of "*Evropa i chelovechestvo*" (Europe and mankind) by Prince N. S. Trubetskoi (Sofia, 1920). Trubetskoi rejects the "cultural fallacy" of European social science, both in its chauvinistic and its cosmopolitan form, [17] and asserts the inviolable autonomy of culture. Westernization is seen as the evil of our age; the "blessings of civilization" are denounced, and all cultures are called to become conscious of themselves, assert themselves, and resist the encroachment of civilization. Unlike Danilevskii, Trubetskoi is consistent in his view that culture is exclusive and non-transferable; for, whereas Danilevskii had tended to attribute a world mission to the Slavs, a mission to make Slavic culture dominant in the entire world, Trubetskoi does not substitute such a pan-Slavic for the rejected pan-European ideal.

A curious development in Eurasian thought was that the representatives of this movement drifted toward a reconciliation of old Slavic values with Communism. The Russian revolution was hailed as a revolt of the Eurasian culture against the West. The former "has' been smothered by two hundred years of a monarchy kowtowing to Europe; and...the Revolution, though in its conscious will it was a particularly vigorous affirmation of the European-made ideal of godless Communism, was in its subconscious essence the revolt of the Russian masses against the domination of a Europeanized and renegade upper class." [18]

In keeping with the reversal of Russia's Western expansion after the First World War, the Eurasians redefined the area of the Russian-Eurasian *Kultur*, and tried to establish this Eurasian community in terms of geographical, linguistic, ethnical, social, and historical unity. [19]

Thus the concept of culture survived in modern Russian thought (outside the Soviet Union) not only in the strictest anthropological-ethnological sense, but also in its more intuitive meanings reminiscent of Spengler's historical scheme. In addition, it has been used in the sense of culturation by that group of Russian neo-mediaevalists of which Berdiaev is the best known representative. In his *"Khristianstvo i kul'tura,"* E. Spektorskii asserts that culture is man's ability to master nature, society, and himself. His thesis is that our unprecedentedly high achievements of material and social culture are threatened by the destruction of spiritual culture, and he calls for a spiritual revival, for a preoccupation with spiritual culture, which in his opinion must be based squarely on the New Testament. [20]

Finally, some elements of Russian nationalism during the first World War similar to their German counterpart, took refuge with the myth of culture by making the spread of Russia's superior culture one of the chief war aims. The word *kul'tura*, especially with the adjective "national" preceding it, turned into a thinly veiled ideology of national domination and national expansion, not only to justify pan-Slavist ambitions, but also to rationalize the tsarist policy of forced russification. [21]

[1] Toennies uses "Volkstum" almost synonymously with "Kultur," whereas "Zivilisarion" is defined as "Staatstum"; all these terms are used universally, without being restricted to German culture.

[2] Usually, it was nothing else than a euphemistic synonym of "antisemitic."

[3] They are, of course, also literal translations of each other.

[4] Stoltenberg, 1937, pt, 1, p. 200.

[5] Note the similar connotation of "the others'* which the Hebrew word "goyim" and the Latin "gentes" — both originally meaning "peoples" — have acquired. Luther' consistently translated both words as "Heiden."

[6] Rousseau straddles both these types of revolutionary ideology and could therefore become a precursor of both the rational and the irrational tradition of nineteenth-century thought. Herder's concept of Cultur also contains seeds of both the political-rational and the irrational-cultural strands.

[7] Herder's preoccupation with primitive cultures is manifested not only in his philosophy of history, hot also in his extensive labors to translate the poetic heritage of primitive or extinct cultures.

[8] It is true that Schiller, taking the Kantian concept as a point of departure, attempted to give it a completely unpolitical, or rather antipolitical, twist. Recoiling from the sight of the terror that had been unleashed by the French Revolution, Schiller in his *Letters on the Aesthetic Education of Man* (first published in 1795) denounced the idea that material culture could advance mankind. Look at the developments in France — he said in effect — and you will see the disastrous results of this kind of culture. In the place of the Kantian idea he then posited the demand for a culture of the beautiful, i.e., for an essentially aesthetic orientation of human endeavor. While these Letters were an all-important harbinger of the Romantic movement in Germany, the concept of "aesthetic culture" developed in them did Dot, apparently, come into general usage.

[9] Cf. Konrad Bittner, "J. G. Herder's Ideen zur Philosophie der Geschichte der Menschheit," in: *Germanoslavica,* vol. II (1932-33), no. 4, pp. 453-80; also: Karl Staehlin, "Die Entstehung des Panslavismus," in: *Germanoslavica,* vol. IV (1936), p. 1-25 and 137-62.

[10] "Istoricheskie pis'ma," (Historical letters) no. VI: "Kul'tura i mysl'," (Culture and thought) in: P. L. Lavrov, *Izbrannye sochineniia na sotsial'no-politiches-kie temy v vos'mi tomakh* (Selected works on sociopolitical topics, in 8 volumes). Moscow, 1934, vol. I, p. 243.

[11] Ibid.

[12] Ibid., p. 144. This and the following translations are those of the author.

[13] "Formula progressa g. Mikhailovskogo," (Mr. Mikhailovski's formula of progress), *op. cit.,* vol. I, p. 404 (italics mine). For some remarks on the theories of both Lavrov and Iuzhakov in English, cf. Julius F. Hecker, *Russian Sociology,* New York, 1915. Columbia University Press, pp. 107 and 161-62.

[14] 2nd ed., Sankt Peterburg, 1896-1903.

[15] Cf. his statement that "ethnographic groups do not coincide with anthropological ones due to the fact that they are products, not of biological development, but of cultural-historical influences," from an anide entitled "Rossiia v antropologicheskom omosheniL.' (Russia in the anthropological sense) quoted by M. G. Levin, "Dmitrii Nikolaevich Anuchin," in *Trudy Instituta Emografii imeni N. N. Miklukh-Maklaia,* new series, vol. I, Moscow-Leningrad, 1947, p. 12.

[16] For a brief characterization of the Eurasian movement, cf. D. S. Mirsky, "The Eurasian .Movement," *Slavonic Review,* vol. VI, no. 17 (December, 1927), pp. 312 ff.; cf. also Karl Haushofer, *Geopolitik der Panideen,* Berlin, 1931, p. 17-26.

[17] Trubetskoi maintains that the terms "mankind," "human civilization," "world order," and such, are quite unreal, and betray as much Western egocentricity as the classical ideas that Hellas or the Roman *orbis terrarum* constituted the whole civilized world. Thus cosmopolitanism and chauvinism are different only in degree, not in principle — an idea which has recently been incorporated in the Communist Party line by Zhdanov. Cosmopolitanism and chauvinism, according to this line, are bourgeois ideologies; the contrasting proletarian virtues are internationalism and Soviet patriotism.

[18] D. S. Mirsky, *op. cit.,* p. 312.

[19] George V. Vernadskii attempted to write a Eurasian history in his *Opyt istorii Evrazii s poloviny shestogo veka do nastoiashchego vremeni* (Attempt at a history of Eurasia from the middle of the sixth century up to the present time), Berlin, 1934.

Roman Iakobson tried to establish and define a group of Eurasian languages to show their close relation: *K kharakteristike evraziiskogo iazykovogo soiuza* (Toward a characterization of the Eurasian language union), Paris, 1931.

Pëtr N. Savitskii saw Eurasia as a separate world in geographical terms. His concept of Space-Development-Types (tipy mestorazvitiia) is, expressly, a geopolitical modification of Danilevskii's "cultural-historical types": "The concept of spaco-development has to be joined with Danilevskii's concept of cultural-historical type...For every one of these types there is a corresponding 'space-development.' " — *Rossiia — osobyi mir* (Russia, a world by itself), Paris, 1929, p. 65. Cf. also his *Geograficheskie osobennosti Rossii* (The geographical peculiarities of Russia), Prague, 1927.

[20] E. Spektorskii, *Khrittianstvo i kul'tura,* (Christianity and culture), Prague, 1925.

[21] Spektorskii refers to this use of the concept in op. cit. p. 10. Cf. also Lenin's criticism of this use of the term referred to in Appendix B, *infra.*

Appendix B: The Use of the Term Culture in the Soviet Union

By Alfred G. Meyer

WHEN Stalin, in his first letter on linguistics, [1] asserted that language was not part of the superstructure of any given society, he took a decisive step in the direction of recognizing the existence of certain cultural features which are older and have a more lasting stability than social structures organized in a common effort to produce the means of life and its reproduction. Fur the last twenty years or so, Soviet ideology has come to give explicit recognition to a *national culture* which transcends the scheme of historical development outlined by Marx and Engels. The length to which it has gone in this may be illustrated by a section on Russian culture and the culture of the nationalities of Russia" in the special volume on the Soviet Union of the new Great Soviet Encyclopedia: [2]

The rich and progressive Russian culture exerted, during the nineteenth century, quite a great and fruitful influence on the development of spiritual culture among the numerous nationalities of Russia. Tsarism, with its reactionary national-colonial policy, strove to sow disunity among the nationalities of Russia and set them against each other. The progressive Russian culture brought the nationalities of Russia together and united them in one brotherly and friendly family whose members were interested in overthrowing tsarism, in abolishing serfdom and its lasting consequences, and who from the very beginning of the nineteenth century became involved in an all-Russian revolutionary struggle under the leadership of the proletariat.

This increasing emphasis which Soviet ideology has been paying to the national traditions of Russia and its many nationalities must be seen as the natural outgrowth of Stalin's theory of "Socialism in one country." [3] At the same time it must be realized that it is directly opposed to all that .Marx and Lenin had to say about national culture.

In Marxism, the concepts devised to express the totality of all social phenomena in their interrelation is not culture, but the mode of production, with its two important subconcepts, the forces of production and the social relations of production. The term "culture" enters into the conceptual framework of Marxism only on the level of the superstructure. But on this level it has much the same content as the current anthropological concept of culture, with the proviso that the economic substructure and the corresponding class relationships are on a more fundamental level; moreover, there is a tendency in .Marxist usage to endow the term "culture" with a meaning of achievement or culturation reminiscent of the use which the Enlightenment made of it. Two Soviet dictionary definitions will illustrate these points; the first is from the *Tolkovyi slovar' russkogo iazyka* (Reference dictionary of the Russian language) of Professor D. N, Ushakov, [4] the second from the *Bol'shaia So-vetskaia Entsiklopediia* (Great Soviet Encyclopedia) vol. xxxv. [5]

Kul'tura — 1. The totality of human achievements in the subjection of nature, in technology, education, and social organization...

Kul'tura — 5. The material activity of labor of men which conditions the evolution of social man with all the multiplicity' of his spiritual interests and needs, constitutes the basis of all human culture and provides the guiding framework for the explanation of the various forms and the development of culture...Culture expresses the historically determined stage and the means of man's mastery over the forces of nature; it manifests itself in the level of technology, organization and habits of labor, organization of social life, in manners, customs, and in morality; its expressions are also the stage and forms of men's ideological development, i.e., language, science, art, literature, philosophy, and the *Weltanschauung* of an age.

Lenin contrasted culture with barbarism, in a passage in which he claimed that the imperialist war was threatening to destroy all the previous achievements of culture:

It seems that the countries [now at war) are once more turning from civilization and culture to primitive barbarism and are once more undergoing a situation in which behavior becomes unrestrained, and men turn into beasts in the struggle for a piece of bread. [6]

True to the internationalist tradition of his movement, which denied that the nation had any significance as a cultural or social unit, he bitterly scored the use which was made of the concept of culture by nationalists everywhere:

The class-conscious workers know that the slogan of "national culture" is clerical or bourgeois bluff, no matter whether they talk about Greco-Russian, Ukrainian, Jewish, Polish, Georgian, or any other culture. 125 years ago, when nations were not yet divided into bourgeoisie and proletariat, the slogan of national culture could be a unifying and total call to battle against feudalism and clericalism. But since then the class struggle of the bourgeoisie and the proletariat has broken out even,-where. The split of the "united" nation into exploiters and the exploited has become an accomplished fact.

Only clericals or bourgeois can talk about national culture at all. The working masses can talk only about the international culture of the world movement of workers. [7]

Thus it is misleading, in Lenin's opinion, to speak about national culture. And yet, in another sense, there is such a thing; but this national culture is even more clearly bourgeois in content than the myth for which the term is used by nationalists. This is how Lenin saw it:

Within *each* national culture *elements* — however undeveloped — of democratic and socialist culture exist, for in *each* nation exist a mass of working and exploited people whose conditions of life inevitably generate a democratic and socialist ideology. But in *each* nation also a bourgeois...culture exists — moreover not just as "elements," but as the *ruling* culture. Hence "national culture" in general *is* the culture of landlords, priests, and the bourgeoisie. [8]

These polemics against the concept of national culture, it must be noted, were directed not only against nationalists, and pan-Slavists from the camp of the bourgeois or pre-capitalist classes, but, even more sharply perhaps, against such socialists who, like the Austrian school (Karl Renner and Otto Bauer), the Marxist movement in Georgia, or the Jewish "Bund," advocated a vigorous struggle for national or cultural-national autonomy. [9]

For culture, according to Lenin, is the superstructure of class relationships and has therefore little or nothing to do with nations, except in the measure as nations themselves are part of that superstructure. Let us once more adduce part of a Soviet dictionary definition of culture which illustrates this point:

In a class society culture too is class culture: each ruling class endeavors to create such culture as would strengthen its power. In the period of the highest flowering of capitalism, bourgeois culture eave the world great savants, inventors, philosophers, and writers. The bourgeoisie made use of the fruits of this culture for the purpose of increasing its wealth and intensifying the exploitation of those who work. At the present time, in the period of imperialism, bourgeois culture is decaying and approaches its end, and the cultural level of the population goes down. The working class is creating its own socialist culture, by appropriating and critically re-working all positive achievements of the past. On that basis socialist culture creates a science, technology, and art which are higher than under capitalism. It uncovers inexhaustible riches of popular creativity in all the peoples of the USSR. In distinction from bourgeois culture, socialist culture is directed toward the satisfaction of the needs of the broadest popular masses. Hence it is all-human culture. Simultaneously, on account of differences in language, customs, and other national peculiarities in the different peoples of the Soviet Union, socialist culture takes on a different national form. "Proletarian in content, national in form, that is the all-human culture toward which socialism is striding." (Stalin). [10]

Similarly, the article on *kul'tura* in the Great Soviet Encyclopedia maintains that in class society, culture is the culture of the ruling class. Conversely, only classes that are ruling have a chance to develop culture. Hence, in order that the proletariat may acquire culture, it must first seize power and become the ruling class. "Only the victorious proletarian revolution creates the conditions for...the cultural revolution," i.e., for the appropriation of culture by the proletariat. For the same reason it must be expected — the Encyclopaedia continues — that the proletariat is still *uncultured* at the time it makes the revolution. It can catch up culturally with the bourgeoisie only after the revolution. "Socialism — to use the words of Lenin — begins where culture spreads among the millions."

This "cultural revolution" at which the encyclopaedia hints became one of Lenin's chief preoccupations after the October revolution. He wrote about it repeatedly from the middle of 1918 until the end of 1923. Abstractly, he had spoken about the problem even before the war, though in much more optimistic terms than after the revolution:

The international culture which is already being created systematically by the proletariat of all countries takes up and incorporates not the "national culture" (of any one national collective) as a whole, but takes out of each and every national culture *exclusively* its consistently democratic and socialist elements. [11]

More concretely, the problem was defined only later. Thus he wrote in 1922:

The task is to bring the victorious proletarian revolution together with bourgeois culture, bourgeois science and technology, which have so far been the attainment of few; this is, I repeat, a difficult task. Everything here depends on organization, on the discipline of the advanced section of the working masses. [12]

Nor did he have any more illusions then about the ease and speed with which the cultural revolution might be accomplished; and yet he did not think that the low cultural level of the Russian masses should have argued against the seizure of power by the bolshevik party.

Our enemies (he wrote in 1923 in one of his last articles) have often said to us that we have undertaken the foolhardy job of planting socialism in an insufficiently cultured country...in our country the political and social revolution has [indeed] turned out to precede that cultural transformation and cultural revolution, which we are nonetheless facing at the present.
...for us that cultural revolution presents unbelievable difficulties both of purely cultural nature (for we are illiterate) and of material nature (for in order to be cultured a certain development of the material means of production, a certain material base, is needed.) [13]

The "culture" Lenin had in mind when he preached the cultural revolution entailed technological skills, political maturity, and other aspects of *westernization.* His use of the term is thus a return to the eighteenth-century' use of the word in the tradition of the Enlightenment. The adjective "uncultured" was, in addition, used very often to characterize the rough-shod methods of Soviet and party bureaucracy, its authoritarian degeneration and its corrupt abuses. Culture, then, was by implication the achievement of a smoothly and democratically functioning administrative apparatus. A lengthy passage from his political report at the XIth party-congress in March 1922. the last of these congresses he attended, will illustrate this. He was speaking here of dangers threatening the revolution from within, in spite of the fact that the regime had all the political and economic power it wanted. But one thing was lacking:

It is *kul'turnost'* which those communists who are in the leading positions are lacking. Let us take Moscow, with its 4700 responsible communists, and take that weighty bureaucratic machine — who is running it? I greatly doubt whether one can say that communists are running that heavy thing. If I must tell the truth, then it is not they who are running it, but it runs them. Something has happened here that is similar to what they still to tell us about history in our childhood. This is what they taught us: Sometimes it happens that one people conquers another people, and then

168

the people who conquered are the conquerors, and the conquered one are the defeated. That is very simple, and everyone can understand it. But what happens with the culture of these peoples? Here matters are not so simple. If the people who did the conquering are more cultured than the defeated people, then the former will impose their culture on the latter, but if it is the other way around, then what happens is that the defeated will impose their culture on the conqueror. Has not something similar happened in the capital of the RSFSR; is it not true here that 4700 communists (almost an entire division, and all of them the very élite) turn out to have been subjected by an alien culture? Indeed, we might even get the impression here that the defeated have a high culture. Nothing of the sort: Their culture is miserable and insignificant, and yet it is greater than ours. However pitiful, however miserable, it is nevertheless greater than that of our responsible communist functionaries because they do not have sufficient skill in governing. [14]

This use of the word *kul'tura* (and the virtually synonymous *kul'turnost'*) to denote culturation has survived in the Soviet Union up to the present and is applied to embrace all and any aspects of culturation. The Soviet press and other Soviet literature is filled with admonitions to raise the level of culture in tractor maintenance, in the fight against workers' absenteeism, in daily etiquette, both public and private, in cutting administrative red tape, and virtually all other activities.

In the mid-thirties, greater stress was laid in Soviet society on the education of leadership cadres. Therefore we read in the Great Encyclopaedia that culture entails the education of leaders and specialists in technology, science, the arts, and also in party work; it includes the struggle against illiteracy, superstitions, and un-bolshevik ideologies, hence, positively, it means ideological rearmament. And the highest achievement of culture, it is implied, lies in making all men into fully class-conscious citizens and proletarians.

Used far less strictly, the term has been applied in the U.S.S.R. also to denote the highest levels of the superstructure; ideology, art, and philosophy. And in a term like "Parks of culture and rest" it signifies nothing else perhaps than leisure-time activities and enjoyments in the broadest sense, though it may specifically refer to the "cultural" enjoyments offered in such parks, as open-air concerts, dancing instruction, or the sight of statues, monuments, and flower beds.

In addition, the concept of culture has been used by Soviet anthropologists — or, as they would call themselves, ethnographers — in the general anthropological sense. One of the definitions of *kul'tura* given by Ushakov [15] is: "A specific way of social, economic, and/or intellectual life during a given era, of a given people or class," and for examples the dictionary adduces "neolithic culture; the culture of ancient Egypt; and proletarian culture."

This is not the place to discuss the methodology of cultural anthropology in the Soviet Union. It is a matter of course that the study of culture and cultures must fit i.. o the framework of Marxist-Leninist historical materialism. Yet culture study is considered important enough for the establishment, in the 1920's, of an Institute for the History of Material Culture within the Academy of Sciences of the U.S.S.R. The institute was, until recently, named after Professor Marr, who was its first president. It appears to be preoccupied with research and publications on the history of culture within the territory of the Soviet Union; and the present emphasis is on attempts to demonstrate the high level and independence of mediaeval, ancient, and prehistoric culture of Russia. [16]

To show the range of topics included under the heading of culture as used by Soviet ethnographers, archaeologists, and cultural anthropologists, it might be useful to list the chapter headings in two of the works just cited. Likhachëv treats Russian culture in the fifteenth century under the following headings: Political theory; enlightenment; chronicles; epic; literature; architecture; painting; new developments in customs and mores; and the art of war. Grekov and Artamanov include the following topics in their book on the culture of ancient Russia; Agriculture and trades; crafts; settlement; housing; clothing; food ways and means of communication; trade and trade routes; money and money circulation; military affairs (strategy and tactics); armament; fortifications. They make clear, however, that they have purposely restricted themselves to a treatment of material culture, and a second volume is to deal with "spiritual culture."

[1] I. V. Stalin, "Otnositel'no marksizma v iazykoznanii," (Concerning Marxism in linguistics), *Pravda,* June 20, 1950.
[2] *Bol'shaia Sovetskaia Entsiklopediia* (Great Soviet Encyclopedia), special volume, "Soiuz Sovetskikh Sotsialtsticheskikh Respublik" (Union of Soviet Socialist Republics), Moscow, 1948, p. 565.
[3] For a survey of this ideological development in its various ramifications, cf. F. Barghoom, "Stalin and the Russian Cultural Heritage," *The Review of Politics,* Vol. 14, No. 4, pp. 178-203, April 1952. I am obliged to Jindrich Kucera and Paul Friedrich who, independently and simultaneously, called my attention to this article.
[4] Moscow, 1935.

[5] Moscow, 1937.

[6] "Doklad o tekushchcm momente 27 iiunia 1918 g." (Report on the current moment of 27 June 1918), in: V. 1. Lenin, *Sochineniia* (Works), 2nd ed., vol. XXIII, p. 77. Cf. also an earlier statement: "The imperialist war...is placing mankind before the dilemma either to sacrifice all culture or else to throw off the capitalist yoke by way of a revolution, remove the rule of the bourgeoisie, and to conquer a socialist society and a firm peace," "Za khleb i mir" (For bread and peace), *op. cit.* vol. XXII, p. 145.

[7] "Kak episkop Nikon zashchishchaet ukraintsev?" (How bishop Nikon defends the Ukrainians), *op. cit.*, vol. XVI, p. 618. For similar polemics, cf. also the following articles: "Kriticheskie zametki po natsional' - nomu voprosu" (Critical remarks concerning the national problem), *op. cit.*, vol. XVII, pp. 136-39; "Liberaly i demokraty v voprose o iazykakh" (Liberals and democrats in the problem of languages), vol. XVI, pp. 595-97; and "Nuzhen li obiazatel'nyi gosudarstvennyi iazyk?" (Is a compulsory state language necessary?), *op. cit.*, vol. XVII, pp. 179-81. All of these articles were written in 1913 or early 1914, a period when Lenin and socialists everywhere became more than ever aware of the force of nationalism throughout Europe.

[8] "Kriticheskie zametki po natsional'nomu voprosu," op. cit., vol. XVII, pp. 137 and 143.

[9] Cf. "O 'kul'turno-natsional'noi' avtonomii" (On "cultural-national" autonomy) (1913), op. cit-, vol. XVII, pp. 92-95.

[10] From the definition of *kul'tura* in Aleksandrov, et al. *Politicheskii Slovar,* (Political dictionary), Moscow, 1940.

[11] Tezisy po natsional'nomu voprosu" (Theses on the national problem), *op. cit.*, vol. XVI, p. 510. Cf. also "Proekt platformy k IV. s" ezdu sotsial-demokratii latyshskogo kraia" (Draft platform for the fourth congress of social-democrats of the Lettish region), *op. cit.*, vol. XVII, p. 66.

[12] "Uspekhi i trudnosti sovetskoi vlasti" (The successes and difficulties of the Soviet regime), *op. cit.*, vol. XXIV, p. 68.

[13] "O kooperatsii" (On cooperation), *op. cit.* vol. XXVII, p. 397, Cf. also "O nashei revoliutsii" (About our revolution), *op. cit.* vol. XXVII, pp. 400-01. Concerning the great length of time which the cultural revolution will require, cf. Lenin's speech at the second all-Union congress of political propagandists (II. vserossiiskii s"czd politprosvetov), 1921, *op. cit.*, vol. XXVII, pp. 51-52.

[14] V. I. Lenin, *Sobranie Sochinenii* (Collected Works), (ed. 1), vol. XVIII. part II, p. 43. Moscow and Petrograd, 1923.

[15] *Op.cit.*

[16] Cf. B. D. Grekov, *Kul'tura Kievskoi Rusi* (The culture of Kievan Russia), Moscow-Leningrad, 1944; also D. S. Likhachëv, *Kul'tura Rusi epokha obrazovaniia russkogo natsional'nogo gosudarstva* (Russia's culture during the era of the formation of the Russian national state), Leningrad, 1946; also: B. D. Grekov and M. I. Artamanov (ed.), *Istoria Kul'tury drevnei Rusi* (Culture history of ancient Russia), Moscow-Leningrad, 1948.

CPSIA information can be obtained
at www.ICGtesting.com
Printed in the USA
BVHW011220181220
595610BV00014B/138